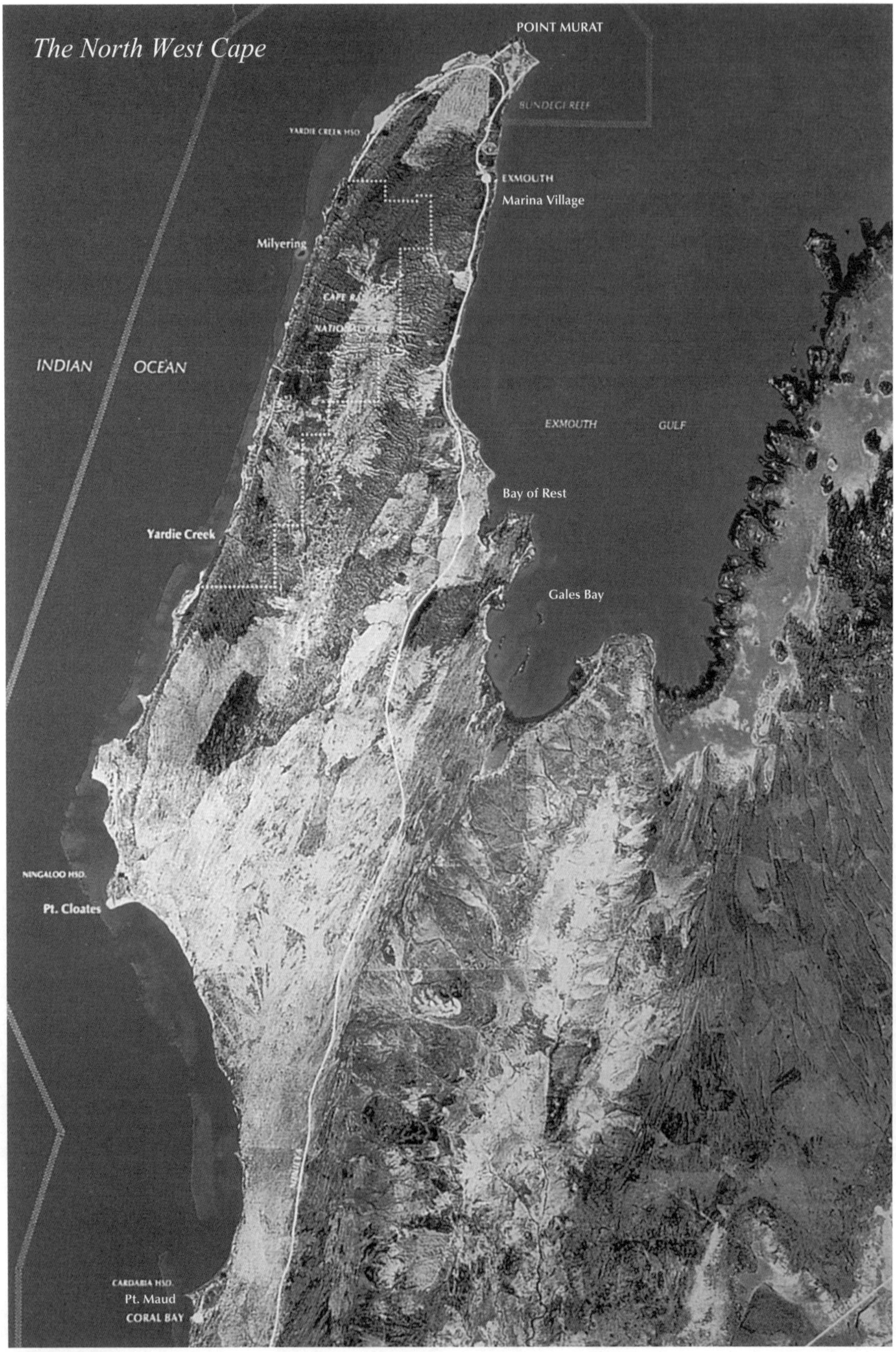
The North West Cape
POINT MURAT
BUNDEGI REEF
YARDIE CREEK HSD
EXMOUTH
Marina Village
Milyering
INDIAN OCEAN
EXMOUTH GULF
Bay of Rest
Yardie Creek
Gales Bay
NINGALOO HSD.
Pt. Cloates
CARDABIA HSD.
Pt. Maud
CORAL BAY

About The Author

Picture: Leone Broadhurst

Hugh Edwards is a Western Australian author of 30 books. Twelve have been re-printed overseas, in the United States, Canada, Britain, the Netherlands, France, Germany, Japan, and Russia. He is published in six languages in 10 countries, and in the *Queen's Birthday Honours List* of 2009 he was awarded the *Order of Australia Medal.*

He first travelled to Exmouth in 1965 as a diver, and was granted a lease to develop a resort on the Muiron Islands. However, on reflection, he decided that the islands would be better left in a pristine natural state and his time would be better spent researching and writing books. The Muirons are now part of a National Park and Edwards is on his 32nd book. He has had many diving adventures off the North West Cape in the years since, as evidenced by his underwater photographs of whale sharks, and the spectacular coral world of the Ningaloo Reef.

His OAM was awarded for *'Services to Australia's Maritime Heritage through the discovery of historic shipwrecks and as an author'*. Hugh Edwards was instrumental in the discovery of important 17th and 18th Century shipwrecks on the Western Australian coast, and was a leader of diving expeditions to the 1629 Dutch East Indiaman *Batavia,* and the 1727 *Zeewyk.* He has been recognised by Act of the Western Australian Parliament as a '*Primary Finder'* of these vessels.

As an author his book *Islands of Angry Ghosts*, on the 1963 *Batavia* expedition, won the Sir Thomas White Memorial Prize in 1966. It was published in America, Britain, France, and the Netherlands, as well as Australia and is still in print today after 43 years. *Wreck on the Half Moon Reef* on the *Zeewyk* was also published in the United States, and the Netherlands, as well as in Australia.

He has written two Aboriginal books, includiong *Joe Nangan's Dreaming,* and three books on Broome, *Port of Pearls,* (winner of the 1984 Premier's Non-fiction Prize) *Broome's South Sea Pearls*, and *A New Broome*. He has also written a number of regional histories, including *Kimberley-Dreaming to Diamonds, Gold Dust & Iron Mountains, Meekatharra – the Gold Beyond the Rivers,* and *Shark Bay Through Four Centuries – 1616 to 2000.*

Recent titles have been *Treasures of the Deep,* about the salvage of the porcelain cargo of an 1822 Chinese junk sunk in the South China Sea. *The Buccaneer's Bell* tells of an expedition to the South Atlantic in 2001 in search of William Dampier's 1700 ship *Roebuck,* and Louis de Freycinet's 1820 exploration vessel *Uranie* in the Falkland Islands. The expedition raised the *Roebuck* ship's bell at Ascension Island.

Breaking with a long run of non-fiction, *The Price of Pearls,* a novel set on the WA Pearling Coast, was published in 2006. Edwards has also written about crocodiles, dolphins and sharks, *Shark—The Shadow Below*, and been involved in many television documentaries, including filming the Great white shark underwater from cages at Albany.

He is currently working on an Aboriginal book, *Barunga,* and as his next project plans an autobiography detailing the highlights of an adventurous life, to be titled *Dead Men's Silver.*

Printed in Western Australia by
Scott Printers Pty Ltd, 4 Aberdeen Street, Perth, Western Australia 6000

H. Edwards, 5 Hooley Street, Swanbourne, Western Australia 6010.
Telephone 08 9384 4766. Email huedwz@bigpond.net.au

ISBN: 978-0-9588487-2-5

Contents

Chapter One	A Step Back From The Edge	1
Chapter Two	The Magic Sound of *'First'*!	10
Chapter Three	Exmouth – Noble & Valiant	18
Chapter Four	A Fatal Miracle	31
Chapter Five	Tracks Without Toes	47
Chapter Six	The Dogs Of War	60
Chapter Seven	Operation POT SHOT	75
Chapter Eight	Ask Me No Questions	88
Chapter Nine	A Tiger In A Trap	94
Chapter Ten	Pastoral Life In A Cold War Peace	109
Chapter Eleven	Leading The High Life	119
Chapter Twelve	Whale Sharks & A Wider World	132
Chapter Thirteen	The Coral Heartbeat	143
Chapter Fourteen	Cyclones – Whirling One-Eyed Monsters	158
Chapter Fifteen	Silver Dollars On The Sea Floor	170
Chapter Sixteen	The Cape Under The Microscope	183
Chapter Seventeen	The Song of the Whale	189
Chapter Eighteen	We Saw It Happen	200
Chapter Nineteen	Coral Bay & *'Save The Ningaloo Reef'*	214
Chapter Twenty	Harvesting the Sea	228
Chapter Twenty One	The Lights That Shone	235
Chapter Twenty Two	Past, Present, & Future	245

A Step Back From The Edge

Chapter One

In the year 1962 the North West Cape drowsed in the sun as it had since the end of the Second World War. The day of October 27th, was ending, and the sun was going down in crimson glory towards the blue rim of the Indian Ocean. Out on the plain red dust rose from the lines of sheep making their way to drink at the troughs by the tanks and windmills. Following head to tail, one behind the other, cloven hoofs placed neatly in the same well-worn tracks. As always.

On the verandas of the stations, the working day was ended. Slumping comfortably down in chairs, elastic-sided boots pushed out in front of them, bosses and workers alike took the tops off their first beers. Feeling the frost on the bottles, they took the first swig. *'Aaah, that's good, mate!'*

It seemed a day just like any other early dry summer day in station life. And yet it was a day the world would remember a long time after. Though no-one in the Exmouth area could have realised it, at that moment the future of the entire world was in peril. While the danger would be overcome literally at the last minute, the extent of it would send ripples far into the future. Including the seemingly unlikely region of the North West Cape and Exmouth Gulf in Western Australia.

The effects of the real-life drama would extend far from the snow-bound Kremlin in Moscow. Far too, from the rusty-brown autumn leaves falling from the trees on the lawns of the White House in Washington, USA. A long way also from the sun-and-shadow patterns on the old gold-hued stones of the Spanish buildings of Havana in Cuba. Those were the three key locations in the situation. All were half a world away, far, far, from the white fringe of the surf breaking on the Ningaloo Reef on that day of October 27th, 1962.

The decisions reached at that critical time would concern millions of people around the world. But the flow-on of military strategy as a result of that year's Cold War confrontation would affect the North West Cape and Exmouth Gulf more than most.

Mind you, the total number of the people actually living in the North West Cape region, a space of some thousands of square kilometres, could have fitted comfortably into a single school bus. The population, mostly based on the sheep stations Warroora, Cardabia, Ningaloo, Yardie Creek, Exmouth, Giralia, and Bullara stations, numbered only 41 people. Aside from the families of the lighthouse keepers at Vlamingh Head, they were the owners and managers of the stations and the people who worked on them. Sheep and shearing, dogs and horses, and to a lesser extent domestic goats, camels and cows, were their life. There was no town closer than Carnarvon on the Gascoyne River 315 kilometres to the south and below the geographical demarcation of *The Tropic of Capricorn.*

There was no post office in the region, not even a general store. Supplies came up on the mail truck once a fortnight and sometimes once a month. Woe betide you if you forgot a tea or flour order! In a harsh land where Nature ruled, it was accepted with a shrug that heavy rain or cyclone damage could play the devil with the truck's schedule. In fact there were few less developed or more isolated coastal areas in all of Australia.

There had been a brief flurry of activity during the Second World War with American and Australian servicemen stationed at Exmouth Gulf. A secret base was established there under the code-name *OPERATION POT SHOT.* There was a lot of cloak-and-dagger activity, including commando raids behind enemy lines. For a time the Gulf saw Allied submarines, and Catalina flying boats in its waters. Kittyhawk and Spitfire fighter aircraft patrolled high up in skies that always seemed to be a perfect China blue.

The real war came briefly to the Cape with different-sounding aircraft engines in the night. The strange aeroplanes carried the red roundel of Imperial Japan on their fuselages, flying south on missions from Indonesian bases on bright moonlight nights. There were five raids on Exmouth in 1943, with bombs dropped on three occasions. The bombs missed their targets, and the Australian ack-ack (anti-aircraft) gunners opening up in retaliation also failed to score a hit. The planes returned to their bases. No-one was hurt on either side, and honours remained even. That was the War at Exmouth!

After VJ Day (Victory over Japan) the soldiers, sailors, and airmen shouldered their kitbags and thankfully went home. They left an airstrip at Learmonth long enough to land a Lancaster bomber, some rusty landing barges blown inland by the 1945 cyclone, some sand-bagged pillboxes along the sea coast, and the burnt-out remains of the radar station below the lighthouse at Vlamingh Head.

And the memories.

The North West Cape went back to its serious business of tending sheep, with race meetings in the Gascoyne and Winning Pool and balls in Carnarvon for light relief. Owners and managers and their wives, if they could, went down to Perth at Christmas and New Year, for the racing carnivals at Ascot and Country Week cricket.

It was a pattern of life that showed little prospect of change. But those who lived out in the remote areas preferred it that way. They had the Flying Doctor radio and the Flying Doctor too if he were needed. Most of the station people managed to keep up a social round, meeting together regularly for a day of fishing and a barbecue.

There was shearing and mustering twice a year, and in between there were fences and windmills to maintain, horses to shoe, gates to repair, and all the daily routine of station life. It seemed that there was always something that needed to be done. Tom Carter (the *Birdman*) who pioneered Ningaloo Station in the 1890s, titled his book of memoirs *No Sundays In The Bush.*

It was a saying frequently quoted in the years since his time. Sometimes with wry humour, sometimes with resentment, depending usually on whether you were an owner or an employee. A Chief or an Indian.

In 1953 there was a major event with the Australian oil search company WAPET (West Australian Petroleum) moving in to drill for oil in Rough Range. When oil was struck for the first time in the nation's history at Shot-Hole Canyon the flow was registered at 500 barrels a day! There was huge excitement, Australia-wide. The newspaper headlines in all the capital cities were the biggest and blackest since the Second World War, and the stock market went crazy.

Sadly, disappointment followed. Successive wells proved dry, and the Shot-Hole strike was not enough on its own to sustain a commercial development. WAPET went away to drill elsewhere still hoping that somewhere, some day, a payable oil field would be found in Australia.

Eleven years later, after drilling 95 wells and after an expenditure of 80 million dollars on exploration – an immense sum for the times – WAPET finally struck what they had been looking for. They tapped a commercial flow of '*black gold*' at Barrow Island. Today Barrow Island and the numerous producing wells on the North West Shelf are major suppliers of Australian oil and gas. At Exmouth, in the 1950s, the well at Shot-hole canyon was capped, and life went back to normal. With the sheep. Baah!

What did this quiet lifestyle – idyllic if that was what you fancied, boring if you craved something more lively – have to do with World War 111 and a possible Armageddon? The end of the civilised world in a nuclear horror?

Today, half a century later, most people have forgotten about the day that the United States and Soviet Russia came to the brink of nuclear war. An event which must surely have devastated both countries and Europe and cities and people around the world. A catastrophe on an unimaginable scale which would have cost millions of lives. A conflict which could have had no favourable ending for either side.

And yes, it would have a big influence on the future of the North West Cape.

In what came to be known as the *'Cuban Missile Crisis'*, there was an ugly situation where the great powers of the United States and Russia were angrily shaking nuclear weapons at each other. It was made more dangerous because there was an imbalance in the most terrifying arsenals of all, the stocks of nuclear missiles. If the super powers had been roughly equal in arms they might have been less inclined for a confrontation. But the hawks on both sides urged the importance of a First Strike. In the parlance of bar room brawls the advice was '*Hit the other fellow first! And hit him hard!*'

The Russian generals were only too aware that the United States had a huge superiority in their arsenal of inter-continental nuclear missiles. The Russian pro-war lobby rationalised that getting in early with strategically placed missiles might put a large part of America out of action and level the playing field. Their American equivalents put their argument on the basis of '*Let's get this over for once and for all while we still have the numbers!*'.

The United States had the biggest arsenal of nuclear weapons – more than 300 land-based inter-continental ballistic missiles (nuclear-headed rockets) and a growing fleet of Polaris missile submarines with nuclear capability. The Soviet Union, in contrast, had only four to six land-based inter-continental missiles, and about 100 short range V-1 type missiles that could be launched from surfaced submarines.

Technically speaking, the USSR, was heavily out-gunned. Theoretically America had enough nuclear weapons to obliterate every major city in Russia. But it only needed one nuclear weapon to devastate the city of New York, or Washington, or Baltimore, or Philadelphia, on the U.S. east coast – or all of them in a surprise strike with only four nuclear weapons.

Nonetheless, there could be no winners in an all-out nuclear war. Who-ever made the first strike would have an advantage, but the retaliation would be awesome. World War 111 would have been the greatest tragedy in the history of the human race. Yet despite the risk October, 1962 – and especially that day of October 27th -- saw relations between the United States and Russia on a knife-edge. Fingers mutually itching on the triggers.

Incredibly (as we analyse it today) some senior military commanders on both sides were anxious to press the button that would have sent a large part of the world into a hell of smoke and flames. It was another episode in the brinkmanship that had dogged relations between Russia and the United States since the end of the Second World War.

While there had been cordiality between the great leaders, Roosevelt, Churchill, and Stalin, in their common fight against Hitler's Germany, the mood soured after the fall of Berlin when that country was divided into East and West Germany.

The Russian refusal to allow supplies into Berlin was overcome by the Allied Berlin Airlift, the first round in what came to be known as '*The Cold War'*.

The political philosophies of the two nations were so different, the Russians representing Marxist communism, and the Americans their own kind of western democratic capitalism.

There seemed no common ground, and the two nations were each paranoid about the capacity of the other to influence smaller nations around the world to join their causes. On that basis each maintained huge armies, navies, and air forces, and there was no question on either side about who was considered to be the enemy. The Cuban Missile Crisis brought all that into sharp relief.

The Russians were very aware of the American superiority in long range weapons. Where could they find a base closer to the United States to suit their shorter range weapons in the event of a shooting war breaking out?

The answer was Cuba, where the revolutionary communist leader Fidel Castro had toppled a corrupt conservative government. Cuba was too poor and lacked the resources to be a threat to the United States in any ordinary sense. But there were those in the US who were alarmed at having any communist-led nation in their part of the world. The Caribbean was considered far too close for comfort. In an ill-advised adventure a group of Cuban exiles, trained and armed by the American Central Intelligence Agency, were parachuted into Cuba to try to overthrow the Castro regime in a coup. A real-life version of the popular television program *Mission Impossible*.

However, as an episode of fact instead of fiction, the operation which was centred on '*The Bay of Pigs'*, did not go according to the script. It turned out to be a complete disaster, with the invaders repelled, killed, or captured. The CIA was humiliated. But not content with that, US armed forces then staged a mock invasion of a Caribbean island as a training exercise called *Operation Ortsac,* the object being to capture a fictitious leader called *Ortsac*.

Since *'Ortsac'* is '*Castro*' spelled backwards it was hardly a subtle title and the message was clear. As if any other hints of hostility were needed, the Cuban leader became aware of CIA efforts to hire Mafia hit-men in an assassination attempt (as officially revealed by the United States in 2007). The cumulative effect was to drive Fidel Castro headlong into the arms of Moscow. He declared Cuba to be a socialist republic, and entered into close ties with the Russians who upgraded his military equipment and defences.

When, in return, the Russians asked to be able to install nuclear missile launching pads in Cuba, within short range of the United States, Castro was delighted. Here was real power at last. The US might not like him, but now they would surely have to respect him!

The Russians were able to use the excuse that the Americans had installed Jupiter long range missile systems in Turkey close to the Soviet border. What was good for the goose was surely good enough for the gander?

So began the crisis. American spy planes, the famous U2s, detected and photographed the building of missile bases in Cuba. Some launching pads were complete, and some missiles had already been landed. From the American point of view it was now a matter of immediate urgency to prevent more missiles or nuclear war-heads reaching Cuba by ship or submarine, while at the same time making official diplomatic complaints to Moscow.

A fleet of Russian ships carrying missiles and nuclear power-heads began sailing down the Atlantic Ocean towards Cuba. The US Navy was sent on blockade to prevent them delivering their cargos. Shadowing the ships were Russian submarines ready to fire torpedoes if their surface vessels were fired upon. The ships met the ring of US vessels, and held back while waiting for orders. The stand-off which became *'The Cuban Missile Crisis'* was under way. For 13 days -- perhaps the most crucial 13 days in the history of the world -- matters teetered on the brink.

'Nuclear catastrophe was hanging by a thread' the Soviet Army Chief of Operations, General Anatoly Gribkov declared afterwards *'And we weren't counting days but minutes!'*.

The US were unaware that the Soviet submarines had nuclear-headed torpedoes, each with the equivalent power of the A-bomb dropped on Hiroshima. It required only one commander to act independently or one provocative incident, to start a shooting war. One such incident occurred on October 27th, 1962, with the shooting down of one of the U2 American spy planes over Cuba, killing the pilot.

The world held its collective breaths!

The leaders of the two countries were John F. Kennedy in Washington and Nikita Khrushchev in Moscow. While they exchanged brittle formal messages others, including Kennedy's brother Robert, were working frantically in backroom negotiations with the Russians on an informal basis.

'We're eyeball to eyeball' declared US Secretary for State, Dean Rusk *' And I think the other fellow just blinked!'*

Fortunately for the world, eyeballs stinging, they both blinked at once.

On October 28th, 1962, Khrushchev agreed to Kennedy's suggestion to dismantle the launching pads and remove all nuclear weapons from Cuba. He said he would do so on the condition that the United States agreed never again to invade Cuba. A further confidential condition agreed upon was the removal of the Jupiter missiles from Turkey. Kennedy agreed on both counts and the world was saved from nuclear war. Commonsense had finally saved the day. But, as the Duke of Wellington remarked after the Battle of Waterloo in 1815, *'It was the closest run thing, you ever did see!'*.

On October 28th, 1962, the dawn brought another day on the stations of the North West Cape, which seemed just like any other October day. The sheep were out in the paddocks, and in good time men on horses with dogs running alongside were out there too. Working as usual and quite unaware of the momentous events which had taken place half a world away while they slept.

But the Cuban crisis would produce some dramatic changes in US military strategy which in time would involve the Exmouth region and those sheep stations on the Cape. The American U2 exercises over Cuba had shown how hard it was to hide rocket installations from aerial surveillance. Systems, including satellites orbiting in Space, could only improve photographic aerial views of what was happening anywhere in the world.

Once sites were pin-pointed they were vulnerable to attack and could no longer be counted upon when needed. Clearly the most potent weapons at the US disposal were its fleet of nuclear submarines. They could fire nuclear rockets and they could hide anywhere in the deep blue sea – even under the ice-packs of the North or South Poles! Nuclear submarines could fire missiles when submerged and undetected from any of the seas of the world. The submarines could be under the cover of the Atlantic, the Arctic, the Mediterranean, the Indian Ocean, or the vast Pacific. But how could they receive the order to fire, or instructions on where to proceed?

In the past a submarine had had to surface in order to make or receive radio contact, and a sub on the surface was vulnerable to detection by satellite and possible attack. But the United States Navy, a country ever innovative and masterful of technology, had developed a VLF (Very Low Frequency) system of transmitters which could make contact with a submarine anywhere, and any time, even at the bottom of the sea. The problem was that VLF was no crystal-set operation. It required a complex web of very high towers – some more than 1000 feet -- and extensive back-up of buildings and facilities. Construction of a VLF base was not a small undertaking. It was the equivalent of establishing a whole town.

From 1961 onwards the United States had been considering 15 potential sites around the world, including the Marianas islands in the Pacific.

Because the Cold War had been focussed on Europe there was a gap in the radio communications coverage of the Indian Ocean. That was now an area considered to be of increasing importance not least because of Arab and Middle Eastern oil. Preliminary surveys had already been conducted in Australia, on a wish-list basis.

Now the intensifying of the Cold War made the Indian Ocean a new priority. There was a prospect of problems arising in Iran in the Middle East. The communist insurgence in Vietnam in the Far East, where the French were about to suffer a humiliating defeat, was causing concern. Among the considered VLF sites was the abandoned British '*Blue Streak*' rocket range at Talgarno in Australia. The North West Cape was also on the list and when the Navy took a hard look at the report which came back, it showed that region as rating highly in the essential requirements.

The Point Murat area was especially suited to a tower installation because it would allow signals to be sent out across an arc of 300 degrees with the sea on three sides. Exmouth Gulf was a remote area. There were only a few civilians who would be affected by the establishment of a base with extensive accommodation and support facilities. Weather conditions were another requirement, and the Exmouth region scored top marks there too, with a preponderance of fine, sunny days throughout the year.

Perhaps more important than any other aspect, was the fact that Australia was a stable country, and regardless of what political party was in power, the country would remain an ally of the United States. As it happened the Liberal Party were in government at the time, and they would be the most receptive to any arrangements with the Americans. But, equally, any future Labour government would be unlikely to rescind or vary any agreements made by their political rivals. In that sense there would be no diplomatic problems. Last but not least, in such a remote area security could be more easily maintained.

It was stated in discussions with the Australian government that the purpose of the VLF station would be to establish better communications with US ships and submarines in the Indian Ocean. There was no need to elaborate further on that. Though it didn't require any degree of strategic genius to understand the true purpose of the VLF installation. After all the Cold War was still well and truly alive. Most of the world was in a state of '*Them or us!*' and allied to, or at least sympathetic to either Russia or the United States. So far as Australia was concerned 'Us' meant alignment with America. The big US! America was about to escalate her military involvement in Vietnam, and Australia would introduce conscription and send soldiers there too. After a visit to America to meet President Lyndon B, Johnson Australia's Prime Minister Harold Holt had returned with the catch phrase '*All the way, with LBJ!*'

In the 1960s the Russian bear and world communism were still seen as the twin bogeys for the western world and in the United States the *'Domino Theory'* was very much in mind.

The Domino Theory?

If one domino falls over, in the familiar game, it knocks down other dominoes until ultimately they are all flat on the table. A parallel was suggested with countries falling under the influence and military dominance of Soviet Russia. A large part of Europe formed the Soviet Bloc, which included East Germany, Poland, Hungary, Czechoslovakia, Bulgaria, Romania, and Albania. In the east China was communist too, under Mao Tse Tung, and so was North Korea. It was suggested that if Vietnam were to become communist, then Laos, Cambodia, Thailand -- even Malaysia -- might follow suit like dominoes collapsing one after the other. After all, a communist attempt at a take-over in Indonesia had been narrowly averted, and had been put down ruthlessly with bloodbaths in Java and Bali.

Against that troubled international background on May 9th, 1963, an agreement was signed between the American and Australian governments for the establishing of a VLF station on the North West Cape. Following the Cuban Missile Crisis the US Secretary of Defence had decided to make the station part of the United States Defence Communications System, which meant that a large High Frequency Radio unit had to be added to the VLF component.

Among other uses it would allow communication with the B 52 nuclear bomber fleet. The aircraft were primed for action on a permanent basis. There were always aircraft in the air at any one time carrying armed nuclear weapons. They flew continuously between the United States and Europe, always ready in case that single word *'GO!'* should come from a US President. The doomsday signal to begin The Third World War.

Before the official announcement about the Exmouth region, and as with all matters of the Defence Department, an air of secrecy hung over the concept of what was about to happen on the North West Cape. Rumours abounded. First strangers, some of them identified as Americans by their accents and sunglasses, turned up with notebooks, brushing away the flies, and making notes. They were uncommunicative with the locals.

Then there were surveyors looking through their theodolites at areas no-one had ever cared about before. With charter planes landing and taking off from the Learmonth airstrip there was more aerial traffic than there had been since the Second World War. Locals, bemused, pushed their broad-brimmed hats back, scratched their foreheads, and asked each other *'What the hell is going on?'*.

Finally an official announcement confirmed what was already suspected – the Americans were going to build a major base at the Cape. Once the news was out, the people on the stations were naturally concerned about how the project would affect their own lives, understanding that it would be a major undertaking. But even at that point they would have been astonished if they had been told that within three years there would be 3000 people working on the North West Cape!

The size and scope of the project was beyond most people's imaginations. At Cape Murat the formation of the VLF towers would be an awesome sight. The central Tower Zero, at 387 metres would stand higher than the Eiffel Tower in Paris. As the highest engineering construction in the Southern Hemisphere, it would be surrounded by a ring of inner towers each 1145 feet high, with a circle of outer towers measuring 905 feet. To put this in a geographical perspective, the highest natural point on the Cape Range is 304 metres.

The power plant alone, in Area A, at Point Murat, had an electricity output able to supply a city of 12,000 people, and had fuel tanks with a capacity of 4,250,000 gallons. A cyclone-proof pier, 1099 feet long with a head of 167 feet in width and two dolphins 1200 feet apart, was built to withstand 30 foot waves. That was typical of the scale of the project.

Area B, where the sheep of Yardie Creek Station once wandered, nibbling the scant foliage, would incorporate the Base Headquarters. The HQ had accommodation for several hundred men, a swimming pool, basketball and tennis courts, and a softball field, as well as a theatre, chapel, medical facilities, and Officers and Other Ranks messes. At its peak the ' United States Naval Communication Station Harold E. Holt' (as it came to be named) had 500 United States Navy personnel there on operations at North West Cape, with more than 400 Australians and other civilians employed in various roles. At times there were probably 1000 people involved, directly or indirectly, in the various aspects of running the Base.

The US Navy presence would take in three main areas, Areas A, B, and C, in blocks from Cape Murat to Learmonth. At the same time the Commonwealth and Western Australian State governments decided to build a support township. The new town of Exmouth was gazetted on January 6th, 1963, and became a Shire early in 1964.

The Americans would build their own homes for married personnel in the town, and having American and Australian families living side by side became a guiding principle. So the town of Exmouth and the Shire of Exmouth were born.

In the half-century since the frenzied construction period of the 1960s a good deal has naturally changed. The Cold War and the threat of global conflict thankfully receded. Economic circumstances -- a wounded rouble -- instead of nuclear missiles revised Russia's path to the future. The Soviet Bloc fragmented into individual nations, each with their own approach to the rest of the world.

The old hardline principles of Marxist communism gave way to a modern democratic, free-thinking approach in Moscow which would have had the former dictatorial Marxist Joseph Stalin turning in his grave. In 1992 the United States decided, with the threat of world conflict apparently minimal, to withdraw their people from Exmouth. They left the station in the hands of the Royal Australian Navy, the Commonwealth Government, and civilian contractors.

The station was still functional, ready for any emergency which might arise. But the universal hope in countries everywhere, was that there would never again be another peril like the Cuban Missile Crisis. Where initially the Station was the whole reason for Exmouth's existence and everything revolved around the Base, by the time the new 21st Century came around it was no longer the major element in Exmouth. Instead tourism had become the focus, with whale sharks, game fishing, the coral wonders of the Ningaloo Reef, the Cape Range National Park, and Coral Bay, the main attractions in the region.

By 2010 the whole face of the town was about to change. The marina, opened in 1997, had been extended to provide for an exciting canal development, the Exmouth Marina Village. There was a new four-star hotel, the Novotel Ningaloo Resort, at Sunrise Beach. The canals with new houses lining their banks, projected retail areas, and tourist facilities would be highly visible from Murat Road, the main entry for visitors coming into town, giving a bright and buoyant picture of Exmouth today.

But the Exmouth story begins a lot further back in time than that. Some four hundred years, in fact.

ABORIGINE warriors considered themselves undressed if their spears were not within arm's reach. They never went anywhere without a spear – or sometimes two or three – in their right hand. Other than that they wore no clothes except occasionally pearl shell Rigas over their genitals. European clothes were a mystery to them.

The Magic Sound Of *'First'*!

Chapter Two

At daylight on January 8th, 1811, while Exmouth Gulf remained as yet unnamed, the big Aborigine camp in the dunes at Point Cloates awoke to high excitement. There was a ship on the reef opposite them, a little distance off shore. Masts canted over, sails flapping, distress in every angle of the vessel. They had often seen sails going past like white clouds on the horizon. Sometimes they had come so close that they could see the dark hulls below the spread of canvas. They were sure that they must become snared on the coral fangs of the treacherous outer reefs. But as the Aborigines watched expectantly the ships had always turned away in time and continued on their voyages north to Java and China and other distant lands.

But this one, like a broken-winged bird, must have come into the surf-fringed danger zone in the night. Now it was askew on the reef, and plainly in dire trouble. Keen eyes on shore saw the sails flogging out of control, making cracking noises like cannon shots. The tiny figures of crewmen running about on deck were making the erratic movements of men in a desperate situation.

The ship's bow was high in the air where she had ridden up on the reef. While she had missed the savage surf break of the outer reef – where she would surely have been battered to pieces and destroyed in a short time -- she was still being struck by smaller waves and surges, and the wind was increasing. Since she was immobile, and she wasn't lifting and falling, it was probable that her hull had been breached and her lower decks flooded. In short she was doomed.

Soon those on shore could see that a decision had been made. Since it was plainly impossible to save the ship, now the people had to look to saving themselves. Three boats, one after the other, were lowered over the bulwarks in the lee of the ship. Then there was a fresh sensation. Smoke began to rise, the ship was on fire!

Gradually the flames increased until the ship was an inferno, flames leaping high from stem to stern, belching black clouds of smoke high in the sky as those on the beach watched and wondered. The boats, which had cast off from the ship to watch it burn from a safe distance, now began to move. Masts were stepped, sails hoisted, and the Aborigines on the beach became restive – were the white strangers coming ashore?

The tactic of the Aborigines, when-ever people from the ships had landed in the past, was to fade away into the bush. Their wisdom, after long discussion between the elders, the Old Men of the tribe, in previous years, was to avoid all contact with the magicians. Who could tell what evil or grief they might bring with them? 'Better not to take the chance!

But this time the boats turned away and followed the direction the ships at sea always took. They headed north, the wind behind them, their sails disappearing around the headland of what would later come to be known as Norwegian Bay. It was the start of a remarkable story.

The ship on the reef, still burning, was the Yankee clipper *Rapid,* 98 days out from Boston, on a voyage that had made her skipper, Henry Dorr, nervous from the very outset. In the lazarette below his cabin, were boxes containing 280,000 Spanish silver dollars, a fortune in anyone's language.

The silver was to exchange for silks and chests of tea in Canton up the Pearl River on the China coast. The *Rapid* was a fast vessel in the clipper tradition. She was able to show a clean pair of heels to most pirates or privateers. But the sight of any sail, particularly one which might turn out to be an English frigate, would cause anxiety aboard her. England and the United States were in a period of hostility, and technically at war. Britain was too involved in the on-going conflict with France to take any immediate military action against the Americans. But any United States vessel on the high seas at that time was considered fair game by the ships of His Majesty's Royal Navy. The *Rapid* had only eight guns, and she would have been no match for a Man-o-war.

Where the British officers and Jolly Jack Tars were concerned, her silver dollars would have made a tempting prize of war, the loot to be divided proportionately, among a grinning crew. A fine incentive!

Rapid's best chances were her speed and good luck. She had managed to elude her enemies through the reaches of the Atlantic and the Indian Ocean. But now, when the main threat seemed over, her luck had deserted her in the worst possible way. On the reef, his ship disintegrating below him, Henry Dorr made a drastic but courageous decision. They had no choice but to save their lives by sailing for the East Indies, the nearest point of civilisation, in the ship's boats.

Why burn the ship?

Henry Dorr couldn't take the Spanish dollars with him – they would have weighed more than seven tons, and the boats needed to be as light as possible, except for essential food and water. If some other ship came along, saw a vessel on the reef, and stopped to investigate they might have found the silver and celebrated the unexpected windfall with uproarious delight.

Dorr's answer to that unwelcome possibility was to burn the ship and hope that he could come back one day with divers to salvage the treasure. Setting the *Rapid* ablaze was a desperate measure in a most desperate situation.

The 22 crew of the Rapid were divided between three boats. The chief officer took 10 men in the longboat, the most seaworthy craft. The second officer and four sailors went in the gig. Captain Dorr, his clerk Mr Flagg and three sailors went in the smallest craft of all. It was only 16 feet long and described as '*very leaky*' and having less than half a metre of freeboard. Henry Dorr must have been a man of considerable honour to send the bulk of his men in the best craft and to have elected to go in the smallest boat where there was the greatest element of risk.

Encountering storms along the way Dorr's crew had to throw overboard more than a third of their water, and even their wet and heavy clothes, in a desperate bid to survive. They had a ration of only three cups of water and three small pieces of bread per person per day. But they made it to Christmas Island where they joyously cooked local rats and crabs and wolfed them down as only starving men could. Thunderstorms filled their water barrels.

On the next leg, assailed by storms and tropic line squalls they were several times forced to heave-to, boats head-to-wind, sea-anchors out, men bailing furiously. Eventually, against the odds, all three boats reached the Sunda Strait and gratefully turned east around Java Head to the Dutch East Indies capital of Batavia. Dorr's journey took 37 days. Another epic small boat voyage from the Western Australian coast. Their survival, through all their dangers must have seemed miraculous to them, and in a time of strong religious convictions no doubt they went down on their knees on arrival and fervently thanked the Almighty for their deliverance.

In that manner all the crew reached Batavia alive. But the story was far from over. The Dutch capital of the Far East was a town notorious for pestilences, in particular malaria, typhoid, and other tropical fevers.

The Dutch had built canals, just like the ones they had left behind in Holland. They were similar to the European models in most respects, but – importantly – they were biologically different in that they bred the tropical malarial *anopheles* mosquito in clouds.

Some of the *Rapid* crew, sadly including Mr Flagg the ship's clerk, died soon after arrival, their health weakened by the physical stresses of the open boat voyage. No doubt the reaction of the others, after all the dangers and now with this new and ominous threat of disease, was to desperately wish themselves homeward bound. Preferably on a vessel sailing for Boston or Baltimore. But any American port would do.

'What now?' they would have asked Henry Dorr.

American ships were not common visitors to Batavia. One possibility would have been to go to Canton, on the China coast –*Rapid's* original destination – where American clippers called more frequently. Another option was to take passage to Europe where Dutch ships regularly sailed. But since that part of the world was embroiled in the smoke and fury of the Napoleonic wars that would have been an absolute last resort. 'Better to go to British India, Calcutta or Madras…?

While they pondered their escape, an unexpected opportunity presented itself.

After six weeks of cooling their heels in the fever port Henry Dorr heard of an American vessel in distress. The captain and apparently most of the crew of the 93-ton American schooner *General Greene,* had died from malaria or yellow fever, and the vessel was left with not enough hands to take her home. The circumstances of the *General Greene* were tragic for her crew but good fortune for Henry Dorr and his band of castaways. He navigated her back to Philadelphia where Dorr and the owners of the *Rapid* immediately began making plans for the salvage of the 280,000 silver dollars. Those boxes of specie, now under green fathoms of water in the wreck of the unlucky *Rapid* on the Ningaloo Reef.

They had to keep their intentions secret because hostilities still existed between the United States and Great Britain. But eventually a vessel called the *Meridian* sailed for Ningaloo. A good deal of the treasure was raised, but some, for whatever reason, was left on site. A new story would unfold dramatically in our own time after the accidental finding of the wreck and a treasure trove of remaining silver dollars by skindivers in 1979.

Following the *Rapid* shipwrecks occurred thick and fast on the Ningaloo Reef. Some 25 vessels would be lost, a number with all hands, in the lead up to modern times. The Portuguese *Coreo da Asio*, clippers, barques, colonial schooners, pearlers, Japanese grain carriers, whalers, steam ships, even an American torpedo boat in the Second World War, all left their bones on that beautiful but deadly stretch of coastline. The corals costing the lives of ships and men of many nations.

Rapid was the first recorded shipwreck. But who, we may ask, was the first European to sail past the Ningaloo Reef? Who was the first to land there? Who applied the names we know today, and what were the reasons for their origin?

Once vessels of the Dutch East India Company – the great *Vereenigde Oost-Indische Compagnie,* or VOC – began sailing from the Cape of Good Hope to the Sunda Strait in Indonesia and the '*Spice Islands'*, it was inevitable that sooner or later ships would sail further east than anyone had sailed before. 'Certain that one of them, one morning, to the surprise of her captain and crew, would find Australia before her bows. A vast, red-brown mass stretching from horizon to horizon, north and south..

The first such skipper, so far as we know, was Dirk Hartog of Amsterdam, in the VOC vessel *Eendracht.* On October 16th, 1616, he sighted the huge island at Shark Bay which would later be named Dirk Hartog Island in his memory. To get a historical perspective on the date, 1616 was the year that William Shakespeare died in England. Queen Elizabeth – *'Good Queen Bess'* – was not long in her grave. Hartog and most of the senior members of his crew had been born before the Spanish Armada sailed.

It was a long time ago, even by European standards of history. And it was 154 years before James Cook and *HMS Endeavour* arrived on the east coast at Botany Bay!

Skipper Hartog left an inscribed pewter plate recording the *Eendracht's* visit. It was nailed to a post on a cliff at Shark Bay, and he (or one of his sailors) is believed to have been the first European to have set foot on Australian soil.

Hartog is best remembered for his Shark Bay contact. But as he sailed north, continuing the voyage to Indonesia, there were telescope sightings of other land to the east. Disembodied fragments were glimpsed on the horizon, which were taken to be '*Islands in the sea'*. One of these sightings was at 22 degrees South Latitude. What the Dutchmen were looking at there was no island. It was the distant crown of the Cape Range of North West Cape. Thereby qualifying Hartog and the *Eendracht* for inclusion in this history of the Exmouth region.

No doubt there was some distortion by mirage, the peak seemingly floating in space and adding to the illusion of an *'island'*. Many other skippers would make the same mistake in the future. Hartog's *Eendracht* finally reached her destination of Bantam in Java, in December, 1616, after a voyage from Europe which had lasted nearly a year. By that time her passengers and crew must have been desperately glad to reach their destination.

At Bantam Hartog merely reported sighting *'Some islands in the sea, which were, however, uninhabited'*. In their turn the Dutch East India Company bureaucrats in Bantam thought Hartog's report so unimportant that it was not included among their correspondence back to the Netherlands until August, 1617. Some ten months later.

At the time, though the Portuguese had been in India and the East Indies for more than 100 years, and the Dutch had been in Java since before 1600, Australia had yet to be represented on any map of the world. Though, strangely, it had actually been named more than a millennium beforehand. The Graeco-Egyptian astronomer Ptolemy in Alexandria in 140 AD theorised on the probability of a great continent south of the equator. It must exist, he said, to balance the weight of the known lands of the northern hemisphere. He went so far as to give his mysterious continent a name, calling it *'Terra Australis Incognita'* – literally *'The Unknown South Land'*. The *Incognita* was tagged on because there was no actual proof that it existed, and geographers would argue the matter for nearly 1500 years before the Dutch seamen of the VOC came along. Their accidental contacts took the *Incognita* out of the name.

Curiously Australia, *Australis*, was actually named in this way before England. Britain, in Ptolemy's time, being under Roman rule, and known then as *'Britannia'*.

Unknown to Hartog, or even his VOC masters, a Dutchman named Willem Jansz had already sighted Australia ten years earlier in 1606. Sent on a voyage to New Guinea with the little vessel *Duyfken* to investigate trade possibilities, his men faced a hostile reception on landing. Nine of his crew were brutally slain with clubs and barbed arrows by war-like tribesmen. Understandably shaken by the massacre and sheering away to the south, he found new land which he assumed was still a part of New Guinea which had been named by the Portuguese in 1545.

In fact, what he was seeing was the western face of Australia's Cape York Peninsula. There is no record that he landed. The vessel was now seriously short-handed and the surviving crew members were probably demoralised by the deaths of their companions. From the skipper's point of view, if nine men were lost from a crew of 16 to 20 there would hardly be enough hands remaining to sail the ship home should a second shore party meet with a disaster. Unaware of the existence of the Torres Strait, Dutch cartographers had Australia joined to New Guinea on their charts for the next 200 years. Depriving Jansz for all that time of the credit of his discovery. But – extraordinarily -- he would have yet another sighting of Australian shores. More of that in a moment.

Hartog, in 1616, had no conception that his *'Islands'* were part of the giant promontory of today's North West Cape. Or that the country beyond stretched away over thousands of unbroken red-earth kilometres, to the far Pacific Ocean. Australia was a huge land mass bigger than most of Europe, and equal in size to North America between Mexico and the Canadian border.

Given that he failed to realise that he was looking at a continent, not '*Islands in the sea'*, and did not understand the significance of his accidental landfalls, including the North West Cape, why should Dirk Hartog be listed as one of the more famous '*discoverers'* in our history?

The answer is that fame, the reason why we remember someone, is a quirky and sometimes irrational thing. Dirk Hartog was simply the first European believed to have trodden Australian soil. There is a magic about that word *'First'*. Australians have a saying '*There's no prize for second!'* and there's a hard truth in that statement. For example we know that Columbus was the first European to sail west across the Atlantic and make a landfall on the other side. But who knows the name of the next explorer to follow in the wake of the *Santa Maria?*

Every schoolchild has heard of Christopher Columbus. But ask the question '*Who was Vespucci Amerigo?'* and don't expect to be overwhelmed by a flood of answers. But it is the second explorer Amerigo's name which remains on the continents of North and South America. Together they cover more space than any other territories named after any of the world's great navigators – at least he has that distinction. But in the general ignorance of Amerigo's undoubted achievements it remains a memorial without the applause.

Edmund Hillary was famously the first to stand on the peak of Mt Everest linking arms with Sherpa Tensing. Everyone knows that. But who was next to stand in triumph upon that frozen peak? In so many instances the man who is first goes down in history. After him – though the mountain may be just as hard to climb, the dangers as real, the triumph just as worthy of celebration – perhaps unfairly, the later names don't really seem to matter to us.

But Dirk Hartog's landfall followed by similar sightings of the North West Cape by other Dutch vessels, including the *Zeewolf* and the *Mauritius* in 1618, one after the other, did prove a vital point. Australia, the previously unknown Fifth Continent which had been argued about by geographers all those years, really did exist.

Following in his wake other Indies-bound skippers made landfalls at different points along the same coast in quick succession. The initial lack of interest shown by the officials in Bantam was replaced by excitement in Holland when the skippers' sailing logs and reports were returned home. There much sharper eyes among the chart-makers of the VOC perceived the significance of the observations. When they set the latitudes down on parchment and the positions of the landfalls joined up, they realised that they had the outline of the continuous edge of a vast continent.

By 1622, Hessel Gerritz, the VOC's chief cartographer, had a preliminary outline of the Western Australian coast. In 1627, with a finished and more complete version, he presented a picture of the coast very much as we know it today. It included the Exmouth Edge. The North West corner of Australia.

Hartog's first sighting of the Cape Range in 1616 gives us a marker for the beginning of European history of the area. Having said that, it raises the question of whether he was really the first? History has a long list of false assumptions entrenched by long habit and it is interesting sometimes to compare the legends with the realities. For instance, in any quiz show the answer to the question *'Who discovered America?'* will have the bell ring and *'Christopher Columbus!'* will be acclaimed to applause as the correct response.

Wrong!

In fact Columbus performed an outstanding feat in crossing the Atlantic. It was then sometimes called *'The Green Sea Of Darkness'*. Folk-lore had people believing that anyone venturing too far out on its molten grey surface would sail off the edge of the world.

It was said that the sea in the region of the equator literally boiled! In the light of those mediaeval superstitions Columbus had to coerce a mutinous crew whose greatest desire was to turn back. His reward was the sighting of land in the west which no European had seen before him. That in itself was a significant achievement. But what he actually found were the Bahamas and the islands of the Caribbean. The landfalls were not the twin continents of the Americas.

In fact Columbus never saw the North American mainland at all and had only a far-off glimpse of a portion of South America. Ironically, until his death in 1509 at the early age of 55 -- a broken man still pleading his case with Spanish royalty – it was his own firm belief that he had reached China -- then known in Europe as *'Cathay'*. It was China which had always been his objective, a largely forgotten fact today.

So he made a magnificent discovery but suffered a geographical confusion. We can say the same about Willem Jansz aboard the Duyfken in 1606 who thought he was sailing past a part of New Guinea when, in fact, it was an Australian shore which lay before him.

Which brings us to the question of who really were the first visitors from the Northern Hemisphere to sight Australian shores? We generally credit the Dutch because that opinion is held on the basis of known records. A matter of what is definitely known, rather than mere speculation. But if we were to keep an open mind on the matter, there remains the possibility – even the probability -- that other unrecorded Northern Hemisphere mariners may have had prior opportunity. Their credits withheld simply because the records have been lost or destroyed.

There has been a good deal of speculation through the years about whether the *'Treasure fleet'* of the Chinese eunuch-admiral Zeng He, as early as the 1420s, may have preceded the Dutch in Australian waters? The Chinese, the Arabs, and the Portuguese, all had the capability to make voyages south of the equator. Books on the subject such as *1421 – The Year China Discovered*

The World, by Gavin Menzies, and *The Secret Discovery of Australia -- Portuguese Ventures 200 years before Captain Cook,* by Keith Gordon McIntyre, make interesting reading.

So do we credit the Chinese, the Portuguese, or the Dutch with discovering Australia? And what about the Makassar men and Indonesian trepang fishermen who fished north Australian waters for centuries? With all those contenders we are looking at events over hundreds of years before our time. But carbon dating proves that the Aborigines were on the North West Cape (no doubt they had a different name for it) 30,000 years ago. Plainly, that WAS long, long before any of the others came over the horizon. The great Prussian botanical geographer, Alexander von Humboldt (1769 – 1859), after whom the Humboldt Current off South America and many plant species are named, made an amusing comment about discoveries .

'*There are three stages in the popular attitude towards a great discovery'* he said, with a smile. '*First men doubt its existence. Then they deny it, and finally they give the credit to someone else!'*.

Perhaps we should go back to the things which we do know are positive facts rather than interesting possibilities. And even within that limitation there are some historical ironies for us to consider. For instance Dirk Hartog died in Amsterdam in 1621 aged 41, without knowing that in 1616 he was looking at a great continent, or that he would be famous forever after because of it. Willem Jansz never knew in his lifetime that he was looking at Australia and not New Guinea. But there is sensationally more to his story than that.

Two years after the *Eendracht* passed by the North West Cape the first recorded landing was made there by Europeans. The VOC vessel *Mauritius* arrived off the Cape in July, 1618, and a party went ashore.

'*We discovered an island, landed on it and found human footprints. On the west side it extends NNE and SSW is 15 miles long and its northern extremity is in 22 degrees ...'* .

The supercargo of the vessel was none other than Willem Jansz, former skipper of the *Duyfken* which had made the first known Dutch sighting of Australia at Cape York in 1606.

What a fantastic co-incidence that Jansz, of all people should sight Australia twice! Each time without knowing what it was! In 1606 he thought he was seeing New Guinea shores. In 1618 he thought he was on an '*island'*! How amazed he would have been if he could have learned that his *'island'* was actually joined by thousands of miles to his Cape York sighting of his *Duyfken* voyage 12 years previously!

That it would have been theoretically possible (given the time and the patience and probably a camel!) to travel on dry land from one place to the other?

After the *Mauritius'* visit to North West Cape Dutch charts carried an indentation named '*Willems River'*. Since there is only one natural feature on the North West Cape which fits that description it is likely that Jansz found his *'human footprints'* near Yardie Creek. Leaving his own footmarks as the first European prints on the North West Cape.

As a result of the new knowledge passed on to the chart-makers by the VOC skippers, there began a regular procession of Dutch and English ships passing by outside the Ningaloo Reef on their way north to the Indies. We may wonder what the Aborigines would have made of the traffic? Those white sails out at sea with lights in the night?

They would have known that the ships carried men, because of landings like that of Willem Jansz's party who came ashore by ship's boat from the *Mauritius*. If Jansz saw *'human footprints'* then Aborigines would certainly have been interested in his own, viewing them in awe and perhaps some dread. They would have studied the Dutch footprints minutely after the visitors had returned to their vessel in their longboat.

'Who are these spirit people?' they would have asked. *'These beings who came and go along our shore in their great canoes?'* Were they human or were they ghosts of their own people long since dead? And if they were ghosts was their intent good or evil?

There were a multitude of questions with no satisfactory answers. The appearance of the strangers was as much a mystery as anything else about them. They carried weapons that glinted and sparkled in the sun. They covered their bodies with multi-coloured skins, with other odd shade arrangements on their heads.

The Aborigines of the Ningaloo Reef had gone naked themselves for thousands of years. Hats, clothes, and shoes, would have been completely alien to them, as would guns and swords and pikes made of iron. The Dutchmen, clumsy and in unfamiliar territory in the bush, usually failed to catch sight of the local inhabitants who showed clean pairs of heels and merged into the landscape. But it is a fair assumption that curiosity would have been too much for some of the indigenous observers. They may have crept back under cover to assay a peep from hiding at the newcomers.

What a story to tell around the camp fire that evening!

OLD ROAD. Before World War II the rough track to Exmouth Gulf was along the west coast via Warroora, Cardabia, Ningaloo, and Yardie Creek stations. Fine for camels, rough for motors.

Exmouth – Noble And Valiant!

Chapter Three

When Jao Jaoquim de Freitas, captain of the *Correo da Azia* lost his ship on the Ningaloo Reef near Point Cloates in 1816 he was not short of excuses. He reported '*Coming from Lisbon to Macau against weather, sea, and wind, and fire, shallows and coastal dangers, and errors of maps!*'.

The charts were certainly suspect where they related to that part of the Australian coast. Matthew Flinders of *HMS Investigator* is generally credited with '*Circumnavigating Australia*' in his surveys. But that was not actually the case.

His charts of the Torres Strait, and Northern Australia, were certainly up to the demanding standards set by the British Admiralty and best exemplified by the skills of James Cook. But shortage of supplies in Flinders' survey of 1801 to 03 obliged him to interrupt his work in Northern Australia and sail for Mauritius across the Indian Ocean to re- provision. The direction of the prevailing winds meant that he could not return to his previous location in Northern Australia and instead he took up his task again with *Investigator* on the South Coast from Cape Leeuwin eastwards.

As a result, while most of his full chart of Australia was the result of his own up-to-date surveys, he had to rely on the Dutch charts dating back to Willem de Vlamingh in 1697 for west coast information. While the Dutch surveys were a credible effort for the 17th Century, they did not match the standards of Flinders' own time. They had serious errors in longitude, placing the North Western Australian coast too far to the east.

While navigators could determine their latitude (position north-south) from the angle of the sun at midday, before Cook in 1770 and for many years after him most ships did not have chronometers to give them a reliable longitude, or east-west position at sea. They relied on '*Dead Reckoning*' or educated guess-work. A practice which sometimes lived up to its name.

Most mariners were aware of the short-comings, relying on their own instincts and seamanship when approaching land in those latitudes. They looked for signs such as land-based seabirds such as crested terns, floating weed, cuttlefish bones, and the long clouds which formed over high points on the coast. These signs of Nature all warned them of land ahead. Skippers sensibly shortened sail at night and began taking soundings when they saw any of these indicators.

Like the American clipper *Rapid* wrecked five years earlier, the *Correo* was also carrying silver. Some 106,000 Spanish silver dollars were stored in chests below her decks when she sighted the Australian coast in the region of Shark Bay, apparently having no difficulty in making that landfall. De Freitas followed the line of the coast northwards to the Ningaloo region, but on November 26th, about 1a.m., she struck the Ningaloo Reef a little way south of Point Cloates. His error after his first sighting of the Australian coast was trying to keep the land in sight after turning north. A course which took him too close in to that deadly section of Ningaloo Reef between Point Maud and Point Cloates.

A fire at night in the compass binnacle – presumably a lantern over-turned – meant that the helmsman had to steer 'blind' for a time of confusion while the flames were doused and another lantern obtained before he could read the compass again. This was undoubtedly a contributing factor to the disaster. The lookouts may also have been distracted and diverted from their primary task by the emergency.

Modern charts of the area and aerial photographs, show that between Point Cloates and Point Maud the mainland coast trends eastwards looking like a tiger shark bite out of the land. But the line of outer reefs continues more or less in a straight line, far out from the low-lying shore. Any skipper trying to keep the land in sight and sailing a parallel course with it was risking his vessel once darkness fell. For those reasons it was an exceptionally dangerous piece of coast and it would claim many more victims as the years went by.

The *Correo da Azia* struck in an area of heavy surf on the outer reef, and her hull was immediately breached and two masts toppled. The crew managed to launch their longboat and, salvaged three barrels of biscuits and some water. In this state they remained alongside with the longboat tied to the mizzen mast, buffeted by surf, the hull of their ship sunk below the waves.

When daylight came they hoisted sail and travelled north looking for a suitable place to build up the sides of their boat for an anticipated long ocean voyage. In this way they rounded Point Murat and came ashore in the vicinity of Bundegi reef. It was recorded that:

' Some of the sailors, two scribes, and the surgeon went inland some five kilometres searching for water or inhabitants. All but two of the men returned reporting that they had seen tracks of animals like those of lions, tigers, and wolves, and many trails of snakes. They had found huts made of mud with small entrances and brush coverings. Repairs to the launch were completed by 6 pm on 27th, November. Thinking that Aborigines or wild animals had killed the two missing men, and fearing that they might face the same fate the group departed …'

The captain and crew of the *Correo* were spared the hardship of the long ocean open–boat voyage undertaken by the people from the *Rapid.* That was probably just as well. With their scanty supply of water and provisions it was unlikely that they could ever have reached any of the distant points of civilisation. But by a stroke of luck they were picked up almost immediately they set out from Exmouth Gulf by the American sailing ship *Caledonia* from Philadelphia which had crossed the Indian Ocean bound for Canton. By an extraordinary co-incidence the *Caledonia* is listed as one of the ships which had stranded on the Ningaloo Reef on a previous voyage. More fortunate than the others, her crew managed to free her unharmed, and she sailed on to her destination. Another adventure story.

The captain of the *Caledonia* knew the story of the *Rapid* and told the captain of the *Correo,* Joao Joaqim de Freitas, of the loss of that ship at *'Cloots Island'* not far from where the *Correo* had gone down.

The abandoning of the two crew members – sailing at dusk on the same day they went missing and not giving them any chance to be reunited with their companions – may seem callous in the extreme. On the other hand they were a group of thoroughly frightened men, at their wits end, at one of the farthest corners of the earth. Men with the dark prospect of death by thirst or drowning, seemingly just around the corner. If the boat had not departed when it did it would have missed the golden chance of the *Caledonia* coming by, and they would probably all have perished at sea.

What happened, then, to the two men '*Who were supposed killed by animals or natives and could not be found'?*. There are no '*lions, tigers, and wolves'*, in the Ningaloo region which could have harmed them.

The Aborigines, at this time were more afraid of Europeans than otherwise. Did the men wander inland and become lost and disoriented? Did the Aborigines care for them when they found themselves abandoned, as they did later for the survivors of the Hungarian barque *Stefano*? What were their thoughts when they found that they had been left behind?

If they were accepted into the tribe did traces of Portuguese blood linger in the Aboriginal people of the Ningaloo Reef, or some Portuguese words become inserted into the language? We will return to that interesting speculation at a later time. The Portuguese authorities in Macau sent another vessel south to Australia to the *Correo da Azia* wreck-site to correct the chart errors and to see whether any of the treasure could be saved. The area of the wreck was located but there is no record of any salvage. The sea and weather conditions there were perhaps too difficult given the lack of air-breathing diving equipment at the time.

Pondering the possible fate of the two unknown Portuguese on the North West Cape reminds us of the two mutineers, Wouter Looes and Jan de Bye, '*Death-deserving miscreants'*, who were marooned on the coast further south by Commandeur Franciso Pelsart. They were set ashore to take their chances after the wreck of the Dutch East Indiaman *Batavia* on the Abrolhos Islands in 1629. *Batavia* was another treasure ship, another story. But this time it was a dark tale of mutiny and massacre followed by fearful retribution. The blackest entry in Australian maritime history.

Francisco Pelsart with 40 people –including women and a baby -- had set forth in an open boat in a desperate bid to bring rescue for the people left behind on the bleak coral cays of the Abrolhos. Pelsart's open-boat voyage is of interest in our context because he brings us a description of the North West Cape as it was 379 years ago. By the time the over-loaded boat had travelled a few hundred kilometres north from the Abrolhos they were desperate for water. Several landings along the coast seeking water were unsuccessful, until they reached the vicinity of present day Point Cloates and the Ningaloo Reef. Pelsart wrote in his journal:

'Sailed thus along the Coast, alongside which stretches a reef. Between the reef and the land there appeared to be very still and smooth water. We did our best to get into it, but found no opening until nearly noon when we found a gap where there was no surf....This coast had a low dune foreland of about one Dutch mile in width before one comes to the High land where we found some small holes in a rock that were full of fresh water that the rain had left there. It seemed that the blacks had been there a little time before, for there lay the shells of Crabs and the ashes of fires. We quenched our great thirst...for since the wrecking of the ship we had been without Wine or other drink except for one or two small mugs of water.. and remained there the whole night'.

They filled their water barrels, and searched to see if there were other sources of water.

'But our search was in vain, it appeared that it had not rained there in a very long time, no was there any sign of running water. Beyond the heights the country was flat again, without trees, foliage, or grass, except for ant hills thrown up, which in the distance were not unlike the huts of people. Was also such a host of flies which came to sit in the mouth and eyes that they could not be beaten off..... We next saw eight black men each carrying a stick (spear) in his hand and these approached within a distance of about a musket shot. But when we went towards them they ran away'.

The Aborigines would have had more to wonder at and to pass down in their legends of the strangers, for this time there were white women who came ashore. And there was a baby! Present day visitors will appreciate how exceptionally lucky the Dutchmen -- lacking any bushman's skills -- were to stumble upon a rock water hole with fresh water in a country largely barren of surface water. It was, literally, a chance in a million.

The opportunity to fill their water barrels enabled them to continue on another eleven days and reach the coasts of Java.

As a result a rescue vessel, the *Sardam*, with Pelsart aboard, sailed south eight days later to relieve the castaways at the Abrolhos. But while the ship's boat had sailed for help a terrible story was unfolding. The story of the Batavia mutiny is too long and too complex to recount here -- see the author's book *Islands of Angry Ghosts* for a full account. Suffice to say that the mutineers killed 129 people on the islands by a variety of cruel means.

They hacked some men down with swords and drowned others. They cut the throats of women and raped the remainder. They strangled babies, and beheaded children for amusement in an orgy of blood lust. And – in the end – they paid dearly for their crimes.

The mutiny was put down by the arrival of the *Sardam.* Pelsart, horrified by what he found, conducted the first judicial trials in Australian history and ordered the first executions. The ringleaders were hanged on a wreck-wood gallows, some with the additional punishment of having their hands cut off before going to the gibbet. Wouter Looes and Jan Pelgrom were marooned and left behind on the mainland

In reflecting on the unfolding of historical events we can sometimes ask the hypothetical question *'What if?'* In this case what if Francisco Pelsart's party in 1629 had failed to find the drinking water in the rocks in the Exmouth Cape Range, as could so easily have happened?

Without that extremely fortuitous discovery those in the ship's boat would likely have perished of thirst before reaching their journey's end. And in that event neither the Dutch in Java in 1629, nor we in modern times, would ever have known about the *Batavia* wreck or the dark circumstances at the Abrolhos.

On the Ningaloo Reef ships and centuries rolled by. For a long time the area remained without a name. The coast in general was called *The South Land* by the Dutch and (curiously) *New Holland* by the English. But the dragon-backed North West Cape remained an anonymous piece of wilderness on the far side of the world. No-one took the trouble to look around the corner to see the vast sheet of water that would be the future Exmouth Gulf.

Most of the vessels passing by were traders and for them there was no profit to be gained in exploration. There were risks enough already, their captains would have told you, in undertaking a voyage half-way around the world. Dangers a-plenty, without going looking for more trouble! Australia was simply a landmark to be used in that capacity. A rugged red milestone on their journey. They cleared that forbidding coast as quickly their sails would carry them, and *'God Speed The Ship!'* on her way to the Dutch East Indies or China!

For a long time the North West Cape was considered to be an island, as the crews of the *Rapid* and *Correo* had opined. The reason was that south of the high ground of Point Cloates -- known to the Aborigines as *'Ningaloo, Najendo, the Nose'*—the coast cuts back sharply at right angles and the indentation goes in some eight kilometres to the east. From out at sea Point Cloates itself is conspicuous. But the low land to the south, lying much further east, often becomes invisible in the haze. Giving the impression of Cloates standing alone as an island.

By 1719, more than 100 years after Dirk Hartog, at last there was a name. Historian Chris Halls records that Captain Nash of the vessel *House of Austria* named Point Coates '*Çloots Island'* after the wealthy Dutch shipowner and merchant Baron Cloots who was a part owner of the vessel. By 1796 the master of the ship *Belvedere* was listing it in his log as *'Çlootes Doubtful Island'*. '*This island'* he recorded *'Lies North by East, and South West by South, about 32 leagues in length with terrible breakers from each end running about three miles out to sea'*.

In the end the useful landmark, through general usage, became Point Cloates and so it remains today. There were not many other early names, and that reflects the universal dislike of the first explorers for the Western Australian coast.

In fact there weren't many explorers either.

The Dutch considered Australia simply a confounded nuisance because it wrecked their ships and was a barrier to easy access to the Pacific Ocean and potential trade with South America. The British, early on, confined their navigational interest to the approaches to Sydney and Hobart town. It was only when the French began poking their noses into Australian waters that they were roused to take preventative action, first with Matthew Flinders in 1804, then with Phillip Parker King in 1818. It may seem surprising that the major explorations by the Dutch East India Company's Willem de Vlamingh in 1697 and the French expedition of Baudin in 1801, didn't pay more attention to the Exmouth region.

But the European explorers – whether Dutch, French, or English – all disliked what they found on Western Australian shores. By the time they had sailed and explored north as far as Exmouth, the last geographical point on their program before heading north for Java or Timor, they were tired and grumpy. They had had enough.

In 1697, Vlamingh's men, exhausted, after unsuccessful forays inland on foot from the Swan River to Shark Bay in debilitating summer heat, were only too glad to shake the *Southland's* red dust off their sea-boots. Though they spent time there, they did not even bother to name Shark Bay, leaving that honour to the Englishman William Dampier two years' later. Their remarks about the country were universally unflattering. *'This is a barren land, not fit for animals, let alone humans to inhabit!'* reads one journal entry from Vlamingh's expedition.

Ouch!

When Vlamingh's three ships reached the northern end of North West Cape they anchored off-shore. But though there was a great waterway to explore they turned away from it. Java beckoned, and no-one went ashore, though smokes of Aboriginal fires were seen, and fires glowed at night. Attempts at making contacts with the indigenous inhabitants further south had failed dismally. All that had been found there were footprints and sometimes fires with the coals still glowing, but the people themselves had fled. There was no reason to believe that it would be any different at the North West Cape.

De Vlamingh wrote in his journal aboard his flagship *Geelvinck* '*I then gave the signal to weigh anchor and leave this Southland for good!'*. Aboard the support vessel *Nijptang* the journal entry read: '*Five guns were fired from the Geelvinck and our ship fired three to farewell the miserable Southland!'*

The miserable Southland...

Francois Peron, the naturalist aboard the *Geographe* on the Baudin expedition of 1801 to 1804, let scientific detachment go out of the window when he wrote of '*A frightful desert!'*. Louis de Freycinet smuggled his new wife Rose aboard his vessel *Uranie* at Toulon in 1818 before they sailed on their great adventure. Their first Australian call was at Shark Bay. *'This stay on terra firma was not very pleasant to me, the country being treeless and bare of vegetation. One can only walk on burning sand ...'* Rose recorded in her diary *'It had been without a single regret that I left that Hell on earth, the coast of New Holland!'*

'Burning sand?' Please! They were there in September when Shark Bay Celsius temperatures are in the mild 20s – cooler, sometimes, than Paris in July!

Jacques Arago, an artist on the *Uranie* expedition was the most vitriolic of the visitors. He wrote in his journal *'Not a bird in the sky, not a wild beast or any harmless four-footed thing, not the murmur of the least cold water spring to gladden the earth! Desert everywhere with its cold, heart-freezing solitude and its vast echo-less horizons .. The soul is oppressed by this sad and silent spectacle of a nerveless, lifeless, nature evidently issued but a few centuries from the sea...'*

We know today that the Shark Bay region is actually replete with animal life. That is the reason why it has been listed as a World Heritage Area. Fish, sharks, dolphins, dugongs, whales, abound in the sea.

Ten species of mammals, mostly marsupials and ranging from red kangaroos to stick-nest rats, hop, scratch, and burrow ashore. There are 98 species of reptiles slithering about, and there are more than 100 species of sea and land birds, including three kinds of eagles, beating the air with their wings.

How could the Europeans, especially the scientists, err so badly? The answer is that Australia, where even the swans were black instead of white, was alien to everything they had ever experienced before. The west coast of *New Holland*, an apparently empty land was so different from their own familiar surrounds that it frightened them.

They carried with them nostalgic memories of black-and-white cows and fleecy sheep in green pastures. Coaches and carts on cobbled roads, with the staccato clatter of horses' hooves...

Windmills spinning, people milling in market squares, singing in taverns, linking hands in festivals. Times of dancing and celebration. They thought of cathedrals with spires piercing the sky and the sweet sound of the choir carrying far on a still morning. The solemnity of religious processions with priests and monks carrying banners and crucifixes...The bustle of a fishing boat harbour... The places and sights they remembered with a homesickness which was almost a physical ache by the time they had been nine months and more away.

There were none of these things in this primeval place. The Austral light was too bright, the horizons too wide, and there was nothing in between. Nothing to remind them of the dear, beloved places of home. So they turned their faces away, looking instead back towards the way they had come.

'Home is where the heart is!' is a saying that rings true, whether you are an Eskimo, a Hottentot, a Saudi Arab, or a New Guinea highlander with a bone in the nose. Or a Northern European. Each relates to their own widely differing environment. We are imprinted (as the animal scientists say) with our childhood environment. Whether it may be desert sand, glacial snow, a green wood, or wind-tossed palm trees that bring a nostalgic tear to the eye.

It is somewhat ironic that many of the tourists who arrive at Exmouth today, eager-faced, from Europe, and America, from Japan and South East Asia, come precisely because it IS a different countryside.

The exploration of the Australian coast in the 19th Century, was delayed by the long-running Napoleonic Wars. But it became a matter of priority after the victory at Waterloo because of British concerns about future French intentions in the Indian Ocean and Pacific.

Mardsen Horden, biographer of Phillip Parker King, quoted Captain Thomas Hurd, hydrographer to the Royal Navy, who had long urged a completion of Australian exploration. Hurd pointed out in a prophetic submission to the Admiralty as early as 1814:

'Nearly the whole of China and Eastern Seas, including between Kamchatka and van Diemen's Land are unknown to us. Particularly a vast extent of coast on the north and west sides of New Holland, which is supposed to be sterile and without fresh water. But which supposition, I have no doubt upon proper examination will be found to have been grounded in error, and that many large Rivers, Harbours, and interior waters remain to be discovered in this unexplored country'.

A further reason for his concern was the fact that in the first 20 years of the 1800s some 303 British naval vessels were shipwrecked with the loss of 12,761 seamen's lives. Many of the wrecks occurred on unsurveyed reefs or coasts. Once the charts were completed, the casualty list from 1820 to 1889, a period of almost 70 years, saw only 109 naval shipwrecks and the loss of only 5147 lives.

Lieutenant Phillip Parker King, son of Philip Gidley King, governor of New South Wales, after Royal Navy experience in combat in the Napoleonic wars, was the man who finally explored and charted Exmouth Gulf in 1818.

King was a youthful commander, aged only 27 years when he first rounded Cape Murat and sailed into the gulf which would be his first major exploration.

The voyage would be the first of a series of surveys filling in the gaps of Matthew Flinders' 1804 charts. King would emerge with a reputation as a hydrographer second only to Flinders. But in the New Year of 1818 the waters ahead of him were unknown, and he too was an unknown. The challenges lay ahead. Exmouth Gulf was to be the first of them -- and almost the last.

What had been recorded in the 202 years up to that point? Vlamingh and the Dutch in 1697 had thought so little of the Gulf that they left no names there at all. The Dutch were always sparse with nomenclature. In contrast French explorer Nicolas Baudin, who sailed the coast with the *Geographe* in 1801-04, and his officers were inclined to be the opposite, scattering French names up the Western Australian coast with 30 of them in Shark Bay alone.

Many of the French names are still on the map today. But Baudin did not waste too much ink or effort on the Exmouth region. He did name Point Murat, after the King of Naples, a French ally in the Napoleonic wars. He mistook the two Muiron islands for a single island. Muiron was Napoleon's aide de camp and close friend, killed by his side at the Battle of Arcole. The Montebello islands were named after the French general Lannes who was named as Duke of Montebello by Napoleon after his northern Italian victory in 1800.

The French latitudes and especially the longitudes on the West Australian coast were frequently astray, and King may not have been surprised to find that Baudin's position for Point Murat was 20 kilometres in error.

In deference to the earlier Dutch explorer he named the northern extremity of the North West Cape 'Vlamingh Head'.

There was an initial excitement aboard *Mermaid* on first entering this huge sheet of water, which stretched away into the distance and which had not been seen previously by European eyes.

The gulf was far larger than King or anyone had anticipated. Previous charts had shown only the small indents on the coast titled *Jacob Remessens River* and *Willems River* from two centuries previously. Instead, once the little *Mermaid* rounded Point Murat, King found the vastness of the gulf opening before his eyes. It was a sheet of water which left them breathless, since it was quite unexpected, and which proved to be 40 kilometres wide, and 67 kilometres in length.

As they sailed down it they were tantalised by the question of whether it might be the mouth of some great river leading into the interior? King's instructions from the Admiralty in England, included an order to investigate '*Any river likely to lead to an interior navigation of this great continent'*.

Through all the first half of the Nineteenth Century there were theories – espoused especially by the New South Wales firebrand politician William Charles Wentworth – that there must be a *Great Inland Sea* in the centre of Australia. In consequence coastal exploration vessels like the *Mermaid* and later *HMS Bathurst* and *HMS Beagle* were ordered to look for the entrance of a large navigable river, in the west, the equivalent perhaps of the mighty River Murray in eastern Australia, and one which might lead into the interior.

Explorers by land, such as Charles Sturt in 1844, struggled through the inland deserts hoping to top a rise and view a blue vista of water ahead of them. They certainly saw blue but it was simply the maddening false hope of shimmering mirages. Sturt even carried a boat as part of his baggage, leaving it out there in disgust for the sun to bleach and rot, and the Aborigines to wonder at.

The Inland Sea was an attractive myth. To give some weight to it there is the Lake Eyre Basin in the dry middle of Australia. It actually lies 15 metres below sea level, has minor flooding every three years or so, and fills fully about four times a century.

When Lake Eyre does fill completely it becomes a stretch of water so wide that it is impossible to see from one shore across to the other. The event attracts thousands of sea birds and pelicans. Aborigines may have told explorers of a '*Big water!'* Perhaps in days of a different climate the water was permanent.

It took a lot of pain and the loss of not a few lives to prove the negative point about the *Inland Sea.* Ludwig Leichhardt set out from the Darling in 1848 with six men, seven horses, 20 mules, and 50 cattle. He planned to cross the continent, taking 12 to 18 months to do so. He expected to establish the truth of the *Great Inland Sea* for once and for all and make a triumphant entry into Perth at the end of it. His party disappeared, never to be seen again.

Despite intensive searches no trace of them has ever been found – their fate remains one of the great mysteries of Australian exploration. Burke and Wills also famously perished on their south-to-north crossing of the continent in 1860. In 1818, as Phillip Parker King sailed down his new gulf, the idea of the *Great Inland Sea* was still very much alive.

A river leading to the interior was high on the list of features he hoped to find. He had instructions from John Wilson Croker, secretary to the Admiralty in London, to make that search a priority. But as they reached the mud flats and mangroves at the far end of the great gulf there was disappointment. It was plain that there was no river to be found there. King wrote in his journal: *'I had sufficiently observed my instructions in investigating this opening and had cleared up a great geographical question as to the mouth of some great river'*.

What he found instead was a safe anchorage in the Bay of Rest, which he named with heartfelt thanks. *Mermaid* had had a bad time of it in the confines of the Gulf. During the day they experienced extreme heat and maddening calms. At night south easterly gales sprang up creating dangerous wind-against-sea tide rips at the head of the gulf. When she lay at anchor overnight the 89-ton cutter was thrown first one way and then the other with fearful jerks on her anchor lodged in rocky ground.

They broke one anchor and lost another. Taking the risky option of trying to sail through the night, he found to his horror at dawn that *Mermaid* was almost in a white swathe of surf. If daylight had been just a little bit later '*We would have been lodged, very snugly, upon the breakers off the west end of Muiron Island!'*.

Though he wrote of the incident in apparently light-hearted fashion, it could have had very serious consequences. Had they struck the reef and wrecked the *Mermaid* they may not have escaped with their lives!

There was no major Australian settlement nearer than Sydney on the other side of the continent. They were not expected back within 12 months and no-one would have come to look for them until well after that time. Anyone struggling ashore would have found that the Muiron Islands are waterless. A place to die, rather than a refuge for castaways. It was a narrow escape for ship and crew. But while thanking their stars, the *Mermaid* was left with only one anchor and a still a major exploration in unknown waters to complete! King wrote:

'*Everything here appeared to oppose our prosecution of this interesting opening. The danger is multiplied in the night by the strength of the wind and the tides, and by day we are retarded by calms ...With shoal water on every side it makes me anxious, but I am determined to penetrate while the last anchor remains…*'

The night alarms had his crew exhausted. But finally they found a safe haven, where his last anchor nestled safely in mud instead of the treacherous rocks at the head of the gulf. '*My feeling was so considerably relieved of a weight of fatigue and anxiety that on anchoring I called this anchorage the 'Bay of Rest'. As truly did it prove to be so for us all!'*.

Now there was another name to add to those already on the chart. King decided to name Exmouth Gulf after '*The noble and valiant Viscount Exmouth'*.

King had served under his command when the viscount was Admiral Sir Edward Pellew at the time of the Napoleonic wars. He held him in the highest esteem and paid him the great compliment of naming his first great discovery after him.

Who was Sir Edward Pellew?

He would have needed no introduction to anyone in Britain in his own time. He was a famous naval figure when Horatio Nelson, the hero of Trafalgar, was the most loved man in Britain. A period when the Royal Navy was at the peak of its power.

'*Hearts Of Oak are our Ships!*
Hearts of Oak are our Men!
We'll fight and we'll conquer
Again and again!
We always are ready
Steady boys, steady! ...'

As a dashing frigate captain Pellew inspired the author C.S.Forrester in later years in writing the Horatio Hornblower series of novels. Some of Pellew's real-life exploits rivalled those found between the covers of naval adventure fiction. Edward Pellew joined the Royal Navy as a midshipman, aged 13, in 1770. By the time he was 20 he was aboard the schooner *Carleton* in the battle of Lake Champlain during the American War of Independence. When his senior officers were killed in action the young Pellew, scarcely more than a boy, took command. He handled the vessel so well that she played a major part in sinking two enemy ships. It was a feat which mightily impressed the Admiralty, and as a reward Pellew was promoted to the rank of lieutenant, and was given the command of the vessel.

During the war against France, in 1791, in command of *HMS Nymphe,* he engaged the French frigate *Cleopatra*. After shooting away the enemy's mainmast he ran *Nymphe* alongside, and made fast with grappling irons. The English crew then swarmed aboard the Frenchman with pistols and cutlasses, and seized her as a prize. Recovering at the same time important code papers.

For this derring-do exploit, still aged only 34, Pellew received a knighthood. Three years later Sir Edward had command of *HMS Indefatigable* and the Royal Navy's Western Squadron. A meteoric rise in the service.

But one of his bravest and most meritorious acts took place in January, 1796, as an individual. On an icy mid-winter day the East Indiaman *Dutton,* loaded with troops went aground off Plymouth Hoe. In heavy seas, waves crashing over her decks, she seemed doomed to break up with inevitable heavy loss of life. Few of the hundreds of men aboard her could swim. Edward Pellew took a line and swam out through the surf to the stricken vessel. His heroic action enabled a life-line to be rigged from shore to ship and most of those on board were saved.

In recognition for the act, which had been performed at great risk of his own life, he was created a baronet in 1796. He took the title *'Exmouth'* from his home in south east Devon. There the town of Exmouth is sited where the river Exe runs into the sea. Pellew continued to receive promotions. He was posted a Rear Admiral in 1804 at 45 years of age, swept the British seas clear of French warships and was created a full baron by 1814, the year in which another one of his dashing exploits took place. .

For centuries the Barbary Coast, and the North African town of Algiers held by the Moors, had been a pirates' nest. The predator vessels manned by motley renegades of all nations, sailed out from Algiers harbour where they enjoyed the protection of the Bey of Algiers in return for a share of plunder. The very mention of the name *'Barbary Coast'* made Christian seamen shiver, and the lawless pirates were the scourge of Mediterranean seas. The passengers and crews of the ships they captured were sold off in the Algiers slave-market to wealthy Muslims. By 1814 the British had had enough.

A fleet under the command of Baron Exmouth, (Sir Edward Pellew) sailed to blockade Algiers and demand the release of all Christian slaves and captives.When the Bey predictably refused to consider the order, Pellew's fleet began a nine hour bombardment which left the Algiers shore batteries destroyed, the city heavily damaged, and every ship in the harbour sunk.

With Algiers in ruins and fearing further reprisals, the Bey was compelled to hand over 3000 Christian men and women of various nationalities who had been Algerian slaves. No doubt their gratitude at being saved from *'A fate worse than death'* was overwhelming.

'For this splendid victory' it was recorded *'Exmouth was advanced to the dignity of Viscount'.*

What a list of honours! What a man!

Those who had the privilege of serving under him, like Phillip Parker King, admired him to the point of adoration. In gratitude for the time spent in his command, King named *'Exmouth Gulf'.*

The viscount had had another admirer in Matthew Flinders, King's predecessor and Australia's most famous maritime explorer. In 1804, Flinders had named islands in the Gulf of Carpentaria, the 'Sir Edward Pellew Group'.

That was the man, larger than life, whose name was given to Exmouth Gulf, and the current town of Exmouth. Not many other Australian towns can boast that they are named after a gentleman of such bravery and distinction!

King's Bay of Rest, deep in Exmouth Gulf, was known as Jogador by the Jinigudira tribe whose fish traps were prominent along the shore. Lieutenants Roe and Bedwell went ashore from the *Mermaid* hoping to meet with the Aborigines. But -- as they usually did -- the Indigenous inhabitants kept carefully out of the white men's way. Cunningham, the botanist had hoped to find new plant species. But he too soon became exhausted in 105 degree heat tramping three miles over '*masses of spinnifex'*. And no doubt getting the sharp prickles of that spiny plant in his shins to remember the place by.

Conditions became so hot on board that to touch a gun barrel or grasp a metal fitting seared the flesh. King wrote '*It is now so hot that in writing on the paper the leaves curl up exactly as if a book was held to the influence of a large fire!*' They were ready to leave, longing for the comparative cool of the open sea.

As *Mermaid* resumed her journey north past the site of the future port of Onslow, there was a fishing story to tell. The region has a history of fishing stories, bigger and better than most. This was about the one that didn't get away. *Mermaid's* men were keen fishermen, having little else to do once the cutter was anchored for the night. Fresh fish on the table was also infinitely preferable to salt provisions.

Author Marsden Hordern, in his biography records that while they had their lines in the water a large shark – probably a tiger shark -- circled the ship.

The sailors: '*Offered it a piece of their salt pork ration, which it removed deftly without taking the hook. They rebaited and again the pork disappeared. After 14 pieces of pork weighing about eight pounds had been lost in this way, the frustrated fishermen changed their tactics. When next the shark swam close up under the stern they harpooned it, hauled it aboard with a block and tackle, cut it open, retrieved the meat, and returned it to the cook. King noted with some amusement that it was then eaten by those to whom it had belonged* '*previous to its going through the process of passing down the shark's throat!'*.

On February 18th, 1818, when the *Mermaid* departed on her way to further explorations, there was a new name on the chart on a stretch of water which was virgin territory when she first arrived there. Two centuries after the first Europeans had passed by Exmouth Gulf was named at last.

Some of the other names he left behind had political connotations. For instance in the Kimberley he may have smiled as he thought of probable French reactions when he wrote down Mount Trafalgar, Mount Waterloo, and Mount Wellington on his chart!

'Touche`!'

IN OCTOBER 1962 the world held its breath as the United States and Soviet Russia faced off in the Cuban Missile Crisis. 'We will bury you!' Nikita Kruschev shouted in the United Nations Assembly, pounding the desk with his shoe.

WHILE WE SLEPT through all those years it was as well that we didn't know that there was always the sinister shape of a United States nuclear bomber somewhere in the air between America and Russia. Ready night and day for that word 'G0!' from a US President. The command, never issued, which would see the deadly nuclear missiles released from below its wings. In the same period Russia built 245 nuclear missile-armed submarines.

THIS IS WHAT THE WORLD FEARED: A nuclear submarine fires its deadly cargo, unseen below the surface. Fortunately commonsense on both sides prevailed, the Cold War ended without a nuclear shot fired, and the world was spared the grim prospect of Armageddon.

SHIPS WERE VERY DIFFERENT THEN: Dutch East Indiamen of Dirk Hartog's time passed by the North West Cape in the 17th Century. Nevertheless ships like this one painted by WA marine artist Ross Shardlow were heavily armed against pirates and enemies of other countries. An Indiaman customarily carried 30 to 40 cannon.

THE DIFFERENCES IN DRESS: Dutch burghers in Amersterdam in the 17th century reflected the prosperity of the time. The Aborigines would have been astonished at the dress of the Dutchmen who came ashore. Especially their shoes which left tracks without toes.

HAPPY ABORIGINES fishing in Yardie Creek in the 1920s using nets made from twined vines as described by the Stefano survivors in the 1870s. One of the girls cradles a dog. In their natural state the first inhabitants of the North West Cape wore no clothes at all.

PHILLIP PARKER KING in his first command with the little cutter Mermaid, was the first explorer of Exmouth Gulf in 1818.

JOHN SEPTIMUS ROE decorated the title page of his log book. Both he and King were exceptional artists in days before photographs.

SIR EDWARD PELLEW was a British naval hero who gave his name as Viscount Exmouth to Exmouth Gulf.

THE TITLE PAGE of John Septimus Roe's log book. He went on to become the Surveyor General in the first settlement of Western Australia 11 years later, and held the post for 42 years.

THE CAVE OF DEATH where the young men of the barque Stefano met a slow death. Today it is a part of Warroora Station. In the picture are John McDiven, Leonie McLeod and Leonie's grandchildren.

A DINGHY OVERLOADED with wool bales at Giralia Landing. The bales had to be ferried out to a waiting schooner. It is easy to see how Harold Harper and a station worker were drowned when a wind came up off-shore in 1921.

HMC MERMAID, was Phillip Parker King's first command. She was also the first vessel to enter Exmouth Gulf. King charted the Gulf in February, 1818, and named it after his naval hero Viscount Exmouth, the former Sir Edward Pellew. His instructions from the Admiralty were to look for a supposed 'Great River' leading to the centre of Australia in the belief that an 'Inland Sea' might exist there. There was no river but instead Mermaid found a secure anchorage which King named The Bay of Rest. (From the painting by WA marine artist Ross Shardlow)

A MOUNTED STOCKMAN, Bill King, junior, sits easily in the saddle on his horse Tommy at Yardie Creek. There was a time when a man's dog and his horse were his two best friends in the bush. (Picture: King family)

THE FIRST MOTOR CAR to come through to Exmouth from Carnarvon, with Bill King at the wheel in 1921. They used gelignite to break down the creek banks and spinifex was laid along the wheel ruts of the tracks of the camel wagons. The vehicle was a Model T Ford. Bill King senior is on the right of the picture and Joe King is in the vehicle next to young Bill. (Picture: Bill King Jnr)

ABORIGINAL SACRED CAVE on North West Cape, where important ceremonies were held.

THE INTERIOR of the cave, the roof blackened by centuries of fire smoke.

VIEW FROM THE CAVE: Ron Campbell looks out over the coastal plain to the distant green waters of the Ningaloo Reef.

King went on to complete four voyages of Australian surveys which were equal in merit to those of Matthew Flinders, though he never received the same recognition. His next assignment was in far cooler conditions than Exmouth Gulf. In 1826 he commanded *HMS Adventure* in company with *HMS Beagle* on a four year survey of the coasts of Chile, Peru, and Patagonia. There, in the stormiest seas in the world, snow and ice and the huge waves off the notorious Cape Horn, were constant dangers for sailing ships which were continually on lee shores. The conditions called for the highest skills in seamanship.

As a result of his Australian surveys King became a Fellow of the Royal Geographical Society in London. Late in life he was appointed Australia's first Admiral, before dying in Sydney aged 64 years in 1856.

Charles Darwin, whose voyage on the *Beagle* provided him with the inspiration for his revolutionary *Origin of the Species,* the theory of evolution, described King as '*My beau ideal of a captain!*'.

And the little *Mermaid?* She leaked so badly on the Kimberley coast on her second voyage that King was forced to run her aground at Careening Bay, to stop the leaks. There is still a boab tree there with the name *HMC Mermaid* cut into the bark.

The cheap iron fastenings from when she was built in Calcutta had rusted so badly that it was possible to pass a straw through the nail holes into the hull. Despite caulking and repairs the leaks were worse when she was put back into the water! There ensued a desperate voyage back to Sydney, pumping all the way, only to be nearly wrecked at Botany Bay when almost home. The vessel actually struck the rocks there but sailed off in the backwash of a fortuitous wave!

'*I have seen Death in various shapes*' King wrote later in a letter to his father '*But never before encountered him at such close quarters!*'

In addition to his navigation skills King was a talented artist, a useful skill in recording coastal features in days well before the advent of cameras. His first survey and the one which particularly concerns us, resulted in the naming of Exmouth Gulf, and the establishing of that great sheet of shining water on Admiralty Charts.

In that sense he is the true father of the Exmouth region. His name remains on Western Australian charts in King Sound, and King's Cascades, in the Kimberley, and the King River at Albany. There is also a King Island in Queensland, and King's Table, a flat-topped hill at Darwin. But King Island in Bass Strait is named after his father Philip Gidley King, governor of New South Wales, not our navigator.

Incidentally the different Christian name spellings occur because Phillip Parker King was named after Arthur Phillip, the first governor of New South Wales.

His biographer Marsden Hordern paid Phillip Parker King the ultimate compliment in the title of his book '*King Of The Australian Coast*'.

STEFANO SURVIVORS Baccich and Jurich and their rescuer Charles Tuckey.

A CRUEL COAST for shipwrecked sailors. The starving boys from the wreck of the Croatian barque Stefano walked over these rocks with bleeding feet. Only two of them survived where now holiday makers play and fish in the sunshine.

A Fatal Miracle

Chapter Four

Following the loss of the *Rapid*, shipwrecks followed one after the other on the Ningaloo Reef. Each wreck had its own story, with the sadness of lives cut short as well as vessels lost. Some tales stand out from the others. The loss of the *Emma*, for instance, was the greatest tragedy in Western Australian colonial history. A third of the newly-settled population of the North West went down with her in 1867.

Her story began when Francis Gregory led his expedition to what is now the Pilbara, in 1861. There he found what every Western Australian pastoralist had been hoping for – millions of acres of good grazing land and six major rivers. Water plus feed made for a potential bonanza!

Settlers with flocks and herds -- many of them from Victoria – chartered vessels and hurried to the region. Within a few years there were sheep stations on the de Grey river, the Yule, the Oakover, Nichol, Sherlock, Harding, and Turner rivers.

It all happened very quickly. Roebourne was officially declared a town site by the Colonial Government in 1866. Sheep grew fat on the native grasses and multiplied at an incredible rate. By 1867, the year the *Emma* sailed, the initial flocks totalling 1000 sheep in 1863 had increased partly by imported flocks but mostly by lambing to 38,580 head! By 1890 there were 2,524,913 baaing *woolly-backs*. Each one a money earner!

By March 1867 the hard work of establishing the stations had reached a point where many of the young men pioneering them felt that they had earned a break and they all agreed to take a concerted holiday in Perth. The flower of the Pilbara's youth booked their passages aboard Walter Padbury's coastal trading ship the *Emma.*

She was a very sound vessel, built in Lowestoft, England, in 1859. *Emma* was a two- masted schooner, but also a fair-sized craft able to carry 600 sheep as well as general cargo and passengers. Her dimensions were 85 feet in length, by a 20 foot beam, and she was 117 tons register.

Emma seemed – as her owner Walter Padbury no doubt hoped – to be ideal for serving the North West ports. Except for one negative factor. The problem lay in the quality of command. Her dismal record from the time of her arrival in WA showed that she was an accident waiting to happen. Though it was hardly the fault of the vessel.

Under different masters, she had collided with the jetty in Geraldton, run aground in the Abrolhos Islands, grounded again at Cossack, and stranded twice at Fremantle. Once striking the *'putty'* hard enough to be dismasted. One of her problems was a compass which had been salvaged from the wreck of the *Calliance* at Camden Harbour, and which had not been *'swung'* to compensate for any magnetic disturbances in its new situation.

As a result the compass may have been a dangerous number of degrees out of register. We may also wonder what happened to her original compass? After all she had presumably sailed out from England with it quite satisfactorily, when she came to Western Australia.

At Nickol Bay Captain Badcock, skipper on her final voyage, told the Resident Magistrate Robert Sholl – whose 21 year-old son Treverton, his clerk of courts, would be on board – that his plan for the voyage would be to sail wide of the Monte Bello islands and then to sail back in towards the mainland and ' *To keep close along the shore if possible'.*

The words can send a shiver up our spines even today. So far as that fatal shore south of Point Cloates is concerned, it would be the very worst possible course to take!

Among those who waved cheerfully from the ship's rail on departure was William Tays. He had come from Victoria to become a pastoralist. But failing to get a land grant, he had become one of the North's pioneer pearlers. With a whaleboat and some Aborigines, the most primitive means, he had raised nine tons of pearl shell by dry shelling and working the shallow banks. With the world price of 150 British pounds per ton for pearl shell, MOP, or Mother of Pearl – a time when 150 pounds was the purchase price of a sailing cutter suitable for pearling -- he could see where his future lay.

Now he was on his way back to Victoria to raise capital to buy a suitable vessel and intending to return to make his fortune as a pearler. Billy Tays must have been the fittest man in the Pilbara. At the Roebourne Races Sports Day in 1886, he won the prizes for hammer throwing and tossing the caber. He also won the sack race and caught the greasy pig – the pig was the prize!

Among the other young men was Charles Nairn a 32 year-old bachelor, and Padbury's manager on de Grey Station, who was going south to marry his sweetheart. His right hand man Dan Brown was with him to be *Best Man* at the wedding. Another nephew of Padbury's was 23 year-old George Grigson. They were a merry group in a mood ready to celebrate. Of the 42 passengers aboard, others were Captain J.E. Abbot and several passengers from the *New Perseverent* wrecked at Butcher's Inlet the previous December. The odds were surely against being involved in two shipwrecks in a row? Also joining the ill-fated ship were the Hungarian naturalist Louis Blagrav, Police Constables William Rogers and Bob Toovey, three Aboriginal prisoners bound for Rottnest Island Native Prison, and two other free Aboriginals from Nichol Bay.

There were also eight crew, making altogether a ship's complement of 50 people. Included in the *Emma's* southbound cargo were the salvaged anchors and chains from the *New Perseverant*, wrecked at Butcher's Inlet. The *Perseverant* herself, condemned for further voyaging, was hauled ashore at Cossack, and a hole cut in her side to become a pub for the pearlers. It was later conjectured that the magnetic influence of the extra iron of her anchors and chains in *Emma's* hold may have contributed to the errors already endemic in the *Emma's* compass.

She sailed from Nickol Bay on March 3rd, 1867, and then simply disappeared from human ken. When she failed to arrive at Fremantle there was no great concern immediately. Sailing ships were often overdue – the major reason why steamships ultimately stole their trade.

The *'normal'* coastal voyage – and every trip was different – was considered to be 30 days sailing north, with the benefit of the southerly winds behind the vessel. Sailing south with the likelihood of the wind *'on the nose'*, beating up against the regular southerly head winds, could take 50 days or more.

On that basis the *Emma* should have reached Fremantle by about the end of April. As the days overdue became weeks, and then a month, there was a sharp prick of anxiety. Then the time stretched into the end of a second month, and other vessels which had left the North West after the *Emma's* departure arrived and still there was no sign of the *Emma.*

Aside from anxiety about the safety of those aboard she was also carrying all of the Pilbara stations' wool clip for the season. Its loss would be a financial blow. More than that she was the supply ship for the whole of the North.

If she failed to return with the supplies already ordered, Roebourne and the people on the stations would face an emergency for basic provisions. As it turned out they would be reduced to cracking and eating the corn intended for horse feed.

All too soon they had to face a terrible truth. The *Emma* must be lost. A cold fear seized the heart of Walter Padbury. Charles Nairn's fiancée sat crying, with her wedding dress. Charles Nairn had been born in Padbury's Perth house. Padbury had no children himself, but he hoped that those young men aboard the *Emma* – boys who seemed like sons to him -- would have been his heirs.

His biographer John Nairn, in his book *Walter Padbury; His Life & Times*, wrote that it was not the loss of his vessel but the loss of the lives of those fine young men which sent him into shock for months. It would lead him, broken-hearted, to quit his lease of de Grey Station.

Magistrate Robert Sholl in Roebourne mourned for Treverton his blue-eyed boy who was his clerk of court and right-hand-man. Whom he hoped would be a magistrate himself one day.'*I fear my dearest son I will hear of no more!*' he cried.

What could have happened?

Vessels were sent to search for any signs of survivors, including the cutter *Mystery*, and the *Albert*. To no avail. Worse, *The Brothers* which had sailed north in February joined the list of missing ships with all her crew. There was a huge area to search, including known danger spots such as the Monte Bello and Abrolhos Islands, as well as the North West Cape. If anyone had gone ashore south of Point Cloates they must surely have seen wreckage on the beaches. But apparently no-one did search there.

An explanation of a kind was offered 10 years later, when the coast was becoming more civilised and white pearlers who recruited Aborigine divers and crew had more frequent contact with the Aborigines of the coast. Charles Tuckey, of the well-known Mandurah family, worked a pearling vessel called the *Jessie*. He reported that on board one day in 1876 one of his Aborigine skindivers from the North West Cape told him the following story.

'About 10 years ago a ship was wrecked on the North West Cape. The people landed at night, in the boats, and as they had no means of defending themselves the natives had no difficulty in making them prisoners. There were a large number of people and amongst them there were some females .The natives were not 'sulky' with them. But nevertheless they killed and ate all of them, the narrator taking part of some of the flesh'.

Tuckey said that when an opportunity occurred he stood in as close to shore as possible and through his telescope saw the ribs of a vessel on the beach in the area indicated. What do we make of that story?

Accepted at face value it adequately explains the loss of the *Emma* and her people. But on review some serious doubts arise. To start with there were no women aboard the *Emma*. The young men from the Pilbara who joined her were used to working with Aborigines and spoke the Ngarluma language used by the Aborigines of the Cape. There were also three Aborigines, reluctant passengers on their way to Rottnest Island Native Prison, and two other Aborigines.

If all 50 people reached the shore it could be assumed that the young men, and the Aborigines would have been able to negotiate some sort of settlement with the local Aborigines while they sought a means of rescue. With their bush experience, and the determination of young men such as Bill Tays, hero of the Roebourne Races Sports Day, they would surely have been able to make a much better fist of living off the land in Swiss Family Robinson fashion than European sailors who found themselves in a totally foreign environment?

The later experience of the *Stefano* castaways showed that the Aborigines of the Ningaloo Reef were far from being blood-thirsty killers of the legend.

On the contrary, the *Stefano* castaways nine years later would owe their lives entirely to the kindness and humanitarian spirit of the Aborigines on that part of the coast.

How many boats did the *Emma* carry? It would have needed at least two and possibly three boats to carry her full complement of people to the shore, and good seamen in unfamiliar waters would have sensibly waited until daylight rather than attempting a landing in darkness. Moreover, on a cargo vessel extra boats take up space and weight that owners often considered could be better utilised for paying items of cargo. If the *Emma* had lighters available at Cossack and the Long Jetty at Fremantle for loading and unloading, her owners may have been tempted to cut boats carried to the bare minimum of a dinghy. That is exactly the situation described by Lockier Burgess who was aboard the *Emma* when she went aground on a reef in the Abrolhos some time earlier. Writing his memoirs many years later he recalled:

' We left Fremantle in a bustle, with trusses of hay piled on the main deck so, in fact, everything was in the wrong place. If rough weather had come on suddenly we should have been in a fix. To make matters worse a large compass that belonged to the Calliance wrecked at Camden Harbour was placed in the Emma. The Calliance was three times the tonnage of the Emma so consequently the compass would not work correctly in such a small vessel. The result was that the next night after leaving Fremantle we found ourselves high and dry on the south end of the Abrolhos. We had only one boat –such were the conditions in those times that we were allowed to go to sea with only one boat! And that not even a lifeboat, but an old tub built of jarrah which would go down like a stone if she capsized!'.

Nonetheless, the *'old tub'* was able to reach Geraldton 50 kilometres away across rough seas to summon help for the stranded vessel and those aboard. The sheep and passengers she was carrying were off-loaded onto an island while the *Emma* was freed. She was saved by good luck on that occasion. But constantly relying on luck could only have one ending. There would come a day when the *Emma's* luck was pushed too far. Sadly, for those aboard, that is what eventually happened.

It is interesting that in the Abrolhos grounding the un-adjusted compass had the vessel veer to port and an unscheduled contact with the Abrolhos islands. If the same tendency of veering to port were present on her fatal trip south from Cossack it would have brought her in toward the land and the reefs on her port side.

The mystery of her last voyage continued until 1979, when diver Serge Katarshi in 1979 found wreckage on the reef off shore from Maud's Landing. The wreck was identified in 1988 by the Western Australian Maritime Museum as being the remains of the *Emma.* Significantly among the wreckage was a gudgeon (one of the fittings that hold the rudder) from a small craft.

If it were from the *'old tub'*, the *Emma's* sole boat, it would indicate that no boat was launched and that the ship and all her people were overwhelmed in the suddenness of the disaster. The wrecksite is in the overlap of reef at the entrance to Maud's Landing, some eight kilometres off shore. A hook of reef extends out to sea, placed by Nature in a way that would entrap any south-bound vessel making the fatal error of following the main reef down from Point Cloates. It was a natural ship-trap for a vessel standing in close to land at night – as Captain Badcock had indicated he would do.

He had not been in command in the previous strandings – Padbury, in exasperation at incompetence, had had to change captains with almost every trip. This was Badcock's first voyage with the *Emma* and perhaps his inexperience was also a contributing factor.

She struck the reef at the outer point where the swell lifts and breaks most heavily from the Indian Ocean. If the swell were running high at the time the *Emma* would have been lifted and smashed down, caught between the hammer of the surf and the anvil of the reef.

Evidence of the force of the way in which she broke up, was a Seibbe Gorman copper diver's helmet and breast plate, recovered from the wreck, which was crushed and twisted almost out of recognition.

What does all this mean?

The weight of evidence seems to be that the *Emma* was overwhelmed so suddenly after striking the reef that there was no time to launch her small boat.

It seems most likely that the ship was dashed to pieces in a very short time. The distance from shore, the currents, the prevalence of sharks – night feeders – in the area means that it was unlikely that there were any survivors.

So what, then, was the foundation of the legend? It seems unlikely that it applies to the *Emma* for the reasons discussed. But could it be a case of '*Where there's smoke there's a fire*' ? Could there have been some other unfortunate vessel which would fit the story?

In 2010 the Western Australian Maritime Museum had two unidentified mid-19th Century ship wrecks on their books in the vicinity of Point Cloates. One was probably the *Stefano*. But the other may be the mystery ship which fits the legend?

There is indisputable recorded evidence that the Aborigines of the Gascoyne region were cannibals on occasion. This could occur as a funeral ceremony with a religious theme when a member of the tribe died – as observed by the survivors of the *Stefano* shipwreck in 1875 – or it could occur when tribes got together at a time of ceremonies. A time when warriors were *'stirred up'* by war-like dances and when local natural food supplies were running short because of the weight of numbers. Maud's Landing, Cardabia – the area indicated by Tuckey -- was one of the places tribes used to meet. Castaways coming ashore there at such a time of ceremonies may have been cruelly unlucky.

But of course they were unlucky to be wrecked in the first place.

Where the survivors of the Hungarian barque *Stefano,* wrecked south of Point Cloates in 1875, were concerned, the Ningaloo Aborigines were nothing but kind and helpful to the disoriented survivors. Young men who would have been easy victims had the Aborigines chosen to behave differently. The only occasion on which there was a recorded confrontation on the Ningaloo reef was after the wreck of the brig *Occator* north of Point Cloates in 1856. By that time the Aborigines of Ningaloo would have been accustomed to the bonanza of items washed-up following shipwrecks., Like the people of Cornwall, in England, who saw a shipwreck as a joyous occasion for the cargo and valuable items strewn along the shore. The difference, of course, was that where unscrupulous Cornwall *'wreckers'* would lure ships to their doom on the rocks on the British coast, with lights and beacons as false navigation marks, Aborigines were never guilty of that abhorrent behaviour.

The *Occator* was wrecked north of Point Cloates on January 12th, 1856, while on a voyage to the Muiron Islands to prospect for guano. The crew of nine men and Captain Place, took to the longboat and completed the journey to the Muirons where they hoped to meet a sister ship, the *Eblana*. After four days when there was no sign of the other vessel and they were suffering badly from thirst they decided to sail south. Because they had chosen a bad place to land they were forced to carry their boat three kilometres over the top of the island and launch it on the other side – no mean feat in January temperatures!

As the longboat travelled south inside the Ningaloo reef a large party of Aborigines, armed with spears, began to follow them. Their attitude was not unfriendly at first. But when the boat ran in to shore to pick up a cask of water washed in from the wreck the crew later reported:

' They put themselves in a menacing attitude and walked into the water armed with stones. When the water became too deep for wading about 10 of the more hardy swam out with the obvious intention of seizing the boat. When they got nearer one pitched a spear at the boat, but this was caught by one of the crew without doing any harm.

' Others cast stones with slings. Mr Jones at this time fired and shot one of them with a charge of slug and shot. They then retired and lighted a fire on the hills'.

The *Occator* party were eventually rescued by the cutter *Favourite* after making their way to Shark Bay. Did the encounter bring on a revenge mentality among Ningaloo Aborigines, if the man wounded by the shot subsequently died?

That did not appear to be the case when the young boys from the barque *Stefano* struggled ashore in 1875. Even allowing for the fact that their shipwreck took place nearly 20 years later.

The saga of the *Stefano* is one of the great Australian shipwreck stories. A tale of great tragedy and equal heroism. It also gives us a rare picture of the life and times of the Aborigines of the North West Cape in days before their lives were changed forever by the coming of the white man. In most areas of Australia there are no records of how Aboriginal people lived prior to the arrival of Europeans. But the shipwreck, a tragic accident, fortuitously provided us with first-hand information about how Aborigines lived in the Exmouth region in earlier times.

A scholarly Catholic priest in Dubrovnik on the Adriatic, Father Stephen Scurla, interviewed the two North West Cape shipwreck survivors from the Mediterranean barque *Stefano.* Michael Buccich, a 17 year-old cadet, and his companion Ivan Jurich aged 18, had lived a tribal life for several months with the Aborigines who succoured and saved them from death early in 1876.

Father Scurla's account, written in Italian, formed the basis for the book *The Wreck Of The Barque Stefano Off the North West Cape of Australia in 1875*, written by one of the survivor's American grandsons, Gustave Rathe, and published by Hesperian Press, in Western Australia in 1990. A second manuscript by Monte Sala, *The Stefano Castaways,* was also based on Father's Scurla's original story. It contains some details which are not covered by the Rathe account. Both accounts are valuable contributions not only for the history of the *Stefano*, but also for their descriptions of the way that the Aborigines of the North West Cape lived before the coming of the white man.

The *Stefano* was listed in records and accounts of the time as *'An Austrian-Hungarian barque'*, a description which sometimes causes confusion today because of the complex history of that region. There were no Austrians or Hungarians on board, though politically, in 1875, the wide-flung Austrian Empire of the Hapsburgs included the Dalmatian-Croatian area of the eastern coast of the Adriatic sea. There was also a strong Italian influence from Venice and Father Scurla's original manuscript was written in Italian..

With the exception of a 12 year-old Welsh cabin boy Henry Grose, all the officers and crew would be listed, by today's definition, as Croatian. As another confusion their names vary in the different accounts from Croatian to Italian spelling. By modern standards they were very young. The captain, Vlaho Miloslavich, of Ragusa, was only 26 years old, though he had had experience of long voyages. The second in command was Carlo Costa, aged 24, listed as *'Second captain'*. The first officer was Martino Osonjak. Michael Baccich, a cadet, was only 16 years old. The crew numbered 17, including the bosun, two quartermasters, a cook and a carpenter, as well as able seamen and cadets.

We may wonder what an eastern Mediterranean vessel was doing on Australian shores?

But at the time a large fleet of merchant sailing vessels operated from the ports of the eastern Adriatic, engaged in trade around the world. They were fine ships and the *Stefano,* at 1000 tons, and 53 metres in length, was one of the largest sailing ships to leave the port of Fiume, now known as Rijeka. She picked up her 12 year-old cabin boy Henry Grose and a cargo of 1300 tons of coal at Cardiff in Wales, intending to deliver it to Hong Kong.

The ship made a fast voyage down the Atlantic but encountered a severe storm in the Indian Ocean after rounding the Cape of Good Hope.

The gale blew for nine days, and there were periods when the crew doubted that the ship could survive. Few people today understand the hardships of deepwater voyaging often experienced in sailing ship days.

'A deep howling could be heard from the wind in the masts and the rigging. The vessel would disappear entirely into the abyss which would open between two waves. Then a wall of water would break over the prow, swamping the bridge with irresistible violence and filling the crew with the utmost apprehension.

'The rolling of the ship was so violent that sometimes the ends of the yards would lean over so far as to touch the crests of the gigantic waves. It was quite impossible to keep standing. Two ropes were stretched across the bridge, which the sailors clutched with all their strength to avoid being swept away. The helmsmen were secured with a rope around their waists ...'

Eventually the gale abated, and they were able to steer north east up into latitudes of better weather. The Australian mainland was sighted on October 26th, and the ship altered course to run parallel with the shore.

But at 2 a.m. on the following morning –disaster! In pitch darkness and driven before a fierce southerly wind, the ship struck a seaward section of the Ningaloo Reef just south of Point Cloates. The reef stopped the vessel dead in her wake with a violent impact. A big swell was running, and as the off-watch crew ran up on deck waves began breaking over the stricken barque forcing her further onto the reef.

All was panic and confusion in the darkness of the night, as the crew struggled to get the ship's boats ready to lower over the side. The 12 year-old cabin boy Henry Grose was put in the first boat. But as it was hoisted out a huge wave threw it back against the ship and smashed it to pieces, The boat crushing the poor boy who was little more than a child. He was to be the first casualty. A second boat was launched, with Captain Miloslavich aboard. But it was swamped and turned turtle a short distance from the crippled *Stefano* drowning the captain and others of the occupants. The main and mizzen masts fell, and it became obvious to everyone that the ship was rapidly breaking up.

Some of the crew climbed into the rigging of the remaining mast to escape the waves cascading over the deck. Others threw companion ladders, gratings, and other wooden objects into the sea and hoped that by clinging to them they would be washed to the shore. Michael Baccich, a 16 year-old cadet, a relation of the owners, was in the overturned ship's boat with the captain, He managed, in desperation to swim back to it and grasp the keel. With the help of a sailor Toma Dediol, and the force of the waves they were able to right it again, though it was still filled with water. In this waterlogged craft they drifted, their bodies still fully immersed in cold water. 'Drifted on all the remainder of the night and the next morning, sometimes numb with shock and cold, sometimes paddling with their hands. The sight of the shore at daylight heartened them and finally at 2 pm next day the boat washed in to the beach.

There they found several others who had reached the shore by clinging to floating objects or by swimming. All were totally exhausted. Baccich recalled later *'One by one we crawled further from the water, and with our aching hands dug burrows in the warm dry sand. We spent the first night under the sand and gave no thought to tomorrow'.*

Next day they counted heads and found that the survivors numbered the assistant captain Karlo Costa, Baccich, Dediol, Lovrinovich, Antoncich, Baccich, and Jurich. Searching the beach for other survivors they found Brajevich, and Vulovich, further along the shore. They were stretched out semiconscious above the tide mark, unable to move. They also found and buried the body of Radovich, which moved them to tears.

On a happier note they found quantities of stores washing up including bottles of wine, jars of oil and lard, a barrel of flour, as well as a barrel of beans, small jars of oil, preserved kidneys, beef, and potatoes.

The sufferers from exhaustion were revived with the wine and assisted back to the main landing point. By now a vast quantity of wreckage was washing in the shallows. Aside from the ship's stores, according to Sala's account. '*On the beach were the main mast, the yards, the topmasts, the oars and small masts of the boats, the main hatchway, part of the after cabin, the helmsman's wheel. In addition there were tables and empty boxes, and chests, two carpenter's* planes ..' In the bosun's chest were two overcoats, a needle case, and a piece of cotton cloth about 16 metres in length.

Using the masts and spars they made the framework for a hut on a flat stretch of sand sheltered from the southerly wind by a high sand dune.

The sides were built up with planks and a sail formed the roof. For the moment they had food and shelter. They found crabs and crayfish in the shallows –and most important – a barrel of water further down the beach. On that first day the survivors were in a better situation than might have been expected. But then a disaster – albeit well-intentioned – occurred. A group of Aborigines, about 50 men and women, appeared from the sandhills, the men all carrying spears.

Some of the survivors were alarmed, Baccich recalling the stories he had heard about cannibals, hid in the shelter. But the Aborigines were peaceable. After conducting ' *A thorough but gentle examination'* of the hair and clothes of the castaways, they went down to the shore, searching for small crabs and clams ' *Which they found rather easily'*. Costa went after them. Baccich later said '*Whenever they found something they never failed to offer it to Costa before partaking themselves. Encouraged by this kindness and their earlier courtesy, Costa spoke to them in English and French alternately asking them the location of Champion Bay which he felt might be in range. The natives merely repeated his words as best they could occasionally adding a few words in their own language. It was frustrating because we felt they wanted to help us...They seemed puzzled. While they were talking one man approached Costa and handed him a piece of paper which he had found washed on the rocks near the shore'*.

Unbelievably it was a piece from one of the Stefano's charts showing the north west coast of Western Australia.

'It was more than unbelievable' Baccich said joyfully '*It was miraculous!*'

Alas, no. It was a fatal *'miracle'*. Eight of the young men there that day would die miserably because of that chart.

Costa, who had assumed command of the group after the death of the captain, decided after perusing the chart they should walk south to the Gascoyne River where he felt there must be a settlement. In fact there was no settlement at Carnarvon. The pioneer settlers Brockman, and Butcher, would not overland sheep into the region until the following year, 1876. While development would follow rapidly in succeeding years, the townsite of Carnarvon would not be gazetted until 1883. Champion Bay, the site of Geraldton, 300 miles further south was even more out of the question. To the north the town of Onslow across Exmouth Gulf, would not come into being until 1885.

The nearest settlement 300 miles in a northerly direction was Tien Tsing, later renamed Cossack, the port to the inland pastoral town of Roebourne. The Aborigines of the North West coast often said ' *Chin chin!'* meaning Tien Tsing, to the castaways, but that name along with *'Palamandur'* for Fremantle naturally meant nothing to the shipwreck survivors.

The closest settlement to the south was at Shark Bay where a rush to the pearl banks was underway. The von Bibra family had a sheep station on Dirk Hartog Island. But both Roebourne and Shark Bay could only be reached by boat.

Where, then, was the nearest white man?

Not too far away at all, if they had only known. Had the castaways only travelled north instead of making the fatal decision to walk south, there was a pearling fleet just around the corner of the Cape in Exmouth Gulf. In late 1875 the Cossack pearling vessels *Wild Wave, Lily of the Lake, Blossom, Dawn, Azelia, Montiara, Dolphin, Governor Weld, Barringarra, Charm, Ada, Aurora, Eveline Mary, Helema, Victorian,* and *Albert,* were all working pearl patches in Exmouth Gulf.

One of their water points was at Bundegi at the north western end of the Gulf. Any European castaways arriving there could hope to find succour when boats called to fill their water casks. The Aborigines knew that, and tried to tell the *Stefano* people so. The man who gave them the chart had worked in the pearling fleet and could speak a basic form of English. But, allowing for Costa's accent, and the few English words the Aborigines possessed, the communication failed. When it is considered that the Aboriginal pronunciation of the English word 'flour' was *'balowa'* it is easy to understand the problem.

While the northern walk would have taxed the survivors along the shore they could have made it – as Baccich and Jurich did months later. But a far better means of reaching help was immediately at hand. After all, Baccich, Costa, and Antonich, had drifted ashore in the Stefano's yawl.

Though it was water-logged and had suffered a hole through banging on the reef, it was still quite repairable as the Aborigines would later prove. Baccich reported oars and the small boats' masts and sails among the items washed up from the wreck. Some significant small boat voyages had already been undertaken along the Western Australian coast. The *Tryal* survivors sailed to Java in ship's boats after the 1622 wreck at the Monte Bello Islands. Francisco Pelsart sailed to Java, from the Abrolhos after the 1629 *Batavia* wreck and mutiny. Men from the 1656 *Vergulde Draecke* wreck did even better, reaching Java in a cock-boat from as far south as the modern fishing settlement of Ledge Point. Followed a year later on the same ocean track by a boat crew abandoned by the search vessel *Waeckende Boey*. And, of course, the *Rapid's* survivors in three boats sailed from Point Cloates in 1812 to finally reach Batavia in Java.

Those were long ocean voyages in tiny craft, with far less quantity of supplies than were available to the *Stefano* survivors. For them there was a comparatively short haul to the head of the Cape with the wind behind them. The *Correo's* boat had rounded Point Murat in a single day from Point Cloates. It would have taken two day's travel at most, inside the reefs, for the *Stefano* survivors, even allowing for pulling the boat up on the shore at night. They could have bailed out the skiff, run it ashore, turned it upside down, elevated it on a frame of driftwood and repaired it.

Domenic Antoncich, the ship's carpenter was one of the survivors. While he had no formal tools there were two planes each with a steel chisel among the flotsam. There were plenty of nails and copper sheathing in the timbers washed in from the wreck, as well as cans of tar. While the boat was being prepared and made ready for sea the others could have spent their days patrolling the beach, gathering the food and water barrels which were daily washing ashore. Accumulating enough supplies to make the journey with plenty in hand. It would take some days for the wreck to empty out, and it would be prudent to wait for suitable weather.

The advantage of a boat would have been the fact that a sailing craft with a favourable wind can travel 160 kilometres in 24 hours.

The same distance on foot, for a group well-shod and with plenty of food and water, would have taken 10 days trudging along over rough terrain. The castaways had no shoes and limited endurance since they had hardly used their walking muscles in all the weeks at sea. More importantly they could not carry enough food and water to last the distance. In contrast the yawl could have carried the whole party. It could have covered significant distance without those on board becoming exhausted, and it could also have carried enough food and water to last a month.

For example the crew of the *Occator* wrecked in 1856, sailed up the Cape to the Muiron Islands, and then back down again to Shark Bay to be saved there by the cutter *Favourite*.

In hindsight it is easy to say what the *Stefano* castaways should have done. But, of course they had no local knowledge and were distracted by the seeming Godsend of the chart. It was also possibly the case that none of them had expertise in handling small boats. As deepwater sailors their experience may have been limited to big ships, and of course, they had no way of knowing about the activities of the pearlers to the north.

Whatever the reason, Costa's fatal decision for the group was to walk south, carrying their provisions. He estimated the distance to the Gascoyne at about 160 kilometres, though he told the others it was only 128 kilometres. The distance was actually 192 kilometres. They buried the flour and food they could not carry in the floor of their camp and set out confidently on November 1st, All Saints Day, three days after reaching the shore.

Their aim was to cover 16 kilometres a day which they hoped would bring them to their destination in not much more than a week. None of them had shoes.

Though they bound their feet with strips of linen torn from the cotton sheet washed in from the wreck the harsh terrain very quickly found them out. They had started a fire on landing, using a sextant lense as a magnifying glass to heat a small amount of gunpowder. The resultant explosion blew the lense away and burned Baccich's hand badly. The lense could not have gone far but they were unable to find it, despite the fact that it was so important.

By the middle of the second day they were already faltering. At the end of the third day, in the vicinity of Point Maud, Costa declared himself exhausted, threw himself on the ground and told the others to go on without him. They persuaded him to continue, but on the seventh day Jurich, Baccich, and Vulovich, too collapsed and said that they were unable to go any further. Michael Baccich realised at the end of that first week that what Costa had told them was incorrect. Looking at the chart he could see that far from being a day or two from their goal they had at most covered only a quarter of the distance. Moreover they had only one small bottle of water left and one litre of flour for six men. Disaster stared them in the face.

The story could have ended then and there. But unexpectedly two Aborigines appeared. They led them to a place where they dug at the foot of a sandhill and found fresh water. Then they started a fire by rubbing two sticks together and cooked the castaways' remaining flour into a damper for them. '*The Aborigines tried to talk to us, but their phrases were unintelligible'.*

It is a fair assumption that they were trying to tell the castaways that they were going the wrong way for succour. Meantime another band of Aborigines came to the aid of the shipmates who had fallen behind and were now prostrate with hunger and thirst. They led them to a nearby well and cooked them a meal of fish more than welcome for starving men. The castaways were astonished to hear the cry '*Brothers! Brothers!*' and to find that with the tribe was one of their shipmates Peranich. He had swum ashore further south than the main group and had been fed and cared for by the Aborigines unaware that anyone else had survived the wreck.

There was an emotional reunion and together they found a cave on the beach at a place which is now modern Warroora Station, where they could shelter in the shade from the sun. Reunited with their friends they pressed on southwards and were excited when they saw what they thought was the Gascoyne River. But it was only a sea inlet near Bulbarli and what they hoped would be a freshwater stream proved to be merely a saltwater marsh.

The Gascoyne – which would have been a similar disappointment had they ever reached it – was still many miles away with a waterless stretch of 144 kilometres south of Bulbarli.

'They thought they had reached Cape Farquhar' said Max Cramer, a partner of the author in the discovery of the 1629 *Batavia* shipwreck and the 1963 expedition. *' In fact they didn't get anywhere near it. It they had tried to go any further south it would have been fatal.'*

Cramer travelled on the tracks of the Stefano survivors. He compared their accounts with his own survey of the terrain in a paper called *Red Herrings,* referring to some of the confusions in interpreting the story. *'What they were attempting was a physical impossibility'* he said. *'In the circumstances tragedy was inevitable'.*

Despairing and now questioning Costa's leadership, seven of the castaways decided to turn back to the place where the cave was and where the Aborigines had shown them where to find water. Costa declared '*I cannot abandon them. We must stay together, to live or die as one*!'.

Somehow most of them survived December in the cave, living on sea food and bush berries. They managed to light a fire for cooking. Peranich used a steel blade from one of the carpenter's planes to strike a spark from a rock into a pinch of the gunpowder which they carried in a tin. The fire, which they kept continually burning, meant that they could cook their food gathered from the reef. But they became steadily weaker and weaker, and spent most of their time lying hopelessly in the cave. It is quite likely that they had the first lethargy and despondency of scurvy. The final straw was the great cyclone of Christmas Day, 1875. In Exmouth Gulf it sank the pearling boats *Wild Wave, Lily of the Lake, Ariel, Fairy Queen,* and *Blossom*.

The *Wild Wave, Lily of the Lake,* and the *Fairy Queen*, were no small cutters or luggers. They were large schooners, each carrying more than 30 crew and Malay divers. The death toll was 76 lives – Exmouth's first recorded major loss of life. The castaways fled their seaside cave for another hollow further inland. On that cataclysmic night the first deaths occurred. Peranich and Vulovich who failed to reach the second cave died of exposure in the storm. Over the next 30 days six more of the castaways died, one after the other, four of them in four days.

Finally desperate with hunger Baccich and Jurich looked at the corpse of Bucich and fell on it ready to devour portions of human flesh. '*Wretches!*' cried Dediol, the only other person left alive. '*May God damn your souls!*' With that he too died.

Baccich and Jurich were overcome with shame and remorse, expecting to die too. They collapsed on the beach outside the cave and lay all day in the broiling sun. But help was at hand. As night fell '*I opened my eyes to a soft evening sky and saw an early rising star constellation. Around this heavenly vision was a row of black faces. Even more beautiful than the stars were the eyes staring down with compassionate intensity*'.

The Aborigines had found them literally at Death's door. Gently they carried them to their camping ground, gave them food and water, and made it clear that the two castaways were to stay with them and go with them when they resumed travelling. The intention of their Aborigine rescuers was to hand the castaways over to a North West Cape group, the emu-totem people the Jinirigudi a part of the Talanji people, in the hope that they could in turn take them north and hand them over to the white pearlers.

This was what eventually happened. Though at the time the castaways could not understand what it was that the Aborigines were trying to tell them, where they were going to, or what the urgency was to go north.

The question may be asked why had the Aborigines not looked after them before? In fact they had. In the first instance they had attempted to tell the castaways of the pearling activity to the north and had been puzzled by their insistence on going in the opposite direction. Whenever the whites had reached a life-or-death situation Aborigines had stepped in and guided them to water and had given them food. And they had cared for Peranich as a single person.

But because their own life-style demanded continual movement to conserve water and food resources they could not take on the task of nurse-maiding the group as a whole. They could only physically take control when death reduced the number to two. The Aborigines of North Western Australia had a similar social pattern to other groups on the continent. It was essentially a family society, of related groups linked loosely together. There was no chief or headman in any of the tribes. Though there were councils of elders, and major decisions were the result of discussions by the group as a whole.

There was also usually a Maban, a wise man, spiritual leader, or – to use the common terms, 'witch doctor' or 'medicine man' -- who had power and influence. He could be a doctor and healer, or on the other side of the coin, a perpetrator of black magic in the shape of death spells. There were strict rules for marriage, to prevent inter-breeding. The old men took the younger women, and young men the older women or widows, until they grew older and were entitled to younger brides. Again, to prevent inter-breeding, there was an elaborate system of totems based on genetics which only permitted taking partners of the right opposite totem.

On the North West Cape the groups were always on the move to prevent over-use of the precious water points or diminishing of the food sources. The two boys found that their hosts grew angry if they talked between themselves in a language the Aborigines could not understand. This was fortunate because it forced the boys to learn the Aborigine words very quickly, and later they gave Father Scurla in Dubrovnik an extensive vocabulary of the language they had learned.

Reviewing the Scurla document Dr Alan Dench of the Centre for Linguistics of the University of Western Australia, was surprised to find that the vocabulary was Ngarluma tribal speech rather than the dialects of the Gascoyne area. The Ngarluma were a tribe in the vicinity of Cossack and Roebourne.

But this was confirmed by Tom Carter who had Ningaloo Station at Point Cloates in the 1890s for 14 years. He wrote in his diary that the tribe there were the Talanji whose common speech was the Ngarluma dialect. This was different from language spoken by the Aborigines at Minilya and other Gascoyne tribes but similar to the speech of Aborigines at Onslow and the Roebourne district.

The boys, though they didn't realise it, were allocated to particular families, and the two men who looked after them – who made sure that they had enough to eat and kept them moving – were known to them as 'Jacky' and 'Jimmy'. Their English names were given them during time spent with the pearling fleet. The medicine man of the group had taken the name 'Challi' for himself presumably after Charles ('Charlie') Tuckey the pearling captain of the cutter *Jessie,* whom the Aborigines much admired. Challi cured Jurich, at different times, of a toothache and a stomach ache by seemingly magical means.

At one time the boys recorded witnessing a cannibal feast. A young girl had died, and her remains were roasted on a fire and portions consumed by the whole tribe. Before the reader recoils at the thought, this was no instance of perverted greed for human flesh, but a solemn ceremony of farewell for the departed.

Similar ceremonies were held in the Kimberley and elsewhere in Australia. The parents wore white clay on their heads as mourning for weeks afterwards. Because the Aborigines were completely naked, slept on the ground between windbreaks of bushes, had no shelters, and lived entirely by hunting and seed gathering, the boys were unaware of the extent of their contacts with the whites. But some of the men had steel knives and axes.

Curiously they wouldn't use them, treating them as precious possessions, treasures to be kept safe. It they wanted to cut a portion of turtle or dugong they preferred their familiar stone knives and hand axes.

There were some fetishes which the boys found strange. In the Mediterranean, as in modern Australia, the octopus is considered good eating, a quality seafood. But here the Aborigines regarded it with horror and loathing, refusing to touch one let alone eat it, though they were plentiful along the shoreline. When the boys caught and cooked an octopus it caused a tribal commotion and they were made to throw it back in the sea. There was also an irrational antipathy to watches. The boys had saved three pocket watches, but when the Aborigines found them they smashed them with great vigour, finally pounding the remains with stones. Did they associate the ticking with a devil inside the watch cases?

In the tribe the men were the family leaders and their word was law. The women's daily task was finding seeds and berries. The seeds were ground into flour on grinding stones which were left at particular campsites. The flour was mixed with water and made up into 'dampers'. There was one meal during the day, in the evening, and the men ate first, sitting with their backs to the women and children, and throwing food to them over their shoulders. Cooking consisted of placing fish or turtle meat on the fire. Sometimes it was baked by covering the flesh with coals. The fire was lit, in time-honoured tradition, by rubbing two sticks together, and the men were very adept at it, producing a flame in a few minutes.

Everyone slept on the ground behind brush windbreaks, digging a hole for their hips. Before sleeping the men sang for an hour, beating time with their boomerangs and throwing sticks. The tribe never stayed in one spot for more than a few days. The criteria were food and water. Water was found by digging in the sand at the base of high sand dunes, or in rock holes. If there was a place where the fishing was good or there were turtles but no water, then sufficient fresh water was carried in a *yanrey* or *coolamon* made from wood, or more often in hollowed out baler or conch shells. The women did the carrying, with the *yanrey* on their hip, with a piece of green bush in the water to prevent it from spilling. Babies were carried in the same way..

The Aboriginal day consisted either of travelling from one place to another, hunting and gathering, or a combination of both. The men provided the meat, and this consisted mainly of fish and turtles.

If a dugong were killed it was a subject of great rejoicing, and the tribe would stay at the spot roasting flesh until it was all consumed. Though crabs and crayfish were plentiful along the shoreline the Aborigines did not hold them in high regard, but something to fall back on only if fishing were unsuccessful. They considered that the best use of a crab was as *'berley'* – crushed to fragments with a rock and thrown off the edge of a reef to tempt fish within spear range.

They caught turtles when the females crawled up the beach to lay eggs, and the Aborigines were very partial to the eggs. The men also often caught turtles by swimming, turning them on their backs and bringing them back to shore. They used nets to catch both large turtles and dugong. While they had canoes at various places it is not clear whether the craft were 'drifters' from some other place since the North West Cape did not have timber suitable for canoe-making. Further north, especially in the Kimberley, Aborigines made quite elaborate rafts from mangrove poles.

But the '*kalums*', as the rafts were called there, required a special type of tall straight mangrove with a very bulbous base, which may not have been available further south. The North West Cape Aborigines travelled so frequently as hunter gatherers that they could not carry anything with them other than their spears and boomerangs. Any floating logs, canoes, or the boats of Europeans washed up from shipwrecks, might be used opportunistically in particular places. But they would not have lasted long.

European boats, in particular, needed to be covered otherwise the hot sun warped the timbers and ultimately destroyed them. Summer shade temperatures on the North West Cape are regularly over 40 degrees Celsius, and an uncovered boat would barely last a season in the open without care.

When the Aborigines and their two charges travelled north from Point Maud they approached the boundary of another tribal group, whose territory ran from Point Cloates northwards to the end of the Cape. The boys first group of friends asked them to take the boys up to the Cape. They agreed, but after a short time turned back and wanted to give the two boys back to the original group because they could not walk fast enough to keep up with them.

There was anger, and a fight, with spears and boomerangs thrown. But eventually peace was restored and a compromise agreed upon. The boys could come with the new group on condition that the two men, Jimmy and Jacky, who had befriended them, would be responsible for catching their food and looking after them if they could not keep up with the tribe. Ironically when the two boys and their group of Aborigines reached the site of their original hut they found that the Aborigines had repaired the *Stefano* yawl and found a mast and sail and five oars for it. Ten Aborigines and Baccich and Jurich went out in the skiff on a hilarious but unsuccessful turtle hunt. The oars jumping out of the rowlocks and confusion reigning amongst the inexperienced rowers.

The Aborignes had been saying to the boys for some time ' *Minara denki nagoru ... 'Soon you will see your dinghy!'.*

'Denki' was an obvious corruption of the English word 'dinghy'. There were other English words adapted which neither the boys nor Father Scarla recognised because they spoke Italian. *'Nirin'* for a needle, *'Komin'* for 'come' are clear enough to us. The Italian pronunciation of the letter C as *'ch'* explains *'Ciugga' (or 'Chugga')* for sugar, *'Ciar'* (or *'Chiar'*) for shirt, *'Thie'* for tea, *'Coconagi'* for coconuts. *'Balowa'* for flour, and so on.

In the case of the repaired dinghy from the Stefano the Aborigines probably hoped that the boys would be able to sail up to the Cape solving the difficulty of taking them there by land. That would have relieved their hosts of the responsibility. But it would have quickly become obvious that Baccich and Jurich did not have the basic boating skills. Apparently it didn't occur to the boys at the time that this was the reason why the tribe had brought them to the boat. Though Baccich did reflect on it in the aftermath.

The boys found that the tribe, even old people, walked incredibly quickly at an estimated five miles and hour, far faster than Europeans.

In the beginning the boys had great difficulty in keeping up, and the Aborigines continually grabbed them by the hand and cried '*Bulura vagai!' .. 'Keep moving! Keep moving!'.*

Baccich recalled later *'I thought to myself how magnificent they looked, almost floating through the tangled brush. They moved so effortlessly!'*

Despite their impatience on the march, the Aborigines were incredibly kind to the castaways. Their youth and pitiable condition probably helped incite their sympathy. Baccich was only 16 at the start of the ordeal and small for his age, while Jurich was 18 years old. The Aborigines treated them as children – uninitiated boys.

To the end of a long life Michael Baccich would remember with gratitude how his life was saved and the trouble his Aborigine friends went to, often at inconvenience to themselves, in arranging his rescue. The boys lived with the Aborigines in the indigenous life-style, for four months. They were frustrated by occasionally seeing ships, large and small, on the horizon. But always they sailed past. Finally, on April 17th, 1876, rescue came at last. Remarkably Jurich had a dream on the previous night.

'*Today we are going to be saved!*' he told Baccich in the morning, excited by the dream.

Baccich, disheartened by false alarms, replied gloomily '*Let us not deceive ourselves my friend... We dream of things that we desire. This land which has now received us is inhospitable and deserted. There is little hope that today or any other day a ship will appear*'.

But Jurich was right . A vessel did appear at the head of the Gulf and began tacking towards shore. Eventually Charlie Tuckey – the '*Challi*' they had heard so much about from the Aborigines – rounded up into the wind and anchored inside the Cape in his cutter *Jessie*

Soon a dinghy came into the beach and two white men stepped ashore. Apprehensive at first at such an unexpectedly large crowd to greet them, they had drawn their revolvers and looked questioningly about them. Baccich and Jurich rushed down to greet them. Tuckey was amazed, Baccich recalled, to see '*The strange apparition of two gaunt boys with patches of brown and pink skin and dishevelled hair that had gone uncut for six months. I was clad only in shredded remnants of what had been drawers and I was holding an enormous floppy hat, a present from one of the recently arrived Aborigines. Jurich was hardly better off, with the tatters of half of a shirt over his shoulders and in his hand a sailor's cap, a relic from the Stefano*'.

There was a frustration because neither Baccich nor Jurich spoke English. Both burst into tears and the captain was so moved that he wept too.

At last they were on their way to *Pulimandur* and were able to understand that the word they had heard so often from their Aborigine friends meant the port of Fremantle!

Tracks Without Toes

Chapter Five

Aborigines developed their tracking skills from the day they could walk. The women were as adept as the men at reading the earth for the tracks of animals and their fellow tribesmen. They knew the individual footprint of everyone in their group, and could tell by the deeper imprint of the right foot whether a stranger was carrying a spear, or a friend had killed a kangaroo and was carrying it over his shoulder.

When the first Dutchmen landed on the Cape in the 1600s the Aborigines would have been agog to examine their tracks after the strangers had left. Aside from their strange wearing apparel, some of the newcomers wore boots with an indented heel and a single pointed toe. That was extraordinary – humans and every animal in the Australian bush from a kangaroo to a crocodile had toes and left toe prints!

The exception was when the *Kadaitcha Man*, the witchdoctor, wished to disguise his tracks for evil purposes. Then he wore sandals of emu feathers or padded spinifex so his track was a splodge not a print and consequently unidentifiable. Could these people – if they were people – be witchdoctors?

The first time Aborigines in the North saw horse tracks they were thrown into total shock. The semi-circular, deep-dug prints of a horse's hooves – all four of them! – had no toes and were unlike anything they had ever seen before. They tried, and failed, to imagine what kind of an animal could be responsible. These must be Devil footprints!

They were equally confused by the tracks left by the first carts, believing that they must be made by two snakes. The Aborigines followed the wheel ruts for miles waiting for them to come together. When they finally saw the horses in the flesh they were no less awed by the sight than what they had imagined – after all a riding horse is enormously bigger and probably ten times the weight of a kangaroo. And the strangers sat astride them!

Aborigines called them '*Yowarda'* – the white man's giant riding dogs!

The first horses and the first carts and wagons did not come to the North West Cape until long after they were a common sight in most other areas of Western Australia. The Cape was too far, and too remote. It did not have the permanent rivers or freshwater sources regarded as essential for pastoral settlement in days before windmills and wire fences. Even the pearlers regarded the Cape as cursed after the 1875 Christmas Day cyclone which wrecked four schooners and drowned 76 men.

Though Julius Brockman took out the lease of Minilya, which included the North West Cape as early as 1876, it would be sometime later before anything really happened in terms of pastoral progress on the North West Cape. By that time development had moved more quickly elsewhere. Communities had been established at Broome and Derby in the Kimberley, at Port Hedland, Marble Bar, Nullagine, and Roebourne, in the Pilbara, and Carnarvon in the Gascoyne.

What happened at the North West Cape after Charles Tuckey's *Jessie* carried our two heroes, Michael Baccich and Ivan Jurich away to Fremantle in 1876?

They were feted in Fremantle, fed, clothed, and the local colonials generally made a fuss of them. Concerts were held to raise money for their passage home, and for rewards for the Aborigines who saved them. It was commendable that the two castaways took ship back to the north with Captain Vincent's schooner the *Rosette,* bearing gifts for the Aborigines of the North West Cape who had saved their lives.

There was an emotional reunion with 'Jacky' to whom Baccich gave a sheath knife mounted on a leather belt. There were mirrors, and hatchets, and trinkets, and bags of flour for the others, delivered with hugs and tears .Only then, they felt, that duty fulfilled, could they go home to their familiar surrounds of the Mediterranean.

There was a curious reunion with another member of the tribe. In an earlier chapter the question was asked whether the two men left behind by the *Correo da Asio* castaways in 1816 were looked after by the Aborigines, as were the two boys from the *Stefano*? Perhaps some traces of Portuguese vocabulary may have remained in the local language as evidence? For example the Portuguese word for turtle was *'Tortuga'*. The word for turtle on the North West Cape as recorded by Baccich was *'Tataruga'*.

Michael Baccich left us with a description of an unusual member of the tribe. Remember that neither he nor anyone else in Western Australia had any knowledge of the shipwreck of the *Correo da Azio* which had occurred before European settlement.

'This man Vallero' Baccich said *' Was an extraordinary person. He was so tall that the next tallest man in the tribe barely reached his shoulders. His body was big in all respects and he was not proportioned the same as the other natives. He had a full bossom that rivalled the women's in size, and his enormous abdomen hung over his hips. There were other peculiarities which suggested he was from another race. There was a total absence of beard or other body hair and the hair on his head was very stubby. He was unlike anyone else in the three tribes. I estimated him to be 40 years old. The entire tribe looked on him with devotion and, to a degree, veneration. Everyone waited on him and he was never assigned to any duties. I speculated that he too, perhaps many years ago might have been a castaway like us. Perhaps he was an African, a slave, or in ship's service...?'*

Vallero, in 1876, was too young to be one of the Coreo's marooned crewmen. However the Aborigines may have taken Vallero's father into their tribe as they did with the Stefano boys. After all, doesn't Vallero sound like a Portuguese name?

The description leads to a more sinister thought. If the two *'missing'* seamen were of Negro origin and thus from the lowest status on the *Coreo,* in a situation where food and water were short and space in the open boat at a premium, might they not have been abandoned deliberately? It remains one of the unanswerable questions.

Sadly, three years after the boys' visit the *Rosette* was lost in a cyclone off the Pilbara coast in 1879, going down with all hands including Captain Vincent. Another maritime tragedy on a shipwreck coast.

As a final touch the Austro-Hungarian government sent a gold watch (now with the Royal Western Australian Historical Society) and a letter of thanks to Charles Tuckey for the part he played in the great adventure of the rescue. After qualifying as a captain Michael Baccich, still aged only 21, navigated a ship to New Orleans in the United States. There he found a large Croatian community, and resolved to quit the sea. He became a very successful businessman first as a maritime provisioner and shipping agent, later as a real estate agent.

He married and had seven children. One of his six daughters – born on October 27th, 1890, the 15th anniversary of the *Stefano* shipwreck – was named '*Australia*'.

He corresponded regularly with Charles Tuckey whom he affectionately called '*My second father!*'.and died in 1935 aged 76 years. His many descendants still live in the United States. Ivan Jurich too had had quite enough of the sea. He '*swallowed the anchor*' (as the old sailor's saying has it), became a farmer and tended a vineyard, living to a ripe old age in his native land.

The story of the two youthful survivors inspired those who had relatives aboard the ill-fated *Emma,* which had disappeared in 1867, to petition the Colonial Government to fund an expedition to see whether there might be *Emma* survivors too, still living with the Aborigines.

The Perth *Inquirer* newspaper of January 19th 1876, had already run a long article quoting Charles Tuckey's Aboriginal informant who said that, 10 years previously white castaways had been killed and eaten by Aborigines in the Point Maud area. The article continued:

'Almost every mail that reaches us from neighbouring colonies brings tidings of the rescue of Europeans after years of bondage on islands in the South Seas inhabited by the most ferocious cannibals. And who shall say that there may not be one or more survivors of the many shipwrecks on our coast similarly situated in the hands of the savages in the neighbourhood of North West Cape?'

By amazing co-incidence, on the very day that the *Inquirer* article was published, seven of the *Stefano* castaways were still alive – but only just. They were lying with diminishing strength, in the sea cave at Warroora waiting for Death to overtake them.

In May, 1876, when the news of the rescue of Baccich and Jurich reached Roebourne where many people had had friends or relatives aboard the *Emma,* there was public outrage at the lack of a government-sponsored search for shipwreck survivors. The Government Resident Robert Sholl, whose son Treverton was lost with the *Emma,* chartered the schooner *Victoria* and sent her to Point Cloates under the command of Pemberton Walcott, with orders to search the area. Walcott – who had ridden with Francis Gregory in 1861 on the first exploration of the Pilbara – was astonished by what he found at Point Cloates in June, 1867.

South of the point, in an area which formed a natural collecting point for flotsam and jetsam, he found a concentrated mass of wreckage which included the remains of several vessels cast up on shore. He reported:

'The wreck of the Stefano was pointed out by natives and the camp of the survivors where sundry articles belonging to her were found such as boards with written particulars, torn charts, stools etc..'

There were two postscripts as a result of Walcott's investigation. He brought back to Roebourne the cabin door on which Carl Costa had carved the details of the wreck and the names of the survivors. It moved Baccich and Jurich to tears when they saw it while visiting Cossack and Roebourne with Captain Vincent in the *Rosette*. They called there on a leg of their voyage to reward the Aborigines of North West Cape.

News of the wrecks initiated a *'timber-rush'* from Roebourne. Sawn timber was expensive and hard to come by in the north, especially of the quality required for building or repairing vessels in the pearling fleet. Several small vessels apparently sailed south from Cossack to recover wreck timbers from Point Cloates.

The next person we find in the area was Robert E. Bush. His father Lieutenant Colonel R.E.Bush, had commanded the 96th Regiment at Fremantle. His son Robert was raised in England and was intrigued by his stories of the faraway Swan River Colony and the vast horizons of the lands beyond.

Robert, aged 23, arrived at Fremantle in 1878 aboard the barque *Lady Elizabeth*. The ship was wrecked off Rottnest on departure after he had disembarked, which no doubt caused him some concern. He had intended to sail north in the *Rosette* which sailed with his baggage on board. Bush missed the boat, for some reason. It was as well for him he did so because the *Rosette*, as noted, went down in a cyclone with all hands, taking Bush's baggage with her.

After visiting the de Grey on the Pilbara he spent some months as a jackeroo on Henry Moloney's station Murgoo in the Murchison. As an adventurous young man, he made a number of explorations up the coast north of Carnarvon looking for land to lease on his own account. On one of his journeys, in 1879, Robert Bush passed on the coastal side of the huge salt expanse of Lake MacLeod and reached the area which now comprises Warroora Station.

'The blacks here have a tale of a lot of white people having been wrecked here years ago, and showed us what looked like the grave of one who died from eating a poisonous berry which grows here. They say his mates buried him. We then made for the beach again and we found the bones of his comrades, who I suppose were frightened of leaving the beach for fear of the blacks. Well, we buried these bones as decently as we could in the sand. We could find no clues as to who they were from the bleached and rotted portions of dress among the bones. We found them in a bit of a cave where they had crept to die from hunger and thirst, little thinking that white hands would ever give their remains (however rough) of burial. The wild dogs had carried away a lot of their bones. We covered their grave with some fine big shells'.

So the bones of Dediol, and Bucich, at last found a final resting place!

Robert Bush became a pastoralist in his own right. He was not a man who did things by small degrees. He established not one but two stations on the Gascoyne River. They were Upper and Lower Clifton Downs, two of the largest pastoral properties in Australia. The upper station was used for cattle and the lower one for sheep.

The acreages of the two properties were enormous by modern standards, standing respectively at 1,160785 and 2,000,000 acres. The upper station ran 12,000 head of shorthorn cattle. Lower Clifton Downs included 140 miles of the Gascoyne River, and could carry 150,000 sheep. The property could accommodate 90 shearers and station workers in its outhouses and shearers' quarters. That station also had 1000 head of shorthorn cattle, 250 horses and 120 camels – used for hauling the wool on wagons the 110 miles into Carnarvon.

Things moved more slowly on the North West Cape. The first man to take up land there was Julius Brockman. He obtained leases at Warroora and in the Point Cloates region as an extension of Minilya Station. Brockman had had 10 years of problems with drought and continuity of water for his sheep at Minilya and was looking to find some more reliable water points.. There was good water on the coast for sheep north of Bulbarli. The highly desirable '*milk bush*' also proliferated between the dunes.

Milk bush?

It was a plant prolific in moisture, and while feeding on it sheep did not need to drink at all. It was also good for ewes with nursing lambs, and other sheep put on condition very quickly while feeding upon it.

The main problem on the North West Cape at that time was its remoteness. It was so far from anywhere. While all the shipping traffic to the North passed by outside the reefs, there were no suitable anchorages – a point Julius Brockman would prove to his cost.

Julius was '*Mr Everywhere'*. A restless soul, he had been pearling in Shark Bay and Roebuck Bay, managed de Grey Station in the Pilbara, taken the first sheep into the Kimberly at Beagle Bay, established a station on the Fitzroy, another on the Meda, and finally joined his brother Charles in the Gascoyne at Minilya.

In 1888 he purchased the cutter *Ada May* for pearling and to carry wool bales from his coastal leases to Carnarvon for shipment. On March 3rd, he set out from Carnarvon to travel up the coast with stores and the necessities to set up his intended new station near Point Cloates. The expedition ended in tragedy. On board were Brockman, a stock inspector Bob Miller, an Aborigine called Johnny Friday, and two Malays, Peter and Meagle, who had come from Singapore on the usual contract for divers and crew. The *Ada May* was towing a dinghy.

They attempted a passage through the reef between Yalobia Hill and Maud's Landing when a surging swell pushed them forward and snapped the dinghy line. The Malay on the helm began to luff the the *Ada May* up to recover the dinghy. Brockman seeing a swell rearing behind them cried to the helmsman to keep going shorewards. But it was too late. The breaker caught them beam-on and because the hatches were off, half-filled her. The next wave caught her and swamped the cutter which sank, with only her mast showing, and all aboard were thrown into the water.

The accident occurred just on sundown with the shore a mile-and-a-half away. Tom Carter, who would later buy the Point Cloates lease, described what followed.

'They were all good swimmers, though Miller was perhaps the poorest hand at it, so Julius Brockman seeing that one of the Manillamen had an oar told him to let Miller have it -- which he did. Then another breaker came and separated them all.

Brockman kept on swimming steadily towards the land which was high, trying not to think of the sharks which abound in these seas. But occasionally bumping into jellyfish which he said gave him a nasty feeling.

*Just as he was beginning to feel exhausted he heard the cry of a red bill (*pied oyster catcher*). This encouraged him knowing he must be near the beach. After a while, letting down his legs, he found he could touch bottom. He reached shore naked as he had got rid of his clothes when he began to swim. He shouted and cooeed but could get no reply, so dug a hole in the warm dry sand above high water mark and slept exhausted. Next morning he could see no signs of the others and so proceeded south to his Yalobia well about three miles distant where he got a drink and saw the tracks of two men who afterwards proved to be the Manillamen. The Aborigine, Johnny Friday and Miller were never seen again, and were undoubtedly eaten by sharks.*

'The sun now began to get fierce and Brockman, whose feet were badly cut by the reefs, put seaweed on his head and walked on to Warroora, 17 miles south where he found some of his station blacks. He sent some of them in to Minilya Station to tell the news and have the buggy sent out for him while he got an old frock from a native woman and waited for the buggy. The heat of the sun had burned the whole of his body and when I saw him he looked like a boiled lobster and

was suffering severely from the irritation of the sunburn. All his skin, being so burned, peeled off after a few days. He was going about in a white sheet for several days not being able to bear the touch of clothes.

'The insurance company, with which Miller had his life insured, behaved very badly refusing to pay the money to his widow until after a very long interval because they said no-one saw his body and so there was no proof of his death'.

Not surprisingly Brockman became disenchanted with his coastal holdings after that, and sold his northern leases. He moved south to Guildford on the Upper Swan where there was less chance of being shipwrecked, and far less possibility of his naked body being broiled by the sun -- or of having to borrow a frock from an Aboriginal lady!

Carter, generally known as '*The Birdman'* purchased Brockman's coastal leases, and made his homestead at Point Cloates, built largely from timbers of wrecked ships. He named his station 'Ningaloo' from the Aboriginal name for Point Cloates, '*Najendo'* – meaning *'Nose'* because of the fact that the land there was like a protuberance pointing out to sea. The name Ningaloo was later given to the wonderful coral reef stretching south from the tip of the North West Cape for 320 kilometres

Carter was called '*The Birdman'* because of his passionate interest in ornithology. He left Yorkshire in 1877 under the auspices of the Royal British Ornithological Society and Lord Rothschild. His aim was to finish the task of collecting data on Western Australia's birds begun by John Gould, tragically speared by Aborigines at the Gulf of Carpentaria on Ludwig Leichhardt's expedition of 1845.

Though he had no need to work, for he had independent means, Carter, a dashing and handsome young Englishman, typical of many from good families who came to Australia for '*Colonial Experience'*, decided that the best way to see the country was to work on stations. He joined Julius Brockman at Minilya.

When Brockman decided that he had finally had enough of the North, in 1889, Carter purchased the Point Cloates holding from him, and three years later added another 40,000 acres up to the tip of the Cape which would eventually become Yardie Creek Station. He ran the two properties for 14 years. Station life was physically very hard indeed at the time of Julius Brockman and Tom Carter. But a revolution was about to occur in pastoral life. The modern aids which would completely change Australian station systems sound simple enough now. They were windmills, wire fencing, and corrugated iron. All were brought to Western Australia late in the century – Charles Harper brought the first windmills to de Grey Station in the Pilbara after having seen one working in England in 1876.

Some of Carter's diary entries indicate how tough a life it was on sheep stations at the time. Station owners and their employees often slept on '*the big floor with the blue curtains'*. Literally on the ground and under the stars! At one period Carter lived '*Under a white gum tree'*. We may wonder what happened when it rained? Some of his associates thought he was *'sissy'* because he had a hammock '*the cause of much scoffing from the regular hands'* instead of throwing his blanket down on the dirt with the ants and the centipedes.

One day he particularly remembered concerned the Yandoo well where water was drawn up by hand in an open drum lifted by a windlass and poured into troughs to water 1000 sheep. It was hard work, as may be imagined. Not only sheep but the white overseer and the Aborigine shepherds also drank the water.

'I had noticed for some time that the water was acquiring an increasingly rank taste and smell, and next morning a sheep's ear came up in the bucket. I thought it time to get out the putrefying carcase, which I could see floating below. Accordingly I told the Aborigine assisting me to get into the bucket and I would lower him down.

'But he steadfastly refused to do anything of the sort. As I could not trust him to lower me single-handedly I got a light line from Grierson's cart, and making a noose at one end lowered it down the well. Then I let out all the rope off the windlass and went down it hand over hand. The first part was all right as the well was timbered some 15 feet from the top and I could get toe-hold between the timbers. But when I got below them the sides of the well were smooth, greasy sandstone. I wondered if I could clamber out again without any assistance from footholds on the sides!

'However I wanted that sheep out of my only drinking water! I got the light line around the carcase and shouted to the Aborigine to haul it up. This he did – the foul drippings falling all over me until he got it to the top. Then I went up hand over hand, and was almost exhausted on reaching the top again. Two days later the same rope broke when lowering the empty drum!'.

Before windmills came into general use, stock drank from river pools and ate the nearby country bare. They had to go further and further afield and died if the distances became too great. Sheep, horses, and cattle were vulnerable in drought when the rivers and pools dried up. The option to natural pools was to dig wells. But water had to be drawn up by hand with buckets, as described by Carter, using a windless, or a lever and fork system, and poured into troughs made from hollow logs cut in half.

Fencing was bush timber post-and-rail, and only practical over short distances. Without fences the sheep had to be constantly watched by Aboriginal shepherds, or herded into stone enclosures at night or temporary ones formed by cutting bushes and laying them on the ground. Windmills which used the wind to bring water to the surface, and into troughs without human assistance, and wire fences which kept sheep in paddocks without the need for shepherds, drastically reduced the need for labour on the stations. They also allowed for a dramatic increase in the size of flocks. Artesian bores provided artificial lakes.

Before corrugated iron became available, station homesteads and other buildings were erected using local stone, mud walls, or timber, with wooden roofs. Corrugated iron was light, easy to use, and it required a fraction of the time and labour of building in stone to erect and nail the sheets in place. By the time of the First World War in 1914 almost every shearing shed in Australia, as well as out-stations, out-houses, and shearers' quarters, were made of corrugated iron sheeting. Iron was used for all bush roofing regardless of the quality of the building underneath it, whether a palatial homestead or an out-house toilet. Metal troughs soon replaced hollow logs cut in half for stock to drink.

While collecting his birds Carter was a meticulous diarist. Some of his earlier diary entries made up the book *No Sundays In The Bush,* edited by his daughter Violet and published by Lothian Publishing Company, Victoria, in 1987. The title first occurred to him when Carter was well-sinking – a back-breaking job – and found that his sweat and toil was occurring on an Easter Sunday when most of the rest of the world was enjoying the religious holiday!

He was a crack shot, though he was actually blind in his left eye from birth. For that reason, where most ornithologists used binoculars to study their bird subjects Cater used a telescope or *'spy-glass'*. After gathering voluminous notes on the birdlife of Point Cloates and the North West

Cape he sold Yardie Creek and Ningaloo, respectively in 1902 and 1904. He returned to England to marry his childhood sweetheart Annie Ward who had refused him 18 years previously. A *'True Romance'* story!

They came back to Western Australia afterwards, taking up a property in Broome Hill – a contrast to the heat and dust of the north -- before returning to England in 1914.

On his death his marvellous collection of more than 1000 Australian birds, including many from the Exmouth region, went to museums. He is still regarded as one of the great British ornithologists. Carter's contribution to the study of Australian birds occupies two pages in Hubert Whitell's *Literature of Australian Birds.* Four species and 14 sub-species bear his name. Birds he collected are in the American Museum of Natural History, the British Museum, and the Western Australian Museum. 'Not bad for a station owner on the remote North West Cape!

His daughter, Violet, wrote that '*He found several previously unknown birds, but his greatest joy was the discovery of Eremiornis carterii – the Spinnifexbird, a beautiful thrush-like bird which is peculiar to North West Australia and the Northern Territory'.*

Curiously Ningaloo Station and Point Cloates were always known to Gascoyne people as '*Madman's Corner'*. Was it because you had to be crazy to live in such an out-of-the-way place? Or was it because of Carter's fascination with the birdlife?

In terms of time – how life-spans can take in several eras – it is interesting to note that Tom Carter, the first white man to live permanently on the North West Cape, died in 1931. Two years later your author was borne. So the lives of only two people cover the modern history of the Cape from 1889 when Carter took up the lease of Ningaloo to the present day! Small world!

The stations of the Exmouth region changed hands frequently on a speculative basis, both before and after the year 1900. Though, aside from Carter, the differing owners did little to improve or stock the properties. Western Australians were in a speculative mood at the time, many of them awash with British money as a result of the great gold rushes of the 1890s.The history of WA at that time was a fairy tale come true.

Early in its history Western Australia had struggled to survive as a British crown colony. It was called *'The Swan River Settlement'* and was more generally known disparagingly as ' *The Ugly Duckling'*of Australian colonies. It had been left far behind by other Australian colonies in New South Wales, Victoria, and South Australia. At the official census of 1881 the white population of WA was still only 30,000 people – two thirds of a Saturday Australian Rules football crowd at Subiaco Oval today. In comparison Victoria's population at the time was 874,000 people.
But a turn-around was about to take place. While it has been said often through the years '*Australia rides on the sheep's back!*' the real truth is that it was gold that made the dramatic difference. The precious metal transformed Australia from a series of separated British colonies autocratically ruled from the Colonial Office in London, to a self-governing nation making its own decisions in its own right. It was gold that created the modern Australian nation.

Figures tell the story. The population of NSW increased by 500,000 people after the discovery of gold at Ophir, near Bathurst in 1851.The population of Victoria expanded five times after the discoveries at Ballarat and Bendigo. The population of Australia which was only 400,000 people before the first gold strikes, increased to 1,200,000 people in 10 years after the first gold nugget had glinted in a prospector's pan.

But the most sensational discoveries of all, and the greatest and latest transformation would occur in Western Australia.

There were a rolling series of gold rushes. The first strike was at Hall's Creek in 1883. There followed more finds in the Pilbara, at Mallina, Nullagine, and Marble Bar. The next rush was to finds with even greater potential in the Murchison, at Cue, Lake Austin, and Meekatharra, in the 1880s and early 90s.

But the most famous and fabulous strikes of all were made last, at Coolgardie and Kalgoorlie. The effect on Western Australia was magical. The old '*Ugly Duckling*' tag which caused West Australians to cringe for so many years, vanished to be replaced by a far more flattering tittle '*The Golden West'!* It sounded so much better!

By 1904, a decade after the first major gold strikes, the WA population had increased to 240,000, an increase of eightfold in ten years. In 1914 it numbered 322,000 people. Four out of five new arrivals in the 1890s had come because of the gold, which amounted to 80 per cent of WA's exports.

Before gold, in the 1880s, the only railway line ran from Perth to York. There was no harbour at Fremantle and steamships had to unload passengers and cargo at Albany, which was linked to Perth by wagons and horse-drawn coaches.

Gold brought a network of new towns and railway lines. It provided good roads and a new steamer port at Fremantle, a water pipeline to Kalgoorlie, and a spate of public buildings. On a personal level gold financed the kind of houses and luxuries West Australians had only previously dreamed about. The glitter of gold replacing the grey mantle of previously perceived failure. The former run-down convict colony now attracted emigrants by the thousand.

Most importantly miners put their returns from gold into other investments, and above all into developing farms and pastoral properties. That was why the golden gleam would be important to Exmouth when sheep stations were finally developed there.

Both Exmouth and Giralia stations benefited from gold. The King family who had Exmouth Station from 1908 onwards, were heavily involved in prospecting and mining.

William King had obtained the lease in 1908, and with the help of his half-brother Joe King, was the first person to make a real success of running stock on the North West Cape.

Bill King, of Mornington, in Victoria, researching his family's history in modern times wrote: '*The North West Cape was an incredibly isolated location. There were no tracks to anywhere at that time, and the only access was by the coastal trader, the vessel Geraldton. Every piece of building material, basic provisions and stock had to be shipped in by sea and rowed ashore by dinghy. There was no surface water on the land and this was left to the well-sinking skills of Joe King whose years of desert prospecting had taught him how to obtain this precious commodity*'.

Joe King, more than 40 years old, joined the army at the outbreak of war in 1914 and rose through the ranks to become a sergeant major in a unit of engineers. After the war Joe's son Billy, aged 17 went up to Exmouth Station to become a jackeroo.

Bill King ('Young Billy's' son) wrote in 2008 '*The permanent white population on the Nor' West Cape at the time was 11 people. There were the three Kings, William, Joseph, and 'Young Billy'. The two Campbell brothers at Yardie Creek Station had taken up their lease at the same time as Joe King. There were six people at the lighthouse, Mrs and Mrs Wilson, their two children, and two helpers who came and went. The Aborigine population numbered about 30 at Yardie Creek, and a similar population at Kooburroo Well, the site of the town of Exmouth today*'.

At that time Exmouth Station comprised 160,000 acres, including the Bay of Rest, and carried 10,000 sheep with 27 horses.

The men of the three stations, Exmouth, Yardie Creek, and Giralia, helped each other out with shearing, well-sinking and putting up buildings. Joe King was much in demand for his ability to sink wells and erect windmills.

There were many stories from those early days. On one occasion a coastal schooner sheltering from a cyclone in the Bay of Rest was driven aground. To refloat the vessel the crew had to dump some of the cargo overboard. They included some mysterious large packing cases.

'Giralia Homestead in those days was little more than a lean-to of galvanised iron and a bark hut. The thought of packing cases floating in the low reaches of the Gulf was an appealing challenge. ' Never mind the contents, the timber would be useful!

' Joe and my father rowed the station dinghy out, snared the packs and towed them back to the beach. It soon became evident that they had rescued a windfall -- not just packing cases but packs of timber and the material for a complete pre-fabricated house!'.

The items had carried numbers to assist in erection. Rae and Denver Blake, the owners of Giralia in 1999 when Cyclone Vance swept through and ripped their homestead apart, were puzzled by the coded numbers on each stick of timber. Until Bill King junior called by on a visit to Exmouth and told them the story of the *'rescued'* house.

Joe and 'Young Billy' also built the shearers' quarters on Giralia . A welded and bolted steel frame was erected and covered with galvanised iron to make the quarters 'cyclone proof'. The strength of the building was proved when it survived the catastrophic cyclone of 1945, and Cyclone Vance in 1999 which destroyed the Giralia homestead. All the steel and other materials for the shearers had to be ferried ashore by dinghy.

'Young Billy' as a free hand, worked on all the North West Cape stations, and even had a season as a deckhand on the pearling lugger *Rouzelle.* In 1924 he went to work on Yardie Creek for the Campbell brothers. When they retired to Perth he became the station manager. His son found a used envelope from his Yardie days with a supply order scribbled on the back. It underlined the isolation of the Cape.

100 bags flour
12 bags sugar
1bag salt
1 bag pepper
20 cans butter
10 cases canned fruit
10 cases jam
12 bags potatoes
12 bags onions
20 cases beer
10 cases whisky10 cases wine (Penfolds Red Label Port)
Plus hardware

While back in Perth for Christmas in 1919, Bill King spent some of his earnings on a camera, and the materials for developing and processing film. Returning to the station in 1919 he set about recording station life on film, developing and printing his own pictures.

Many of them of are of remarkable quality, considering that they were exposed by the light of a hurricane lamp. As a result he has left a magnificent heritage record for Exmouth of pictures of those early days.

'Young Billy' had many adventures, including becoming a driver for a time for Gascoyne Transport, a trucking firm begun by the aviators Charles Kingsford Smith and Keith Anderson. Lindsay Skipworth and Bill King drove the first motor car to get through to the lighthouse at Vlamingh Head from Carnarvon.

The supply ship had run aground and the lighthouse was in dire need of supplies. His son, also named Bill in a family tradition, would establish his own outback tours travel business many years later. He recalled :

'*The one thing that used to stop me in virgin country was washaways with their steep, sometimes vertical-sided banks. I asked dad how he and Lindsay managed to negotiate the innumerable washaways flowing down from the Cape Range?'*.

'Simple' the elder King replied. ' *We just took a case of gelignite and blew the banks in!'*.

In 1926 Bill King decided to go to the Royal Melbourne Show to broaden his knowledge of merino bloodlines from the high-quality stock on exhibition. While he was there he went to post a letter at the Ormond Post Office and met the post mistress, Eileen Lawless. When he went back to the North West Cape he corresponded with her.

' The correspondence must have got pretty serious' his son remarked in 2008 *'Because in 1928 he returned to Melbourne, proposed, and he and Eileen married on the 28th of July'*.

Joe King, meantime, had never got over the lure of '*chasing the weight'* on the goldfields and leaving the station he struck it rich with the *Eldorado* mine in the Murchison. With the proceeds he bought the *Bangemall* pub, so-called because a miner had come in one day grasping a bag of nuggets. He pounded the bag on the counter and cried excitedly '*This bangs 'em all!'*.

Joe invited the newly-married Billy and Eileen to come and help him run the pub. But the location, 400 kilometres inland from Carnarvon, near Mount Augustus (which few people realise covers four times the area of Uluru) was very remote for a girl who had never been out of Melbourne. When she was five months pregnant with the next Bill King she decided to go back to Melbourne for the birth. In later years she would say '*Bangemall wasn't quite the end of the world -- but I think you could see it* (the end of the world) *from the veranda!'*.

Bill King arrived in Melbourne in 1929, for the birth of his son, the youngest William. He brought with him all his worldly possessions – a suitcase of well-worn clothes, a travel rug, his camera, and a Winchester rifle. In good time he established a bus company, prospered, and after the Second World War became president of the South Melbourne Football Club. Years later it was relocated to become the *' Sydney Swans'* who won the AFL Premiership in 2005!. His son, Bill King junior, inherited his father's love of the bush and combined it with the family bus business. He began running tours to Central Australia under the slogan '*We're Going Exploring!*' and seeking out the most remote corners of the Red Centre, the Kimberley, and the Northern Territory.

He became renowned for his innovative tours, christened *Longitude 131*, and often following the tracks of explorers such as Burke and Wills. In 1974 he moved his headquarters to Alice Springs.

When he went to travel trade shows in Britain, Germany, and the United States, promoting outback Australia, the response was overwhelming. *' It became embarrassing. I ended up with more people than I could carry !'*.

Bill King became a legend in the outback travel business, winning countless awards, and the business remained in the family when he retired. Today one of his favourite destinations is still Exmouth, where his father began his own career so many years ago.

There was a sad tale to begin the history of Giralia. Nathaniel Harper was one of the important figures in Western Australia. A mining engineer all his life, he was latterly the manager of the *White Feather* mine at Kanowna. He was the man who first persuaded Premier John Forrest of the importance of the water pipeline to Kalgoorlie. Harper's son Harold served with the 10th Light Horse in the First World War, attaining the rank of major. He saw action at Gallipolli, Egypt, and in Palestine, and was mentioned in despatches by Field Marshall Lord Allenby. A distinguished military career.

Nathaniel Harper leased Giralia Landing, on April 1st, 1918, intending it as a pastoral career for his son after returning from the war. Harold was a good horseman, used to organising men, and accustomed to the arid spaces of the Middle East. Just the man for the job! He took on the post of manager of Giralia with enthusiasm.

On December 23rd, 1921, Nathaniel Harper received the telegram which every parent dreads. Harold and a Malay employee, Matt Ah Hoe, had rowed the station dinghy, loaded with four bales of wool, out to a waiting schooner. A heavy wind was blowing. In the late afternoon haze people on shore and on the schooner lost sight of the dinghy. Next day the wool bales were found washed up on shore, but there was no sign of the dinghy which had never reached its destination.

Constable Nicholson from Onslow sent a telegram to Perth: *'The captain of the schooner is of the opinion that the wool was dumped and the dinghy has drifted out to sea'.*

Those who know Exmouth waters could see the likely scenario. In the hot summer months winds blowing from the interior often reach gale force in the early evening – as Phillip Parker King discovered while charting the Gulf in the *Mermaid* in 1818. The seas rising steeper and more confused as a boat goes away from the land.

The over-loaded dinghy, at risk even in calm conditions, was soon in a situation of dire peril. The decision to dump the wool was probably made too late. The oar-powered dinghy would be unable to make headway if there were an attempt to return against the wind. As darkness fell the dinghy would be swept helplessly by wind and sea towards the head of the Gulf.

Nathaniel Harper arranged for searches by launch from Onslow and by aircraft loaned from West Australian Airways. But no trace was ever found of the dinghy or the missing men. It was a doubly sad day for Nathaniel Harper. His wife Margaret, Harold's mother had also died. A telegram had been sent to Harold but he never received it. A friend and distant relative, George White, was standing on the shore waiting to deliver it when Harold returned.

Time passed. In 1932 the silent partner of William King of Exmouth Station, Arthur Watson, died, and William himself died soon after. The property went into the hands of executors and was sold to the Lefroy family. At that time the holding had been increased to 266,398 acres, and was carrying 16,000 sheep, 40 horses, 37 cattle, and three camels. A third generation of Lefroys, John and Linda, were still living on Exmouth Station in 2008.

During the 1930s life continued on North West Cape much as it always had. But in the outside world dark clouds were gathering over Europe. In Italy Benito Mussolini, leader of the fascist party, had declared himself '*Il Duce*', effectively dictator.

There was a similar story in Spain. Generalissimo Francisco Franco staged a military coup against the communist government. After winning the resultant civil war he too became established as a dictator. Even more ominous was the rise to power in Germany of Adolf Hitler, *'Der Fuhrer!'* and the establishment of the Third Reich.

The British attempt at appeasement with Germany in the Munich Pact of 1938 proved a failure, earning only the contempt of the Nazis at British *'Weakness'*. By 1939 all Europe shivered with apprehension as it became apparent that the *'Dogs Of War'* were about to be unchained.

Hitler's troops marched into Poland on September 3rd, 1939, and Britain at once declared war on Germany. Australia followed suit on the same day. For a long time the war in Europe and the Middle East appeared remote to Australians.

But in 1941 the war would come to the Gascoyne coast in an unexpected and highly dramatic way.

IN 1914 THE FIRST HMAS SYDNEY sank the German raider Emden at North Keeling Island in the Indian Ocean with heavy loss of life. In 1941 the German armed merchantman, Raider 41, better known today as Kormoran would exact a terrible revenge on HMAS Sydney II, pictured above.

The Dogs Of War

Chapter Six

On November 25th, 1941, two RAAF Hudson aircraft buzzed the sleepy Gascoyne town of Carnarvon, bringing it to life with a jolt. The message dropped by the RAAF was that two lifeboats containing about 80 men were landing on the coast north of Quobba Station. The aircraft had been engaged in the search for survivors from *HMAS Sydney 11*, sensationally sunk on November 19th, by the German surface raider *HSK Kormoran* off Shark Bay.

Under the RAAF's impression that the lifeboats contained *Sydney* survivors, a party including Police Sergeant Stan Anderson, Dr J.W.Piccles, Gascoyne Traders' manager Pat Young, in Gascoyne Traders' trucks, and Reg Anderson in the town's single taxi, left for Quobba. In Carnarvon billeting arrangements were hastily made with private citizens to accommodate the castaways, and shearers' beds and bedding were brought in from neighbouring stations. Ladies groups baked cakes and cut sandwiches, and the whole town volunteered to assist in any capacity required of them. A warm welcome was prepared for the expected heroes.

Then came the shock news from Quobba that the lifeboats were not from the *Sydney* at all!

Instead they contained 103 German officers and crew from a ship whose name *Kormoran* was completely unfamiliar to anyone in Western Australia. The German ship, a converted merchantman formerly named the *Steiermark* and now also known as armed *Raider 41,* had been sunk by scuttling after an engagement with the *Sydney.* The *Kormoran's* crew abandoned ship after shells from *Sydney* started an engine room fire that could not be contained. She had more than 300 magnetic mines stored in her holds and that was good reason to be somewhere else when the fire reached the mines. *Sydney's* fate was not known. But the Germans reported that she was last seen on fire, and seriously damaged, heading on a south east course in the direction of Geraldton.

At Quobba the first lifeboat containing 46 men told Sergeant Anderson that they had come ashore the previous morning and were without food or water. However it was soon established that they had found water and had rounded up four station sheep, one of which they had killed. The second lifeboat which came ashore 24 kilometres further north at Red Bluff contained 57 men, including 13 officers, and was well-provisioned.

Arrangements in Carnarvon had to be hastily changed. Instead of a heroes' welcome the Germans – locals peering at them from around corners -- were taken to the insalubrious quarters of the small town gaol (formerly known as the '*Drunk's Tank'*) where they were guarded by members of the Carnarvon Volunteer Defence Corps.

With the natural generosity of country folk the sandwiches and the beds and mattresses intended for *'Our boys'* were passed over to the Germans, some of whom were suffering seriously from sunburn and dehydration. The Volunteer Defence Corps, *'Dad's Army',* with their .303 rifles and soup-bowl tin hats, were somewhat uneasy at finding themselves unexpectedly in direct contact with the Hun in the flesh.

HMAS SYDNEY MORTALLY WOUNDED. A painting by Jochin Sachse shows the terrible effect of the torpedo salvo and the first broadside. All the Australian officers in the command centre would have died instantly.

THE COMMANDERS, HSK Kormoran's Theodor Detmers , HMAS Sydney II's Josph Burnett.

PATHETIC REMAINS. A shoe lies on the seafloor. Who wore it last? (Picture: Australian War Memorial/ Finding Sydney Foundation)

A GAS MASK tells its own sad story. (Picture: Australian War Memorial/Finding Sydney Foundation)

A KORMORAN 5.9 GUN. Part of the German armament which played a vital part in the Royal Australian Navy's greatest wartime disaster. The gun was a veteran of the Battle of Jutland in 1916 in World War I. (Pictures: Australian War Memorial/Finding Sydney Foundation)

PRESERVED ON THE SEA BED. Sydney's X-turret which sent Kormoran to the bottom. The open observation shields show how, cut off from all communication, the gun crew opened their protective port shields so that they could see their target regardless of risk from enemy fire. The gun remains trained as it would have been after their last shot. (Picture: Australian War Memorial/Finding Sydney Foundation)

SYDNEY'S BADGE still remains bright and clear on one of the boats on the sea bed beside the hull of the sunken ship. (Picture: Australian War Memorial/Finding Sydney Foundation)

Kormoran was formerly the Hamburg-Amerika passenger liner Steiermark. In wartime she became Raider 41, and though her guns were recycled from the World War I battlecruiser Steydlitz and last saw action in the 1916 Battle of Jutland, and her torpedo tubes were also recycled from the same era, she proved a deadly enemy at short range. (Jochin Sachse painting)

GERMAN PRISONERS FROM THE KORMORAN disembarking at Fremantle. For them the war was over though they remained supremely confident that Germany would win. In 1941 that seemed a likely outcome.

SURVEYING THE TARGET Major Ivan Lyon, Operation Jaywick commander, looks through a telescope from the nearest island before the successful folboat raid on Singapore Harbour. (Picture: Australian War Memorial)

OPERATION JAYWICK COMMANDOES underwent extensive training on the Hawkesbury River before their daring Singapore raid via Exmouth Gulf. Their converted fishing boat's familiar silhouette is in the background. (Picture: Australian War Memorial)

FOUR BRAVE MEN: Bardie Hawn, Bluey Truscott, Peter Turnbull and Charles Learmonth. All were awarded the Distinguished Flying Cross. Truscott crashed in the Gulf, Turnbull died in New Guinea and Learmonth lost his life off Rottnest.

TRUSCOTT in the cockpit of his Kittyhawk in New Guinea. Flying conditions were as much as a danger as the enemy with low cloud, constant rain and mist, and their airstrips slippery as a skating rink.

The photograph shows the narrow strip of Marsden matting from which aircraft strayed at their peril. Once off the matting there was a sea of mud.

AUSTRALIANS at Exmouth, manning the radar station at Vlamingh Head.

THE ANZAC SPIRIT: one of Exmouth's Australian defenders shows his style with a submachine gun. Exmouth was bombed three times by Japanese aircraft during World War II, and the Australian anti aircraft guns opened up in reply. The bombs missed their targets and the 'Ack Ack' gunners also missed, so honours remained even.

AN AMERICAN SUBMARINE returns to Fremantle after a patrol. The strong esprit de corps of the submariners is shown by the large group of men waiting to welcome them back from enemy waters. Men in submarines suffered the highest proportion of casualties in the US armed services. Of 16,000 submariners 3500 or 22 per cent died in World War II.

THE CREW OF the American submarine USS Barbel, a regular visitor to Exmouth Gulf. Barbel sank ten Japanese ships before finally being sunk herself by Japanese aircraft off the Philippines. There were no survivors of her 85 man crew. (INSET: The picture of Lieutenant William Tiffany illustrates the tragedy of wartime losses.)

THE BATTLE FLAG of USS Barbel. All the submarines and aircraft of the day had their own flags or symbols painted on their hulls. Barbel may have added to her ten ship total before she was sunk herself.

Even though the Enemy appeared to be human beings very much like themselves, the VDC were nervously aware that they were heavily outnumbered. If the Germans had made a determined and concerted rush they could easily have overwhelmed their guards. However the Germans were in a strange country with nowhere else to go. Even if they gained the upper hand temporarily it could only be a matter of time before regular army troops were brought in. It was more sensible to accept their fate as prisoners. Perhaps they also thought that they might not be prisoners for very long. In 1941 Germany held the upper hand in Europe, with France humiliatingly defeated, and Britain reeling after Dunkirk. Germany, at that time, despite losing the battleship *Bismarck*, Hitler's pride, was winning the war at sea with U-boats and surface vessels decimating Allied convoys.

On December 7th, less than three weeks after the *Sydney-Kormoran* engagement, Japan would enter the war following her devastating strike at Pearl Harbour. After sweeping through South East Asia, conquering the tired old Colonial possessions of Hong Kong, Malaya, Singapore, the Philippines, and the Dutch East Indies, Japanese troops would soon be pushing forward in New Guinea on Australia's very doorstep.

Dark times indeed!

Most of the *Kormoran* men would have believed without question that Germany would win the war and that they would be liberated, perhaps sooner rather than later. While they were considering the matter in the Carnarvon lock-up, regular AIF troops were already on their way. A contingent of the 11th Garrison Battalion in 12 vehicles was rushed to Carnarvon from Perth – perhaps *'rushed'* is not the right word. Due to the primitive state of the gravel highway in those days it took them 35 hours to reach their destination!

Meantime word was coming in of other lifeboats, though alas none of them were from the *Sydney*. The Blue Funnel line steamer *Centaur* arrived in port at Carnarvon towing a lifeboat with 31 *Kormoran* survivors. *Centaur's* captain had refused a request for them to come on board because they outnumbered his crew and – not unreasonably -- he was afraid they might try to take over his ship.

Aircraft sighted another lifeboat 100 miles out to sea which was picked up by a fishing boat. The liner *Aquitania,* returning from taking troops to Singapore, picked up 26 men from a raft. The tanker *Trocus* picked up another 25. And so it went on until 315 Germans of the original 400 crew had been rescued from lifeboats and rafts and brought in to detention. They included the *Kormoran's* captain, Commander Theodor Detmers, and his senior officers.

Some of the men in the rafts and lifeboats had had a hard time of it, as evidenced by the diary of Lieutenant von Malapert. '*We existed on scraps of bacon and biscuit. We were terrified at the thought of being cast ashore on a desert and dying miserably of starvation. Some of the men were half crazed with the pain of swollen and blistered limbs. We had to watch them all the time to prevent them jumping out of the crowded boat. There were 57 men in our boat. It was impossible to lie down, and we had to take our turns standing and sitting'.*

Land was sighted *'With great jubilation!'* on the morning of November 25th, the fifth day after the action, ' *At 8.30 a.m. we landed in front of a cave which lay quite sheltered in the south corner of the bay. We pulled the boat up on the beach and unpacked everything. Everyone got something to drink and had to lie down on the white sand in the shade of the cave and rocks. After being such a long time in the boat one is so weak on the feet that when one steps ashore for the first time one feels as if drunk'.*

So much for the sufferings of the Germans. But what of the men from the *Sydney?*

That is where the controversy begins. It would rage with undiminished intensity for nearly 70 years. One of the key questions is why it took the Navy four days after the *Sydney* was overdue at Fremantle to authorise an air search for Australia's most famous warship? Even then the search was conducted in the wrong area.

HMAS Sydney was a vessel enshrined in the nation's heart as the victor over her Italian counterpart the *Bartollemeo Colleoni* in the Mediterranean, and she had distinguished herself in other actions in that theatre of war. She had been returned to Australia to guard troopships taking Australian troops to the doomed British fortress of Singapore. The British expected a possible attack there if and when Japan should enter the war. As indeed occurred within three weeks of *Sydney's* last escort duty.

Though she failed to dock on schedule in Fremantle on Friday, November 20th, 1941, as scheduled, the Navy did not arrange for the Lockheed Hudson aircraft of the RAAF, based at Pearce, to fly until the following Monday. Men drifting in lifebelts in the water would not have survived that length of time. The search, when it did take place belatedly, was 400 kilometres north of where the action had taken place and where the ships had sunk.

Bungle after bungle.

Incredibly messages from the *Sydney* were picked up by RAAF signalmen in Geraldton and relayed to the Naval command in Fremantle on the evening of the battle. After the war the Navy denied the messages existed. But it has since been proved, to the satisfaction of Group Captain Rig Bourne, of the RAAF, that they were sent and were received.

Men from an Army unit have since come forward to say that they were members of a detachment sent up to Shark Bay to bury washed-up bodies from the Sydney. They said that as many as 82 decomposing bodies were buried in one mass grave, some still wearing lifejackets with *HMAS Sydney* stencils on them, others with officers' epaulettes.

The burial party were supposedly appalled at the bad condition and the stench of the bodies which were said to be individually unrecognisable. Some were buried still on their stretchers. Members of the grave-digging party were said to have spent much of their time vomiting in the low scrub. Afterwards they said that they were sworn to secrecy and threatened with dire penalties if they disclosed what they had seen. Officially, of course, it '*Never happened'*.

Was that the case? Was the story of buried bodies part of a baseless *'Conspiracy theory'?* . True or false, Mystery Beach at Dirk Hartog Island, and Crayfish Bay and False Entrance further south are natural collection points where debris and bodies would be expected to wash up.

In fact, after the war, so far as officialdom was concerned, no body from the *Sydney's* crew of 645 officers and men was ever found. When a Carley float drifted ashore far to the north at Christmas Island early in 1942 containing the body of a lone sailor, the Navy denied that the man could have come from the *Sydney*. This despite the fact that he was wearing a navy blue boiler suit of the kind used by engine room crew in the *Sydney,* or that the craft contained sandshoes with an Australian government broad arrow stencil. Or the even more significant fact that the metal of the float had the message *LYSACHT DUAL ANNEAL ZINC. MADE IN AUSTRALIA* printed on it!

In 2007 the body at Christmas Island was exhumed and found to have indeed come from the *Sydney*. Sensationally there was a bullet or piece of shrapnel in the interior of the skull which must have killed or totally disabled the victim. The question was asked how a dead man with an ounce of lead in his head could get into a Carley float? In fact it seemed he had received his fatal wound while on his hands and knees, crouched perhaps, to avoid the fate that finally overtook him? Rigor mortis froze him in that position, and though the body was tossed around in the float by the waves he was buried in that stance.

In the German report of the action, at the conclusion of the battle the *Sydney* had steamed away over the horizon, on fire, and listing to port to disappear into the falling darkness. No lifeboat, raft, or Carley float – according to German evidence – was launched at the scene of the battle.

In fact the German evidence was to become the crux of future problems. Was what the commander Theodor Detmers and the others told Australian intelligence officers the full truth? Or was there a cover up for some reason never revealed?

The *Kormoran* survivors picked up by the *Aquitania* and landed in Melbourne, gave an entirely different and obviously false position for the battle as being south of Busselton. Was Detmers' position also deliberately incorrect, and if so why?

One of the reasons why the German official account was regarded with suspicion in some quarters was the fact that too many men said the same thing, as though it were a prepared statement. It was too pat. Usually, it was suggested, after a time of danger and high excitement in action accounts of survivors sometimes differed wildly.

Unfortunately when the German survivors, officers and men, were initially detained they were able to mingle together and – if they had chosen to do so -- determine on a standard story. In short they had the opportunity to give an account which would sensibly cause them the least trouble in captivity.

What did the Germans say?

The *Kormoran* encountered the Sydney accidentally, late on the afternoon of November 19th, 1941, according to their account. In fact the lookout in the crow's nest at first took the mast on the horizon and the white flash of the hull to be a yacht. The news was jocularly received in the bridge below.

'A yacht! Gott in Himmel! What is a sailing boat doing out here in the middle of the ocean? Don't they know there's a war on!'

The smiles soon vanished. The oncoming vessel was not a yacht at all. It was a Perth-type light cruiser, the breed of warship the Germans most dreaded to see. A cruiser had twice their speed and a far superior armament at long range.

Though the *Kormoran's* guns packed a considerable punch they had been shortened for concealment and were only effective at short range. A cruiser could stand off at 20,000 yards and blow the German out of the water. The *Kormoran* had 350 magnetic mines in her holds which made her doubly vulnerable. Any direct hit could blow ship and men to smithereens.

The ship's medical officer Dr Habben recalled '*First Officer Foerster went through the ship with the hard news that it was a cruiser. The one thought was in everybody's mind, but speaking for myself I simply could not believe that I was about to say Goodbye to Life!*'.

Detmers tried to run for it, heading south west into the setting sun, but there was no escape. The *Sydney* soon caught up, and when the *Kormoran* identified herself under her disguise as the Dutch merchantmen *Straat Malakka* she was requested to fly the secret signal given to all Allied shipping.

Since the *Kormoran* did not have the code her signalman tangled the signal flags to obscure the message. But while that gained a brief delay time was running out. Then, incredibly -- according to the German account -- the *Sydney* ranged up alongside the *Kormoran*, broadside on, at a distance of not much more than 1000 metres. '*Point blank range*', in gunnery terms.

It was close enough for the Germans to see cooks in white aprons leaning on the rail and looking out over the water. A boat was about to be lowered. Though Sydney had her guns trained on the raider it was obvious to the Germans that everyone on the Australian ship still thought that they were dealing with an ordinary merchantman – a *'Dumb Dutchman'*.

At that short range, in that situation, the *Kormoran* was a formidable foe. She had six 5.9-inch heavy guns hidden behind steel covers which could be raised in a matter of seconds.

There were seven anti-tank guns with armour piercing shells which could be used as anti-aircraft weapons or lowered and used against shipping as surface guns.

Deadliest of all *Kormoran* had concealed torpedo tubes firing from below the waterline, one on each side of the ship.

Detmers, when questioned by Australian Intelligence officers, said that at that point with the element of surprise on his side, he had everything to gain and nothing to lose. Seizing the moment he gave the order to replace the Dutch flag with the German battle flag and fire all armament, including the starboard torpedo tube hidden below the *Kormoran's* waterline.

At such short range the gunners could hardly miss their targets. There was no need to aim. It was just a matter of point and shoot.

The initial targets were *Sydney's* gun turrets, which would be pounded by *Kormoran's* quick-firing heavy guns. The anti-tank guns would concentrate on the bridge where the Germans could see massed officer's white hats in the command centre. The effect was utter devastation aboard *Sydney*. The first salvo tore the *Sydney's* bridge apart, probably killing Captain Burnett and most of his senior officers at their command stations before they even realised what had happened.

A torpedo -- '*The great equaliser*' as described by Friend and Foe in both wars -- struck under the for'ard gun turrets with a tremendous explosion, putting them out of action too, and one by one the other gun turrets were pounded by the German 5.9s.The Walrus aircraft amidships was hit, and aviation fuel gushed out over the deck and started a fire amidships. The major damage was inflicted in the first few minutes – the significant hits in perhaps two minutes or less. After the first salvos only one gun on *Sydney's* rear deck, X-turret, remained firing. Crippled, the Australian ship turned towards the *Kormoran* as though attempting to ram, and passed under the raider's stern. As she passed by, in a last defiant gesture, four torpedoes were fired from Sydney's stern. All passed close to their target, but missed.

The mortally wounded *Sydney* then continued on a south east course as darkness began to fall. When last seen, the Germans said, she was blazing from stem to stern, listing to port, down by the bow, and proceeding slowly at 5 to 6 knots.

It was a David-and-Goliath action, and an incredible victory for *Raider 41*. But it was a victory at a cost. Sydney's X-turret guns had scored a direct hit into the *Kormoran's* engine room. The shell pierced a fuel tank, destroyed her fire-fighting machinery, and started a fire that could not be extinguished. Detmers made the decision to abandon ship mindful of the magnetic mines which the flames would ultimately reach. The crew disembarked into lifeboats and rafts. Scuttling charges were detonated, and the *Kormoran* sank to the bottom of the Indian Ocean, her job well done.

If you were to look at it from a German point of view.

In her career as a raider she had sunk 78,000 tons of Allied merchant ships – 12 vessels -- and now her greatest prize of all, *HMAS Sydney,* the *'Unlucky 13th'* victim, was about to join her on the sea floor of the Indian Ocean.

What happened to the *Sydney*? Did she capsize and roll over, or explode when flames reached her stored ammunition? Or did she just sink below the waves as she gradually filled with green seawater from the many shell-holes in her side?

For the next 66 years it was only known that she was never seen again, nor – according to official records -- were any traces found of the 645 officers and men aboard her except '*Christmas man'*, the Christmas Island corpse.

How could the disaster have occurred? If it did all happen as the Germans said it did, Captain Joseph Burnett acted in contradiction of his standing orders. The presence of armed German surface raiders in the Indian Ocean, masquerading as neutral or Allied shipping, was well known, and the procedure for dealing with them was quite clear. Burnett was well aware of the instructions from his time in Navy HQ, Canberra.

Cruisers were to stand off from a suspicious vessel. If she failed to identify herself with her secret signal, she was to be checked out with the Walrus catapult-launched aircraft standard on cruisers. On no account was a cruiser to come as suicidally close to a suspect as *Sydney* was supposed to have done with *Kormoran.*

So, in the aftermath, and as might be expected, the Navy blamed Captain Joseph Burnett for an error of judgement which, it was said, cost the lives of himself, his men and his ship. That was the easy way out. It was a case of *'Human error'* – find a scapegoat -- and therefore no blame could be attributable to the Navy or the Government. End of case.

But was it really that simple?

The list of books written about the *Sydney* and the varying conspiracy theories in the post-war years showed the extent of public interest, and the grave doubts in various quarters about the official statements of fact.

The uncertainty resulted in many publications, with varying opinions. Some claimed that there was the involvement of a Japanese submarine two and half weeks before Pearl Harbour. Others suggested that there had been a massacre of Sydney survivors – witness the Christmas Island sailor with a metal object (bullet or shrapnel) in his skull. At the time in 1941 the government dithered for 10 days before making a public announcement.

When an American radio station broadcast the news of the loss of the *Sydney* their hand was forced – how did the Americans know when it was a secret in Australia and America was not yet in the war? Australians generally were devastated. Every state had men aboard the *Sydney.* For the hundreds of men there were thousands of parents, wives, children, and relatives.

Former Navy Minister Billy Hughes summed up the feeling. '*The magnificent ship had seemed to have a charmed life. She had run the gauntlet of the toughest fighting in the Mediterranean and escaped with not much more than a scratch on her paint. Everyone of our countrymen had thrilled to her exploits!'*

After the war when there was no longer need for secrecy, the public demanded to know more details, but the Navy hid behind the Official Secrets Act. What answers were available were less than satisfactory. There was always a deep-seated suspicion that there was a scandal lurking somewhere and the Defence Department was anxious to keep the lid on it. Doubts festered through the years to the point where the Federal Government agreed to an *HMAS SYDNEY Committee of Inquiry* in 1998.

Nothing much that was new emerged from the talk-fest which critics labelled as '*Yet another whitewash'*. But there was one important determination, one aspect on which there was agreement on all sides. If the wrecks of the *Sydney* and *Kormoran* could be located in their last resting places on the bed of the Indian Ocean a lot of the unanswered questions could be met by a detailed examination of the evidence of what remained on the sea floor.

Finding the two ships would not be easy. But there were precedents including the discovery of the *Titanic* 12 miles below the surface of the Atlantic and the German *Bismarck* also deep, deep down, in wreck searches in modern times. The technology was in place. It was just a matter of finding the money and the right man for the job.

The Federal Government agreed to provide the basis of a fund to be filled out by public subscription. In February 2001 the non-profit organisation *Finding Sydney Foundation* was formed, with *HMAS Sydney Search Pty Ltd.,* as trustee. The directors of the foundation, based in Perth, were all volunteers. In this way, the better part of a lifetime after the event, the search for the *Sydney* was at last under way. If she were really discovered the news would be almost as sensational for the Australian public as on that black day when the cruiser and her total complement disappeared from the pages of our history.

The inspiration for the *Finding Sydney Foundation* came from hydrographic surveyor Ted Graham and a group who used to meet at the *Café Sol,* in Stirling-highway, Nedlands.

'*We felt strongly'* Graham told Perth's *Post* newspaper *'That if our generation didn't do something about finding the Sydney it might just get forgotten'.* Among the original group were Professor Kim Kirsner, a University of Western Australia expert on human memory and language, and Don Pridmore of the former aerial survey company Aerodata.

Others were Keith Rowe, Ron Birmingham, Bob King, Bob Trotter, and Glenys McDonald who had written a book titled *Seeking The Sydney*. The unpaid volunteer group with Ted Graham as chairman, put together the tax-exempt structure of the non-profit *Finding Sydney Foundation* and spent two years raising funds for the final assault.

As well as fund raising there was a practical side to *Finding The Sydney* activity. Professor Kirstner instituted a research program aimed at ascertaining the position of the wrecks. It was determined that if the *Kormoran* could be located that would lead searchers directly to the *Sydney.* In the case of the *Kormoran* there were multiple statements from German survivors to Australian Intelligence to be analysed There were also physical calculations of wind drift and the positions of lifeboats, rafts, and debris at the time to be considered by Pridmore and the others. When the human and physical evidence were combined a position was calculated which would prove surprisingly close to the actual location of the sunken *Kormoran*.

There was a false alarm in August, 2007, when a wreck discovered by fishermen off Dirk Hartog Island, was claimed by *The West Australian* newspaper to be *Sydney*. But an examination by the Navy vessel *Leeuwin* showed the wreck to be too small and with different configurations to the Australian light cruiser. So it was a case of back to the drawing board.

However the false alarm was not entirely in vain. It high-lighted the case of the *Sydney* again, and the Howard Government agreed to additional funding over and above what had been promised previously.

On August 25th, 2007, Minister Bruce Billson made the announcement on the deck of the Royal Australian Navy's new guided missile frigate *HMAS Sydney111* at Garden Island in Sydney Harbour. He told members of the *Finding Sydney Foundation* that the Federal Government had approved a further $2.9 million grant on top of the $1.3 million grant approved in August 2005 for a total of $ 4.2 million. In addition the WA Government would contribute $500,000 and the NSW Government $250,000. Together with private donations there would be a fighting fund of more than $5 million towards finding the *Sydney*. Bringing the ship back *'Home'*, in an important sense, after 66 years lost to the nation.

The increased funding enabled international wreck expert David Mearns to be engaged to lead the field search. A 49 year-old American, with three children, who lived in London, Mearns had an impressive record including finding the wreck of the British battleship *HMS Hood* in the deep waters of the Atlantic Ocean.

The *Hood* was Britain's greatest naval disaster. She was sunk by a single shell from the German warship *Bismarck* in the Greenland Strait in May, 1941. The shell ignited her explosives magazine and a total of 1416 crew died in the disaster. Three days later the Royal Navy gained revenge when they cornered and sank the *Bismarck,* with a loss of more than 2000 German sailors.

Mearns was originally trained as a marine biologist and marine geologist and first worked with a company that did research and recovery for the US Navy. He eventually went into business on his own and had 19 years of finding shipwrecks and salvage. He formed his own company *Blue Water Recoveries* and by 2007 had found more than 50 shipwrecks ranging from modern warship to a 1503 Portuguese ship the *Esmeralda,* and ancient galleys.

His success rate, based primarily on intensive preliminary research, was claimed to be better than 80 per cent.

Ted Graham, chairman of the *Finding Sydney Foundation*, had a fortuitous meeting with him in England while Graham was on a stop-over between airline flights, and – using all his persuasive powers -- aroused Mearns' interest in the potential of a *Sydney* search.

Prior to the actual search Mearns spent several years researching *Sydney,* including finding previously unpublished reports by *Kormoran* officers in Germany, one of them in code. The reports were consistent in the information they contained and this led to a decision to ignore the conspiracy theories and to begin the search on the basis that the German accounts were most likely correct. He published several search boxes, changing them through the years. The information included an estimated position given to him by the FSF in 2004 which proved astonishingly close to the actual site of Kormoran. *'If we can find the Kormoran I believe that she will lead us to the Sydney'* Mearns said.

When the Howard Government in Australia approved the extra funding in 2007, the services of Mearns' company were engaged by FSF and the specialist oceanic survey vessel, the Singapore-based *MV Geosounder* was brought to Geraldton on charter to FSF. *Geosounder* was equipped with side-scan sonar, magnetometers, and all the necessary gear for oceanic surveys. Arriving in Perth after studying all the evidence available Mearns said that he believed that the chances of finding Sydney were '*In the 85-90 per cent range'*. He had his doubters.

Some, perhaps weighed down by all the negative years, simply described it as *'Unfindable'*, and there were even some critics who described the search '*As a waste of tax payers' money'*.

' We don't know how far the Sydney managed to go on her south east course before sinking' Mearns said. *'But we do have the position indicated by the Germans as to where they sank their own ship. On that basis we'll try to find her first and then attempt to track down Sydney, following her final and fatal course'.*

In addition to studying all the records intensively he interviewed *Kormoran* survivors, including Lieutenant von Malapert, now aged 92, who was on the bridge during the action. Mearns met him where he now lives in Chile and over five days of interviews said that he found him a credible witness. *'Right from the start I was quite confidant in the quality and veracity of the German accounts about where the action took place'* Mearns said. *'Though there were many other researchers who strongly took an opposing view'.*

In fact the Finding Sydney Foundation's research group's calculations would prove to be extraordinarily close to the real site. In association with his associate professor John Dunn, Kim Kirstner analysed 70 statements made by the crew of the *Kormoran* after they were taken into captivity. They concluded that the positions given to the men in the lifeboats by Detmers as captain and the navigation officer Myers after the *Kormoran* sank were pin-point accurate. This was necessary for their survival because they were 120 kilometres from the nearest land and in unfamiliar waters. It was vital to know where they were.

However Kirstner concluded that for whatever reasons Detmer and the senior German navigation officers did not give the Australian authorities the correct position when they were interviewed later. He believed that this resulted in Mearns, relying on the navigation officers accounts more than the crew, to provide two positions for the *Kormoran* in a submission to the Commonwealth in 2005. They were 17 and 26 nautical miles from the actual site. A 2007 submission had positions 22 and 27 nautical miles from *Kormoran.*

The position given by the Finding Sydney Foundation's research group was far closer. It was only 2.7 kilometres – '*Spitting distance'* in wreck search terms -- from where the wreck would eventually be found!

On that basis the official search began in March 2008, and it was a rough start, with the tail end of a tropical cyclone whipping up strong winds and heavy seas. Technical gremlins plagued the first week, but as professionals the group were aware that the sea doesn't give up her secrets easily.

Geosounder began a process known as *'lawn-mowing'* in the trade of wreck-searching. It consisted of steaming endlessly up and down in a boxed area of search at a speed of three knots towing an underwater sled at the end of several kilometres of cable. The sled carried the 'eye' of the side-scan sonar. One of the most sophisticated pieces of equipment in the world, it covered a six kilometre swath of the seabed 2500 metres below the ship. The equipment was operated by a professional crew led by Art Wright from the Seattle firm Williamson & Associates who came with the vessel.

Then, on Wednesday, March 12th, 2008, only 64 hours after they officially began searching, came the electrifying news that the wreck of the *Kormoran* had been located. Lieutenant John Perryman, RANR – Senior Naval historian and Official Observer, made his report:

'At 17.30 a small dark contact appeared at the top of the SM30 side-scan sonar display

which we were monitoring in our survey room. David Mearns immediately classified the target as man-made due to the characteristics it displayed such as hard straight edges, shadow, and its orientation on an otherwise featureless seabed. During the next hour the first evidence of a debris field began to appear and before long we were viewing a centralised concentration indicating a central and catastrophic explosion. This was consistent with the German account of the final destruction of the raider HSK Kormoran, scuttled by her crew following the engagement with HMAS Sydney. At the time of her scuttling she was carrying a full cargo of some 300 mines each packed with high explosives. Approximately 1200 metres to the south of the debris field a much larger target was detected, seemingly intact, which was tentatively classified as being the forward section of the Kormoran. The position of the centre of the debris field which represents the site of the scuttling and resultant explosion is South Latitude 26 degrees 05 minutes 49.4 seconds, and Longitude 111.04 degrees 27.5 minutes East in a depth of 2560 metres of water'.

The bottom was littered with items of debris, some of them probably from *Sydney* as a result of the heavy damage she had received in the engagement. The *Kormoran* was clearly in two pieces with most of the aft section atomised by the explosion of the mines. The flared bow was intact and standing upright.

'How quickly our fortunes have changed in one day!' observed observer Glenys McDonald, amid the general euphoria on board the *Geosounder.*

The greatest moment of excitement of all came at 10.30 am., on the morning of March 16th, 2008 – only three days after the final discovery of the *Kormoran* -- the shell-battered silhouette of *HMAS Sydney* herself, the final prize, appeared on the *Geosounder's* side-scan sonar's display screen to cheers and congratulations. She was only 12.2 nautical miles from the scene of the engagement and the wreck of her adversary *Kormoran.*

The Prime Minister, Kevin Rudd, the Navy, the *Finding Sydney Foundation,* and all those connected with the search on the mainland, were notified. The news, together with pictures of the shadowy silhouettes of the two ships as seen on the side-scan sonar, were carried on the front pages of all Australian newspapers. David Mearns rang Ted Graham, Chairman of the *Finding Sydney Foundation* and Patrick Flynn the Project Manager. Ted in turn called the Deputy Chief of Navy Russ Crane. Everyone was in a state of disbelief that after only 64 hours the object had been achieved.

'I spoke to Ted' said Glenys McDonald *'And this six foot seven giant of a man was overcome. We unashamedly cried together'.*

The Prime Minister Kevin Rudd made the first official announcement and in a remarkable 24 hours the news flashed around Australia. Ted Graham in later years reflected that a small group of volunteers backed by excellent Australian research, combined with David Mearns as project director, and the wonderful Williamson underwater equipment aboard *Geosounder*, had together achieved an outstanding result.

However, while the first part of the job had been done and done well, and in the midst of the publicity and congratulations, there was still the second most important part of the project to be covered. The wrecks had been found. Now they had to be filmed and examined at a depth of 2500 metres by an ROV (Remotely Operated underwater Vehicle). Australia awaited agog for the pictures. Among other things they would prove or put to rest for ever the conspiracy theory that a Japanese submarine had been involved in the battle.

Geosounder returned to port in Geraldton – where *HMAS Sydney* had once been a familiar visitor – to receive the new and vitally important equipment flown in from overseas to take pictures of the two sunken ships. The images recorded by the ROV, 2500 metres below the surface, would prove to be extraordinary both for clarity and content and for the tale they would tell.

The ROV was a story in itself. It was a 2 x 1.3 metres yellow box, carrying lights and cameras designated as a '*Sub-Atlantic Comanche*'.

Powered by four horizontal and three vertical thrusters, it was able to move at three knots, and could operate as deep as 3000 metres. A seven man team was required to operate it. The basic principle was that the Comanche went to the bottom inside a *'garage'* or shelter on the end of a long cable.

When an area of interest was reached the ROV emerged and moved around on the end of a 200 metre umbilical cord to film and photograph. Surely the higher end of human technical achievement!

The first pictures received on the surface and relayed to Australian newspapers showed the wreck '*Bathed in blue light!*'. The clarity of the water was extraordinary and the fearful damage inflicted on the light cruiser was all too apparent. The bow, struck by the *Kormoran* torpedo, had completely broken off and was lying some little distance away.

Grim evidence of the efficiency of the German gunners was seen in the damage to *Sydney's* gun turrets, the images from the deeps showed direct hits which must have killed three out of the four gun crews and put the turrets out of action.

When the bridge control points were destroyed together with the senior officers, X-turret was left with no option but to operate independently. The gunners had apparently opened their armoured forward covers to enable them to directly see their enemy, even though the move left them unprotected.

It was X-turret which scored the fatal hits on *Kormoran* and which led to her eventual sinking. The ROV pictures showed the turret still pointing to port in its last position with the covers still open,. The scene frozen forever in time.

Early in the search it was noted that the lifeboats were out of their cradles, which led to speculation that some of the Sydney's personnel may have launched them. But later in the search five lifeboats were found on the sea floor some distance from the main wreck. The most remarkable feature was that the ship's crests, each one hand-painted, were clearly visible on the bows of each boat.

For Western Australian Maritime Museum representative Dr Michael McCarthy the images of the lifeboats were particularly poignant. *'Seeing the frames and the remaining ghostly strakes of planking on the carvel boats was one of the most striking images of my archaeological career'* he told Perth's Post newspaper. *'The hand-painted badges on each boat were another of the most evocative shipwreck images I have ever seen. It was wonderful how they had retained their emblems and colours undiminished!'*.

But perhaps the items which most touched the group watching the images come up in the *Geosounder* control room, 2500 metres above the wreck, were personal items. There was a gas mask and items such as black Navy-issue shoes brought tears to the eyes of Glenys McDonald. *'Who last wore the gas mask, who wore the shoes'?*

When the *Comanche* had completed its work on the *Sydney* wreck site attention moved to the *Kormoran,* the first wreckage to be found on the now famous search. *Kormoran* was literally blown apart by the explosion of her cargo of mines, and conditions for filming were not as clear as they were with *Sydney*. But the pictures answered some important questions. They showed the two underwater torpedo tubes, one on each side of the vessel. It was the one on the starboard side which delivered the first devastating blow to *Sydney*. The images also showed two of the 5.9 inch guns which destroyed *Sydney's* firepower, still in excellent condition with their removable covers.

The pictures corroborated what the Germans said in 1941. In fact the images showed that their account, questioned for many years by doubters, was substantially correct. The scene of action was where *Kormoran's* captain Theodor Detmers, had said it was. The Kirstner group's analysis of the early reports was also that the Germans had been telling the truth. The horrendous damage to *Sydney* tallied with the German reports.

There was so much good and bad luck on both sides. X-turret's shell that landed in *Kormoran's* engine room was not enough to sink the vessel outright. But it destroyed the ship's fire-fighting system and started a fire that could not be put out. *Sydney's* last brave salvo of torpedoes passed close to her enemy, but missed. If one of them had struck and detonated *Kormoran's* cargo of mines the ship would have been blown to smithereens and there may have been no German survivors either. In that event the world would never have known what had happened to either ship. They would have both remained forever on that long, long list of missing ships.

In the aftermath, alongside the joy of the discovery and the solving of a 67 year-old mystery for the relatives and friends of those aboard the *Sydney*, there was some controversy.

The Finding Sydney Foundation members were delighted, feeling that their research had been vindicated by the result. But they were disappointed that the credits were not more evenly distributed in the aftermath. Surely the fact that the search began in their location, established prior to 2004, and that their position was only 2.7 kilometres from the actual wreck site deserved some more generous acknowledgement in the final triumph?

While the search answered many questions some others still remained. The most important one, of course, was why the Australian commander Captain Joseph Burnett took his vessel so close to the *Kormoran* in the first place? Could there be some reason not yet revealed? Some, in the past, had suggested that he may have been misled by British Royal Naval Intelligence as to the identity of the vessel passing itself off as the *Straat Malakka*.

What if it had been suggested to him that the ship was the *Buren,* a German supply ship known to be in the Indian Ocean and which was unarmed? The message there, perhaps, being *'Get in close and board her and get her code books and enigma machines before the sun goes down'?*

One of *Sydney's* boats was actually being lowered when the action began, perhaps confirming that suspicion.

At the time of the engagement *Sydney* was under British orders, through the Royal Navy '*China Station'* HQ at Singapore. *The White Ensign,* the journal of the Naval Association of Australia, noted that '*Prime Minister Robert Menzies did not consult Parliament before obliging Australians to fight in a European war in September 3, 1939, On November 7 He transferred all Australia's ships and sailors to the British Navy.*

'Thus the Australian Navy was part of, and totally controlled by, the Royal Navy from November 7, 1939 to September 29, 1942'.

This meant that *HMAS Sydney* was under Royal Navy control at the time of her fatal meeting with the *Kormoran* on the 19th of November 1941. When British wartime events were de-classified after the statutory 30 year period after the Second World War *Sydney's* file was given a further long period as '*Classified'*. Why? What is in the file that the British don't want the world to know?

One of the questions that was never satisfactorily answered was why it took so long for a search for the *Sydney* to be initiated? One of the men who asked that question previously was former RAAF Group Captain Rig Bourne who flew on the belated aerial search. He was well aware that men in life-jackets do not last four days in the water.

Bourne was with the RAAF establishment at Pearce air base in Western Australia, from where the search was ultimately mounted. But on the night that *Sydney* encountered the *Kormoran* radio messages were picked up by RAAF signallers in Geraldton saying that the *Sydney* was in action with the Enemy.

Rig Bourne claimed that a message '*Sydney's Gone!'* was received on the night of the fatal encounter. It was passed on to the Navy's *HMAS Leeuwin* depot, and the District Naval Officer was telephoned at his Cottesloe home at 1a.m. on the Friday morning. His response was that *'Sydney is not overdue'*. It was not until the afternoon of Monday that the Navy gave the RAAF the instruction to began an aerial search.

An obituary in *The West Australian* newspaper in 2008, after Rig Bourne's death at the age of 88 years, stated: *'When Rig Bourne's search found nothing he pushed for more searches and asked why the initial search had not begun until four days after the Sydney sank? As a senior RAAF officer he had access to files and could interview service personnel.*

'He claimed that the series of morse code messages detailing a battle was picked up by two RAAF signalmen in Geraldton and relayed to RAAF Pearce, from there it was sent to Western Command headquarters in Perth, and then to the Naval shore base HMAS Leeuwin in Fremantle.

'The messages resulted in the phone call to the home of the District Naval Officer at his home. Reg insisted that he had contacted all the people who had passed the message along the chain. They confirmed that it had been sent on the night. "I was called a liar by the Navy but I told the truth" he said. He documented his findings about the *Sydney* in a manuscript *The Bourne Papers* which is now in Perth's Battye research library.

The discovery of the wrecks of *HMAS Sydney* and the *Kormoran* stirred other memories around Australia. Letters and stories from families and relatives of the 645 men who died with *Sydney* on November 21, 1942, flooded in to city and provincial newspapers around the nation. Collectively they would fill a book – or perhaps several books – and perhaps that should indeed be done some day. But at least a couple of tales are relevant in the Gascoyne-Exmouth context.

Perth's *Post* newspaper, whose editor Bret Christian had been running *HMAS Sydney* stories for several years as part of a personal crusade to mount a *Sydney* search, recounted the story of Reg Anderson of Carnarvon under the title:

<u>REG'S JOY TURNED TO HEARTBREAK.</u>

When Reg Anderson heard shipwrecked sailors had landed on the coast north of Carnarvon he was possibly the most excited man in town. His younger brother Ron was a sailor on HMAS Sydney.

An RAAF pilot searching for the Sydney had reported two beached lifeboats 130 kilometres north of the town. Word spread like wildfire around Carnarvon that Australian sailors had been found.

Reg owned the town taxi and when the police commandeered the vehicle with others to go to the scene, his daughter Lynette McCorry told *Post* that he was more than happy to oblige. He drove the police sergeant Stan Anderson and Dr J.W.Piccles in the lead of the convoy, hoping to be reunited with his brother. Instead the trip had a bitter ending when he found that the castaways from the lifeboats were not *Sydney* men but German sailors from the *Kormoran.* Though he was unaware of it at the time, his brother Ron was already dead. Despite the sad result there was one positive aspect. Reg took pictures of the lifeboats, the cave where the Germans came ashore, and their scattered stores and equipment, which are historically unique and important in the *Sydney-Kormoran* story.

What sort of men were the central characters in the drama?

In 2008 Perth man Colin Stratton was one of the few people alive who had spoken with Kormoran captain Theodor Detmers. At the time Stratton was a 20 year-old sergeant in the 22nd Motor Transport Company sent to bring Detmers and his second-in-command Lieutenant Commander Kurt Foerster to Perth by road.

'Detmers was a perfect gentleman' Colin recalled for the author. *'His English was so good that if you had put him in a pin-striped suit and a bowler hat you might have thought him a typical English gentleman. In fact he was in a formal blue uniform with his iron cross at his throat – the full mufti. I talked with him about the action and he was still shaking his head in amazement that his converted merchantman had been able to take on an Allied light cruiser and win the day'.*

Detmers and Foerster were taken to Perth in the back of a three-ton Army truck with a wire cage and canvas canopy to be delivered to Swanbourne Army camp, the site of the modern SAS regiment. Stratton was in a utility which followed behind with orders to shoot if an escape attempt were made.

'In fact there was no question of that' Stratton recalled. *'There was no resentment or animosity. He just accepted what had happened as the Fortunes of War'.* Once when a stop was made on the road well south of Carnarvon so that prisoners and guards could relieve themselves *(' Take a Nelson Riddell'* as Stratton put it, using the old Army term) Detmers joked with his captors that he could tell them exactly where they were, though he had had no view of the surroundings from the closed-in truck.

"We're heading south" he said', Stratton remembers *'And he gave us his estimate of the distance travelled. He was dead right'.*

In modern times a lady came to Carnarvon who was not at all the usual tourist or visitor. She was German, going on in years, and her husband had died of complications following a stroke. She visited the town library and sought out a book titled *The Raider Kormoran*, written by the former captain of Raider 41. The man who sank the *Sydney* and who wrote the book was Theodor Detmers.

The woman wrote on the fly leaf, an action which would have been questioned if it had been anyone else, and her grammar was in the German rather than the British style. But her message to Carnarvon and the world was clear enough.

'Wars did much harm. May Mankind learn to keep always Peace!'

The name in the signature was Ursula Detmers. She was, of course, the wife of the former captain of *Raider 41*.

After the success of the search there were memorial services, official and unofficial, for the 645 men of *HMAS Sydney* all around Australia. The first of them was aboard the *Geosounder* above the wreck of the Royal Australian Navy ship far below in her final resting place. Navy representative Lieutenant John Perryman laid a wreath on the waters on behalf of all aboard, the haunting strains of the *Last Post* were played, and a poem by Petty Officer H.B.Shipstone was read above the site where HMAS Sydney, and perhaps PO Shipstone lay far below.

Let me live, 0 mighty Master
Through this war. Yet if I'm slain
Tasting triumph and disaster
Joy and not too much of pain
Let me roam the raging waters
For a while to love and laugh
And when I'm beneath the ocean
Let this be my epitaph
'There sleeps one who took his chances
In that war-crazed, tragic Hell
Battled luck and circumstance
Loved and laughed, but fought and fell
Victor then, he did no crowing
Wounded then he did not wail
Cursed and swore, but kept on going
Never let his courage fail.
He was fallible and human
Therefore loved and understood
By his fellow men and women
Whether good or not so good
Kept his spirit undiminished
Had a laugh for every friend
Fought for Freedom till it finished
Lived, loved, laughed until the end!'

THE CREW OF HMAS SYDNEY II: All 645 men died on that fatal night of November 21, 1941. There were no survivors. (Picture: Australian War Memorial)

Operation Pot Shot

Chapter Seven

After Japan attacked Pearl Harbour, on December 7th, 1941, there was no need to tell people in Western Australia that there was a war on. They were still shaken by the disastrous news about *HMAS Sydney*. Houses were blacked out at night, and every house had a slit trench in the garden, dug by a sweating head of the family, in case of an air raid. In Perth your author remembers as a child helping to dig Vee-shaped trenches at Claremont Practising School, and seeing a prefabricated Anderson air raid shelter installed at the family home in Crawley.

An American admiral came to live next door to us in Crawley-avenue, and Catalina flying boats – some with bullet holes in their fuselages -- came in to land on the Swan River below our house.

Carnarvon historian Jack Valli, in *Gascoyne Days*, recorded that Carnarvon householders were advised to pack a case with enough emergency rations to last at least 24 hours and to be ready with blankets for immediate pick-up should the order to evacuate the area be given. Needless to say, there was no price on real estate! Every male of the right age – and some who were really too young or too old – were talking about '*Joining up!'* The town band played patriotic tunes from the First World War such as *It's A Long Way To Tipperary*, and *Pack Up Your Troubles In Your Old Kit Bag*! As well as *God Save the King, Advance Australia Fair!,* and what would become the wartime favourite, *Waltzing Matilda.*

There was no band and none of that kind of urgency on the Cape or in the Exmouth Gulf. The stations carried on as always, unconcerned for the moment. After all, what enemy in their right mind would think of invading where there were no made roads, hundreds of miles from anywhere?

As someone pointed out, *' There was just miles, and miles, and bloody miles of bugger all!'* A No Man's Land that stretched right across from the North West Cape to the other side of Australia! That was summed up by the fact that even before you crossed the West Australian border a lot of the names in the interior carried the legend '*Desert'* alongside them. There was *the Great Sandy Desert, The Little Sandy Desert, The Gibson Desert, The Great Victoria Desert, The Tanami Desert,* and so it went on.

The Japanese would have been aware of the situation, for had not Japanese divers and crews been sailing the WA coast on pearling luggers since the 1880s? They knew every harbour, every anchorage, from Shark Bay to Darwin. That included the Bay of Rest in Exmouth Gulf, a favourite pearlers' anchorage when King Tides prevented diving.

It was American military strategy which brought the Second World War to Exmouth in 1942, just as the Cold War would bring them back again in 1963.

It is often said that America '*Saved Australia'* in the Second World War in the sense that it was an act of chivalrous generosity towards a threatened smaller nation. Without the United States entering the war against Japan, Australia with her best troops serving overseas would indeed have been an easy target for invasion. But it was not actually the case of a White Knight putting out a hand to aid a damsel in distress. Rather it was a situation of dire strategic necessity for the United States in the Pacific.

The Japanese had over-run the US bases in the Philippines and South East Asia. There was no American foothold remaining north of Australia by the end of 1942. The Americans needed a stable base from which to regroup, re-form, and initiate a counter attack. Australia was the only possible choice.

Of course there was no argument about that from a nation desperate in the face of the Japanese threat and feeling abandoned by Britain. General Douglas McArthur arrived with appropriate fanfare saying *'I shall return!'* (to the Philippines), and Australians said *'Thank God you're here!'*

Whichever way you look at it, generosity or a practical issue, or a combination of both, the United States undoubtedly did save Australia and a bond was formed which endures to this day. The Americans had had the opportunity to watch the European war unfold from a distance, and the lessons learned were the effectiveness of submarine warfare and the absolute necessity for aerial supremacy.

Fremantle Harbour, in Western Australia, became the biggest submarine base in the Southern Hemisphere. Twenty five US submarines were sent to Western Australia from Manila, with Dutch and British subs making up extra numbers later in the war. Exmouth Gulf was an obvious forward staging point. Submarines from Fremantle and Catalina flying boats based at Crawley on the Swan River, could top up their fuel 1200 kilometres from Fremantle, with the Dutch East Indies, Singapore, and the Philippines a lesser distance away.

The large, long-distance American submarines had a colourful variety of names. They included *Pecheral, Pike, Permit, Porpoise, Taron, Salmon, Sargo, Saury, Sailfish, Soulpin, Searaven, Seal, Seawolf, Seadragon, Skipjack, Snapper, Spearfish, Sturgeon, Stingray, and Swordfish.* The USS *Harder* had an especially poignant story. The lighter S-class submarines were known by numbers only: 537, 538, 539, 540, and 54. In April, 1942, the Americans announced their intention of setting up a base at the southern end of Exmouth Gulf, and by November, with characteristic energy they were building it.

Exmouth historian R.C.Gordon of Exmouth Junior High School, who recorded the events of the period, wrote in his *History Of North West Cape*. *'The Commander of Task Force Fifty One, Admiral C.S.Lockwood, instructed the Advance Base Planning Committee to prepare a plan. When this plan was submitted it provided for the construction of a landing strip and maintenance facilities for fighter aircraft and shore based patrol planes, a radar station, roads, water storage, a pontoon pier and moorings for a submarine tender, with anti-submarine defences, and underwater detection gear. Living quarters were to be constructed providing accommodation for an estimated 400 to 500 men. Anti aircraft defences were also included'.*

The plan was ambitious by any standards, but especially so when applied to Exmouth Gulf. To start with the Exmouth region had no made road connecting it with the outside world. In those circumstances how were the United States Navy going to get the significant amount of construction material into place? There was a typical tight-lipped Navy answer of the kind you would expect: *'By ship of course. How else would you do it?'*

Use of Exmouth Gulf as a fuel depot began in May, 1942, with the arrival of the submarine tender *Childe,* accompanied by three Catalina flying boats. All used the Bay of Rest as an anchorage. A 500 ton oil lighter arrived from Darwin in August. Construction of the base began in December 1942, with materials landed from the WA State Ship *Koolinda,* and the USS *Gulf Star.* The Exmouth base would be kept highly secret and was given a code name *'OPERATION POT SHOT'* .

What was the origin of the name? It may have been suggested by the US Naval Commander Admiral Christie who supposedly said *'Let's take a pot shot at it!.*

Early in the war the emphasis on secrecy everywhere reached a high point of paranoia.

People from Italian families and who had been born in Australia were herded into camps as *'enemy aliens'.* Any flickering light in Cottesloe was seen as someone signalling to an enemy submarine. Master pearlers from Broome who had had Japanese crews on their luggers were regarded with grave suspicion and were insulted by being told that their movements were being watched.

RAAF Wireless/telegraphy operator Eric McNabb found out about the secrecy obsessiveness one day in Perth when he was hauled off the streets of Perth by a pair of RAAF service policemen.

'What's all this about?' he asked indignantly.

'You'll find out soon enough!' gruffly spoken. That was the only answer he could get.

It was the end of a rather pleasant period for McNabb. Previously he had been a W/T (Wireless/ Telegraph) Operator in Broome, following the disastrous Japanese air raid of March, 1942,which destroyed 23 Allied aircraft. Since then things had quietened down considerably. On leave in Perth, he had been enjoying staying at his parents home in Maylands and catching up with family and friends. All that ended abruptly. He was taken to Western Area Headquarters, given tropical gear and an old radio transceiver he had previously had problems with in Broome -- which caused an outburst of bad language – and was told that he would be installing the gear aboard RAAF 017-02.

'What the hell's that?'

'You'll find out when the time comes!'

He was sworn to secrecy about the operation – though at that point he did not know what it was or where he was going. He was not even allowed to make a 'phone call home.

'What will my parents think when I just disappear without telling them anything?' he asked, not unreasonably. He received the standard answer *'Don't you know there's a war on? Just follow your orders, Signaller!'*

Fortunately he knew a girl in the WAAF (Women's Auxiliary Air Force) at Western Headquarters who was able to quietly tell the family that McNabb had suddenly been sent away on orders. It was wartime, and they understood. Though he had already served three-and-a-half years with RAAF signals, Eric McNabb was still only 21 years old. He stepped out of a C47 aircraft at Learmonth, blinking in the sunlight, with his piece of ancient Avro Anson radio equipment, still not entirely sure where he was.

'What met my eyes was a scene of utter desolation. It was very hot and dusty with plenty of flies. It did not impress me at all!' .

McNabb now found out why he had been sent. He was to be the radio operator, part of the crew of an RAAF air sea rescue craft. When we think today of the usual image of Air-Sea Rescue, the mental picture is of a substantial motor launch throwing up a huge bow wave and travelling at 30 knots in all weathers.

In this case think again! McNabb's vessel, No 017-02 was the ex-Geraldton crayfishing boat *Columbia.* She was 11 metres in length, a cutter-rigged sailing craft, and though she had a diesel motor she was more comfortable progressing – like all fishing boats of the day – under sail. Her maximum speed under both sail and engine power was between six and seven knots! It is not unlikely that at one time she had been a Shark Bay pearling craft because she had only 23 centimetres of freeboard at the stern. Shark Bay pearlers dragged metal scoops along the shallow banks to get their pearl shell, and their craft were deliberately built with sterns low to the water to make it easier to get the scoops on board. Equally effective, it might be suggested for pulling half-drowned airmen out of the ocean?

Columbia, moving with the unhurried calm of a middle-aged lady, handled Exmouth Gulf conditions well, and by good fortune she never had to be used for her intended purpose of rescuing downed pilots.

McNabb found no fault with *Columbia*, though he was less than enthusiastic about the isolation and harsh conditions at Learmonth. Even so, he had it better than most Australian servicemen in the area.

He and the *Columbia* crew lived aboard, but were sometimes accommodated in the US Navy quarters, at Pot Shot when tied up to the Learmonth jetty. The American conditions were immeasurably better than those of the Australian Army and RAAF servicemen posted to Exmouth Gulf.

The Australians lived in wind-flapping tents infiltrated with red dust. Their rations were bully beef out of tins where the Americans lived in clean Nissan huts and had turkey and ice-cream for lunch. If McNabb needed a new radio valve from US stores he would make sure to turn up at lunch time!

One of the names indelibly associated with wartime Exmouth was the famous fighter ace Keith *'Bluey'* Truscott who in civilian life had been a football star for the Melbourne Football Club in its premiership year of 1939. His enlistment in the RAAF attracted a lot of publicity, and he obtained leave from the air force to play again in the 1940 premiership for the *Demons.* Curiously for a man with all the co-ordination needed to reach the top level in football, he struggled with his early flying lessons. But for his sporting reputation he may never have graduated. But his instructors were patient and eventually he got his *'wings'*. But he never made smooth landings. He consistently bounced his aircraft on the tarmac and later the Marsden matting of the wartime strips, with his ground crews shaking their heads.

Though his flying wasn't pretty, once he got into combat it was another matter. Truscott was a lethal fighter pilot. He joined No 452 Squadron in Britain in May 1941, flying Spitfires, and had an immediate impact. He destroyed six German aircraft in one month, and was awarded the Distinguished Flying Cross. He rose to be acting squadron leader and finally became commanding officer of 452, adding a bar to his DFC. By that time he had shot down 11 German aircraft, and had had another three '*Probables*', and two '*Damaged'* against his name. Meantime he had been shot down once himself, parachuting into the chilly waters of the English Channel to be picked up by Air Sea Rescue craft.

At that time he was probably the most famous fighter pilot in Britain. The Marquis of Donegal organised a public fund, inviting red-headed men all over Britain to subscribe to a 5000 pound fund to buy 'Bluey' a new Spitfire. By 1942 with the Japanese threat to Australia he was back on home soil to join No 76 Squadron flying Kittyhawks.

When the Japanese push began in New Guinea, he was appointed second-in-command of the squadron and sent to Milne Bay. They operated in appalling flying conditions with constant rain, heavy mist, low clouds, and Marsden matting steel runways slippery as a skating rink. Truscott's personal tally of enemy aircraft destroyed rose to 16, with an additional three '*Probables*' and three '*Damaged*'. When 76's squadron leader Peter Turnbull, DFC, was killed in action, Truscott took over command of the squadron. After the successful conclusion of the New Guinea campaign, with the Japanese suffering their first land defeat of the Second World War, No 76 Squadron were posted back to Australia.

To their disgust they were sent to Yanrey Station in Western Australia. Yanrey was in the arid country east of Exmouth Gulf and the fly-boys from 76 Squadron regarded the isolation of the post with horror. They dubbed it '*Death Valley*'. Bluey Truscott flew over to Learmonth, had a look at the American facilities and made a personal decision to remove the squadron to Exmouth. He didn't see the need to consult any of the relevant authorities.

There was never any official approval for re-siting 76 Squadron, and only Truscott with his strong personality and immense public popularity could have got away with it. Unfortunately it ultimately cost him his life. While carrying out training exercises with Flying Officer Ian Louden in another Kittyhawk out of sheer boredom, they decided to make a mock attack on an incoming Catalina PBY flying boat.

The date was March 28th, 1943. Truscott was apparently deceived by the fact that the flying boat was losing height for landing and the glassy surface below made conditions deceptive.

As he rolled his aircraft and passed below the Catalina, the wingtip of his Kittyhawk, A29-150, caught the surface of the Gulf. The aircraft cart-wheeled and slammed into the water and Australia's most famous fighter ace was killed instantly.

Though it is sometimes incorrectly described as having been a failure, Operation POT SHOT was actually very effective in terms of Allied requirements especially for the submarines. It was serviced by the well-known State Ship *Koolinda,* and a commandeered Chinese trader, the *Chunking.* In addition various other ships spent time there as tankers for bunkering, and as service and repair vessels for submarines and aircraft.

Most of these ships had stories of their own. The *Koolinda* had rescued the Japanese crews of pearling luggers surviving but drifting helplessly after the 1934 Lacepedes cyclone north of Broome. The storm sank 19 other luggers and cost 224 lives. A grateful Japanese government sent letters of thanks. During the war there was a belief that the Japanese would never bomb the *Koolinda* for that reason. True or not, the Japanese did have opportunities to sink the *Koolinda* on her regular calls to Broome, where at times Japanese reconnaissance planes flew over while the ship was sitting on the mud at low tide by Broome's long jetty, unable to go anywhere. She survived the war unscathed.

The Dutch tanker *Ondina* had been torpedoed out in the Indian Ocean, and had a huge hole in her side when she limped into Fremantle. But she remained afloat and functional, and spent time at Exmouth Gulf refuelling submarines. In leisure moments the crew used to net fish which came inside the ship through the hole in the hull.

Where did the name *'Learmonth'* come from? Wing Commander Charles Learmonth, DFC and Bar, Commanding Officer No 14 Squadron, had a distinguished war record. When he was with 22 Squadron in New Guinea he led five Boston bombers in the Battle of the Bismarck Sea to sink a Japanese destroyer. He was awarded the Distinguished Flying Cross for his part in the action. In January, 1944, as a wing-commander flying out of Pearce, he was the pilot of a Beaufort bomber which crashed into the sea off Rottnest Island on January 6th, 1944.

The Beauforts had had a series of unexplained crashes, killing pilots and crews and puzzling the experts. Learmonth, finding himself in a dive from which he was unable to pull out, remained coolly at the controls and radioed, so long as he was able, a description of the problem in the tail assembly from which engineers were able to diagnose and rectify the fault. He was only 26 years old when he died. For his widow the fact that he was awarded a bar to his DFC was a consolation which could hardly have compensated for her loss. The air strip at Exmouth was named in his honour, the name remaining in modern times as part of Exmouth's proud wartime legacy.

There would have been many other stories about Exmouth Gulf during the war that have never been told. The submarines came and went silently. Some never returned at all, and their rusting wrecks, like the *USS Harder*, lie at the bottom of the South China Sea or the Pacific or the Indonesian Archipelago, together with the brave men who sailed in them. The 22 per cent casualty rate in submarines was the highest of any of the United States forces in the Second World War. A total of 3500 men died of 16,000 in the service. Many of them passed through Exmouth Gulf on their patrols.

One of the sad stories was that of the *USS Barbel* (named after a freshwater fish) which operated out of Fremantle during the Second World War. *Barbel* had a distinguished war record. She was awarded three Battle Stars during her period of service from 1943, and sank 10 Japanese ships, including two destroyers, for a total of 55,200 tons, and damaged two others (total of 14,000 tons). She may have added to the list on her last patrol.

Barbel was commanded by Lieutenant Commander Conde L.Raguet. She left Fremantle on January 5th, 1945, and was in Exmouth Gulf by January 8th, to top up her fuel tanks.

She was ordered to join two other submarines, *Bluegill* and *Bream,* to form a wolf pack at the entrance to the Balabec Strait in the South China Sea..

Submarines in the area were at constant risk because of shallowing water and the danger of being sighted and attacked by aircraft. On February 3rd, *Barbel* reported to the other submarines that she had had numerous aircraft contacts daily, and had been attacked three times with depth charges.

On February 4th, a Japanese aircraft sighted an American submarine, later confirmed as *Barbel*, and dropped two bombs. One landed on the submarine near the bridge. It was reported that *'The submarine plunged under a cloud of fire and spray!'*. *Barbel* and her crew were never heard of again.

Commander Raguet had the unhappy distinction of being the youngest US submarine commander to lose his life in the Second World War.

Eric McNabb recalled *' One afternoon I was enjoying a free beer in the US Recreation Room – one bottle at a time was allowed, and when empty could be returned and exchanged for another full bottle. Ice-cold of course.*

' A United States Navy submarine had arrived and was moored alongside the fuel barge, topping up its fuel. Some of the crew had been ferried ashore for a short break and a free beer. It was not long before the dice were being rolled and a game of 'crap' was in progress. I had never seen so much money changing hands before and I just stood back and watched as five and ten pound notes were wagered. That kind of money in those days was a small fortune to me.

I asked one of the young submariners why he was so keen to part with his money. He replied 'What the Hell? We are off on operations and I may not return to use it otherwise. So why worry about it?'

Was the young submariner one of the 3500 casualties by war's end?

One of Exmouth's regular callers, the US submarine *Tautog,* made 13 patrols, and sank 26 Japanese ships, totalling 72,616 tons.

The Japanese bombed Exmouth on a number of occasions, though never with the devastating results they achieved at Darwin or Broome. In fact no lives were lost, and there was no damage of any consequence in any of the raids.

The Japanese usually came over on a moonlit night, and the approaching aircraft would be picked up by the RAAF radar station at the Lighthouse on Vlamingh Head, and other radar in the Gulf while they were still well out to sea. The first raid by two aircraft occurred on May 20, 1943, and on the following night nine bombs were dropped but failed to find a target. The Australian Army anti-aircraft unit responded but failed to make any hits. In soccer terms it was an 0-0 result.

Later the American authorities in Perth were furious because they said that by opening fire the *'Ack-ack'* gunners had revealed the existence of the base to the Japanese and *'compromised'* its safety. As a result of this concern the submarine tender *Pelias* was withdrawn from Exmouth. The anti-aircraft gunners scratched their heads and asked why, in that event they were there at all? What was the point of having AA batteries if they were not supposed to fire?

In any case, on a full-moon night the Japanese pilots would have seen the moonlight glinting off the Nissan huts, observed the Pot Shot jetty snaking out from shore, and spotted the *Pelias* out in the Gulf.

The unit which probably had the toughest conditions were the crew of the RAAF radar unit located at Vlamingh Head. Des Doyle, at the time a corporal-clerk, later recalled receiving his orders in November, 1942:

'You are posted to 310 RDF Station WEF (with effect from) December, 1942'.

Bewildered, Corporal Doyle asked : *'Where is 310 RDF, and what is it?'.*

He received much the same treatment as Eric McNab.

'No-one knows, or they are not saying, other than you are to proceed to HQ Western Area for instructions. A service policeman escorts you to an area of closed doors and very secretive individuals who appear most reluctant to elaborate. You are handed a file "Schedule of Equipment" and told 'Please go ahead and equip the unit with all its domestic requirements'.

'Consternation, maybe shock, is the order of the day!

'Following a show of frustration, indeed even petulance, I discover that other people will be involved and that transport will be by MV Koolinda. Knowing that the usual passage of that vessel is to the North West it is reasonable to assume that that is where we are headed'.

Doyle's RAAF unit was taken ashore at Exmouth Gulf by barge and driven by US Navy truck to their radar station at the Cape. *'Living in the country as a youth accustomed me to rough roads, but they were nothing compared with the conditions we experienced at the Cape and what we would live with in the months to come.*

'On arrival at the unit we were confronted with a galvanised shed – kitchen and dining areas – showers, latrines, and tents all located in sand dunes just off the beach. It was hot as hell, and we were hungry, thirsty, tired and dirty. A meal of bully beef and biscuits really lifted us! The tea tasted very strange too! Bore water took its toll and very shortly, including our sergeant medical orderly, we were all well and truly scourged with the ' trots' and the unit was effectively useless. This lasted about four days when obviously our internal organs had re-arranged themselves'.

The water problem was solved by the genial Eric Payne, who had Yardie Creek Station. He allowed the unit access to better quality water at the homestead. However, since their only transport was a Massey Harris tractor the nine mile trip to fill up a water tanker was an all-day effort.

The *'Doover'*, as the radar was nick-named for excess-secrecy reasons, gave up to an hour's warning of the approach of enemy aircraft and plenty of time to retreat to slit trenches. The troops tended it in six-hour shifts, and could pick up aircraft movements as much as 296 kilometres out to sea. Though they heard the Japanese aircraft passing overhead *'quite loudly'* on occasions they were never bombed themselves. However, the threat of the Enemy aside, health problems continued to dog the unit.

'In remarkably short time the whole unit became literally 'rotten', Doyle recalled *'With Barcoo Rot (a form of scurvy) mosquito bites, spinifex needles breaking off in the skin then forming large sores filled with pus..'*

He managed to get down to Pot Shot where the US Navy doctor was horrified at his appearance. *'One look at me, emaciated and covered with sores was enough. Quite frankly he was disgusted and his immediate reaction was to arrange with his Executive Officers for our unit to be given sufficient supplies of all kinds of nourishing food, including vegetables. Imagine the surprise at the Unit when I arrived back with all these 'goodies'!*

Not only that, he was driving a 4 x4 Ford utility on indefinite loan. It was not popular at the US base because of its number -- USN 13. The Australians at the radar had no reservations about that. They had transport at last! *'Thank goodness for superstition!'*

The Australians were young and flexible, and soon settled down to life in a harsh environment. Though they were the most distant appendage of POT SHOT they were surprisingly often visited by Army and Navy celebrities including, on one occasion, Admiral Nimitz, Commander in Chief of the United States South West Pacific Fleet.

Security was practised to an obsessive degree. The Americans insisted on passwords for anyone moving in the area and a new password was issued every day. All radio communications had to be in code, and Des Doyle recalls that the radar station at Vlamingh Head received their password from a Catalina flying boat going out on long range patrol at 5am every day. The password for the day was dropped in a weighted pouch with a coloured streamer from the blister gunport on the side of the Catalina.

'It soon became a fun thing to either try to hit me with the package or blow over our tent. The Cats often flew so low that the grinning crewman in the blister was practically shaking my hand! Sometimes they erred in the drop, and I would have to salvage the streamer from the sea'.

One of the controversial issues of the war in Exmouth Gulf was what was referred to later as *'The Big Flap'*. In May, 1944, all Western Australia was alerted to rumours of a supposed Japanese invasion fleet headed for the west coast. Signaller Eric McNabb, posted to Pot Shot, was told specifically that a Japanese invasion was expected. The leisurely pace of the airstrip at Learmonth suddenly saw a dramatic escalation of aircraft and senior personnel arriving in transport aircraft .

'On arrival all personnel were advised of the extreme secrecy of this operation. Mail services, inwards and outwards, were suspended, as were movements of people in transit'.

With a thunder of Rolls Royce Merlin engines 19 Spitfires from Darwin arrived on May 10th, followed by 12 Beaufighters, and then a further 17 Spitfire re-enforcements. Learmonth was beginning to look more like a front-line station, with the population of Air Force personnel rising from less than 100 to nearly 800, including administration, maintenance workers, pilots and air crew. In addition another radar station, No 161, designed to help fighter aircraft intercept incoming enemy raiders, was flown down from Truscott Base in the Kimberley, and sent out to Vlamingh Head.

Operators staring at the screen in the radar station at Vlamingh Head were agog to pick up images of vessels stretching from horizon to horizon. They were the US South Pacific Fleet which had advanced from the south, taking up the entire radar screen, and which had now hove-to off North West Cape.

'What the hell is going on?' the radar operators asked each other.

Eric McNabb, aboard *Columbia* recalled a sight to be remembered for a lifetime: *'The South West Pacific Fleet came in and lay off the North West Cape. The Fleet was making so much smoke we said to one another that the Japanese would surely be able to see it from Tokyo!*

The Fleet itself was a sight to behold. There were three battleships, and four aircraft carriers in the centre, surrounded by cruisers, then the oilers and tankers, and support vessels. A ring of destroyers completely surrounded the fleet.

'They disappeared over the horizon one way, and over the horizon on the other side. I have never, to this day, seen such a huge concentration of war and support ships!'

One of the radar crew estimated that when the fleet began to move it took 20 hours before they disappeared off his radar screen.

On May 21st, 1944 it was all over. The South West Pacific Fleet returned to its normal station, giving Surabaya, in Java, a barrage on the way. The Spitfires and Beaufighters flew away with a waggle of their wings, and the administrators climbed into their DC 3s, and went back to their *'shiny-bum'* bureaucratic jobs in civilisation. The embargo on mail and transit personnel was lifted, and by the end of the month Learmonth and the Gulf were back to boring normality.

So what had really happened?

There was never an official explanation, though there were too many eye-witnesses to the arrival of the South West Pacific Fleet off the North West Cape, and the dramatic build-up of aircraft at Learmonth in May 1944, for the *'Top Brass'* to come up with the usual brusque denial: *'It never happened!'*. For anyone with the temerity to ask, the response is still a denial.

The defensive movement on the west coast apparently followed US submarine reports of a major movement of Japanese warships east from their main base at Truk Lagoon in the Marianas in the Pacific. This may have been taken to indicate an intention to make a strike at an Australian target. Perth was placed on air alert at the time and rumours abounded. But apparently the Japanese movement was only to Singapore where their vessels were considered safer from American air and submarine attack.

The war in Europe ended with Germany's surrender on May 7th, 1945. Meantime the Japanese were being driven out of their mid-Pacific island bases at Guadalcanal, Iwo Jima, and Saipan.

Japanese shipping was being devastated by American submarine attack, with many of the submarines passing through Exmouth on their way to or from the theatre of war. Tokyo and the major cities were mercilessly pounded from the air by B 29 bombers. As the Americans prevailed in the Pacific theatre of the war, Exmouth became less important in the overall war effort.

Learmonth was devastated by the major Exmouth Gulf cyclone of February 1945, which completely wrecked the base and cost the lives of three RAAF men at the Bay of Rest. Ironically Nature claimed more human lives and did more damage than any of the efforts of the Japanese enemy. Knowing that a 'blow' was expected, Eric McNabb's trusty 017-02 crash boat *Columbia* and a landing barge were double-moored in the creek by the unit's base at the Bay of Rest. But the precaution proved in vain as a tidal surge roared up the creek. The veteran *Columbia* was smashed to bits and her wreckage washed miles inland together with the landing barge. The storm provided one remarkable story of survival.

Four personnel from the RAAF Marine Section were asleep in their tents at the Bay of Rest when the storm struck on the night of February 2nd, 1945. McNabb records that Coxswain Alf Hawkins recalled that the usual 'deadly stillness' prevailed with the approach of the cyclone. Though Hawkins was anxious about being in the path of the cyclone he took some re-assurance from the fact that there had never been a problem at the Bay of Rest in previous years,

Nevertheless, Alf Hawkins said later that he felt very uneasy that night and before going to bed opened his Air Force issue jack knife and placed it on an old kerosene case which served as a table alongside his bed. Wind and waves rose during the night and about two o'clock in the morning the sea suddenly overwhelmed Alf's tent. Thinking quickly he grabbed his tent mate, Lance Corporal Tonge, and slashed through the roof and fly of the tent with his jack knife. Both found themselves swimming immediately in the onrush of water from the tidal surge which washed them right over the sandhills and far inland.

Both men were naked as it was common practice to sleep 'In the raw' in the summer heat. The two stayed together as long as they could, but in the blackness of the night, in the howling wind, and the turbulent water they became separated. Hawkins never saw his companion again.

He swam all night until he felt some mangrove branches and clung desperately to them until dawn. When full daylight came he was able to make his way ashore, and stagger naked to Exmouth Station homestead for help. A search party from RAAF No 76 Operational Base Unit set out to look for the other three missing Marine Section airmen. But only one body, that of Corporal B.J.Carr, was ever found. But for his premonition and the ready-to-use jack knife, Alf Hawkins would have been among the dead.

Their encampment, consisting of a large US Bell tent used as a mess, with all its stores and refrigerators, and the sleeping tents, had vanished completely, and the beach, which had formerly been a coral strand, was completely covered by sand.. The wreck of *Columbia* finished up two-and-a-half-miles inland, and the landing barge finally came to rest four miles inland.

The 1945 cyclone completely wrecked two thirds of the buildings at Learmonth. It turned heavy trucks on their side on the airstrip and wrecked or damaged all service equipment. At that stage of the war it was not considered worthwhile re-building the base and most personnel were withdrawn. So Exmouth's war ended 'With a whimper not a bang!' though the airstrip at Learmonth continued to be used by international flights.

Among the VIP's who passed through were Lord Louis and Lady Mountbatten who – it was reported -- enjoyed an Australian beer in the recreation hut while their aircraft refuelled.

But POT SHOT had done its job.

From the beginning there were frequent arrivals and departures of submarines, Catalina flying boats, and aircraft from very active war zones, and there was the excitement of the 'Big Flap' of May, 1944, when the Japanese invasion force was expected.

There was also a commando raid, so secret and so 'hush hush' that few of the servicemen established at Exmouth Gulf were aware that it was happening.

THE RAAF RADAR UNIT at Vlaming Head were delighted when Corporal Des Doyle came back with this American four wheel drive from the US Base at Learmonth. The Yanks gave it to them 'gratis' because its license number was USN 13 and they reckoned it was an unlucky number. Note the left-hand drive.

Ask Me No Questions

Chapter Eight

In August, 1943, an unusual-looking craft, painted a sinister black in colour, slipped into Exmouth Gulf from the north. She travelled south, snake-like down the Gulf until she reached the United States Navy POT SHOT Base. Her distinctive silhouette, pencil-slim and recognisable even at a distance, caused raised eyebrows among US Navy personnel. Men who had served before the war in the Philippines and the South China Sea.

'What the Hell is a Jap fishing boat doing in Exmouth Gulf in the middle of a God-damned war?' they asked each other.

What indeed? However they were right in their identification.

Eighteen months earlier the black-hulled craft, weather beaten and reeking of innumerable cargoes of iced fish, had been the *Kofuku Maru,* Registered Japanese Fishing Boat 2283, laid up by the fortunes of war in Singapore Harbour. Now she had a new name – the *KRAIT* after the deadly little jungle snake. She also had a new and entirely different purpose in life.

There were no Japanese faces on board when she arrived at Exmouth Gulf and POT SHOT. Instead her crew were a cheerful bunch of mostly Australian Army and Navy servicemen in casual oddments of uniform dress. There were nine sailors, and five military men. One of them the leader, was by his distinctive upper-class accent, obviously English. This may have puzzled the Americans who had not seen many Britishers in Australia. They were, after all, mainly fighting that other war against Germany in the Middle East, the Mediterranean, and the Atlantic.

Admiral Christie, the Commander of POT SHOT had been advised in confidence of the nature of the *Krait* mission. That was a necessary courtesy. Because of the highly secret nature of POT SHOT only accredited vessels were allowed within the confines of the Gulf, and *Krait* might have had a need to use the US facilities -- as would prove to be the case.

But for the dependable engineering services of the USN submarine tender *Chanticleer*, and some smartly-handled welding torches, Operation Jaywick would never have got under way.

Everyone else at the Base was left to wonder what the *Krait* was all about. Of course the ordinary American servicemen didn't ask the direct or obvious question. Security was a high priority in their own POT SHOT operation, and they understood that if there was a secrecy aspect to the *Krait* visit it needed to be respected. But they would undoubtedly have been curious.

There was a saying in wartime, especially where '*Secret Ops.*' were concerned: *'ASK ME NO QUESTIONS, AND I'LL TELL YOU NO LIES!'*

For anyone bedsides the Admiral, the *Krait* crew found it convenient to tell at least one lie. They were bound for Fremantle they said. 'Better to divert attention away from the fact that they were actually headed in the opposite direction. They had an audacious intention to attack Japanese shipping behind enemy lines.

At that point even the general hands in the *Krait* crew themselves didn't know their true destination. They rather thought it might be Surabaya in Java. Whatever the target, they expected to be told once they left Australian waters. In fact it would be Singapore.

Below the decks of the *Krait* were commando black rubber folboats (fold-up boats) and an impressive store of limpet mines and small arms weaponry. The attack was the brainchild of Captain Ivan Lyons, of the Gordon Highlanders, who had been at the fall of Singapore and who knew the local waters and the myriad islands in the Malacca Strait all too well. He had taken the capitulation badly in a personal sense, his wife and child were missing since their ship disappeared, presumed torpedoed, in the Indian Ocean. He was itching to get back at the Enemy. This was a chance for revenge on a personal scale.

In that regard Singapore was an ideal target for a small commando force. There were numerous islands, many of them uninhabited, in the approaches. The Japanese there considered that they were so far from the active war zone that an Allied attack would be a practical impossibility. And so it would have been, in the ordinary military way of things.

But the *Krait* was a Trojan Horse, and she had had an interesting history. By bad luck -- or good fortune as it would later turn out – she happened to be in Singapore Harbour and was placed under arrest when Japan declared war on December 7th, 1941.

A year previously Winston Churchill had said: '*Singapore is a fortress armed with 15 inch guns and garrisoned by almost 20,000 men. It could only be taken by an enemy of at least 50,000 men. Such a siege would be liable to be interrupted if at any time Britain chose to send a superior fleet to the rescue ... It is not considered that the Japanese would embark on such a mad enterprise!*'

History records that the 27 naval guns were in emplacements covering the waters south of Singapore, anticipating a naval attack from that direction. Perversely the Japanese came down the Malayan Peninsula from the north to the undefended northern shore of Singapore Island. The guns could fire to the north, but their ammunition consisted of amour-piercing shells for use against warships. They would not explode when fired against infantry and so were useless for that function. That was typical of the British bungles which would lead to the humiliating fall of Singapore.

Singapore's garrison were peacetime troops, mainly Indian, with no actual battle experience and not a great deal of intrinsic loyalty for the Colonial power. The British troops had never been in battle either, and were softened -- especially their officers -- by the good life in a far-too-comfortable tropical billet. They had become '*Pukka Sahibs*' with servants to wait on them hand and foot. That was hardly a good mental or physical preparation for jungle fighting, with mud, blood, and leeches. There were no tanks, an essential tool of modern warfare, in Singapore or Malaya, even when matters became crucial. The air defence of Singapore consisted of 88 mainly obsolete aircraft. They were Vildebeeste bi-planes, held together by fabric and wires, and tubby little Brewster Buffaloes, where 336 modern aircraft were regarded as minimal to defend Singapore and the Malay peninsula.

While Air Marshall Brooke-Popham, Britain's pompous commander-in-chief of the Far East airily stated '*The Japanese are neither air-minded nor properly trained*' he could not have been further from the truth.

The Japanese Zero aircraft was one of the best fighters in the world, probably the equal at that time of the British Spitfire and the German Messerschmitt 109. The pilots were experienced from campaigning in China and Manchuria, and were as good as their aircraft. Japanese troops were also battle-hardened and experienced.

There were some major causes of the fall of Singapore, the first being the ignorance and massive arrogance of the Colonial military commanders, including Popham. Another was General Wavell, Commander-in-chief, in India, where he had been sent following his evident lack of flair as a field commander in the Middle East campaign.

Wavell said in 1941 '*Personally I should be most doubtful if the Japs ever tried to make an attack on Malaya, and I am sure they will get it in the neck if they do*!'

Haw, haw!

Lieutenant General A.E.Percival, commander of British forces in Singapore, expressed the extraordinary opinion that '*Defences are bad for morale – for both troops and civilians!*'

Percival, who had never previously been in a fighting command or heard a shot fired in anger, refused proposals for defences for the northern sector of the island and the city of Singapore on that basis. When the officer in charge of undercover affairs and counter-espionage, Colonel Hayley Bell, who had been raised in Japan, spoke perfect Japanese, and was aware of Japanese strengths and ambitions, warned of the increasing threat, they '*Shot the messenger*'. He was described as an '*Alarmist*'and a '*Crank*' and sent back to England on the orders of the Governor of Singapore, Sir Thomas Shenton. There was no effective intelligence replacement.

Sir Thomas was the man who had all news coming into Singapore censored, and who extraordinarily presented the Japanese landing at Kota Bharu in the Press as a British victory. When the Japanese bombed Singapore city he refused to order a blackout '*Because it might cause panic*' among the citizens.

It is now history that the Japanese landed at Kota Bharu in Northern Malaya on the same day as their Navy attacked Pearl Harbour. The date was December 7th, 1941. In fact the troops landed a few hours earlier, and similarly without a declaration of war. The invasion went as British intelligence had warned with other landings north in Thailand. The Japanese infantry raced down the Malay Peninsula, introducing a new element to modern warfare. They rode bicycles down the excellent British roads, covering more ground in a day than conventional marching troops could achieve in a week.

They drove the untrained Indian troops, the British troops with no fighting experience, and the Australians of the Eighth Division, who fought hard without tanks or armored support, back down the peninsula. Finally they were forced to retreat over the 1200 metre causeway linking Johore to Singapore Island. Soon after the Japanese stormed the '*Impregnable Fortress*' itself. If defence was considered bad for troop and civilian morale, as Percival assured his colleagues, then defeat was surely the most bitter taste of all.

By February 15th, 1942, less than 12 weeks after the first Japanese landing in Malaya, the unthinkable occurred. The British were comprehensively defeated in Singapore. Percival surrendered, and it was all over. It was the beginning of the end for the British Empire. A humiliation deeply felt. Churchill himself described it as '*The greatest capitulation and disaster in British history!*'

It is hard to argue with the statement, but there is no denying that he had played his own part in the debacle. While there were constant and increasingly desperate requests from responsible military officers in Singapore for re-enforcements of men, tanks, and aircraft, none of them were ever sent.

In her book *The Heroes of Rimau,* which included the *Krait* history, Lynette Silver wrote '*Wavell, now Supreme Commander in the Far East, discovered that since 'little or nothing' had been done to construct defences there was nothing to safeguard the northern shore and that Singapore, the fortres,s was an illusion. When Churchill learned of this he was aghast'.*

In his memoirs, *A History Of The Second World War* published in 1951, Churchill was surprisingly frank where Singapore's lack of northern defences were concerned

'I ought to have known' he said *' And I ought to have been told, and I ought to have asked .... The possibility of Singapore having no landward defences no more entered my mind than that of a battleship being launched without* a *bottom!'*

It is true that Britain was in a desperate situation at the time. While the British Raj in Singapore was exemplified by Governor Shenton and General Percival, who strutted about obsessed by peacock protocol, blinkered to all else, Britain at home was fighting for her very life.

She had been driven out of France at Dunkirk, and resisted by a hairsbreadth the German air attacks in the Battle For Britain. She was now in a desperate confrontation with the German Afrika Korps and the Italians amid billowing clouds of dust on the battlefields of Libya and Tunisia.

In Churchill's view if Rommel's Panzer divisions broke through the Eighth Army to Egypt and captured Cairo and the Suez Canal it would be the end of the war for Britain. Beyond Suez lay Mesopotamia (Iraq and Iran of today) the main source of British fuel oil. Further on still was the Caucasus with even more oil wells to drive the Nazi war machine.

Given Hobson's Choice, Churchill felt that the maximum effort had to be made in the West, and that everything *'East of Suez'* -- even though the East might contain the Empire's '*Jewels in the Crown'* such as Hong Kong and Singapore -- would have to take their chances as best they could. It was just hoped that India itself could hold on. Despite that reasonably rational view, irrationally in April he launched the disastrous Greek campaign without air cover that resulted in heavy losses of British and Australian troops in Greece and Crete.

The Australian government was outraged by that failure and by the fact that promises to assist Singapore were being abandoned – after all the Australian Eighth Division was in there too!

In a furious cable to Churchill, the Australian Prime Minister John Curtin wrote '*After all the assurances we have been given the evacuation of Singapore would be regarded here and elsewhere as an inexcusable betrayal! We understood that it was to be made impregnable and in any event was capable of holding out until the arrival of the main fleet'*. ... The mythical *'main fleet'* always spoken about, but which in fact only ever existed in political speeches.

'An inexcusable betrayal!'

They were harsh words, and Churchill never forgave Curtin for them. But what had happened at Singapore was indeed inexcusable as Churchill himself admitted. The effect was immediate. Australia turned to the Americans, demanding the return of the Ninth and Seventh Divisions from the Middle East – much against Churchill's wishes -- to help defend Australia from the increasingly imminent Japanese threat.

The entire Eighth Division, a body of men which could have provided some protection for Australia at home had been lost, killed in action, or taken as prisoners of war, in the Singapore debacle. A disaster for which Australia held the British High Command directly responsible.

While Britain undoubtedly had her problems there were very real concerns in Australia.

With the cream of her fighting forces overseas on Britain's behalf Australia was practically undefended. The Japanese had astonished and dismayed the western world by over-running all of South East Asia in less than three months. In turn they had out-planned, out-maneuvered, and out-fought the British in Malaya and Singapore, the Americans in the Philippines, and the Dutch in the Indonesian archipelago. With command of the air and co-ordinated landings the Japanese took the old colonial territories willy nilly, including Borneo, Sumatra, and Java. And gave the Colonial powers a literal black eye.

They sank the two British warships *Prince of Wales* and *Repulse,* which had gone out without air cover, off the coast of Malaya. The Japanese attacked them with Vietnam-based torpedo bombers.

The Fleet Commander Tom Phillips had never experienced an air attack and dismissed as '*poppycock!* the notion that aircraft could ever be a serious threat to '*a properly armed battleship*'. He went down with his ship.

In the Philippines the Japanese caught the US Army Air Force on the ground at Clark Field. Eighteen of 35 Flying Fortress bombers were destroyed, as well as 53 fighters and 25 other aircraft for the loss of only seven Enemy planes. Every country from China south to the jungles of New Guinea fell into Japanese hands after what must be acknowledged as having been one of the most brilliant military campaigns in history. The Japanese surely the most under-estimated enemy.

If Japan had not attacked Pearl Harbour and brought America into the war who knows what would have happened? But the Japanese commanders had seriously underestimated the enormous resources of the United States. As a country with a population of more than 200 million people, America had sources of coal and steel and oil, and factories, airfields, shipyards, and places of manufacture beyond counting. As an example, at the time of Pearl Harbour the United States had three aircraft carriers. Within a year after the declaration of war 50 more carriers had gone down the slipways!

The Battle of Midway in June 1942, was the beginning of the inevitable rolling back of Japanese conquests through overwhelming numbers of men, aircraft, warships, and aircraft carriers. At the critical Battle of Midway the United States Navy destroyed four Japanese aircraft carriers, and 228 aircraft. The American losses were 307 men against 3057 on the Japanese side. While the Japanese victories were initially a triumph to delight the Emperor Hirohito, the number of countries involving occupying forces stretched Japanese resources beyond their limits. There was simply too much real estate to manage.

Gradually the American heavyweight began to flex its muscles, and the tide of war began to turn. By August 1943 when *Krait* arrived in Exmouth Gulf there were encouraging signs from both the American and Australian point of view.

So the *Krait* was a part of this Allied counter attack?

Yes and no. The American onslaught on Saipan involved 535 ships landing 128,000 United States troops. It included hundreds of aircraft, and vessels ranging from aircraft carriers to battleships, cruisers, and destroyers, as well as landing craft too many to count. Aboard *Krait* there were just 15 personnel, and the attack would be made by only six men in three kayak-like folboat canoes, each one paddled by hand.

As a military exercise it was certainly not on a grand scale. But – while it required consummate skill and bravery for all of those involved -- its importance was intended to lie in its potential propaganda value. British pride had been badly stung by the disgraceful turn of events in Singapore, and the shameful loss of her Far Eastern colonies to the previously despised Japanese.

Before the reality shocks of the Second World War for as long as anyone could remember, Britain had been the dominant power on the world stage. Since the Napoleonic Wars, for 136 years, British pride had been reflected in songs like '*Land of Hope and Glory!..God Who Made Thee Mighty Make The Mightier Yet!*'

In the classrooms across Britain teachers showed pupils maps of the world with the countries of the British Empire coloured in red, stretching around the globe. Children were brought up on Rudyard Kipling and '*The Empire On which The Sun Never Sets!*

But by the 1940s, the unpalatable reality was that Britain's strength had been seriously eroded by the First World War. In that conflict she had paid the highest price economically and it had cost the lives of her most outstanding young men. '*The bravest and the best'* were lost in the mud and blood of France and Flanders. The outbreak of war in 1939 was a further crucial drain on the economy and resulted in the loss of more good men.

By the end of the Second World War the glory days were gone and they would be gone forever.

But there were still many people in Britain – including, and especially Winston Churchill and his cabinet -- who were reluctant to admit that was happening. So far as they were concerned, once the war was over they would be able to go back to the good old days of Empire in the Far East. And *'God Save The King!'.*

Meantime there was a chance to let the damned Japs know who would be the real Masters again once the war was over! The *Krait* might be only a gesture just now. But it could show what the reality would be later. And Captain Ivan Lyons was just the man for the job!

It was really all a bit like a Hollywood movie starring Errol Flynn, and it read like a film script. Ivan Lyon was a glamorous young aristocrat with a huge tiger tattoo on his chest. He was related to the Royal Family through Elizabeth Bowes-Lyon. She had become queen of England when her husband ascended the throne to become King George V1 after the shock abdication of his brother Edward in 1936.

When he went to Melbourne Ivan Lyon stayed at Government House with the governor of Victoria, Sir Winston Duggan, who in turn introduced him to the Australian Governor General, Lord Gowrie. With those gold-plated references he was sent along to the Director of Naval Intelligence, Commander R.B.M Long, and the Australian Naval Board. The information – whispered discreetly behind the backs of hands – that Lyons' idea had the blessing of Winston Churchill and Lord Louis Mountbatten of SEAC (South East Asia Command) could only help to impress the men at the top.

The board supported Lyon's scheme for Operation Jaywick, and enlisted the aid of General Sir Thomas Blamey, commander-in-chief of all Australian land forces. So Operation Jaywick was underway. At least in theory.

Ivan Lyon came from a military family. His father was a general in the First World War, his forebears had been army men for generations back. It was natural that he should go to the Royal Military College at Sandhurst after leaving school. On graduating he joined the Gordon Highlanders as a lieutenant and was sent out to Singapore in 1936.

Lyon had a natural propensity for sky-larking and mischief and on one occasion, after a drinking bout with young British officers he had a huge tiger's head tattooed on his chest, in colours of scarlet, black, and yellow. *'Rimau'*.. the tiger! ... Grrr!

He joined Lieutenant Colonel Hayley Bell's intelligence network whose work was principally anti-espionage, tracking down the Japanese agents who proliferated in Singapore and Malaya.

They discovered plans for a possible Japanese invasion via Malaya years before it actually happened. But the information they supplied was not popular with the British governor and military commander who viewed them as *'alarmist'* and contrary to the official policy which was *'Against provoking Japan'*. For his pains Hayley Bell was bundled off back to England, and his unit disbanded.

Lyon remained in army intelligence, learning to speak Malay fluently, and spending time examining the islands of the Malacca Strait and the coasts of Malaya. When the final disaster came and Singapore fell in February, 1942, Lyon played an active part in assisting the vast concord of panic-stricken refugees choking the Malacca Strait and trying to escape the Japanese advance.

It was in this role that he first encountered his future command in the *Krait*. At that time she was still in her original livery as the Japanese fishing boat *Kofuku Maru*. A lean Australian former sea captain Bill Reynolds had plucked her from detention in Singapore Harbour and was ferrying refugees to the Indragiri River in Sumatra from where they could cross the mountains to be rescued by Allied ships on the west coast.

Krait carried a total of 1100 refugees to safety. A job well done. Lyon was particularly impressed by the fact that while Japanese aircraft mercilessly sank other refugee shipping, with bombs and machine gun fire, staining the waters of the Straits red with blood, *Kofuku Maru* was totally ignored. From that sprang the germ of the idea to use a vessel which the Japanese took for one of their own for a clandestine raid on Singapore. Bill Reynolds was enthusiastically recruited to the idea.

'In the unlikely event we both get out of here alive' he said, putting out his hand *'Let's take it further!'*.

They did escape, Lyon in a battered sailing boat, and Reynolds in *Kofuku Maru*, and they met again in India. Ivan Lyon took the plan in his head to Australia and Operation Jaywick was born.

Jaywick? The name given to the operation illustrates Lyon's mischievous sense of humour. 'Jaywick' was a disinfectant deodorant used in Singapore's public lavatories.

Once the *Powers-That-Be* approved the Jaywick concept a training camp was set up on the Hawkesbury River, where volunteer recruits practised unarmed combat and paddled folboats from dawn till dusk, working themselves up into peak physical readiness for the operation. Lyon's second in command, through a process of elimination, was Lieutenant Robert Page. Like Lyon he had important sources of influence. Bob Page was the nephew of Sir Earle Page, a former Australian Prime Minister. At the time of Jaywick Sir Earle was the Australian Government's representative in London.

With his group assembled and his plan refined to the last detail Lyons was frustrated by trying to get the re-named *Krait* from India to Australia at a time when German surface raiders and Japanese submarines were making life difficult for merchant shipping in the Indian Ocean. Eventually she arrived as deck cargo, and had an infuriating series of mechanical breakdowns on the east coast. It was decided to jettison her original worn-out Deutsz motor and replace it. Engines were not easy to find in war time, but eventually a brand new 103 horse power Gardiner diesel was found in Tasmania and flown to Cairns for installation.

Preparations had taken nearly a year, and Bill Reyolds finally lost patience and went into another branch of undercover work. But at last *Krait* and her crew were in Exmouth Gulf in August 1943, and ready to embark on the Jaywick adventure.

They barely made 100 metres before the mechanical curse stuck again. Her tail-shaft snapped, and *Krait* was left drifting helplessly with no propulsion. After the previous mechanical problems Lyons was left grim-faced. But in many ways it was a blessing – what if it had happened behind enemy lines? The American engineers on the USS *Chanticleer* were delighted to help, and worked non-stop with welding torches sending out hissing sprays of blue sparks for a day and a night.

Satisfied at last the engineers said *' Ok Boys! The repair will get you to Fremantle. But it's temporary -- don't count on it lasting much further than that!'.*

So the Krait left for Singapore at last, sliding out of Exmouth Gulf past the tawny twin silhouettes of the Muiron Islands, on September 2, 1943. Approaching the Lombok Strait and Enemy territory the crew were gathered together and told of their target. They had been through the methods of paddling and attaching limpet mines hundreds of times in training. They had performed a mock night raid on the shipping in Cairns Harbour for more realistic practice. This enraged the defence authorities by exposing their weaknesses, but was invaluable experience for the real thing.

The final 14 crew, now assembled, consisted of Major Ivan Lyon, Lieutenant R.C.Page, Lieutenant D. Davidson, Lieutenant H.E.Carse, telegraphist H.S.Young, Corporal R.Morris, Leading Seaman K.P.Cain, Corporal A.Crilley, Able Seamen M.Berryman, A.Jones, W.Falls, A.Huston, and F.March, Leading Stoker P.McDowell.

Hearts pounding, they ran the gauntlet of the Lombok Strait in their guise as a Japanese fishing boat. They were wary, always, of a possible interception and inspection by a Japanese seaplane or patrol boat. But that nerve-racking part of the journey was accomplished without problem, and they idled up along Borneo shores, each man covered in a sticky brown substance and wearing sarongs intended to make them look like Asian fishermen. Then *Krait* changed course and swung across to the islands of the Riau Archiplego in the approaches to Singapore.

As hoped for in the plan, the ship disguise – in the real sense no disguise because *Krait* was a genuine Japanese fishing boat – worked perfectly. Malay fishing boats and junks hurriedly scampered out of their way, Japanese aircraft took no notice of them.

Soon they were off the island of Pandjang, 60 miles south of Singapore. There the attacking party of Lyon and Houston, Page and Jones, Davidson and Falls, went ashore with their folboats, limpet mines, and a large quantity of stores. It was arranged *Krait* would wander Borneo seas, returning to pick them up after dusk on October 1st, 1943 – if they had survived their daring attempt on the shipping in Singapore Harbour! They had 12 days in which to do it.

The commandos wore black silk waterproof clothing – even black socks and sandshoes -- and each man carried a .38 revolver and 100 rounds of ammunition, with a knife and compass on his belt. Each folboat carried 300 kilograms of limpet mines and food and water for a week. As a final sinister piece of equipment each man was given a suicide pill, a cyanide capsule in a bakelite container, in case of capture and torture by the Enemy.

With their black folboats the paddlers, muscles tuned by the weeks of practice, were practically invisible in darkness, the tension increasing, as they moved from island to island at night, coming ever closer to the target. Lying in the bushes and observing their target by telescope from the closest uninhabited island of Subar, the Jaywick raiders saw Singapore Harbour and the city as a blaze of lights.

Clearly the Japanese were so confident that they saw no need for serious security measures. The attack was made after midnight on the night of September 26th, after bad weather and strong tides had defeated a couple of previous attempts. It was an unqualified success.

Limpet mines were attached to seven vessels in Keppel Harbour and the approaches to Singapore without the raiders being detected. It took 20 minutes to attach the mines to each ship, and Davidson recalled hearing the chimes of the bells of St Andrews Church, including the quarter hour notes, coming clearly across the water. Their mines set with delayed fuses, they paddled off into the night as fast as they could go. Twenty kilometers out from Singapore Harbour they heard the first explosions. *'Our speed increased phenomenally, but there didn't seem to be much excitement occurring in Singapore Harbour'* Davidson reported.

They sank seven Japanese vessels totaling 46,000 tons of shipping.

Mission accomplished, their task was now an exhausting paddle south extending over four nights to reach the rendezvous with *Krait* on October 1st. Because of the delays to the attack this was touch-and-go, with Lyon and Huston and Page and Jones missing the first pick-up. But they were safely retrieved two nights later. It was on the way home they experienced perhaps the most dangerous moment of the Jaywick operation. Radio operator Horrie Young recalled the incident in his own recollections of events.

'We made good time to the entrance of the Lombok Strait so much so that Carse the skipper reduced speed to ensure that we reached it just after dark. But the good fortune that had remained with us through the trip thus far seemed about to desert us. Somewhere around midnight the lookout on watch on top of the wheelhouse observed what he thought was a white sail some distance behind us.

' He watched it for a period and it seemed to be gaining on us quite rapidly! He then wasted no time in informing the skipper who, after observing it briefly, made a memorable quotation. " That's no sail! That's a ship with a bone in her teeth!" Meaning that the mistaken sail was in fact the bow-wave of a fast-moving vessel of much greater size than ours!

'All the officers and crew were alerted and went to their action stations. I went below to the wireless room and switched the radio equipment on for what I was sure was going to be my last radio message and waited for Lyon to draft the text along with our estimated position. Sitting on top of my radio was a wooden box a little larger than a one dozen beer bottle carton which was packed tight with plastic explosives and was connected with a detonator and fuse, the timing being to explode virtually immediately.

'Major Lyon had his hand on the 'button' and would make the fatal decision when to press. It was proposed that in the event of a situation as was seemingly about to overtake us, Carse was to try to maneuver Krait alongside the enemy craft and Lyon would detonate the explosive charge to result in the destruction of both vessels.

'It was an experience I will never forget. In fact it still haunts me in my sleep. The pursuing craft, a Japanese destroyer, very quickly overtook us and took up a position just off our port

quarter at a distance that seemed to be barely 100 yards. It then reduced speed to match our own. We were all waiting for the loud hailer to call in Japanese 'What ship? Where bound?' or perhaps a search-light to be turned on us, but neither eventuated. After pacing us for what seemed a lifetime, but which was probably not more than quarter of an hour, the vessel dropped behind us for a short period, before coming up a second time for another brief look. Then it did the unexpected, increasing speed dramatically and sped off at high speed in the direction in the direction of the northern coast of Lombok Island.

'It is not easy to explain the relief we felt at our reprieve from what had seemed certain disaster. We could scarcely believe our good fortune! Why the vessel failed to challenge Krait to identify herself has been widely discussed down through the years. But it still remains a mystery unlikely ever to be resolved'.

After being '*saved from the jaws of death*' *Krait* quietly chugged on out into the Indian Ocean at her steady six knots, as Carse set a course for Exmouth Gulf. The disguise and the Japanese flag at the stern had stood the test, the destroyer had departed about its business with a froth of white wake, and soon they were able to pull the flag down permanently and resume an Australian identity.

By October 19th, after 6400 kilometres, and 48 days, most of them in Enemy waters, they were back in the familiar surrounds of Exmouth Gulf. There, with the Cape Range in the background, they were in a mood to celebrate.

It had been a copybook operation!

WINNERS are grinners. Page, Lyon, and Davidson, celebrate their triumph of Operation Jaywick. It would be a very different story on the next operation. There were no survivors from Rimau. Their lives were thrown away, some would say needlessly, only weeks before the end of the war. (Picture: Australian War Memorial)

Tiger In A Trap

Chapter Nine

The authorities, ranging from Winston Churchill in London at Number 10 Downing Street, and Lord Louis Mountbatten in Kandy in the hills in Sri Lanka, right down to General Blamey in Melbourne, in Australia, were hugely delighted at the success of Operation Jaywick.

The team had done so well that the original intention of telling the world – and in particular the Japanese – by trumpeting the achievement as a huge publicity stunt was shelved. That decision was made on the basis that there might be other possibilities for other, even more telling raids behind Enemy lines. That was certainly where Ivan Lyon's own ambitions lay.

But there were other rewards. Ivan Lyon was promoted to Lieutenant Colonel, and the Australian Prime Minister John Curtin recommended him for the ultimate decoration, the Victoria Cross. The committee in England demurred, considering that while it had undoubtedly been a gallant action worthy of the highest praise it was not quite up to the peak standard required for the VC. In the end Lyon and Bob Page and Don Davidson were each awarded the Distinguished Service Order.

The Army members Andrew Crilley and Taffy Morris were each awarded a Military Medal, while Paddy Mc Dowell, Wally Falls, Joe Jones, and Andrew Huston received Distinguished Service Medals.

Despite the positives in the success of Jaywick, there were some significant negatives in the aftermath. The first was that at a time of the war when news of the coup would have given a great morale boost to the civilian population, both in Australia and Britain, Operation Jaywick was locked away as an official secret and the publicity value was lost.

The anticipated effect upon the Japanese enemy was also lost, since they didn't know how their ships had been sunk. In fact no-one, friend or foe, knew about Jaywick until long after the war was over. As an important negative, the Japanese, furious at the material damage caused by Jaywick, and the loss of face, decided that the cause must have been sabotage from within the Chinese community. Investigation and torture of suspects began on October 10th – later known as the *'Double Tenth Massacre'* and hundreds of quite innocent Chinese citizens of Singapore were murdered and their heads stuck on spikes of the railings around the town as retaliation against Jaywick.

The ease of the success of Jaywick inspired Ivan Lyon to further ambitious schemes for commando operations. Because Jaywick had gone so well it possibly led to an under-estimation of the dangers of operations behind enemy lines. A variety of schemes were put up to SRD (Services Reconnaissance Department) the top-secret body responsible for undercover operations of Z-Force. Suggested targets included the main Japanese base at Rabaul which was later shelved for lack of American submarine co-operation, because they had other priorities of their own. Lyon's own contribution was an ambitious scheme, code-named Operation Hornbill, for establishing an island base in the Natuna Islands in the South China Sea.

He planned to use a number of '*Country Craft*' to raid harbours and installations in Malaya and Vietnam. The vessels, similar in outward appearance to the normal junks and fishing boats in the area, would be built in Australia. Lyon, as his biographer Lynette Silver (*The Heroes of Rimau*) suggested, would be a '*Pirate King*' working from his own secret base and creating coastal chaos for the Japanese. The powers-that-be approved Hornbill, and work was well underway on the Country Craft at Melbourne. Exmouth Gulf and POT SHOT would once again be in the picture, nominated as a training base for the commandos-to-be.

A new secret weapon designed in Britain would carry the attackers and their limpet mines in the final stages. The Welman Submersible Boat, christened '*Sleeping Beauty*' by its operators, was a submersible mechanical canoe-shaped craft designed by Major *'Blondie'* Hasler of the Royal Marines in Britain for Combined Operations there.

Powered by four car batteries and an electric motor the SB had awesome potential for raids of the Jaywick type. It could run silently on the surface at 4 knots or submerged at 3 ½ knots, and it had a range of 50 kilometres. With a pilot sitting in it, clad in rubber suit and wearing breathing apparatus the SB could travel on the surface or fully submerged using a compass. Lyon traveled to England to test the new wonder and was thrilled to discover its capabilities. The folboat canoe paddled by human hands, was to the SB what the horse and cart were to the modern four-wheel drive motor vehicle.

But as Lyon's plans for SB strikes unfolded, Operation Hornbill was quietly killed by the authorities. The plan had relied on a reconnaissance of the Natuna Islands by American submarine. The Americans had agreed to co-operate on this occasion, perhaps only because they wanted to see what the British and Australians were up to. But when the time came no American submarine was available. They were all too busy in the blockade of Japan.

To be fair, when priorities are considered, there is no question but that the disruption of oil and other supplies to Japan by US Navy submarines was a major factor in bringing that nation to its knees in 1945. Operation Hornbill would have been a gnat-bite in comparison. While they were cool on Hornbill, American submarines did assist without demur on quite a number of other occasions in dropping and -- the far-riskier operation of retrieving -- Australian Z-force personnel behind enemy lines .

However the Americans generally were not impressed by British cloak-and-dagger schemes, which they saw as '*Boys Own Paper*' activity aimed at propaganda. They labeled it '*All Show And No Go!*' so far as the real war effort was concerned. Some of the British commando raids, while engendering publicity to boost national morale while the war was going badly, were the questionable schemes of Lord Louis 'Dickie' Mountbatten as Director of Combined Operations, which resulted in quite unacceptable casualties.

'*Operation Jubilee*', for instance, the ill fated raid on Dieppe in August 1942, saw nearly 5000 Canadian troops involved in the action. When the raid was over 907 were dead, 1874 captured, and 2460 wounded. A total of 3367 men, dead and alive, were left behind on the beaches. Though 227 craft were involved, including six destroyers, they were not able to rescue the entrapped commandos and they were left to their fate. Propaganda aside, and viewed objectively, it was a politically-inspired disaster.

Where behind the scenes politics were concerned in Australia, the Americans made no bones about the fact that they did not want the British involved in the Pacific theatre in any way at all.

By 1944 the tide of war had turned in the Pacific and the Americans were doing very nicely as they were, thank you.

General Douglas MacArthur in particular, the supreme commander, was not in a mood to be sharing any of the credits with his British counterparts when the long-awaited day of victory dawned.

America had done the hard work, the grim hard yards, seen the tens of thousands of body bags, and he was not going to let the British come roistering in at the last minute waving the Union Jack, and claiming a part of the glory.

So Hornbill was dead in the water. But Ivan Lyon had done so much work on the project that he was not going to abandon his schemes. *'When you come up against a brick wall find a way around it!'* So Operation Rimau was born. It was named after the tiger tattoo on Lyon's chest! *'Rimau'* was the Malayan word for tiger.

It was as well that Hornbill never got off the ground because it had some essential flaws. The British assumed, with old-school Colonial naivety, that all of the Malays and Filipinos of the region would be on their side and would both welcome and support any action against the Japanese.

That was not necessarily the case. Malays are not an aggressive or assertive people, and in pre-war Singapore the British, primarily concerned with their own self-importance, had failed to read the signs.

But after 300 years of being dominated and exploited by the Colonial powers, people in the British colonies and in Dutch Indonesia were beginning to feel stirrings of independence. Many of them, while they didn't like the means, were at first quite glad to see the British and the Dutch Colonial masters bundled out of their area.

Neither the Malays, nor the Chinese, who were actively persecuted by the Japanese invaders, liked their new hosts. Indeed, as time went by, they were deadly afraid of them with good reason. But that didn't mean that they would necessarily risk their lives and the lives of their families in undercover work for the deposed colonial powers.

On the other hand, for reasons of money or currying favour with the new masters, there were people – Quislings, as there were in all nations -- prepared to inform the Japanese of European under-cover activity in their area. Allied agents landed behind enemy lines were consistently betrayed until the very end of the war.

In island populations like Natunas there were vessels of all descriptions afloat. They ranged from trading junks down to fishing boats and even log canoes. Craft of all shapes and sizes were continually going backwards and forwards on a daily basis, just as they had for centuries.

Each skipper knew most of the other boats, and pretty much what they were about, as they criss-crossed each others' paths. If strange boats came into the area they would have been aware of them at once.

In those terms Lyon's romantic idea of a secret island base was quite unrealistic. The locals would have known about it as soon as the commandos had unloaded their first dump of arms and fuel on an island shore.

Someone, a *'Judas'* (the name used in Covert Operations for informers), would have talked for money or self-importance. A single Japanese float plane would have been able to investigate the truth of the report, with probable fatal results for those involved in the mission. The difficulty of avoiding aerial surveillance was another factor Lyon does not have appeared to have considered. That may have been because aircraft were given such low standing in his own time with the military in Malaya. The Japanese air force was far more active and efficient in occupied South East Asia.

The local factor was the weak point in all the SRD plans to drop undercover agents behind Enemy lines. Bill Reynolds, original skipper of the *Krait,* was one of those who found that out the hardest way. Dropped by the US submarine *Tate* in the Lombok Strait he was betrayed by locals and was in Japanese hands within three days. From there to face inevitable torture and execution.

That was the fate of many other brave men sent out with patriotic dreams and flawed plans. Operatives sent to their deaths behind Enemy lines. It would happen too in Lyon's last operation.

So Operation Rimau was also flawed?

Sadly, the answer has to be *'Yes!'*.

The basis of Rimau was that Lyon's group would go to the target region – another attack on Singapore shipping – by submarine, complete with limpet mines, and the SB *Sleeping Beauties*.

They would capture a local junk, transfer their SBs, weapons, and stores, and set up an island base as before. This time instead of seven ships sunk they would aim ambitiously for 60 victims! The junk would be scuttled, and the heroes of Rimau would be picked up later at an agreed date by a submarine nominated as the Royal Navy's *Porpoise*. For with the war in Europe now drawing to a close, Churchill and his War Cabinent were now anxious to have a presence in the Far East in order to re-claim the former British possessions there when the shooting stopped. This applied especially to Singapore.

But where Jaywick had gone without a hitch things started to go wrong with Operation Rimau almost from the beginning. A training and selection process was set up at Careening Bay, Garden Island, Western Australia and that proceeded apace. But there were infuriating delays with the equipment. The officer blamed for most of the foul-ups was Major Walter Chapman. He was a handle-bar-mustachioed British army equipment officer who had been sent out from England in charge of the SBs. He had the Australians' backs up from the very start, and he would assume an unfortunate importance at a later stage.

Lieutenant Commander Hubert Marsham, captain of the *Porpoise,* was very concerned about the requirement that his submarine to be exposed on the surface so close to Singapore. No British submarine had been in there since the fall of Singapore. He did not like anything about the project and was not slow to say so. It was every submarine commander's nightmare that one day he might be caught on the surface by Japanese aircraft in a situation where he was unable to crash dive as happened to the United States submarines *Harder* and *Barbel.* Operation Rimau called for the capture of a junk, and then the transfer of the SBs and operatives from the submarine. That would necessarily take some considerable surface time, probably in shallow water where a submarine was most vulnerable to air attack.

When one of the Navy operatives, Branson, broke security by telling Marsham he knew he was bound for Singapore, Marsham was furious. He wanted the operation cancelled because he said it was seriously compromised.

As the Navy saying had it '*LOOSE LIPS SINK SHIPS!'*.

Western Australian Z-force operative Jack Sue had trained at Frazer Island in Queensland, for an operation called AGAS ('Sandfly') to discover the fate of Allied prisoners of war in Borneo. He and his commanding officer Major Gort Chester went to Garden Island in WA where the Rimau group were in training with SBs and folboats.

Sue, an Australian-born Chinese, an Australian citizen all his life, spoke Malay as well as Chinese. He was ideal for behind-enemy lines work, because of his courage, and keen intelligence, and the fact that in appearance he was indistinguishable from the local population. In later years he was associated with your author in diving expeditions to 17th Century shipwrecks on the WA coast including the 1629 Dutch East Indiaman *Batavia.* He sometimes spoke of his nine months behind Japanese lines in Borneo in 1944-45.

'We went across to Garden Island to see whether the SBs were applicable for our operation' Jack Sue recalled, in one of our conversations. *'They were certainly unmatched for their purpose of limpet raids on shipping. But in the end folboats suited our long-term covert operations better'.* He grinned. *'Mind you there was nothing easy about a folboat in rough conditions with two blokes on the paddles. If you want to make your best mate your worst enemy, take him folboating!'*

At one stage there was a suggestion that Gort Chester should join Rimau. But both he and Jack Sue were alarmed by security lapses.

'The scuttlebutt in the pubs in Rockingham and Fremantle was that another Singapore raid was brewing. The mission was compromised from the start', Jack Sue said *'And that decided Gort against any involvement'.*

Instead Rimau took on a British Royal Marine, Major Reginald Ingleton. *'He was a last minute inclusion'* Sue said. *'He was a huge bloke and would have stood out like a lighthouse in a desert as a European in a Malayan situation no matter what disguise was applied. Since he had no special skills we always wondered why he had been taken on board'*.

Jack Sue's Z-force task was to go behind enemy lines in Borneo, landing from a submarine and infiltrating by folboats. His mission was to find out what was happening to 2400 Allied prisoners of war known to be at Sandakan. It was planned to mount a rescue mission by paratroops code-named 'Operation Kingfisher'.

Unforgivably the rescue plans were shelved by Australian High Command. Sue had to watch helplessly from the jungle as the Japanese marched the prisoners away on the infamous Sandakan Death March. Only six POWs of the total complement of 2400 survived.

'The failure to help those poor prisoners was one of the most disgraceful episodes of the war from the Australian side!' Jack Sue wrote, unable to contain his anger, in his book *Blood on Borneo.* '*Contrast that with the Americans' rescue of their own people in the Philippines! Japanese POW camp commanders everywhere had been instructed to liquidate their prisoners and destroy all traces in the event of any Allied invasion. Aware of that, the Americans set up a special commando detachment, the 'Alamo Scouts', and sent them in ahead of their regular troops to secure the POWs. In that way they saved the lives of 7000 men in the Philippines. The same thing could have been done at Sandakan using American DC 3s for a parachute drop. The plan was in place. But MacArthur and the Australian commander General Thomas Blamey fell out badly and that was the end of that.*

'Blamey wanted Australian troops involved at the end of the war and suggested an invasion of Borneo. MacArthur, quite rightly, said it would be pointless. The Japanese forces in Java, Borneo, and Singapore were isolated. They had no ships and no aircraft and couldn't go anywhere or become involved in any way in the defence of the Japanese Homeland. MacArthur's strategy was to go hell-for-leather against Japan itself. When the Emperor surrendered, as he inevitably must in the face of over-whelming odds, the other places would have to lay down their arms in a bloodless victory for the Allies.

'That was exactly what happened in the Dutch East Indies and Singapore. The war ended there without another shot being fired. But Blamey insisted in making landings in Borneo and Australians suffered unnecessary casualties at Tarakan and Balikpapan. More importantly nothing was done for the poor POWs at Sandakan. They were left to a horrendous fate and only a handful survived the Death March. It was a national disgrace hushed up after the war!'

It would not be the only disaster authorities tried to conceal after the end of the Second World War.

Regardless of security lapses, *Porpoise* sailed on September 9th, 1944. She left Garden Island with the 23 commandos of the Rimau force. Things were a little different from Jaywick. This time the expedition was led by British officers, had a much higher British content, and aimed for a very British result.

The Australians involved would have been quite unaware of the expectations which stretched right back to Number 10 Downing-street, with the direct personal interest of Winston Churchill in London. Or that Lord Louis Mountbatten in Ceylon who was now in charge of SEAC (South East Asia Command) was also following the operation closely.

In fact from the point-of-view of the British supreme commanders it was much more of a political exercise than a military operation. The Americans were well in control in the Pacific. By late 1944 Japanese defeat was inevitable and simply a matter of time. Whether Rimau succeeded or failed would not alter the course of the war a single tiger's whisker.

But British post-war prestige in the Far East when the fighting was over was what the mission was all about. The Union Jack would fly high again over Singapore! If the men of Rimau who were about to put their lives in deadly peril for that cause had known the reason, would it have made any difference?

Beset by grave misgivings himself as *HMS Porpoise* left Careening Bay, Commander Hubert Marsham wrote that he was reminded of the swashbuckling Elizabethan, Sir Francis Drake and his daring raids on Porto Bello in the Caribbean and Cadiz Harbour in Spain. Lynette Silver quoted him in *The Heroes of Rimau:*

'The whole business smacks of the days of Drake and Hawkins. An ambitious, dare-devil scheme proposed by a band of very gallant gentlemen, with support and backing from those in high places ..But marred by muddle and inefficiency...'

'They were words' Silver said *'That would haunt him for the rest of his life'.*

As they departed from Garden Island in Cockburn Sound it would be the first time a Royal Navy submarine had penetrated those waters since the surrender of Singapore. At a later date *Porpoise* would become the 74th and last British submarine destroyed by Enemy action in the Second World War. She was depth charged in early 1945 while laying mines in the Malacca Strait, her position betrayed by an oil leak from her creaky machinery. Marsham was not aboard.

Perhaps he had had a premonition. Stressed by the Rimau Operation he requested a transfer from sea-going duties on return to Fremantle in October 1944.

Despite his well-documented unease, the early part of the voyage went as planned. A Malay vessel, the *Mustika,* was captured. She was an Indonesian design, a prahu or tonkan rather than a Chinese junk. She sailed well, but there was a fundamental problem in that she had no motor. For that reason Marsham thought her a very bad choice. The transfer of men, the Sleeping Beauties, and the limpet mines took place. Though Marsham was in a state of constant anxiety, and at times ill-temper, eventually everything was completed to Lyons' satisfaction. There was one departure from the original plan which had called for the crew of the captured craft to be shot for security reasons – '*Dead men tell no tales!'*. Readers will be pleased to hear that instead they were taken back to Fremantle and repatriated after the war.

Major Walter Chapman had accompanied *Porpoise* and was to be the liaison officer for the pick-up. The submarine, with Chapman still aboard, left the commandos on September 30th, to '*Three Rousing British Cheers!'* in Service tradition, promising to return for the pick up at Merepas Island on November 7 to 8th, some 40 days later. It was hoped that the attack on Singapore would be made on October 10th.

The group of 23 men included veterans Bob Page, Don Davidson, Wally Falls, Andrew Huston, and Fred *'Boof'* Marsh, from the successful Jaywick Operation. Men who knew their stuff and who had been there before.

Other members of the final team were Major Reginald Ingleton, Royal Marines, Lieutenant Walter Carey AIF, Lieutenant Bruno Reymond RANR, Lieutenant Robert Ross, British Army, Lieutenant Albert Sargent AIF, Sub Lieutenant Gregor Riggs RN – the SB expert , Warrant Officer Alfred Warren AIF, Warrant Officer Jeffrey Willersdorf AIF, Sergeant Colin Cameron AIF, Segeant David Gooley AIF, Corporal Colin Craft AIF, Corporal Archibald Campbell AIF, Corporal Roland Fletcher AIF, Corporal Clair Stewart, Lance Corporal John Hardy AIF, Lance Corporal Hugo Pace. Douglas Warne AIF had the unusual distinction of being the only Private soldier in the party.

At last everything was ready in position, and *Mustika* was sailing northwards through the islands of the Riau Archipelago, poised for the strike on Singapore. Almost at the last moment – only three hours from attack time – disaster struck!

As far back as Operation Jaywick Lyons and Page had discussed what they would do if challenged by a Japanese patrol boat. Some of the suggestions were hardly practical.

For instance rowing a dinghy over with a diver disguised below it clutching a limpet mine to be placed under the patrol boat. The explosion would have killed the diver. Another idea was to let the Japanese come on board, lure them below decks and then garrotte them, taking over their uniforms.

The difficulty there, of course, was that – despite the brown-stained skins and sarongs – those aboard could be recognized as Europeans even from some distance away. Their stance, strong bodies, and physical attitudes were quite different from slimmer Asian physiques. For someone looking through binoculars from a stand-off distance of 50 to 100 metres, as would happen with a patrol boat, the disguise simply would not stand up. As indeed proved to be the case. Perhaps with this in mind Lyon had made a firm rule that only three of the smaller, darker members of the crew could be on deck in Enemy waters. The others should be below decks.

This especially applied to Major Ingleton, the huge Royal Marine who had been wished on Lyon through SEAC (South East Asia Command) by Lord Louis Mountbatten. Ingleton weighed more than 100 kilograms, was well over 2 metres tall, and could never pass himself off as Asian whatever colour he was painted. The precaution was sound, but at the vital moment it was not observed. It would have tragic results for Operation Rimau.

With no motor *Mustika* could not be guided when the wind dropped. Closing the distance to Singapore on the day of the attack, with everyone's nerves strung tight as piano wires, she drifted with the tide with sagging sails past the last island of all. It was the final point, but they passed it far too close for comfort. The island's name was Kasu, and as she rounded the southern point the tonkan came suddenly across a Malay fishing village, passing in plain sight of the shore. In fact witnesses said later that the tide took her within 20 metres of the end of the communal jetty.

In the village were a detachment of *'Heihos'*, Malays recruited by the Japanese as local police. They had the same uniforms as the Japanese military, but were not to be trusted with real rifles. They carried wooden imitations instead. *As Mustika* drifted past the jetty at 5.30 in the afternoon, apparently with most of the crew including Ingleton still on deck, the Heihos jerked to their feet with astonishment. They could plainly see that the men on board were '*Orang Putehs'*, Europeans, badly disguised as *'Northern Indians'!*

The *Heiho* 'Chief Inspector' Sidek Bin Safar, alerted his underlings Yunus, Yaha, and Atan, and sent for Ati, a Singaporean Chinese who was the only man in the village who could speak English, to act as interpreter. The party boarded the official launch, a non-descript wooden craft of about eight metres with an open rear cabin, and set off with all the official pomposity they could muster towards the *Mustika.*

To the Rimau party they would have appeared as Japanese soldiers, and they would not have known that their *'rifles'* were wooden imitations. But there was still no excuse for the undisciplined action that followed. Despite all the months of planning on how to deal with just such a situation, someone on *Mustika* panicked and fired on the Heiho launch.

Witnesses later said that the culprit was the *'English engineer'* or at least that the shots were fired on his orders. Ingleton, all too distinguishable by his huge frame, should not have been on deck in that situation in any case. The burst of Bren gun fire decimated the Heiho. Ati, the interpreter, managed to fling himself overboard as he saw the weapon leveled over the gunwhale. Three of the *Heiho* were killed in the shots that followed, but Sidek Bin Safar the 'chief inspector' also managed to dive overboard and shelter behind the launch which drifted towards the shore. He and Ati would be witnesses in the ultimate inquiry.

Aboard the *Mustika* pandemonium reigned. Ivan Lyon was probably incandescent with fury at the breaches of operational rules which saw the men on deck identified as Europeans and at the unauthorised shooting of the hapless *Heiho.* The gaffe occurred right in front of the Malayan village with the entire population watching. They had been within three hours of starting the attack on Singapore, and now, as Lyon probably saw it, their plan was in ruins!

He must have been almost deranged with anger and frustration and it apparently affected his better judgment. Only he could have given the order for the events which followed. The Malays on shore – despite a torrential rain squall which followed – saw the *Mustika* remain motionless while the commandos launched six folboats in haste from her deck.

They paddled off towards Subar Island where they had earlier established a base and left some of their number with a cache of stores. Those remaining on *Mustika,* including Lyon, launched a large rubber raft, filled it with stores, weapons, and limpet mines, and followed in their wake. Behind them there were two explosions aboard the *Mustika*, observed by those on shore. The first mine was fired to sink the craft, the second to destroy the SBs that had taken so much time and trouble to bring out from England. As the villagers watched amazed the *Mustika* slowly slid beneath the surface to end her brief participation in the Second World War.

Lyon had made a desperate change of plan. The attack on Singapore would still be carried out, but now folboats would be used as in Operation Jaywick. The raid was made at 3 a.m. that night by three folboats and at least three ships were sunk. Something had been achieved after all.

But why had Lyon changed the plan at all? They were three hours from the start of the attack and the SBs – by which they hoped to attach limpet mines to at least 60 ships – would have done the job so much better.

If the Japanese had been alerted they would have anticipated the folboats and prevented that attack. Since that was not the case, plainly the SBs could have got through and created far more damage. Surely Lyon could have pressed on with the original plan, even though the risks seemed enhanced? In fact by taking the particular action the risks were actually significantly increased.

At the time the *Heiho* were gunned down none of the villagers or the survivor Sidek had any idea of what was going on. But by abandoning and sinking *Mustika* and paddling folboats away in full sight of the village the commandos showed the astonished villagers a pre-view of their method of transport and attack. They left the submerged wreck with the ruined SBs for the Japanese to investigate with divers.

As it turned out sinking *Mustika* and the SBs was all for nought. Sidek Bin Safar, the chief *Heiho,* did not have direct radio or telephone contact with his Japanese masters. No doubt shaken by his narrow escape and the deaths of his associates, he did not immediately go to Blankan Padang Island in the *Heiho* boat to report the incident. He left it until the following day many hours after the commando attack on Singapore. Even then the message was not passed on to Singapore for another three days. So that there would have been ample time after all for Rimau to have used the SBs, to have carried out the original plan, and to have cleared out of the area.

Only Lyon or another member of the Rimau group could have explained the reasons for the course of action taken. But none of them would ever see Australian shores again, nor would anything more be heard from them. The remaining evidence came from the Japanese as they chased the commandos from island to island of the Riau Archipelago. The other sources of information were the statements of Malay witnesses at the later inquiries.

While most of the island Malays steadfastly refused to give the Japanese police -- the notorious Kempei Tai -- any information about the commandos and suffered torture and imprisonment as a result -- there were others all too eager to tell all they knew. One of these was a village headman named Raja Mun.

Four days after the attack, on their way to the pick-up rendezvous Lyon, Ross, Davidson, Campbell, and Stewart, paddled ashore and called at villages on the islands on their escape route seeking information on Japanese shipping. Lyons talked freely in Malay to villagers who were curious about their folboats and the fact that they were carrying Sten guns and pistols. As soon as they departed Raja Mun was on his way to give the vital information of their whereabouts to the Japanese.

As a result those five commandos were cornered at Soreh Island by a large Japanese force in landing barges and forced to make their last stand there. At midnight on October 16, fighting to the last, Lieutenant Colonel Ivan Lyon and Lieutenant Bobby Ross were killed by a Japanese grenade after they had killed 40 of their attackers and wounded more than 20 of them.

Davidson and Campbell escaped, though wounded, and dragged themselves up on rocks on another island, too weak to go further. When the Japanese arrived there they found them sitting up in lifelike positions leaning against some rocks and approached with caution. But Lieutenant Commander Donald Davidson and Corporal Archie Davidson were both already dead. They had bitten into their cyanide capsules rather than be captured.

The other Rimaus managed, by a combination of determination and good luck, to keep a jump ahead of the Japanese searchers and reach their rendezvous point at Merepas Island. They waited for that hoped-for day in early November when the submarine would arrive to take them away.

But, incredibly, the submarine did not arrive on the due date, nor did it show up for another 13 days. An unlucky number indeed. The Rimaus did not know that *Porpoise* had been withdrawn because of mechanical problems, and that Marsham had been relieved of command following his own request to be removed from active duty.

The British submarine now given responsibility for Rimau was *HMS Tantalus,* commanded by Lieutenant Commander Hugh *'Rufus'* Mackenzie. Major Walter Chapman was on board as liaison officer for the Rimau group.

Mackenzie disliked being involved with undercover work, and he was desperate to increase his number of *'kills'* for the war. He considered looking for *'targets'* in the area more important than making the rendezvous on time. That was where the situation became decidedly murky. The American code-breaking system in Australia, code-named *'Ultra'* picked up intercepts of Japanese radio messages as early as October 15th. One of the intercepts read, in part:

'Abut 20 people including Caucasians have been engaged in a defensive stand in the northern part of the Riau Archipelago since the 10th of October ... Even though the Army is searching them out maintain strict watch in the Riau Archipelago and Bulan Straits!'.

Plainly the Rimaus were in grave danger. Logically SRD in Melbourne, and Captain L.M.Shadwell commander of the Royal Navy submarine group in Fremantle should have been notified. Following that, a message that an urgent situation existed should have been passed on to *Tantalus* and Rufus Mackenzie. There is no record that anything of that sort ever happened.

Why not? The Americans were always nervous that the Japanese might learn that their codes had been broken and that their communications were being read. They had no knowledge themselves of Rimau, because of Australian secrecy, and may have decided that the intercept was not sufficiently relevant or urgent to risk passing on to the Australians. Unaware, Mackenzie decided to ignore the initial rendezvous date and continue his patrol. Major Walter Chapman, who should have insisted that prior arrangements should be adhered to, apparently concurred with him.

Meantime the Rimaus had fought a desperate action against a superior force of Japanese who arrived on Merepas – the pick-up island – by landing barge. Riggs and Cameron were killed fighting a rear-guard action, and the other commandos retreated to another island, Mapor. From there two men paddled every night from November 7th., to wait at the rendezvous point, *'the hammock tree'* on Merepas, returning to Mapor at daybreak. At that point there were 17 men of the original 23 still at large and ready to be rescued.

Meantime *Tantalus* continued her patrol, which was singularly unsuccessful in finding targets. Frustrated, Mackenzie contacted his base on November 11th requesting a further postponement of the rendezvous date. Surprisingly Captain Shadwell in Fremantle agreed.

Even more astonishingly Walter Chapman, as Rimau's representative, failed to press the needs of the beleaguered commandos.

Disgracefully *Tantalus* would not arrive off Merepas until 13 days later. Even more disgracefully, though a map and Davidson's detailed instructions had been left with *Porpoise,* the submarine surfaced on the wrong side of the island! Chapman and his companion Corporal Croton landed at a difficult boulder-strewn spot. By the time they had hiked across the island daylight was breaking and the two paddlers who had been there that night, by abysmal luck, were already on their way back to Mapor.

Chapman found many signs left by the commandos on the island. But he concluded that they had left the area, estimating a date of departure of 14 days earlier. Though how he came to that opinion was never quite clear. When he was picked up again by *Tantalus* the following night he reported to Mackenzie. They concluded that nothing could be achieved in making further attempts at a rendezvous. *Tantalus* sailed for Fremantle. The Rimaus, unable to believe that they had been abandoned, manned the rendezvous point for 30 days until time ran out for them. Some were killed in firefights with the Japanese. Two drowned, and two others –Willersdorf and Pace – actually sailed in stolen local sailing craft 3000 kilometres to Ramdung Island near Timor.

They were only 600 kilometres from Australia when islanders turned them over to the Japanese. They both died in captivity from ill-treatment.

Ten others, including Rimau's second-in-command Robert Page, were captured and taken to Singapore there to be tried as spies. They were executed at Bukit Timai, on Singapore Island, by beheading with Samurai swords. With that bloody deed all the gallant men of Operation Rimau were dead.

Five weeks later the war ended.

Instead of the huge burst of triumphant pro-British publicity that Churchill and Lord Louis Mountbatten had hoped for, Operation Rimau had turned into an unacceptable tragedy. Worse, there were shabby aspects which those in high places determined to cover up because they did not reflect well on people at all levels of command. There were no medals for the heroes of Rimau, men with an average age of 26 years, who gave their lives for their country. There were no thanks for their sacrifice, nor even recognition of any kind, though they had shown courage and fighting qualities which should have made their nation proud.

Instead the government and SRD put a blackout on anything to do with the calamitous expedition, and Jaywick – though an outstanding success – was similarly blanketed as though it too had '*Never Happened'*. It was not until the war had ended that the relatives were able to discover the fate of their loved ones. Australians in general did not hear about Jaywick or Rimau or the grim tragedy of the Sandakan Death March until many years after the war.

An important researcher into the truth of what occurred was a modern Australian Army commando, Major Tom Hall, himself trained in folboats, who came upon the story quite by accident. As he investigated more details emerged of first the triumphant Operation Jaywick and then the tragic Operation Rimau. He was amazed and disturbed by what he discovered.

In his research he went first to Australian war records as a logical starting point. Then he traveled to Indonesia in search of eye-witnesses in 1981. In 1990 he went further to Britain to comb through official records and interview people connected with those wartime events. They included Ivan Lyon's son Clive, who had joined his father's regiment the Gordon Highlanders.

For, in the greatest irony of all, while Lyon thought his wife Gabrielle and Clive were dead, in fact they were still very much alive. They were sent to a Japanese prison camp after the capture of their ship in the Indian Ocean, and survived the war hoping that Ivan too, was still living.

Major Hall also travelled to Singapore, the Riau Archipelago, and the regions where the heroes had fought and died. At Soreh Island he actually recovered and brought back the skull of Sergeant Colin Cameron, whose body had remained unburied. Returning it to Australia for decent burial. Most of the other Rimaus, including Ivan Lyon and Robert Page are buried in Kranji War Cemetery in Singapore.

Hall was listed as one of the '*200 Unsung Heroes*' at Australia's Bicentennial celebrations in 1988 for his work on the commando records. He turned his material over to the Australian War Memorial and to author Lynette Silver who wrote two of the most compelling books on the subject. They were titled: *Krait, the Fishing Boat That Went to War* and *The Heroes of Rimau.* Another recommended excellent source of information is *Kill The Tiger* by Peter Thompson and Robert Macklin.

There were two postscripts. The *Krait,* which after the war went as a carrier to a Borneo timber company, was rescued and brought back to Australia. She was restored to her wartime state, largely by public subscription, and is now at the Australian Maritime Museum in Sydney.

The Australian Commando Association, of which Tom Hall was a member, were furious at the mean refusal by the Australian government and the Defence Department to grant awards to the Rimau men.

In defiance the Association created its own medal, the *Commando Cross* of *Honour,* and in July, 1978 presented medals to Rimau relatives at the Great War Memorial at Hyde Park in Sydney. Prominent on the medal, appropriately, is the word VALOUR. Jack Sue was awarded the Distinguished Conduct Medal, the DCM, for his work in Borneo.

In Britain, in May 1964, police were called to a car parked outside the district hospital in the town of Amersham, in Buckinghamshire. It was reported that there was a dead man inside the vehicle. There they found the body of Major Walter Chapman, who had left the Rimau commandos to their fate 20 years earlier. Information had been gleaned earlier in England than Australia about the bungled operation and the fact that 17 men, the bulk of the party, could and should have been saved. Chapman had been interviewed by a war historian a few days previously, in what must have been an uncomfortable experience for him.

Following that he took his life by unscrewing the small black Bakelite container he had been given as a member of the ill-fated Operation Rimau 20 years previously.

When he bit on the cyanide capsule it contained he became the last Rimau casualty.

In Exmouth, Western Australia, there is a monument to the *Krait* and her gallant crew by the shore at Learmonth where the US Navy's POT SHOT Base once stood. A number of Exmouth streets are named after the heroes of Operations Jaywick and Rimau.

This book was written in part at 8 Page Street in John Barrymore's house. The street named after Lieutenant Robert Page, DSO. A very gallant officer and gentleman, executed in Singapore by Samurai sword, at Bukit Timah, on July 7th, 1945.

Other Jaywick-Rimau Exmouth street names include Lyon, Ross, Marsh, Warne, Willersdorf, Stewart, Harding, Gooley, Fletcher, Ingleton, Huston, Reymond, Riggs, and of course the *Krait* herself. *'The fishing boat that went to war',* to quote Lynette Silver.

We should not forget them!

American Ambassador Edward Clark congratulates the Australian Prime Minister Harold Holt at the official opening of the American base at Exmouth on September 17, 1967. Three months later Holt was drowned in a diving accident at Portsea, Victoria. The Americans re-named the base in his honour, the US Naval Communication Station Harold E.Holt. (Picture: Doug Bathgate)

SEEN FROM THE AIR the VLF (Very Low Frequency) towers at North West Cape dominate the scene. The central Tower Zero was Australia's tallest man-made structure in 1967, and 40 years later it was still the tallest construction in the Southern Hemisphere. World-wide, at 387 metres or 1276 feet, it was taller when completed than the Eiffel Tower in Paris or the Empire State Building in New York. Exmouth was the largest VLF transmitter in the world. (Picture: Peter Billingham)

THE HELIX ROOM showing the massive Helix coil. The electronic gear dwarfs the man standing in the door way, lower right. (Pictures: Karin Calvert Borshoff).

HUMPBACK WHALES delight in throwing their huge bodies into the air, crashing back in a welter of foam. Why do they do it? Just for fun the scientists say! (Picture: Douglas Coughran)

TALE OF A WHALE. Humpbacks sometimes like to stand on their heads for long periods with their tails out of the water. It's handy for scientists because each tail has different markings which identify individuals like fingerprints identify humans.

"COME DANCE WITH ME!" Jane Liddon trips the light fantastic with a Potato Cod partner. (Picture: Hugh Edwards)

MANTA RAYS are among the largest and most spectacular sea creatures to be encountered on the Ningaloo Reef. They interact well with divers. (Picture: Geoff Taylor)

DUGONGS are another large denizen found in Ningaloo waters. Shy animals, they test a photographer's patience, but are worth the effort for a unique experience. Calves stay with their mothers, swimming in unison, until they are quite large. (Picture: Hugh Edwards)

RHINCONDON TYPUS, the giant whale shark, at 13 to 14 metres is the world's largest fish, and king of the Ningaloo Reef. Here Doug Seiffert of the United States takes a memorable picture. Divers come from all over the world to swim with Exmouth's whale sharks. (Picture: Hugh Edwards)

WHALE SHARK reflections. (Picture: Geoff Taylor)

LEAPING BLACK MARLIN is the reason why Exmouth is a Mecca for game fishermen from all over Australia. Today's fishermen operate on a principle of 'tag and release'. (Picture: Jeni Gates)

A BROADBILL SWORDFISH and Matt and Jeni Gates of Exmouth's Bluewater Tackle.

IF YOU BELIEVE the author's story that he caught this magnificent 75 pound Spanish mackerel with a cotton reel and a bent pin, then you'd probably believe anything! Ask Charlie! (Picture: Leone Broadhurst)

SEEING IS BELIEVING. Barbara O'Dowd really is hand-feeding this giant moray eel. But beware – morays have sharp teeth and short tempers. Feeding them is not advised for inexperienced divers. Count your fingers! (Picture: Hugh Edwards)

Pastoral Life In A Cold War Peace

Chapter Ten

Christmas 1945 was always remembered as being one of the great celebrations. Bing Crosby was singing *'I'm Dreaming Of A White Christmas!'*. The Second World War was over at last, and most of the 'boys' had come home for their first Christmas in years. Some of the Australian soldiers, sailors, and airmen, had memories of death and destruction they would not forget until the day they died.

But for wives and sweethearts and loved ones there was simply a huge sense of relief. Whatever happened in the future, at least their men would not be lying under a white cross in some war cemetery in a foreign land.

Japan had surrendered on August 15th, after the Atomic bombs on Hiroshima and Nagasaki. The documents of surrender were signed by General Douglas MacArthur on board the battleship USS Missouri in Tokyo Bay, on September 2nd, 1945.

In Australia, as everywhere, the news was received with joy. In the months that followed there were some more mixed reactions. The Australian government had heavily censored all war news. The southern newspapers never carried a line about the news that Darwin had been bombed 45 times. Let alone the details of the awesome destruction on February 19th, 1942, '*Australia's Pearl Harbour*', when 21 ships were sunk in the harbour and 251 people killed, and 350 wounded. It was something of a shock when people found out after the war.

The fact that there were 97 Japanese air raids on Australia also remained '*Classified*', so did the information that 49 vessels, including the hospital ship *Centaur*, were sunk off the Eastern Australian coast by German and Japanese surface raiders and submarines at a cost of 1287 lives.

The air raid on Broome, on March 2, 1942, saw 16 flying boats burned on Roebuck Bay, in which screaming refugees were incinerated. Eight other aircraft were destroyed and about 100 people were killed. The official version hardly matched actual events.

The statement from the Prime Minister John Curtin read: *'Rumours to the effect that loss of life in the Broome raid yesterday were very heavy is utterly untrue. It is not in the National interest to make any statement giving details of casualties at any place as this will give valuable information to the enemy. I can assure the Australian public, however that while losses have been incurred – whether they be life or property – the raid was not of a kind to give that satisfaction to the enemy'*.

As Napoleon is said to have cynically remarked *'In wartime truth becomes the first casualty!'*

War has always been an ugly business, and news for the civilian population during the Second World War was effectively controlled by the Authorities. We were carefully protected from the reality. In Australia we were kept in a Fool's Paradise, never knowing how real the threat of invasion was or how close the Japanese came to our shores in New Guinea. Or how fragile our defences actually were.

It would be alleged later that wartime strategists had believed that the forces available were not sufficient to defend the continent as a whole in the event of a Japanese invasion. It would only be feasible, it was thought, to defend Australia's south eastern corner. Naturally theories about a '*Brisbane-Adelaide Line'* were denied by government once the war was over. There were, after all, future voters in Queensland, Western Australia, and the Northern Territory who would have been unimpressed to learn that they and their property had been considered expendable!

There was plenty of other news about the war while it was being waged because it was everybody's immediate concern. But all reports were strictly sanitised. Newsreels showed tanks rolling into battle, but never a fire-gutted tank with a row of crisped and blackened bodies beside it. Nor did we see the surgeons in the field hospitals stained crimson with blood from head to foot as they amputated limbs and desperately tried to save lives.

Instead we had shots of Winston Churchill, cigar clamped between his jaws, giving the *'V for Victory'* sign with two fingers to cheering crowds. Or General Montgomery, *'Monty'*, wearing a Digger hat, poring over a terrain map on the front of a weapons carrier in the desert sands of the North African campaign. His moustache twitching as he devises plans to defeat his arch enemy Erwin Rommel. *'The Desert Fox'* , the classic Teuton with the Iron Cross at his throat.

Or perhaps General Dwight D. Eisenhower in sunglasses with a flower-burst of ribbons and medals on his chest, being driven in a jeep on a country road in Normandy.

The rationale, of course, was to keep up morale up among the civilian population and to keep recruits coming to fill the ranks to replace those they failed to mention. Casualty lists being bad for public morale. There was another aspect which involuntarily assisted the administration. That was the technical fact that the fact that most news films made before 1944 were in black-and-white. We could never have seen the colour of blood even in the unlikely event that someone really wanted to show it to us.

But when Germany was overrun and Japan surrendered it was an entirely different matter. Now both the British and American administrations were pleased to allow views of some of the ghastly realities to show how tough it had been. They were also outraged by what they found at the end of hostilities and determined to show the world the full extent of Nazi and Bushido brutality.

By coincidence colour film had also become generally available for news photography. After the years of keeping the savage reality of war from the civilian population it was suddenly thrust upon us, no-holds -barred, and graphically illustrated in every gruesome detail.

We saw the German death camps in full colour. The horrors of Belsen with the skeletal figures of prisoners nearer to death than life tottering in bizarre red-and-white striped uniforms. The gas chambers and gallows in the background. Or US marines turning Japanese defenders into orange human torches by flushing them out of pill boxes on Pacific islands with flame throwers. Or the figure of 28 million Russian dead.

The real war – as opposed to the phony censored version – was necessarily so cruel, so barbaric, so ugly, that the reaction in the immediate post-war period was sombre. The joy of victory was replaced by a dark realization of what had actually occurred. You had to be glad it was over – But oh! What a dreadful price the world had paid!

And over all the sinister mushroom-cloud shadow of that terrible new weapon, the Atomic Bomb!

Retrospection did not have an important place by the shores of Exmouth Gulf in the years immediately after the Second World War as the stations got *'Back to normal'*. Things were very much the same as they had been in the 1930s. But the important difference was that in 1949 there was a world record price for fine merino wool.

In the heady days of *' A pound a pound!'* station wool growers in parts of the country blessed with good roads began driving high-priced Jaguar and Riley motor cars bought with bountiful wool cheques. When they went to town they stayed in the best Melbourne and Sydney hotels. There was no question of any of that in Exmouth Gulf where the roads were still better suited to camel wagons than pedigreed vehicles designed for London's Pall Mall. The luxury models with low-slung engine sumps, gear boxes and exhausts were never intended to leave the bitumen. They sometimes embarrassingly dragged their underside genitalia off on the fearsome bumps and *'Washaways'* of the Nor' West. Territories where roads had real teeth!

On stations in the Kimberley and remoter areas of the *Outback* like Exmouth most of the work was still done on horseback. Musterers rode their mounts and pack-horses carried the gear for mustering camps as they had since the 1890s. But things would change rapidly, as they did everywhere, after the war.

Ex-army jeeps and 4-wheel-drive Chevrolet ex-military trucks known as *'Blitz Buggies'*, from military surplus auctions would make a difference. British Landrovers came on the market in the 1950s as small but willing work-horses. They were followed by Toyota Landcruisers (*'Tojos'*) with more brute strength and towing capacity. Nissan Patrols, and the post war Willys Jeep – most of the wartime ones had been built by Ford – made up the numbers.

While horses came to be used less and less, there was never a mechanical dog. Man's best friend was indispensable in working sheep, particularly at shearing time. Kelpies and blue heelers still played their part. On stations such as Exmouth Station, run by Gerry Lefroy who bought the property in 1932, and passed it on to his son John, and at Giralia, run by Denver and Rae Blake, Aboriginal workers continued to play a significant part in the post war years. They were important at mustering and shearing times, and were in demand on all the stations for their general bush skills.

This conflicts with a legend widely-held in Exmouth town since it was established in the 1960s. There was a story that the area was considered cursed by Aborigines because some natural disaster had occurred around or before 1900. It was said that none of the Carnarvon or Onslow Aborigines would go there because of the '*Bad spirits'*.

'I heard the story myself in Exmouth' said Denver Blake of Giralia Station. *'But I never heard it from any of the Aboriginal men and women I employed in all the 50 years I was on Giralia. There were a lot of them through there in my time. Syd Dale a Carnarvon elder in later years always said that he was born on Giralia. Certainly our Aborigines had superstitions, but not that one'*.

Nonetheless the legend persisted and it was a fact that Exmouth was alone among towns of the North West in one aspect. While there were several families, unlike every other town in the North there was no significant population of Aborigines.

It was variously suggested that the tribe at the Cape had been over whelmed by a *tsunami* tidal wave -- the violent Indonesian volcanic explosion of the island of Krakatoa in 1883 which caused the deaths of 36,000 people was put forward as a possibility. The other theory for tribal extinction related to a smallpox or measles epidemic, the diseases contracted from Asians brought down as indentured labour for the pearling fleet. It was mentioned by Jack Valli in his book *Gascoyne Days*. Local historian R.C.Gordon in a *History Of North West Cape* also espoused the view.

Gordon wrote *'Much speculation exists over the disappearance of Aborigines from the Cape. It is known they were here originally because Tom Carter studied the Talandji tribe, as they were called. Today relics can be found of their tools and utensils and human remains in the proximity of the ruins of the Point Coates whaling station. However between Carter's period of permanence (1889 to 1904) and the recent occupation no sightings of Aborigines in their native state have been recorded. Two theories exist and are freely quoted in explaining the absence of Aborigines but neither has any conclusive proof.*

'One concerns a huge wave that swept over the Cape drowning many natives. A legend based on their superstitions has developed from this event and their absence is explained by their fear of a repetition'.

Professor Alan Dench of the Centre for Linguistics at the University of Western Australia, grew up in Carnarvon, and had a strong association with the area. He had an especial interest in Aboriginal languages and local history and had obviously heard the legend too. An essay titled *The Aboriginal People Of The North West Cape* by Dench was included with the manuscript of Monte Sala's book *The Stefano Castaway* about the two Stefano survivors.

Professor Dench wrote '*Aboriginal people in the Gascoyne and Ashburton districts today know very little about the people of the Cape. The area is often described as a dangerous place, somewhere where Aboriginal people from the surrounding areas would not, until very recently, willingly go. For the people of the Pilbara the disappearance of the Yinikutira remains a mystery. Popular legend has it that it is possible to stumble on heaps of bones on the beach or in the bush as if the people had died in their hundreds....'* He concluded the essay *'From this limited information we can confidently assume that the Yinikutira fell victim to some epidemic disease, brought to them by contact with the pearling fleet..'.*

That is not to be critical of Alan Dench. He was putting the majority view. There was even an official endorsement of the legend from Commonwealth Government sources in January 2008. A *History of the Ningaloo Marine Park* put out by the Department of the Environment and Water Resources stated: *'Aboriginal people are reported to have left the Cape Range peninsula either before or shortly after European settlement possibly due to the introduction of diseases by whalers and pearlers operating out of Exmouth Gulf'.*

The same report claimed that '*There are no shipwrecks in the Commonwealth waters of Ningaloo Marine Park'*. This is technically correct but is nonetheless a very misleading statement. There are more than 20 major shipwrecks, scattered along the Ningaloo Reef starting with the 1811 *Rapid* and 1816 *Correo da Azio*, and ranging from sailing ships like the 1875 barque *Stefano*, to modern steamers such as the 1909 *Mildura.* and the Japanese *Chofuku Maru* of 1931. However, technically-speaking, Commonwealth waters start three nautical miles offshore and extend to about nine miles out to sea, while the WA State Government waters form the three nautical miles immediately off shore. The wrecks, of course, tend to be in the shallow inshore waters.

Finally, on the subject of the Aboriginal *'Disappearance'* from the North West Cape we have a statement from Aboriginal people themselves. At a presentation by the North West Cape Exmouth Aboriginal Corporation, on May 5th, 2006, it was stated that *'People from the North West Cape (also known as Madman's Corner) left the NWC and shifted to the Ashburton and Gascoyne areas in the late 1800s and 1900s. This action was due to the unacceptable conditions imposed upon them from the pastoral and pearling industries'.*

Reflecting on the theories from so many disparate sources, it would take a brave man indeed to challenge the legend. But perhaps the story does call for a closer examination.

For instance it is certain that the Aborigines of the Cape would have experienced both tidal waves and storm surges associated with cyclones and possibly undersea volcanic events several times a century. Over 30,000 years there must have been numerous cataclysms of Nature. Even in our own time there are records of storm surges crossing the sand dunes and reaching several kilometres inland together with wind forces of over 200 kilometres per hour. Certainly not situations of a '*Storm in a tea cup!*'.

But Aborigines would have been familiar with the signs of an approaching cyclone from their own experience and from observing the movements of insects and animals. For example they told Tom Carter, the '*Birdman*', that when they saw frigate birds, usually only found much further north, wheeling over-head, they knew a *'Big wind'* was coming and would make for the shelter of the high ground in the ranges.

There is no doubt that there would have been epidemics, and deaths from introduced disease. Aborigines initially had no immunity to European and Asian illnesses and suffered greatly in consequence. The Malay, Chinese, and Japanese, involved in pearling, brought the unwelcome gifts of leprosy, smallpox, and venereal disease to offset their value to the industry. Records exist of epidemics from King Sound, Beagle Bay and Broome, to as far south as Shark Bay from the 1880s onwards. With the pearling activity in Exmouth Gulf Aborigines there would not have been spared. Europeans brought measles and influenza, both deadly for dark-skinned people.

The Great 'Flu Pandemic of 1918 killed hundreds of white people as well as Aborigines, and no-one was safe anywhere in Australia. The 'flu penetrated even to areas as remote as Western Australia's gold mining town of Meekatharra, where the community was particularly hard hit. The saddest sight in the cemetery there are tiny bassinet-sized graves, fenced by iron railings, erected by heart-broken parents. They are the graves of the babies who died in the epidemic.

The top of the Dampierland Peninsula north of Broome was a place as far from anywhere as you could find in Australia. It was reachable only by mission boat or pearling lugger. But the 'flu arrived there anyway, and showed no discrimination. Among others it killed Harry Hunter, pearler and beachcomber, and patriarch of the area. His relatives were so afraid of the deadly sickness that they hurriedly took up the deceased Harry, still in his iron-ended double bed, and buried him bed and all, in the high crest of the sandhill above Hunter's Creek.

Who knows how many may have died from the various sicknesses and illnesses on the North West Cape? But the suggestion that they died in hundreds seems unlikely. The Aborigines the *Stefano* boys encountered scarcely numbered more than 50 people in each tribal group. There were never very many of them in the first place, even before the coming of the white man because of the limited food and water resources in a harsh region.

Until recent times individual Aboriginal skeletons could often be seen in sand dune blow-outs on Cape coasts, particularly near the old whaling station at Norwegian Bay where the author saw a number in the 1980s. But this is where the tribes traditionally buried their dead, and there is nothing sinister about natural deaths exposed by natural causes.

Human skeletons have also been found in and around the sand dunes along the Gulf side of the Cape. These mainly date back to the early cyclonic pearling disasters. Bodies of drowned seamen were often decomposing and in poor condition when found. The burial parties had an unenviable task. They tended to bury the bodies above the high-tide mark usually in haste and not particularly deeply at the places where they had washed up.

But the fact is that the essence of the legend is in error.

Aborigines at the Cape, while perhaps reduced in numbers by sickness and social changes, were never entirely wiped out. In fact they remained a visible presence until the Second World War.

In that sense the best answer in dealing with the legend lies in the records of the King family recorded in an earlier chapter.

The excellent photographs taken by Bill King in the 1920s show Aborigines still engaged in various activities on the North West Cape. One of his pictures portrays a group of six young men and three women (and a dog) fishing in Yardie Creek. They are mostly young men and fishing with '*Spears and nets made from bowed sticks to put tension on the vines with which they were laced'*. Exactly as described by the lads from the *Stefano,* in 1876.

King has a number of other photographs of Aborigines and states that '*There were about 30 Aborigines living in the traditional way at Yardie Creek in 1920'*. He said that there also were a similar number also living a tribal existence at Kuberoo Well where the town of Exmouth would one day be built.

The Japanese wheat-carrier *Chofuku Maru* was wrecked near Point Cloates in February, 1931, while endeavouring to assist another Japanese ship, the *Shunsei Maru*, which had stranded on the reef. The *Shunsei Maru* was eventually freed and re-floated, but the *Chofuko Maru* became a total loss. The news of the vessels in distress was carried to the whaling station by Aborigines.

In a paper read by Maurice MacBolt, the former whaling station engineer, to the Augusta Historical Society in 1976 he recalled:

'The stranding of the Shunsei Maru was reported to the whaling station by an old Aboriginal 'Long Tommy' and his wife Mary Ann, on the morning of February 5th, 1931. I went with two men to the ship in a small launch. The Japanese crew, totalling about 50 men, were not happy about coming ashore as they could see about 20 Aborigines who had spears, as they had been fishing and getting turtles. I went ashore to the natives and told them that the Jerridy-Jerridy (' rice-eaters'), as they called the Japanese were a bit scared about coming ashore because of them. The Aborigines thought that a huge joke! The leader of the Aboriginal tribe was known as 'Dingo Charlie'. All the natives – about 20 adults – were full-bloods and could all speak English'.

So Charlie (*'Challi'*) from Charlie Tuckey days was still a popular name for the strong man of the tribe, and groups of Aborigines were still living in a traditional manner on the North West Cape into the 1920s and '30s. Contacts with Aborigines appear frequently in the records of the lighthouse keepers between the wars and one lighthouse keeper was officially in trouble for having sexual relations with an Aboriginal woman.

Indigenous people probably continued to live along the Cape until the Second World War intervened. When Japan entered the war and the Americans set up POT SHOT, the highly secret base at Exmouth, then – and probably only then – the authorities would have said '*You can't stay here now!'* and the Aborigines in the area were ' *Moved inland* ' for *'Security reasons'*.

This happened all along the North West coast from the Kimberley southwards. The authorities had an irrational and paternalistic fear that if the Japanese invaded Aborigines might be *'Coerced'* into acting as guides. Jack Valli states in *Gascoyne Days* that Carnarvon and Gascoyne Aborigines were moved inland.

'In those scary days' he wrote *'It was also decided to send many Aborigines inland for their protection, particularly so that they could not be coerced by the enemy into use as guides'.*

The same situation applied at Onslow. At Exmouth the Allies were paranoid about secrecy, with daily passwords and en-coding all radio communications from Pot Shot Base.

It seems certain that this mind-set would also have applied to end the residence of the remnants of the tribal Aborigines on the North West Cape. Was there an official order, something on the record, to that effect?

Probably, but like so much else of a possibly future controversial nature, it was most likely expunged from the files at war's end. After four years away the North West Cape Aborigines did not go back to their old haunts except to work on stations like Giralia. Their 30,000 year tenure of life in the wild on the North West Cape had ended.

There would be other quite extra-ordinary changes at Exmouth Gulf. But they would not be immediate. One, sadly, was perhaps Australia's most widely publicised false alarm, when the stock market went wild and Exmouth was tipped for a million dollar future. A geological survey of the Exmouth Gulf region in 1940 had revealed promising features and aroused the interest of oil drillers: But the war and Pot Shot's secret nature forced a postponement. In 1953 following further surveys by Ampol, West Australian Petroleum (WAPET) took a major gamble and moved into the old RAAF area at Learmonth.

Apart from a promising geological report, Exmouth had the practical advantages of an air-strip at Learmonth which could take the largest commercial aircraft. There was a jetty – somewhat cyclone-damaged, but repairable -- and some of the remaining RAAF quarters which also fitted that description.

The WAPET base finally consisted of four 20-man dormitories, 17 two-man huts, a general building with dining room, kitchens, recreation room, and library. There were also administrative buildings, generator houses, garage, carpenter shop, and four warehouses. All this before finding a single drop of oil! And for just a moment the effort and the expenditure looked to be rewarded.

There was wild jubilation around Australia when the first hole was drilled at Shot-hole canyon and on December 4th, 1953 the newspaper headlines shouted OIL FLOWS AT 500 BARRELS A DAY! The strike was on the front page of every daily newspaper in Australia in giant type, and the stock-market went predictably crazy.

Alas, the celebrations were premature. The next nine holes drilled disappointingly were *'Dry'* and the supply from the first hole was not deemed sufficient to make it a commercial prospect. WAPET reluctantly moved on. They shifted their drilling rig from Rough Range to the Cape Range, and though they drilled to 15,169 feet on their second well, the result was the same. WAPET then moved their rigs to the off-shore islands. The company drilled another 93 wells and spent nearly $80 million dollars over the next 12 years before at last striking *'BLACK GOLD'* on Barrow Island. A remarkable record of faith and persistence. Today the North West Shelf is Australia's most important source of oil and natural gas, and WAPET's history is a wonderful success story.

While they found no commercial oil at Exmouth WAPET left a permanent legacy. They spent a considerable sum of money building roads to deliver their heavy equipment into Shot-hole Canyon and the Cape Range. The Charles Knife Road, climbing 1000 feet in the space of one mile along knife-edge ridges, is the most spectacular, with breath-taking views and scenic beauty. A gift for future generations of tourists.

Young Denver Blake and his good friend John *'Buster'* Ednie-Brown, both 20-year-olds, set off for Giralia Station in a Willys Jeep in 1953. They were buoyed by the hopes and dreams of youth, but when they reached journey's end they found that it was like taking a step backwards in time. *'The bitumen ended just after the Murchison River'* Denver recalled. *'After that it wasn't a road, just a quarter mile width of dust and gravel and you made your own track around the pot-holes and washaways. The corrugations were like waves in the sea. Every so often you'd find a vehicle abandoned by the side or the road, or a broken trailer or a collapsed caravan for which the conditions had proved too much.*

'The wrecks stayed there for years and became landmarks. If it rained trucks went down to their axles in mud and nobody moved.

'When the rivers were in flood the water went over the top of the bridges at the Murchison, Woomeral, and Gascoyne crossings, and made them impassable until water levels went down. Nature ruled in those days'.

Giralia was unchanged from the 1930s. It had been severely damaged with the *'Big Blow'* of 1945 which drowned three RAAF men in their tents by the Bay of Rest. It had been hit again by another cyclone just before Denver and Buster arrived. Their early days were spent restoring buildings, and repairing fences and stockyards.

Giralia covered a wide range of terrain. It included mangrove creeks on the eastern side of the Gulf where barramundi splashed and on rare occasions salt-water crocodiles sunned themselves on the mud banks. On the northern boundary the famous Rabbit Proof Fence ran down to the Gulf. *'They built it too late'* said Denver *'We used to ask which side the rabbits were supposed to be on?'*

In 1953 Giralia had 24,000 sheep. By improving watering points, including two 30,000 yard dams, more stock could be carried. *'Our best shearing was in 1972 when we shore 37,000'* said Denver, who completed 50 years on the property in 2003. Asked what were the best and worst things which happened in all the years at Giralia, he nodded towards his wife Rae and said *'She was the best thing!'.*

No question which was the worst. Cyclone Vance in 1999 ripped the Giralia homestead apart and destroyed many of their valuable personal possessions.

Denver married the 22 year-old Rae Taylor in 1958. Her family had their hearts in their mouths believing that she would never last the first 12 months. *'The only time I had ever been out of Perth before'*, Rae remembered *'Was on a school trip to Pingelly. I got so homesick on the first night that my parents had to come and get me! That didn't exactly inspire Dad with confidence that I was cut out to be a wife and mother on a distant sheep station!'.*

Happily she would prove him wrong and she would bring up three sons on Giralia. They were Denver, born in 1960, Nathan, in 1963, and Lukis, in 1968. Just the same, as in most marriages, things didn't always go smoothly. One incident reached the Press as far away as Perth where the *Daily News* back page columnist Bernard Kirwan Ward had spent many years one-finger-pecking away on his typewriter, poking fun at the world in his kindly fashion.

'It may just be better all round' Ward remarked in his column in April, 1960, *'If I just say that this happened on a station in the Exmouth Gulf Area and leave it at that'* .

(Author's note: Of course everyone from Geraldton north would know exactly what and who he was talking about! But let Bernie Ward tell the story.)

'The cook had shot through leaving the manager's 24-year-old wife to cook for all hands as well as looking after a young baby. This she did with great competence, but by the time the men came in to sit down for a roast dinner she was in a touchy mood. When her husband told her that he'd had such a hard day that he couldn't even look at the food she so proudly presented she blew her top.

'Hopped into the family station wagon and roared off away to the airstrip (which in that part of the world is what the Champs Elysees is to Paris) there to cool off. The men looked at the boss and asked him if he didn't think he should go after her.

'Nah!' he said confidently 'She'll be back when she's simmered down'. Just then they heard a familiar noise, saw the familiar dust, and saw the familiar wagon flash past the homestead travelling south.

'Cripes!' yelled her husband. 'She's dinkum this time!'. Quickly fuelled the jeep and set off in pursuit.

'Moving along like Jack Brabham late for an appointment with Bridgette Bardot, he finally spotted the dust on the horizon and caught the station wagon after a 37 mile chase at Winning Pool. It was only then that he noticed the registration plate and realised that this was actually a Perth station wagon, the same model as his own, but being driven by a perfect stranger.

'Headed home, feeling quite hungry now, arrived at the station to find his wife restored to good humour and the men just polishing off the last of the meal'.

In the early days at Giralia, like remote stations Australia-wide, all cooking was done on wood stoves. This was an industry in itself because expeditions had to be made out into the bush to cut and bring in the firewood for the week. Someone had to chop the branches and tree trunks down to the right size bits for the stove, and someone had to light the fire and keep it going. All labour intensive. Even lighting the place at night was the same as in a previous century with kerosene lamps.

Aladdin lamps gave a light good enough for reading, but they had to be filled, wicks trimmed, and the mantle glass cleaned. If the flame was turned up too high the wick smoked and blackened the mantle, sometimes breaking the glass. For outside and general use the famous Hurricane lamps were unmatched. In the early days there was no refrigeration, simply Coolgardie safes. Any meat killed had to be cooked the same day or salted to preserve it.

'We acquired some kerosene fridges' said Denver *'And they were regarded as a great improvement. But in reality, in Exmouth with summer temperatures regularly over 40 degrees Celsius they only just kept things cool. Ice-cream was definitely not on the menu!*

' There was no air conditioning, of course, but we had the usual bough shed -- a summer house covered in spinifex with water sprayed over it – for sitting out on summer evenings. Rae was always scared of snakes who liked to be cool too!'

'*When we first got Kleenheat bottled gas it was an absolute blessing*' said Rae *'It meant I could make a cup of tea or heat up a baby's bottle by just striking a match, and for the first time we had fridges that really worked!'*.

Though Giralia originally had a telephone line through Winning Pool, the poles and wire were brought down in a cyclone and it was considered too big a job to replace them at the time.

From then on communication was by the Flying Doctor pedal radio. While this was an excellent service, and included School of the Air, bush people could only communicate with each other by sending a telegram with every word spelled out letter by letter.

In the 1950s everything was done on horseback and most of the stations had stallions and quality brood mares to keep horse numbers up – some with an eye on winning the next bush race meeting! Mustering on Giralia was a major effort with all hands cooking and sleeping out in the bush with their dogs and horses.

'I wouldn't see the homestead for six weeks during mustering' Denver recalled. During that time he and everyone else slept on ground sheets with spinifex bunched up underneath the canvas to take the hardness out of the ground. Cooking was in camp ovens over an open fire.

In those early days there would be 14 to 20 people at the station, including manager, overseer, head stockman, three full time stockmen – including jackeroos, and others signed on for mustering, as well as a cook and house girls.

Many of the staff were Aborigines in family groups, and the Blakes remember them affectionately as excellent workers. The jackeroos lived in the main homestead and were treated as family, eating their meals with the Blakes. Most pastoralists kept up a social round, travelling long distances to meet each other once a month for fishing and socialising at favourite locations. Bush race meetings were great social events with intense rivalry between station owners of quality horses, and local riders.

'The meetings I remember were first at Bullara and then at Winning Pool for 21 years until 1981' Denver Blake recalled. *'We also had a strong following for meetings at Exmouth. Then the WA Turf Club took over and professionalism came into the equation, with horses from down south and professional jockeys and bookmakers. We still had the Winning Country Club and sports weekend, but horses were less and less important on all the stations as motor bikes took over'*.

Giralia had been like a page out of a history book of the early 1900s when Denver Blake first went there in 1953. As they approached the new millennium and took stock, Denver and Rae noted in satisfied fashion that they now had all the modern amenities available in the city. They had air conditioning, deep freezes, electric refrigerators, gas stoves, electric light, television, radio, flush toilets, and a bitumen highway past the front door linking them with Exmouth or Carnarvon. Everything in the garden, it seemed, was lovely.

But their satisfaction would be snatched from them at a black date in the future.

Leading The High Life

Chapter Eleven

On October 27th, 1962, if you had told any of the people living on thc North West Cape – all 41 of them -- that within a year there would be 3000 people on the Cape they would have looked at you with utter disbelief. Either that or dismissed you as crazy.

But events were about to move with dizzying speed. The significance of 27-10-'62 , of course, was that it was the critical day of the Cuban Missile Crisis. A time when the United States and Soviet Russia were eyeball to eyeball and Nuclear War was just an eye-blink away.

That was a call too close for comfort, as discussed in our first chapter. One of the hard lessons learned was the vulnerability of land-based missile sites because of satellite surveillance – the' *Spy Eye in the Sky'*. For that reason there was escalating importance in the role of harder-to-detect nuclear submarines. They carried inter-continental missiles with nuclear war-heads, and they could be anywhere under the surface in the world's Seven Seas.

Previously communication with submarines could only be carried out when they were on the surface. In that situation they were vulnerable to air attack or satellite identification. To counter this the United States devised a Very Low Frequency (VLF) radio system which could contact submarines when they were below the surface or even under the ice at the North Pole.

However the system required bases which needed huge towers and back-up facilities, the size of a small country town. The US had been looking at potential sites around the world for some time before the Cuban crisis. The remote Exmouth Gulf, a United States Navy submarine base code-named 'POT SHOT' in the Second World War had already been noted as having the necessary requirements. These were a suitable location, a suitable terrain and – importantly – a stable political situation favourable to the United States.

With the Cuban Missile Crisis an all-too-recent memory and worrying unrest building up in South East Asia, establishment of VLF stations assumed a new priority for the United States. Exmouth was selected as the site for one of the ring of five VLF bases around the world. There was no time to waste, and an agreement was reached with the Australian Government and formally signed on May 9th, 1963. The sleepy North West Cape was about to be to be transformed and the spectacular tower complex at Point Murat now stands as a symbol of those dramatic days half-a-lifetime ago. Most visitors to Exmouth today take time to look at the VLF aerial complex at Point Murat. It is, after all, one of the engineering wonders of Australia.

When people stand below the 13 towers, with Tower Zero in the centre, and crane their necks to look up into a sky laced with cables and support systems, they are awed by the size and complexity of the VLF system. At the time of building Tower Zero was Australia's tallest man-made structure. Forty years later it was still the tallest construction in the southern hemisphere, and on a world scale it is taller than either the Eiffel Tower in Paris, or the Empire State Building in New York. The first question which enters the mind of the practical person is '*How on earth did they do it? How did they get all those hundreds of tons of steel hardware up into the sky in the first place?'*

All this in an area so primitive that there were not even any sealed roads at the time – simply bush sheep station tracks. Tower Zero, at 389 metres in height, balancing on a giant ball-bearing at its base, is actually loftier than the highest natural point in the Cape Range which looms, a tawny giant, on the skyline behind the towers.

The Range's maximum height is 306 metres. For once Nature is *Second Best.* Yet the construction was completed within two years. A remarkable achievement. The towers, in two outer rings around a central point, were there to support the *'top hat'*, a complex spider web of wires which formed the signal-sending antennae high in the air.

John Hallworth arrived in Exmouth in 1967 as a 21-year-old with previous engineering experience on high constructions. He began as an ordinary hand, but rapidly became a supervisor engaged in building the VLF tower complex. He would spend a lot of time high in the air. '*We had the very best views of the Exmouth peninsula when we chose to look around'.*

He would remain based in Exmouth for the next 40 years, at the same time travelling the world in his profession as a high rigger, and was affectionately known to locals as *'John-the-Pom'.*

'We built the towers four at a time' he recalled in 2008. *'The first 120 feet (40 metres) went up easily enough using a mobile crane. After that it became more complicated. We had a 120 foot long 'Jin pole' inside the structure. The top 56 feet of the pole were clear at the high point and sections were winched up and bolted together. Every two sections completed we'd move the derrick pole higher. There were some pretty big lifts, some as much as 22,000 kilos at a time. The structure was intrinsically very heavy. The vertical components are solid steel, not just hollow pipe, and the steel was the highest quality, able to withstand 90 pounds pressure per square inch. The lifts were done with three drum winches carrying 5000 feet of 25 mm steel wire'.*

Asked about the local legend that the high work was done by Navaho Indians who were born with no natural fear of heights, John laughs. *'It makes a good story'* he says *'But most of our workers were Aussies. Some of the American riggers were from the US Southern States, Oklahama, and so on, and may have had a touch of Indian blood. There were a couple of genuine Red Indians, but generally speaking we were a mixed bunch. During construction of the towers we would have six men at the top and four on the ground. As a supervisor I was always up at the top end'.*

Fear of heights?

'Some people are born without it, others become accustomed to heights as structures work from the ground up' John Hallworth said. *'Of course you have to be careful. But there are a lot of professions where you have to be very careful indeed – look at surgeons with a scalpel in their hands or truck drivers with a big load behind them! What about airline pilots?'*

'Riggers had a saying, "It's not the fall that kills you, it's when it stops!' he said. *'We only lost one bloke on the VLF towers, and that from a comparatively low height. He only fell 30 ft but there was concrete at the bottom. Another chap fell from the 700 foot level, but he got* wedged in *the derrick cables and survived. Generally speaking we had an excellent safety record'.*

The High Life would take John Hallworth to many parts of the world after building the VLF towers. The US Navy sent him to Maine and Annapolis in the United States, and to Hawaii to work on VLF installations there. When care of the Base was contracted out to Boeing Pty Ltd., the high rigging work was sub-contracted to an international firm called Le Blanc, who sent Hallworth off to Pakistan and Sri Lanka *'Building towers and pulling them down'.*

What was his highest job? *'A 700 metre television tower in the United States'*. Now that really WAS high!

Aside from what went up in the air, there were interesting aspects of the VLF tower complex at ground level. In preparing their initial plans the designers were delighted to have such a large flat area barely above sea level. This allowed the sinking of 345,643 metres of copper wire spreading out like spokes of a wheel from the central control ' Helix' building at the foot of Tower Zero, to act as the perfect radio earth. Every second wire was grounded by copper rods to the water table. The towers themselves were guyed by massive cables to huge concrete blocks embedded in the ground which acted as anchors and had to be able to withstand cyclonic winds.

The whole complex was able to bend and move a little, its strength like a spider's web.

The concrete pours were more difficult than in most other places. The outer blocks for Tower Zero each required a massive pour of 765 cubic metres of concrete, with three blocks – inner, middle, and outer – for each guy fastening. When this preliminary work was being carried out in the summer of November 1964 to April 1965, Exmouth temperatures were up in the 40 degrees Celsius range. To counter the heat the temperature of the water in the concrete trucks' hoppers had to be one degree above freezing point. This was so that when the concrete trucks arrived at the location four miles from the batching plant the load had to be less than 35 degrees Celsius when it was poured. Exmouth historian R.C.Gordon recorded *'Thus a certain amount of excitement and a great deal of activity accompanied each pour!'*

The central building in the VLF complex was generally known as the Helix Building, where transmitting and communication took place. The power plant at the complex had a gross output sufficient to serve a city of 12,000 people! Nearby were fuel storage tanks with a capacity of 19,320 kilolitres, and the Navy pier. The pier was 335 metres long with a T-section of 51 metres and two dolphins 366 metres apart. It was designed to withstand 9 metre cyclonic waves. As an unintended and unexpected benefit it would turn out to be one of the world's best SCUBA dive sites in future years.

When the Australian Government signed the agreement with the government of the United States in 1963 it was agreed that the U.S. could build and operate a station at the North West Cape for a period of 25 years. The area granted was 7284 hectares divided into three specific areas. The land was excised from Yardie Creek Station, a pastoral lease operated by Murray and Trudy Broad, and from Exmouth Station, a similar lease operated by Gerry Lefroy and his family. Ultimately it would see the demise of Yardie Creek as a sheep station.

The three sections of the station consisted of Area A, which included the complex of VLF towers, the Helix building, storage tanks, power station, and the pier. Area B, six miles south of the towers included a high frequency transmitter section across the road from the station headquarters, which comprised the administrative section and communication control centre. In Area B there were also workshops, maintenance units, and equipment storage facilities, as well as barracks for enlisted men and chief petty officers. For Navy personnel there were recreational and other facilities – basketball and tennis courts, theatre, chapel, dispensary, hospital, Officers' club, an Enlisted Men's and Petty Officer's club, swimming pool and bowling alleys, to make it a *'Home from home'*.

Area C at Learmonth, 43 kilometres south of station HQ, near the old US Navy POT SHOT site of the Second World War, was a high frequency receiver site at sufficient distance from the high frequency transmitters and VLF towers to avoid interference with incoming signals.

The first priority, naturally in view of the tense world situation, was to get the VLF towers up and working, and to have them integrated with the station HQ, and the high frequency transmitter system. The first signal was transmitted successfully on November 7th, 1966.

After the station the next item on the agenda was the construction of the town of Exmouth itself. The United States Navy needed a location for accommodation for married officers and their families away from the work place. In addition to Navy personnel there would be a need to accommodate the Australians employed in the system – an estimated 400 to 500 people -- many of whom would also have families. The workforce at the time of construction was about 3000 men from 38 nationalities – ultimately 16,000 workers would go through the area before the job was finished. Though conditions were hard, especially in the summer heat, workers were attracted by the high rates of pay and overtime. It was assumed that some of these, like John Hallworth, would probably stay after the base was completed and find work in the new town.

By agreement between the United States, the Australian Government and the WA Government, the Shire of Exmouth was gazetted in December, 1963.

At the time accommodation in the area was a shambles with a population which would peak at 4300 people (twice the 2010 permanent population!).

Many of the single workers engaged in construction were originally accommodated at a caravan park known as Datronics after the major employer. Though regulations theoretically forbade it, many workers had brought their families up, and a tent city arose. The authorities moved them into the adjacent Burtenshaw caravan park. When that filled a third park in the same area known as Reids took the overflow. The three parks were named after contractors working on the Base. In 1964 there were only four permanent houses.

The United States Navy began building 130 concrete houses for their Navy personnel in the town using a distinctive *'blockhouse'* design. Some people joked that they were designed to withstand an atomic blast (and then reflected that, with the Base a potential target nearby, perhaps the joke wasn't so funny after all!). They later built 70 'Dravo' styled houses which contrasted significantly in design and construction. The houses built by the Commonwealth were tropical designs, raised on stilts to allow the air to circulate underneath, similar to post-war buildings in Darwin and northern Queensland. Some were brought down from Talgarno, the town made defunct by the cancellation of the British Blue Streak rocket program. By 1967, the Exmouth townsite was still red and raw and very new. But quite a number of houses had been built on the 284 allocated lots, sealed roads had been laid down, and basic facilities were operating.

The town of Exmouth was officially opened by the Prime Minister, of Australia, Harold E Holt, on September 17th, 1967, the day after the station itself was officially commissioned. The North West of Australia had never seen anything like the pomp of that opening ceremony. The guests of honour included Harold Holt, the WA Premier Sir David Brand, Sir Charles Court, the US Ambassador to Australia Edward Clark, the Commander in chief of the US Pacific fleet, Admiral Roy Johnson, the Commander in chief of US Naval Communications Admiral Robert Weeks, and many other senior United States Navy officers, as well as the Australian Minister for Defence, Allen Fairhall.

The Royal Australian Navy band provided the music with spirited renditions of *God Save The Queen,* and *The Star Spangled Banner.* All in all, it was a day to remember. Would Exmouth ever see anything like it ever again? That was a question nobody asked, for the same reason that most people were unconcerned about the future and what would happen when the United States Navy's lease expired. Townsfolk told themselves that if there was going to be a problem in that regard it was many years away. No-one was looking that far ahead.

It was generally considered that, having spent so much money and effort in establishing the 66 million dollar station, the Navy would probably be there another 100 years. They would be wrong. If the date 1992 had been suggested for a withdrawal – albeit that it was 25 years away – it might have removed the smiles from some faces. But for the moment Exmouth was a brand-new town. As Jack Valli – himself a long-term Exmouth resident – put it in his book *Gascoyne Days:*

'Exmouth was the first new town in Western Australia for many years, it was the first complete town in Australia and probably the world constructed specifically to withstand winds of hurricane force. It was the first town in Australia constructed simultaneously by two nations for the benefit of two nations'.

The perceptive reader will immediately see some matters of interest arising from this international aspect. Would Americans in the town be under Australian or United States law? Would Australians be governed by United States Navy regulations? Would the town be run by the usual local government system current in Western Australia, with an elected Shire President and councillors?

Or would it be a semi-military establishment, taking into account the nature of the unusual arrangements at the North West Cape?

Though Exmouth was officially designated a Shire in 1964, with the area excised from the Shire of Gascoyne-Minilya (the balance of the Shire of Gascoyne-Minilya was incorporated into the Shire of Carnarvon), what followed was something of a compromise.

For one thing most of the population were construction workers. That meant that there were no ratepayers, the Shire had no income, and therefore there could be no election for shire president or councillors. Instead a Civil Commissioner was appointed as the sole authority, and the man chosen for the job was an energetic Australian Army officer, Colonel Ken Murdoch.

Ken Murdoch had had a distinguished military career. In the Second World War he served with the AIF in the Middle East and New Guinea, and was awarded an MBE. After the war he remained as an army staff officer, including some time spent as commanding officer of the Papua New Guinea Volunteer Rifles. One of the high points of his career was with Western Command as the executive officer, ceremonial, for the 1962 Commonwealth Games in Perth. For his contribution to the Games he was awarded an OBE. In his new role at Exmouth he represented both the Commonwealth Government and the Western Australian Government and was appointed Commissioner for the Shire of Exmouth in lieu of an elected shire council. Colonel Murdoch was *'Mr Everything'* at Exmouth, and began his tenure living in a caravan before any houses were built.

He had a position of power few men have enjoyed in any town in Western Australia, and some of the locals – with a tinge of irony – referred to him as *'God'*. He wore two hats, representing both the Australian military and civic authorities. Some of his exercise of authority was resented by US Navy personnel. Colonel Murdoch insisted that, because the security force at the station were Australian civilians both United States and Australian Commonwealth passes had to be presented at all entry points. The Commonwealth Pass had to be obtained from the Civil Commissioner's office prior to obtaining a US Navy pass.

R.C, Gordon noted in 1968: *' With a great amount of say in what occurs at the Base, Colonel Murdoch is a powerful man. In making sure that Australia's rights are safeguarded through stringent enforcement of custom, defence, and judicial laws he is quite unpopular in many Navy circles'.*

He must have been doing his job well!

By the end of 1966 the main building process of Exmouth Town was completed. From two houses in 1964 there were 130 Navy houses built, and 130 constructed for employees of the station. In addition there were 10 Commonwealth Government houses, 36 two and three bedroom units and catering facilities at the Commonwealth Hostel, and 15 private residences.

The first one-room school was opened in 1965, and Doug Bathgate – later to become a Shire President – was brought up as the teacher. In the following year there were two classrooms and by the end of 1967 there were 10, with 12 in 1968, reflecting the expansion of the town. By 1969 the nursing post at the Australian Inland Mission was discontinued and a new hospital had been constructed. There was a police station, post office, infant health centre, kindergarten, library, community hall, two banks, a court house, butcher, baker, general store, two service stations, a cool drink factory, the Pot Shot Hotel, and the first holiday accommodation was available at Norcape Lodge.

Exmouth was a fully fledged town, but there was still very much a military presence. An example was the leaflet which the Tourist Bureau were handing out to visitors. It read:

' Two Nations—Two Goals. Freedom and Peace!'

'The Australian Government has a prime responsibility to provide the nation with security from armed attack and from the constraints on independent national decisions imposed by the threat of armed attack'.

What that actually meant was anybody's guess. What constraints? The sinister words *'Armed Attack'* occurred twice in one sentence. Attack by whom?

However in a further paragraph, it was observed: *'Australia has no defined enemy at the moment'.*

Oh, yeah?

Readers were left to scratch their heads and wonder whether there was something the authorities weren't telling them about. Was another Cuban Missile Crisis just around the corner? Or was it just a case of a bureaucratic obsession with paperwork? Meantime there was a tragedy with an Exmouth link.

The Australian Prime Minister Harold E. Holt, who had established a particularly strong relationship with the American President Lyndon B.Johnson (*'All the way with L.B.J.!'*) and who had played a major part in the agreement to establish the Exmouth station, was drowned in a surfing accident at Cheviot Beach in Victoria, on December 17th, 1967, aged only 59 years.

His body was never recovered. But a memorial service in Melbourne was attended by Lyndon Johnson, the British Prime Minister Harold Wilson, and Prince Phillip. As a mark of respect the establishment at Exmouth was re-named. Previously it had been designated *US Naval Communication Station North West Cape*. In future it would be known as the *US Naval Communication Station Harold E. Holt.*

As the Soviet threat diminished and tensions with the United States eased, authority at the Base was re-constituted and in 1972 it was announced that it would become a *'Joint Facility'*, with a

Royal Australian Navy officer taking the position of second-in-command, and 35 RAN personnel being integrated into general operations. Exmouth's period of being run by a civil commissioner – Colonel J.P.K.(Ken) Murdoch, 1963 to '76, and Air Commodore A.T. (Tom)Walters, 1976 to early '79 -- was followed by the first elections for Shire president and councillors in May, 1979.

The character of any community is often determined by its leaders. Exmouth has been fortunate in the men who made the decisions and charted the path of the development of the town through the years. The differences in personalities and approaches to problems have been plain to see, but the strong desire to serve community interests has been consistent.

The '*Father*' of Exmouth was undoubtedly Colonel Ken Murdoch. He was at the helm as Civil Commissioner for the first thirteen years and had an enormous influence. He rigorously maintained an Australian position with the Americans, keeping the management of the town firmly in his hands against significant pressures. On no account were his people going to become second-class citizens in their own country!

He was also very aware that unless the town looked attractive, and had a positive atmosphere for those who lived there, people wouldn't stay in the area. He wanted a town that had its own character, where citizens would be proud of what had been achieved, and where families could bring up children with all the amenities that would be found in the city. A place where people could say *'This is OUR town!'*.

From raw beginnings Colonel Murdoch saw the town come of age. He encouraged the greening of Exmouth with street trees and parks. He fought for the expansion of the school, the provision of a hospital, kindergarten, and other facilities. He made sporting and recreational facilities a priority, including a swimming pool, ovals for cricket and football, and he was keen to see the golf club get under way.

Ken Murdoch did have a certain military style about him which didn't always make him popular. Historian R.C. Gordon made this observation in 1968 when Colonel Murdoch was still very much in charge:

'He has immense drive and foresight. Naturally being in such as dictatorial position and being Army-trained he expected people to jump to his commands and he achieved results.

'To admire the great task tackled and nearly completed by the Colonel one only has to observe the town today and marvel at all the amenities. Obviously firm bargaining with Canberra must have been responsible for much of the finance'.

He often reminded those in authority that his brief was to '*Build a town of a good standard'* and he stuck by that instruction when he outlaid funding for his various projects. By his very nature the Colonel was impatient of delays in the plans he envisioned for the town.

Canberra was a long way away, and sometimes he felt it took longer than was actually necessary to get permissions and additions to the budget. In those circumstances Ken Murdoch went ahead and did what he felt was required anyway. If he needed to establish loan funds or whatever was needed in the interim, then so be it. The bureaucrats could catch up later. Meantime the Exmouth program couldn't wait for Red Tape to sort itself out.

When his tenure came to an end it was found, with some consternation, that the Colonel had over-spent his budget by a fair degree. This on the basis that '*The end justifies the means'*.

His replacement the new Civil Commissioner, and Commissioner for the Shire of Exmouth, Air Commodore Tom Walters, had the job of sorting out the finances, and applying a system of good civic housekeeping to Exmouth. A plan which would keep expenditure on the rails when the time came to elect a council and a shire president.

It was expected that this would take at least five years. But Tom Walters did his job so successfully that within three years the books were balanced and Exmouth was ready for its first election.

Interest was so high that despite the fact that there were only 485 ratepayers, 27 people nominated for positions on council. There was keen rivalry for the position of President between Bob Burkett, the affable '*Mine Host'* of the Pot Shot Hotel, and Doug Bathgate the first school teacher at Exmouth. Bob had a narrow victory in the first election, and went on to succeed in being elected as a councillor and President in the next three elections. He spent a total of 11 years as a councillor and Shire President.

Exmouth's first Shire Clerk was Stan Dellar who served for five years under Colonel Murdoch. He was recruited from Carnarvon where he was assistant Shire Clerk. In 1971 he was offered endorsement by the Western Australian Labor Party for the seat of North Province, and successfully contested the election. North Province was strangely-named because its area extended from Exmouth to Eucla, from the Nullabor to Laverton, Menzies, and Wiluna.

At 87,283,000 hectares it was one of the biggest electorates in the world, bigger than many European countries. Stan Dellar spent six years in Parliament, and was deputy leader in the Upper House when John Tonkin's government took office. After retiring from politics he returned to Exmouth, working at the Base for the United States Army

Long terms in local government positions are by no means the rule in Western Australia. But Exmouth was fortunate in having a very able Shire Clerk – the position later more aptly re-named Chief Executive Officer – in Kerry Graham. He began the job in October, 1970, as deputy Shire Clerk to Stan Dellar, and retired in 2004 after 34 years service. He spent 31 of them as CEO of Exmouth Shire Council .

Kerry Graham had the job of organising the first elections, and '*breaking in'* the new Shire President Bob Burkett, and the elected councillors. None of them had had any previous experience in a local government capacity. Bob Burkett, renowned for his strong personality, took some time to adjust his non-conformist (he would have called them *'non-bullshit'*) views to accommodate to the necessary formalities of council meetings.

Bob had a pathological hatred of '*red tape',* but he quickly became an adept leader at council meetings. He enjoyed a brisk exchange of opinions with other councillors, and his deputy Stan Dellar, who was by now a councillor and who would become a member of parliament in due course.

'If you can run a pub' Bob would say with a smile '*You can run anything!'*

'Bob Burkett was the best thing that could have happened to Exmouth at that time' Kerry Graham remembers. *'He had immense enthusiasm and energy and was totally dedicated to improving the town and serving the local community. As the publican in a one-pub town he was always approachable and available to ratepayers who had a proposal or a problem – and there were plenty of both'.*

Bob had arrived in town almost by accident. He and Ray Lynch, and Tom Kenny and some other friends arrived in Exmouth for a few days fishing as construction of the base was winding down. Over a few beers – most things were over a few beers with Bob – he learned that some of the workers' accommodation units, each one the size of an average house, were coming up for sale. Given the remoteness of Exmouth they were expected to go for bargain prices.

Bob and his group discussed the possibility of buying the units and using them to set up a fishing camp on Dirk Hartog Island in Shark Bay.

As discussion deepened, and fingers ticked off the likely costs of getting the units to Shark Bay, and then across the water to Dirk Hartog, faces grew longer and the expressions more gloomy. The units might be cheap where they were. But by the time they were on the proposed site they would probably be prohibitively expensive.

'What about leaving them here?' someone suggested. *'The fishing's just as good, and scenically there's a lot more to attract tourists!'*

So *'Nor Cape Lodge'* was borne, sited down near the town beach, with the re-cycled units the basis of the accommodation. A Besser Block concrete plant came with the units and was used to build the restaurant and the bar. A swimming pool gave visitors the choice of a fresh water dip or a walk over the sandhills to where the waters of the Gulf washed the shoreline.

Bob became the prime mover in setting up Nor Cape Lodge and publicising it, and the oftener he stayed there the more he found he liked life at the North West Cape. Exmouth suited Bob Burkett, and Bob Burkett suited Exmouth. While he still had interests in Perth hotels, including the Savoy, and the Naval Base hotels, and Gramps Wine Bar in East Perth, Bob decided to run Nor'Cape Lodge himself on a full time basis and moved his family to live in Exmouth.

His family – wife Joy, sons Larry and Lee, and daughters Mary and Roberta – all played their parts, helping in the restaurant or behind the bar. From there it was a short step to the Pot Shot Hotel when the lease eventually came up for tender. Bob would have his happiest times there, finally buying the hotel which was formerly owned and leased by the Swan Brewery.

Bob was still committed to Nor Cape Lodge, but eventually sold it six months after acquiring the freehold of the Pot Shot in order to be able to devote himself full time to the hotel.

Kerry Graham said that Bob Burkett was the ideal president for a North West shire, able to combine the casual with formality when it was required. He was equally at home with visitors ranging from senior US Navy officers and Admirals, to State and federal politicians. He was on familiar terms with Bob Hawke who would become Prime Minister of Australia. On the other hand he was just as much at ease, and on a first name basis with the bloke who drove the local rubbish truck. Regardless of whether they were rich or poor, famous or infamous, they all drank at the Pot Shot Hotel .

'They don't have a choice really' said Bob happily *'Mine's the only pub in town!'*

Bob became a legend in his own lifetime, and many stories are still told about him in Exmouth. His daughter Roberta Edwards compiled some of them in a charming book which was fittingly titled *A Beer With Bob Burkett.*

'Bob enjoyed helping people' Roberta wrote *'But none so much as an old guy named Bill. Bill enjoyed a comfortable life-style, but his wife controlled the purse strings. She would give him just enough money to buy two beers a day. Bill would come into the bar, drink his two beers, and leave.*

'Bob knew how much Bill enjoyed his time at the pub, so every few weeks Bob would set off in his car just before Bill finished his second drink. He would wait until he saw Bill coming down the road then throw a five dollar note on to the footpath.

'Bill never saw Bob but he always saw the money. He would pick it up, put it in his pocket and hurry back to the pub. Bob sometimes put coins on the footpath and sometimes a ten dollar note.

'He put the money at different spots. At one time he put it almost in Bill's driveway and Bill still picked it up and went back to the pub. Bill never mentioned a word to anyone of his little windfalls in case his wife found out. To Bob it was a win-win situation. Bill was happy. The money was always spent at the pub, and Bill's wife was none the wiser'.

As a forward thinker Bob Burkett sometimes discussed with Kerry Graham what direction the town should take if and when the Americans departed. They realised that would be a crucial time for the town and tourism was the only industry which could keep Exmouth afloat post-Uncle Sam. At one time, together with prawning magnate Michael Kailis they unsuccessfully promoted a plan to build a casino at Exmouth and convinced a *Royal Commission Into Gambling* that it was a good idea. The commission recommended the proposal, but the State Government decided not to implement the finding.

When the announcement of the impending American departure sent most of Exmouth into shock, Bob continued to have faith in the town's future. With his son Larry now running the Pot Shot he continued ambitious plans for expanding the hotel with 45 more motel rooms and constructing the Pot Shot Resort. Bob had maintained his interest in Perth hotels, including a new venture, the Market City Tavern. But spending time between Exmouth and Perth he began having dizzy spells, and a hospital check revealed that he was having kidney problems. An operation brought devastating news for the family. Bob had suffered a severe stroke. After weeks in hospital where his family visited him on a regular basis he died on February 4th, 1992. It was his birthday and he was 61 years old.

In recognition of his 11 years as Shire President and outstanding service to the community Bob Burkett was named a *Freeman of the Shire*. He was also President of the Exmouth Tourist Bureau, Chairman of the Gascoyne Ward of the Country Shires Association, Commissioner of the State Planning Association, Member of the Gascoyne Regional Development Advisory Committee, President of Exmouth Rotary Club, President of the Gascoyne Travel Association, Patron of the Exmouth Golf Club, Patron of the Exmouth Bowling Club, and a Justice of the Peace.

'How he found time to run a pub as well, God only knows!' his daughter Roberta remarked in her book.

A grateful town named the east-west road which linked the main road to Exmouth with Great Northern- highway – a tourist thoroughfare second in importance only to the main road itself – *'Burkett Road'*. Bob would have liked that.

There were many tributes to Bob at the conclusion of Roberta's book. One he would have appreciated came from Doug Bathgate, Bob's rival at the initial elections for Shire President. *' In hindsight'* Doug said *'I would be the first to admit that Bob was the best person for the position of President of the Exmouth Shire Council. He had a wonderful gift of making people feel important and feel well looked after. He had a charisma and he was streets ahead of us in being able to lobby people in government for the benefit of the town'.*

That was a generous statement coming from the man who would succeed Bob Burkett as Shire President. Doug Bathgate was almost an opposite in personality, yet he became a most effective president utilising different but equally important skills. Where Bob was a total extrovert, Doug was reserved with a manner more suited to his occupation as a school teacher. He gave the impression that he could just as easily have been a research scientist.

Indeed, as Kerry Graham remarked, *'If he had his time again that might have been the road Doug would choose to go down'*.

In 2004 Kerry Graham announced his retirement as Chief Executive Officer to the Exmouth Shire Council after a remarkable period of 34 years of service to the community. An essentially modest man he requested a *'No-fuss'* farewell, though Doug Bathgate said *' I believe a farewell of the magnitude given to Ken Murdoch, where everyone in town gathered at the oval, would have been more appropriate'*.

Nevertheless, on his send-off in October 2004, Kerry Graham was conferred the honour of *Honorary Freeman Of The Shire Of Exmouth*. Earlier the Governor of Western Australia had presented him with an Australian Public Service Medal for outstanding service to local government. Kerry was necessarily involved in every facet of Exmouth's development from the 1970s including the stressful recovery period after Cyclone Vance in 1999. Perhaps his most significant role, after presiding over the first Local Government elections, was during the difficult time when Exmouth faced the transition from US Navy Town to having to stand on its own two feet.

While the pearling and prawning industries were well-established, there were no permanent port facilities which meant that they closed down in summer. They were seasonal activities, and there was no industrial back-up. Exmouth's only prospect of a major support industry was through developing tourism, and in that role the town would be in keen competition with Shark Bay, Kalbarri, Broome, and other northern tourist destinations.

Doug Bathgate said at Kerry Graham's farewell function: '*The US Navy's withdrawal had very serious ramifications for the future viability of Exmouth. In a very short period the town lost more than a third of its population. Not only had the US Navy personnel left, but over 200 Australian civilians were made redundant. Exmouth faced massive changes and it was necessary to seek other sources of economic activity to ensure the town's future. One hundred and ninety four US Navy houses were sold and the proceeds were placed in a trust fund for the long-term social and economic development of the town. The Exmouth Transition Consultative Forum was formed to provide community consultation with the State Government during the transition. Kerry Graham played a pivotal role in the function of the forum.*

'He was the executive officer of the Exmouth Trust Fund Committee which was responsible for the $ 13,000,000 Trust Fund. A State Government-appointed committee which included three shire councillors managed the fund. The Deputy Premier of the time (Hendy Cowan) had the final say on expenditure. The fund financed major projects such as the Exmouth Boat Harbour, the Bob Burkett Road, and the Exmouth Air Terminal.

'A community development fund was established using $ 400,000 of Trust Fund money, and in turn this provides interest-free loans to community and sporting groups in Exmouth. Kerry Graham was the administrative officer for the scheme which is wholly managed and controlled by the Shire of Exmouth. As a result the work of the Exmouth Transition Consultative Forum has played a significant role in helping to develop a diverse tourist industry and to overcome the major economic downturn after the US Navy departure'.

As an incoming Shire President Doug Bathgate – deputy president since 1981 -- had excellent qualifications for the environmental development of the area. He had degrees in both zoology and anthropology, and at one time was a member of the Education Department's Nature Advisory Service, together with Harry Butler and Vince Serventy. He ran the Western Australian Museum Education Section for five years before coming to be headmaster at Exmouth. As a result he had a particularly well-informed background in dealing with the environmental and conservation matters confronting the Shire.

His election as Shire President in 1989 came at an appropriate time, because it had become clear by then that with the impending withdrawal of the Americans, Exmouth's future lay in tourism.

It was equally clear that the future of the Ningaloo Reef and the west coast and the Gulf generally needed to be safe-guarded against pollution, over-fishing and over-use of the natural resources. Prior to Doug Bathgate becoming Shire President he was actively involved in the creation of the Cape Range National Park and later in the extension of the boundaries out to the coast, which included the acquisition of Yardie Creek Station. When he became President he supported Dr Barry Wilson of CALM in the establishment of the Ningaloo Marine Park.

As chairman of the Coral Coast Advisory Committee he saw the marine park extended south to Red Bluff, north of Carnarvon, in 2003. He was also a member of the Gascoyne Development Commission and was awarded the Order of Australia for his conservation roles. Doug continued his interest in conservation after his retirement and was Chairman of the WA Recreational Fisheries Advisory Committee in 2007, and a Justice of the Peace.

He was succeeded as Shire President in 1993 by Dave Richardson who had been a councillor since 1979. His years at the helm as President spanned the critical period from May 1993 to May 1999 following the American withdrawal. The changeover from a service community for the Naval Communication Station Harold E Holt, to a town based on tourism and standing on its own, were critical years, and cool heads and sound local government were essential.

Mike Purslow could not have foreseen, when he succeeded Dave Richardson as Shire President that he would be taking office at the most testing time in Exmouth's 35 year-old history. Cyclone Vance wrought havoc on the town in March, 1999. Mike Purslow used his banking experience as chairman of the re-building committee which allocated government compensation funds for Exmouth businesses affected by the cyclone.

John Cooper became President from 2003 to 2007, when Exmouth was in a period of building transition from the old town to new residential areas north of the town. The construction of the Novotel Ningaloo Resort and the Marina Village and other canal developments resulted in a flood of applications for building approvals.

Environmental considerations, public submissions, and surveys resulted in a greatly increased work load for the Exmouth Shire Council and executive officers.

He was succeeded in 2007 by Veronica Fleay, who made local history by becoming Exmouth's first woman President. Her deputy, in the person of Doreen Blum, was also female.

In their new roles the two ladies brought a new persona to positions which had been filled by men for the past 28 years.

'I'd like to believe that, as a woman, I do bring a different approach.' Ronnie Fleay said. *'However I also believe that gender shouldn't really impact on the decisions that have to be made and which are judged on their merits. I'm humbled by the confidence placed in me in representing the community, and hope that one day when I leave this role it will be with the satisfaction of having contributed something positive to this beautiful place which may endure for future generations'.*

Ken Murdoch

Kerry Graham

Stan Dellar

Bob Burkett

Doug Bathgate

John Cooper

Ronnie Fleay

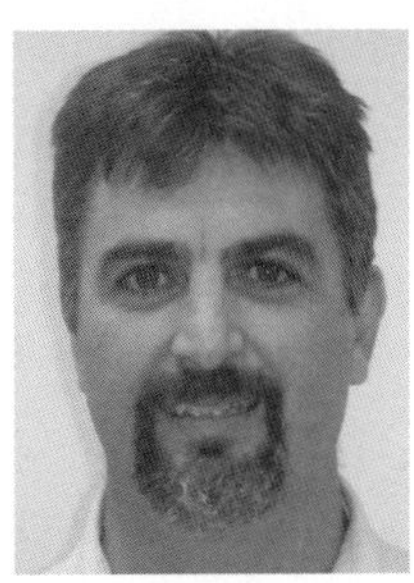

Phillip Anastasakis

Portraits of Exmouth dignitaries

Whale Sharks And A Wider World

Chapter Twelve

When concerns about the possibility that the Americans would withdraw from the Harold E. Holt Communications Base became general in Exmouth, various schemes to promote tourism were put forward. None of them carried the name *Rhincondon typus.* In fact if you had run a quiz around the town about who or what *Rhincondon* was in the late1980s, there would likely have been some blank looks.

Until divers began having experiences with whale sharks off the Ningaloo Reef *Rhincondon* was thought to be one of the world's rarer creatures. Up to the year 1987 only 320 sightings, dating back to 1828, had been recorded in scientific literature. The famous Australian underwater film makers, Ron and Valerie Taylor, and Ben Cropp, each had brief contacts with whale sharks off the NSW coast in the 1970s. It was considered such a unique event that pictures of the divers and the shark appeared on the front page of most Australian newspapers.

In the 1970s and 1980s most charter boat activity at Coral Bay and Exmouth was related to game fishing – with the emphasis on marlin, Spanish mackerel and sailfish – and bottom fishing for those who pursued snapper and red emperor. At the time fishing of any kind was the activity which drew most tourists to town. Whale sharks would be sighted from time to time, and George King, a keen diver in his early days, swam with whale sharks when he was based at Coral Bay for the challenge of the experience.

Local charter boat operators who took game fishermen out in pursuit of blue marlin and sailfish first called them '*Basking sharks'*. In view of the whale sharks' habit of swimming slowly on the surface, with their white spots showing bright in the sunlight, the name might have seemed appropriate. However another large plankton-eater, a quite different species from the far distant North Atlantic, had already taken '*basking shark'* as it's common name. *Cetorhinus maximus* is second in size only to the whale shark.

Geoff Taylor, the Exmouth medico who would begin his own research program into whale sharks, first heard of whale sharks on a Western Australian Museum expedition to the wreck of the *Rapid* at Point Cloates in 1980. Taylor heard the account of one of the museum divers, Geoff Kimpton, who had swum with a whale shark off the reef north of Norwegian Bay. He was immediately envious.

'A whale shark at Ningaloo!' Taylor recalled in his book *Whale Sharks – The Giants Of The Ningaloo Reef. 'I decided then and there that if I got a chance to return to this remote coast I would search out one of these huge yet elusive creatures!'.*

The spell at Ningaloo and the brilliant diving was a factor in his decision to leave his work as a doctor in large city hospitals and take up a post as a country doctor based at Exmouth.

'To me working as a country general practitioner seemed one of the greatest challenges' he recalled. *'The country doctor has to cope with the whole spectrum of medicine from trivial problems to major emergencies. There is no greater test of medical resourcefulness'.* And there were the whale sharks. Another challenge!

His first sighting of a whale shark two years after Point Cloates was on a family outing off the Ningaloo Reef in an 18 foot cabin cruiser on their first trip to the outer reef. *'At the northern end of the reef we were astonished to find two small whale sharks basking on the surface'.*

But his first dive would have to wait. Geoff was with American friends and his wife Joanna, and his two-week-old baby daughter Julia was in a basinet in the cabin. Joanna was not absolutely convinced that the creatures were whale sharks. Sharks –yes. But how could she be sure that they were not some of the species with sharp teeth?

'Because of my new responsibilities as a father I was quickly instructed that this was not a safe place to go diving!' He would have to wait for another day.

Geoff Taylor, in between treating patients at the Exmouth hospital, spent his weekends diving with a friend Peter Moore on the Ningaloo Reef. Meantime they developed a code for discussing sharks when their wives were present. *'We tried to avoid alarming our wives with our intentions of diving with and filming the whale sharks and jokingly referred to them as 'Woolworths supermarkets', while tiger sharks were 'Target supermarkets'.*

After three years of dreaming and planning, determined not only to find whale sharks, but also to film them with his Super-8 cine camera, the moment was all the sweeter when it finally arrived. On a windless day in March 1983, with the surf rolling in on the brown rampart of the reef, the Indian Ocean blue and sparkling, Geoff Taylor found his whale shark at last.

'Suddenly it was there' he wrote in his book '*The creature I had spent so long searching for. It appeared as a huge shape coming up to the surface right under the bow of the boat. I was overcome by excitement as I stood up on the seat, clutching the windscreen and looked down on one of the largest living creatures I had ever seen ...The head seemed wider than the boat, its length completely dwarfed the 18 foot cabin cruiser. Peter kept the boat alongside while I donned mask and snorkel and grabbed for my camera. I snorkelled along next to the whale shark. It seemed unperturbed by my presence, slowly powering itself forward with the side-to-side motion of its huge tail. I was close enough to touch it.*

'The white spots on its head sparkled in the sunlight, and its mouth seemed to be two metres across. A cloud of small fish rode the pressure wave at its head, and under the belly several suckerfish were hitching a ride. The shark was like a moving reef, the prominent ridges along its body giving it a prehistoric look. The tail seemed 10 feet high, and the creature was truly a master of its environment!'

It was the first of three sharks he would dive with that day. A fortnight later they dived with seven sharks, and saw others – a total of 12 sightings in two weeks of what was generally believed to be a rare creature. *'Something very special seemed to be happening'* Geoff Taylor observed.

Perhaps whale sharks were not so rare after all?

He decided that his boat was too small and in 1984 bought a much larger vessel, a 7 metre Baron Sea Eagle with twin 125 horse power Volvo inboard-outboard motors. *'Did she fly!'.* It had sufficient stability to mount an observation tower on the cabin roof similar to the ones used by marlin fishermen. Whale sharks would change Taylor's life. In 1985 he was offered a job in

Queensland. They wanted him to start as soon as possible. He was on the verge of accepting and packing up to leave Exmouth when a call came through from ABC Television in Melbourne. Elizabeth Parer-Cook, wife of wildlife photographer David Parer, was on the line. She said that she had heard that Geoff had film of whale sharks and wanted to know whether he would be interested in being part of a documentary?

'It was the sort of thing I had dreamed of doing' he recalled. *'All thoughts of leaving Exmouth rapidly disappeared and I started preparing for the following season. I needed a professional camera so that I could film in16 mm format. Organising that kind of thing from Exmouth was certainly a challenge!'*

The hardest thing to organise, of course, were the whale sharks themselves. Making a professional film cost thousands of dollars a day. Before bringing some very expensive people and equipment to Exmouth it was a good idea to know quite definitely when the sharks would appear, where they could be found, and how long they stayed. The vital logistics.

Marine scientists on the Barrier Reef, in the early 1980s, made the important discovery of one of Nature's most fascinating occurrences, the Coral Spawning. Moreover they found that they could time it exactly. It was found that the phenomenon occurs in a particular month, seven days after the full moon, and one hour after dark. At that critical moment the coral polyps release their eggs and semen, in a *Safety-in-numbers* phenomenon, forming great slicks which spread across the surface of the sea. When the contents mingle life begins in millions of fertilized cells and live plankton is formed. At the same time many other forms of sea life, marine worms, sea slugs, molluscs, and other creatures hitch on to the coral spawning wagon and also release their own eggs to form a *'Plankton soup'* which spreads far and wide across the surface of the sea.

That, in turn, triggers a huge amount of other marine activity, with fish feeding and mating, and a flurry of prawn and tropical krill crustaceans hatching. On the Barrier Reef the coral spawning occurs in spring, in the months of October and November. Marine biologist, Dr Chris Simpson, researching in the Dampier Archipelago in March 1984, found that the phenomenon also occurred in WA, but at different time of year. On the west coast the coral spawning takes place in autumn after the March and April full moons and on the seventh to the ninth night after the full moon.

In 1986 scientists from the WA Department of National Parks came to Exmouth to observe the coral spawning on the Ningaloo Reef. *'It struck me immediately'* Geoff Taylor wrote in his book *' That this was a natural occurrence of sufficient magnitude to explain the appearances of the whale sharks at a particular time of year!'*

He decided to make his own observations. With a friend Les Eadon he ventured out to Bundegi Reef at dusk. *'There is something very lonely about keeping vigil surrounded only be the inky blackness of night, waiting for an event such as coral spawning floating in a tiny inflatable dinghy. 'I kept diving down in the darkness with a light to inspect the coral and it looked the same as always. It was 8.25 pm and still nothing had happened. I had promised to be home by 9.00 pm, but we decided to give it five more minutes. Suddenly I noticed some tiny pink specks floating on the surface that had not been there before. Two minutes more and the pink specks were everywhere. We grabbed our SCUBA gear and descended to the coral to watch the mass releasing of eggs and sperm. The sight of all that spawn swirling around the coral heads was like an underwater dance and to see it for the first time was absolutely enthralling!'*

Sure enough, the whale sharks next appeared soon after the coral spawning! The trigger of the phase of the moon and the spawning was on record. With that practical information Taylor was able to predict almost to the day when the whale sharks would be most abundant, and he wrote a paper based on the findings for the *West Australian Naturalist* magazine in 1989.

Now that he had the first part of the whale shark timetable Geoff Taylor was anxious to know more about *Rhincondon's* distribution and movements. He had already decided that the Baron was too thirsty on petrol and too expensive to spend long periods at sea. He opted instead for a sailing catamaran christened *Tribeaut.* But the most effective study means of all was found to be aerial surveys. The sharks were big and since they usually obligingly swam on the surface they were highly visible. On one flight with Peter Arscot in March, 1988, they saw 16 sharks along the Ningaloo Reef flying south, and 28 on the way back. Such an extensive range of sightings would have been impossible from a boat.

Clearly that was the way to go. Geoff Taylor applied to the Australian National Parks and Wildlife Service to finance an aerial survey and was successful in obtaining a research grant for 1990. Other surveys followed in 1991 and 1992 confirming the arrival of the whale sharks after the coral spawning. What the whales were eating, filtering through their gill plates, was not only the plankton itself but other creatures, including massed marine worms, tropical krill, and small fish such as anchovies which fed on the plankton. The food chain extending from creatures so small that they were barely visible to the naked eye, to a whale shark 12 metres in length and many tons in weight. The wonders of Nature!

Others in Exmouth saw the potential of whale sharks in a different light. Could they prove a magnet for international divers seeking something different on the world circuit? Tony Medcraft, the proprietor of *Exmouth Dive* travelled to Japan with pictures and film to promote Ningaloo Reef and Exmouth and the whale sharks. The result was an influx of Japanese divers in 1990 and succeeding years. The Japanese television company NHK made documentaries on the Ningaloo whale sharks, and National Geographic and Rodney Fox from South Australia engaged George King and his boats *Nordon* and *The Gun* on charter to make films for world release. Suddenly Exmouth was on the map for international divers looking for something spectacular and different!

Not everyone among the locals realised the significance of what was happening. One day at a Shire function in Exmouth Geoff Taylor suggested to one of the Shire executives that they should put a picture of a whale shark on the front of Exmouth's tourist brochures. The man was horrified at the idea! *'What?'* he exclaimed. *'Why on earth would we want to do that?'* He shook his head. '*We couldn't have sharks associated with our tourist advertising! It would frighten people away!'*

Of course that attitude would change 180 degrees within a short time. The whale shark would become the symbol of Exmouth to the world, and in succeeding years *Rhincondon typus* with its familiar pattern of white spots would be foremost in all the promotions of the town..

When Geoff Taylor reviews his own achievements he is quick to point out that he didn't *'Discover'* the Exmouth whale sharks. Fishermen doing the snapper run to Shark Bay and others had made sightings of them through quite a number of years. Clem Hill, at one time an Exmouth prawning skipper with his boat *Sea Wyffe*, had photographs of a whale shark on the surface published in the Perth *Daily News* in the 1960s.

'George King and the professional charterers had seen them long before I turned up in Exmouth' Taylor said modestly. *'My achievement, if that's what you want to call it, was in the research side of things'.*

What he did do was to document the large numbers of sharks arriving at Ningaloo and identify quite a number of individuals who made regular appearances. His linking of the coral spawning to the sharks and the ability to forecast the timing of the sharks arrival, would prove immensely helpful for charter boat skippers drawing up their winter programs and for the Visitor Centre advising people when to come to Exmouth to see the sharks.

There was another area in which Geoff Taylor was a contributor. Photography as well as science would be a major factor in promoting Exmouth to the outside world. His film of whale sharks was included in the Parers' ABC documentary in 1986. By 1987 he was in the unique position of being the only person in the world with a library of colour 16 mm film of whale sharks.

Documentary makers from all over the world began to contact him in his remote outpost of Exmouth. His footage was used in television films in Britain, as well as in France and Italy. But Geoff Taylor's long-term ambition was to convince one of the international film producers into actually coming out to Exmouth, and he hoped to be able to take part in the filming. He went to London twice, in 1988 and 1989 in efforts to get the documentary off the ground.

While progress was frustratingly slow he managed to meet a world-renowned wild life photographer Tony Bomford. In turn Bomford introduced Geoff Taylor to Frances Berrigan of *Cicada* films who was excited about the idea of an Exmouth whale shark film. When Taylor met him again in London in 1990 Berrigan set about raising the funding from a consortium of United States, Japanese, and New Zealand television interests.

The film, made in 1992, was widely distributed to viewers in those countries, helping to create worldwide interest in the Ningaloo whale shark phenomenon. For Geoff Taylor the most memorable sequence was his own footage of whale sharks in a feeding frenzy with plankton at night. This film remains unique in the world. A substantial amount of Geoff's film was used in the documentary, and – while he would rather have been the film maker – he found himself more often in front of the camera than behind it.

Geoff had insisted that some of the film budget should be used to fund the aerial surveys of sharks. In 1991 he initiated a photo-identification program. Ultimately he had a personal library of photographs of over 150 sharks with measurements of their dorsal fins and had marked a considerable number with fish tags for future recognition. The next step was to fit some sharks with electronic devices for satellite tracking to see where else the sharks travelled around the world.

Dr Taylor published his book *Whale Sharks, the Giants of Ningaloo Reef*, in 1994, illustrated with dozens of his own colour photographs. He also published numerous scientific papers on aerial survey results, population estimates, the influence of El Nino and the feeding behaviour of whale sharks. He is most proud of a collaboration with Dr Alan Pearce of the CSIRO. Together, in 1999, they were responsible for identifying and naming the *'Ningaloo Current'*.

This is a counter current to the main Leeuwin Current which carries plankton along the reef. The Ningaloo Current *'Creates a circulatory movement of water and determines where the main blooms of krill and plankton occur. It is one of the key factors in determining where the whale sharks will be'*.

While Geoff Taylor was busying himself with science, another feeding frenzy was about to take place, this time with cameras. His whale shark film had created enormous interest among wild life film makers around the world. Underwater films had proved to be major successes on television in the United States, Europe, Great Britain and Japan. They included *'Specials'* on Humpback whales in Hawaii, Right whales in Patagonia, Killer whales in Canada, Polar bears on Arctic ice, and schools of Hammerhead sharks in the Sea Of Cortez in Mexico. Each new discovery of interesting marine animals in exotic locations saw international film crews racing to the spot to capture the creatures on film.

Exmouth was the end of the earth if you happened to live in London, New York, or Tokyo. But the more remote and *'different'* and difficult the location the better from the audience point of view! *'Go boys, get 'em!'* in several different languages. So other film makers flocked to Exmouth, and the local charter boat operators led by George King with his boats *The Gun* and *Nordon* were delighted to receive them. Some of the biggest names in world diving, including Dr Eugenie Clark and Stan Waterman from the United States, Ron and Valerie Taylor, and Ben Cropp, from Australia, made the pilgrimage to the Ningaloo Reef.

Your author made his own first underwater sighting of a whale shark in 1995, when the first excitement was at its peak. It was an unforgettable experience. A friend Les Valmadre had connections with an American travel firm called *Tiny Bubbles Expeditions*, run by Doug Sieffert. Doug was typical of the Americans coming to Exmouth. He had previously been diving on Great white sharks in South Australia, and had just done a stint of diving and filming with sperm whales in the Azores. Les rang me to say that Doug had had cancellations and there were two vacancies in accommodation and on a charter boat. Did I want to come and photograph the whale sharks?

It was an unexpected and wonderful opportunity. Some of our most memorable moments come by chance. No-one who hasn't dived with a whale shark can imagine what a totally amazing experience awaits them. I had seen the films and the photographs. I had even seen whale sharks on the surface from a boat on two previous occasions. But – while I thought I knew what to expect – nothing had prepared me for what I would see on the actual day.

We went out to the reef aboard *Nordon 11*, towing a bright red inflatable tender. Spotter aircraft circled overhead. John Starling was skipper, Graeme Russell supervised the deck and got people ready to dive, and Kevin Stone drove the inflatable. The pilot talked to us by radio from somewhere up in a blue sky. His voice crackled over the loudspeaker.

'Get ready Nordon. You have one just ahead of you, on the port bow'.

'Go!' said Graeme. *'Go now!'*

We tumbled into the rubber duck to take our places sitting along the sides and pulling on our fins. Kevin operated the twin outboard throttles with one hand and held a two way radio in the other.

The Cessna stood on its wingtip in a tight turn above us.

'Two hundred metres ahead of you, at two o'clock .. You read me Kevin?'

'Roger! Read you loud and clear!'

'Slow down now. Ten boat lengths on your starboard bow. One o'clock'

'Affirmative. Divers get ready!'

Kevin pulled back the throttle levers, and the inflatable glided towards a huge dark shadow that looked like a mass of seaweed -- except that it was moving!

'Divers GO!'

We were all experienced divers. Everyone knew what to do. On both sides of the inflatable fins went up in the air and divers rolled over backwards into the water clutching their cameras to their chests. Splash! Splash! Splash!

The bubbles of entry cleared and suddenly there it was right on top of us!

HUGE!

There was a moment of actual shock. I knew the whale shark would be big, and –as I said – I had seen the film footage, seen the pictures and I thought I knew what to expect. But I was quite unprepared for the reality which now appeared before my face mask. The damn thing was more than 9 metres long! Longer than my boat *Beachcomber 111* at home! And it seemed about as wide as the driveway of my house! For a moment it shut out the sun.

WHOOPS! There was a momentary risk of a collision as a scooped pectoral fin the size of a yachtsman's dinghy swept past me. I goggled at a pitted side suffused with white dots and lined with prehistoric raised ridges. Suddenly there was a tail high as a factory gate sweeping methodically from side to side and I realised that the giant was on its way. While I was gawping in astonishment there was a danger I would be left behind in its wake.

'Get your act together!' I told myself *'And kick, bloody kick! Or you'll lose him!'*

It took a lot of effort, even with the outsize fins I had bought specially for the occasion, to catch up and get past the monster's head to level my camera. I was puffing and breathless, sucking air in gulps, by the time I got my first shot.

The shark's head was enormous, a partly-open mouth seemed easily wide enough to accommodate a diver sideways. Though the huge animal showed no sign of aggression. It merely opened and closed enormous gill slits in a gentle rhythm. A behemoth moving through the water.

Despite the size there was no suggestion of threat.

In fact the shark looked at me seemingly benevolently with a *'Peace brother, peace!'* expression in yellow eyes which were surprisingly small in such a huge body. Little yellow fish with black stripes swam in a cluster just under its chin.

A black remora suckerfish detached itself from the giant's belly and swam over to briefly inspect me. Then, apparently deciding that I was not a good alternative, it turned about and clamped itself back again to the shark's underside. A case of '*Better the Devil you know*'?

The shark was always moving, a huge mass, going through the water at an effortless four miles an hour. We could just keep up with it, but getting ahead of it to take pictures with a frontal angle (always more interesting than a rear view) required busts of speed which were exhausting. The unexpected effort had me gasping for breath through my snorkel.

The shark seemed to take little notice of the Lilliputian human figures around him, kicking urgently like frogs and poking their cameras at him. He knew we were there, of course. But he was no more concerned about us than the cloud of fish which accompanied him. Perhaps he put us in the same bracket -- dutiful courtiers attendant on the king! Some of the fish even brazenly swam in and out of his mouth pecking at the ticks which had fastened to the interior of that great cavernous space.

After a time he appeared to make a heavy sigh and dived down on an angle of forty five degrees. The last thing we saw were his white spots disappearing into the darkness of the deeper water. For the moment that was the end of the show. Our first whale shark! We were left back on the surface in a daze of wonder, getting our breath back and waiting to be picked up by the red inflatable. Everyone had that shining look in their eyes, the broad grins on their faces, which said that we had just experienced one of the great moments of our diving lives. Fantastic!

It was a wonderful time. We dived every day for a week, celebrated at the Pot Shot in the evenings, and shot roll after roll of 35 mm film of Ningaloo whale sharks. With up to seven sharks a day and practice making us more proficient and selective, each roll was better than the last. On the final day at the boat ramp at Tantabiddi I bumped into Geoff Taylor in town to promote his new book *Whale Sharks, The Giants of the Ningaloo Reef.*

'It's a long way from the shearing shed' he said with a grin, referring to our accommodation at Ningaloo Station on the Museum expedition to the *Rapid* wreck in 1980. The place where we had first met.

'A long way to all this' I agreed, waving an arm to indicate the scene at the Tantabiddi ramp. The parking area was a mass of cars and buses, trucks, and boat trailers, with people milling between the vehicles, many of them carrying diving bags. And all of them there because of *Rhincondon typus.*

There might easily have been a dozen different nationalities present that day. The Japanese were easy to pick, the Americans fairly evident by their dress and their tone of speech and long shorts below their knees. It was a little harder to differentiate between the Brits, the French, and Germans. 'Except that the British seemed to get sunburned feet with crimson insteps, and often wore socks with their leather sandals. You could tell the Aussies by their rubber thongs (nick-named *'Japanese riding boots'*) and sunglasses on strings and the fact that their sun tans were better established, having had a summer to work on them . They were cheekier as well. It was their country after all. Their sharks too? Well, they didn't mind sharing ...It was a good atmosphere.

Out on the water were a dozen charter boats lying to their moorings, like dogs on leads, with aluminium and inflatable dinghies busily going to and fro with white vee wakes, bringing the customers back to shore. There had been eight boats out that day with from 20 to 30 people aboard each of them. The vehicles, the boats, the buses, the people, the whole milling mass, were all there because of the whale sharks.

Geoff Taylor, with his research and his book, had played a part. We know so much more about whale sharks thanks to Taylor and the scientists.

We also had to learn about the best way to maintain the interaction and the whale sharks in the interests of both parties. From the earliest days of tourists swimming with whale sharks the Department of Environment and Conservation (previously titled Conservation And Land Management) was concerned that adequate controls should be imposed to protect the creatures from over-exploitation. Whale sharks, after all, were protected under both Commonwealth and State Government laws. It was fundamental that the number of boats involved had to be limited and as a result charter boats had to be licensed.

To avoid conflict between the operators there had to be rules about boat movements, and it was necessary to establish a code of conduct for swimmers in the water. It was agreed by tour operators that mother boats would stay at a distance of 250 metres from the sharks, and tenders dropping swimmers would approach no closer than 30 metres.

In early encounters photographers had liked to get pictures of divers hanging on to the fins of whale sharks and being drawn along with them. The spectacle made for spectacular shots, but it was quickly realised that the normally placid sharks could be disturbed by the physical contacts. Later regulations prohibited divers from touching the sharks or coming too close and affecting their normal movements. Divers were required to keep a distance of at least three metres, with no more than 10 divers allowed in the water at any one time. It was also found that the sharks disliked the bright light of camera flashes. But because they usually swim on the surface in sunlit conditions flashes are not necessary. The sharks also disliked SCUBA bubbles.

The Department of Environment and Conservation (DEC) kept regular figures of visitor and shark numbers at Ningaloo from 1996. Scans of photographs by ECOCEAN, using the patterns of spots to recognize individuals, identified 356 different sharks between 1992 and 2006. One shark from 1992 appeared again 14 years later in 2006. A study by the Australian Institute of Marine Sciences (AIMS) has estimated that the pool of whale sharks visiting the Ningaloo Reef consists of 300 to 500 individuals..

DEC Whale Shark Project officer Emily Wilson said that a survey of visitors revealed that 50 per cent of the people taking whale shark dives were from overseas. Of the 50 per cent of Australian divers, half were from Western Australia. In her annual report for DEC Emily Wilson noted that in 2006-07 a total of 13 licensed charter boats were operating on whale sharks on the Ningaloo Reef. Ten of these worked out from Tantabiddi, and three were based at Coral Bay where there was also an important tourist centre.

Figures showed that the boats were 81 per cent successful in finding sharks for their average 15 clients per trip over a total of 520 tours. In cases where no sharks were sighted on the day most operators allowed a repeat at no charge, in a commendable policy of *'No show another go!'.*

Eighty two of the sharks seen in 2006 were sighted more than once, according to the AIMS photo index, with 48 from previous years re-appearing. ECOCEAN photo analysis identified 79 individual sharks in 2006, and confirmed that 51 per cent had been pictured at Ningaloo in previous years, indicating that the same sharks were coming back on a regular basis.

So what is it that we positively DO know and DON'T know about whale sharks?

Well, just to start with *Rhincondon typus*, the whale shark is a very large creature It grows to more than 12 metres and perhaps even 15 metres in length, and may get to weigh an incredible 34,000 kilograms. This makes them the largest *'fish'* in all the oceans of the world. They surpass in size their rival filter-feeders, *Cetorhinus maximus,* the *'Basking* shark' of the North Atlantic, and the Pacific *Megamouth*. Despite their enormous adult bulk whale sharks begin life not much bigger than a salmon, the young measuring from 40 to 60 centimetres. While we expect to see them on the surface they can also dive one and a half kilometres below the waves and they apparently spend quite a bit of time right down deep.

The original scientific name, *Rhincondon* or '*Rasp teeth'*, referred to the hundreds of small teeth in the whale shark's jaw. These have no natural function, the food inhaled through the giant mouth is sieved through the fine mesh of the gill rakers. These can sort organisms as small as 1 millimetre in diameter. Only one pregnant female, killed by fishermen off Taiwan, had ever been scientifically examined up to the year 2000. She was 11 metres in length and found to have no less than 300 embryos in her womb. Some of the baby sharks were in egg cases, others free-living. But it was believed that they would all be hatched out before being released into the world by their mother. Clearly, as with other creatures with multiple births, such as turtles, there would be a high mortality rate in the young. Where do the little ones go? Do they hide in the deeps of tropical oceans?

FRANK PAXMAN was a spearfisherman, not a treasure hunter. When he found that he had dropped his anchor into an old wreck where Spanish silver dollars lay scattered on the sea floor he was totally amazed.

THE KING OF SPAIN'S MONEY. Barry Paxman sorts through Spanish silver dollars from the wreck of the American clipper Rapid. He said that the coins, lying in profusion, looked like 'black biscuits'. Later they cleaned up with the gleam of old world silver. (Picture: Patrick Baker, WA Museum)

A RARE FIND: Patrick Baker films the ship's bell of the Rapid. A ship's bell is always the Holy Grail for wreck divers. (Picture: Jeremy Green)

MUSEUM DIVERS Bob Richards and Larry Patterson working the airlift on the bottom timbers of the 1811 Rapid wreck. Note the bag of coins in the foreground. (Picture: Patrick Baker)

DAVE MONGAN'S tour bus takes tourists from one end of the North West Cape to the other. Tours include a boat trip on Yardie Creek, and snorkelling at Turquoise Bay. (Picture: Karin Calvert Borshoff)

ABORIGINAL SHELLS lie on old camp sites along the Ningaloo coast. The hollowed out baler shells were used as domestic utensils. Some may have been children's toys. They may be more than 150 years old. People today are unaware of the history on the ground they are passing over. When this photo was taken a tourist had just passed by and crushed the shell at top left under his foot, reducing it to fragments and unwittingly destroying part of the story of the land and the people who once lived there. These items should be in a museum. (Picture: Hugh Edwards)

LAW OF NATURE. An osprey decided that this old chimney at Tantabiddi was a fine place on which to build a nest. Little birds decided that inside the chimney was a fine place to build their nest too, since ospreys eat only fish. But they had reckoned without the little hawk waiting outside! (Picture: Hugh Edwards)

Ospreys fall on fish from the air, talons outstretched, and sometimes are submerged as much as a metre. With the fish locked in their grasp they surface with strong wing beats and take to the air again. It is noticeable that they always grab their fish with the head pointing forwards presumably for aerodynamic reasons.

Pandion haliaetus and their conspicuous nests are a feature of the North West Cape. They readily adapt to man-made structures building nests on towers, beacons, and radio masts. In the wild they build a pyramid of dry sticks and sea-weed and some Australian nests have been up to two metres in height and may be nearly 100 years old. (Pictures: Karin Calvert Borshoff)

(Pictures: Hugh Edwards)

KANGAROOS are the visitors' favourite animal in the Cape Range National Park. They may be seen in numbers, especially in the late afternoon , on the road to Yardie Creek. Visitors need to drive carefully because Kangaroos are uncertain in dealing with traffic. They may become accident victims if the setting sun or vehicle headlights after dark shine in their eyes.

YARDIE CREEK rock wallaby sitting on its tail. Why do they do that? Perhaps for grooming. (Picture: Karin Calvert Borshoff)

FATAL CONFRONTATION – Kangaroos and speeding motorists don't mix well.

EMUS WALK as though they own the streets in Exmouth. Locals give them right of way. The male bird brings up the chicks, and daddies can often be seen strolling with a clutch of little ones down the road. (Picture: Hugh Edwards)

WHITE HERONS are a part of the spectacular bird life of Yardie Creek, often making their nests in clefts in the cliffs. (Picture: Karin Calvert Borshoff)

NOISY COMMUNAL BIRDS pink-and-grey galahs like to flock together and search for grass seeds on road verges.

THIS BUSH TURKEY thinks he is safe because he is on the other side of a fence. A Winchester 44 rifle, the bushman's favourite, would have fixed that. In the old days he would have been Sunday dinner. Today all creatures in the Cape Range National Park are protected. (Picture: Hugh Edwards)

HORSES, like dogs, were man's best friend in the bush in the old station days on North West Cape. Today they have been replaced for mustering and general station work by the mechanical motor cycle. (Pictures: Hugh Edwards)

Scientists believe that the sharks are slow-growing and do not become mature enough to breed until they are 20 to 30 years old. They may live 60 to 100 years in natural conditions. Their only relatives in the shark world, the wobbegong or carpet shark, and the leopard shark, are both bottom dwellers, with body lengths of less than three metres.

Whale sharks are found world wide in warm tropical and sub-tropical waters, of 100 countries from the Gulf of Mexico to China, Ningaloo to East Africa, Indonesia to the Coral Sea. The author swam with one in the Gulf of Siam while on a wreck hunting expedition out of Cambodia in 1996. But the sharks are only found in aggregations in places where some natural event like the Ningaloo coral spawning brings them together. As an example, at Christmas Island in mid-Indian Ocean each December it is the spectacular seasonal spawning of the red land crabs at the sea edge that brings them there.

Whale sharks may have the thickest skin of any marine or terrestrial creature, as thick as 12-15 centimetres on the dorsal surface of the skin of adult animals. The purpose of the white spots on the epidermis is unknown, though it may help to disguise the outline of the creature against the sea bed. Interestingly each shark has a different pattern of dots in the head and gill area, like a finger print in humans, enabling scientist to identify individual sharks and maintain a record of sightings through the years. Australian Brad Norman, of Cottesloe, Western Australia, a research associate of Curtin University, has been working on identification and global protection of whale sharks since 1994.

As part of his study he enlisted the help of American scientists involved in the NASA space program. The computer program used on the Hubble Space Telescope to map the stars in the galaxy can be adapted to decipher the patterns of the spots on individual whale sharks, *'finger-printing'* the animal. *'This means that if people have photographs of whale sharks anywhere in the world'* Norman said *'They can send them in and we can see whether the same shark has been seen elsewhere and perhaps chart its travels'*. He set up an internet web site ECOCEAN as a public awareness project. *By 2007,* he said, *he had received copies of photographs from 26 countries.*

A mature whale shark has no natural enemies, but nonetheless the species may be seriously endangered. The problem is the fishing activities of that greatest and greediest of all predators, *Homo sapiens*. As many as 1000 sharks a year are believed to have been killed in Indian waters in 1999 and 2000. An unsustainable number. Taiwan caught 270 whale sharks in 1999 and 100 in 2001.

There is no record of whale sharks taken in Indonesia where there are no restrictions. But the electronic tag from one Ningaloo shark showed it was swimming normally at 9.30 in the morning and by noon the satellite signal ominously showed that the tag was on the beach on the island of Roti in southern Indonesia (!).

Satellite tracking of tagged sharks has confirmed that they have a wide range of movement. One tagged shark swam from the west coast of the United States to Tonga, a distance of 13,000 kilometres. Many sharks tagged at Ningaloo have swum as far afield as India and Sri Lanka or wandered up through the Indonesian archipelago into the South China Sea and into areas where they have no protection status.

Dr Mark Meekan, who was involved with the joint AIMS and CSIRO tagging and electronic tagging program of whale sharks, and co-author of a report with Dr Corey Bradshaw, said that it was important that the Australian Government worked with countries such as Indonesia to promote eco-tourism and help stem the predation of endangered species. Fishermen and local politicians needed to become aware that whale sharks were worth much more alive than dead.

Is there a possibility that indiscriminate hunting could see the end of a creature that had survived millions of years since *Jurassic* times? The same danger that saw tigers endangered for the black market in their whiskers and claws for Chinese herbal remedies, elephants for their ivory, bears for their paws?

Hope may yet lie just over the international horizon. With international pressure has brought to bear on countries within the whale shark's annual orbit. India officially banned the capture of whale sharks in 2001.There is also a ban by the Philippines government, the Maldives, the Galapagos, and now Taiwan. They are protected in areas of the United States, Mexico, and Honduras.

If sufficient international awareness can be aroused, *Rhincondon typus,* already a 30 million-year visitor to our waters, may yet continue to grace the Ningaloo Reef long into the future.

Meantime *RT* remains Exmouth's major tourism drawcard. The piscatorial King of the Ningaloo Reef.

'God Save the King!'

RHINCONDON TYPUS to the rescue! (Picture: Paull Weall)

The Coral Heartbeat

Chapter Thirteen

The early Dutch, French, and British explorers were as disparaging about the fringing coral reefs of '*New Holland*' as they were about the perceived barren nature of the land. Where the reefs were concerned they had only one instruction to steersmen – '*DANGER!... Stay Clear!*'

To them reefs of any kind, coral or otherwise, were rocks. It was fundamental to a seaman that rocks sank ships and drowned sailors. So they marked reefs with rows of crosses on their charts, and their rule was that you kept right away from them.

Even the great naturalist, hydrographer and pirate, William Dampier who sailed past the North West Cape in the former fireship *Roebuck* in 1699, had little to say about them.

He would have seen, and doubtless stubbed his toes from time to time, on plenty of loose coral in his years in the Caribbean, Sumatra, and the Philippines. But we presume that he saw the reefs as merely background to the mobile creatures which he found more interesting. He described and sketched hundreds of birds, plants, animals, and fishes, but devoted little attention to the undersea environment in which the marine creatures lived.

Charles Darwin, whose *Origin of the Species* would change all scientific thinking in his approach to Evolution, did give coral reefs consideration. But he saw them chiefly in terms of their evidence of the earth's altering sea levels. In those terms he found that live corals did not grow below 36 metres of seawater. But he didn't study the corals themselves or the creatures adapted to living amongst them. In fact he devoted far more time to the finches of the Galapagos Islands in the Pacific, than to the corals of Cocos Island in the Indian Ocean when he called there with *HMS Beagle* in 1832.

There is a simple reason for the apparent indifference and, to be fair, we can hardly be critical of the two scientists in the circumstances. In 1699, Dampier's day, and 1832, when Darwin sailed, there was no easy means of seeing what really went on below the surface of the sea.

On a perfect windless day with no ripple on the water you might get a tantalizing glimpse of the colours of the corals and perhaps even see some shapes of fish flickering around them. But it was not until our own time with swim goggles and face masks and underwater breathing apparatus, that scientists and ordinary people have been able to see life at the bottom of the sea as fish see it themselves.

Imagine how different the published works of Dampier and Darwin might have been if they had had the advantages of being able to strap on a SCUBA rig and breathe underwater? Exchanging cocked hats for modern face masks? Our imagination may struggle a little to grasp the image!

First times are always important. My own first underwater experience was at Rottnest Island after the Second World War. As a 13 year-old I had been inspired by films of '*frogmen*' commandos in breathing apparatus riding underwater chariots into Axis harbours.

Once past the searchlights and submarine nets and other hazards they affixed limpet mines to enemy warships, sinking them in spectacular explosions.

They were the '*Cockleshell heroes'* of their day in fact as well as fiction. There were books about them like James Benson's *Above Us The Waves* as well as movies on the same theme. I was impressed, like most small boys. On reflection it seemed to me that the masks the charioteers wore were much the same as the pig-faced Air Raid Protection gas masks which could be purchased for a couple of shillings at any war surplus store. I bought a mask, took the chemical canister off the end of the crinkly hose, inserted the end of my mother's laundry hose, and -- Presto! – I was in business!

Some time later, when the opportunity occurred during the Christmas school holidays, I gave the outfit its first trial. I pulled the gas mask on over my face, making a few adjustments with the straps. Then -- with the end of the hose grasped in my left hand and held above the surface as an impromptu snorkel -- I launched myself into the sea to be instantly amazed by what I saw. My friend Bruce Lawson and I had dived into that rock pool at Rottnest Island many times in past school holidays, swimming with eyes open, seeing rocks and moving objects with blurred vision. Now everything came into focus, sharp and clear, as though I were a fish myself.

'There's fish here! Millions of 'em !' I shouted through the hose. Then cough, choke, splutter, as the end of the hose went underwater. *'You should see'* cough, cough *'What I can see!'*

We had often walked past the diving pool, or dived from the high rock which gave the Diving Pool its name. Sometimes, before surfacing, we had seen silver flashes of fish through our blurred vision so that we knew there were fish in the pool. But nothing had prepared me for the number of fish that I could see in their own element with the glass eye-pieces of the gas mask between my eyes and the water.

It was a view the designer and manufacturer of the gas mask had never intended. No doubt they would have been as surprised as I was at the success of this novel use of their apparatus. But – surprise, surprise -- it did work, and I was amazed that there seemed to be fish everywhere. They were all sizes and shapes. Some were as bright and colourful as the parrots we saw ashore. The striped and brighter coloured fish seemed to be mostly stationary, balancing on slowly moving fins and hovering near cave entrances and crevices ready to dash for cover should danger threaten. The swiftly moving fish were all silver, swimming around me anti-clockwise in a continual stream. I recognized silver drummer, skipjack, and herring, from seeing them brought up on the end of fishing lines.

A fish in trouble, like a human in the same fix, is a pathetic sight. These swam around me boldly and confidently, assessing this strange goggle-eyed being which had appeared among them. Some of them were quite large. My chief recollection is of eyes, dozens of eyes, bright and gleaming, and all looking at me. There was a movement on the bottom. Another pair of eyes were looking up at me. Goat's eyes -- an octopus, eight-legged and camouflaged against the seaweed, broke cover and slithered under a rock.

More eyes, this time in the sand in the center of the pool. A small stingray shook the sand off its back and I backed away to give it the respect I felt it deserved. I had seen dead stingrays ashore and thought them hideously ugly. But this one, an eagle ray with brown and black markings flew birdlike underwater on slender wings. I thought it was really quite beautiful.

But what would be the most enduring memory of that day would be the surface – or at least the underside of the surface. It looked like a silver skin, a molten sky, a metallic ceiling, to the underwater world. We had so often crashed through that surface in dives having no idea of what it might look like from below. Like the rest of the human race we just thought of air and water meeting vaguely -- like in the bath. Now there was a image recorded in my brain – '*Under the silver skin!'*. I liked the sight and sound of it.

I can still remember details of that first dive, even though it took place the better part of a lifetime ago.

At that time, in the immediate post- war world of 1946, (aside from the improvisation of my gas mask) there was no diving equipment available, and a view underwater was something few other people, child or adult, had experienced. That made it an adventure to be recounted with shining eyes and a glow in the cheeks.

Today, is it the case that going underwater is regarded as unremarkable and anyone can do it?

Certainly people are no longer as astonished as we were at our first view of the underwater world. Today everyone has seen the pictures in magazines and the films of divers blowing bubbles on their television sets. The equipment is in dive shops everywhere. It is comparatively easy to use, and since today's acolyte is far removed from being the first to discover what lies underwater there is no longer the former hero-status once attached to divers. But those prosaic facts shouldn't detract from the wonder of another world so different from our normal air-breathing surroundings. A world which Nature never really intended us to discover for ourselves.

Perhaps the reaction depends on the person. If you can see an Indian Ocean sunset in all its crimson glory and turn away unmoved, then almost anything might seem unremarkable. Speaking personally, a sunset will always stop me in my tracks, and the underwater world will forever make me catch my breath.

On my own scale the Ningaloo Reef still ranks with anywhere else in the world, and I have seen many underwater scenes in many countries besides my own. Aside from the visual, the aesthetic beauty of a coral reef, such as the Ningaloo complex, there is the fact that a lifetime would not be long enough to learn about all the creatures and plants, great and small, which inhabit the reef structure and its environs. While the reef itself is highly visible what we are actually looking at are the fused calcium carbonate skeletons of billions of coral polyps which have lived, built, and died over thousands of years. They have become one big limestone lump on which the current *'hard'* coral polyps live and build again. A lump on which ships are sometimes wrecked.

Some of the various forms are easy to recognize by their common names, such as '*staghorn'*, *'cabbage'*, or the *'brain'* corals which grow inside the lagoons. Mostly visitors don't see the coral polyps, the builders of the structures. This is partly because they are so small, mere dots on the coral surfaces, and partly because their six to eight flowering tentacles are retracted during daylight hours. But the main reason we don't usually recognise them is because people simply aren't aware of the existence of the reef-builder polyps, let alone the fact that there are 250 species of coral in the Ningaloo Marine Park!

That ignorance (doesn't '*Lack of knowledge'* sound a lot better?) extends to other areas. Most people are surprised to learn that corals, anemones, hydroids, and jellyfish, are all related. The reef-building corals, the sea anemone, the Portuguese-man-o-war, and the dreaded box jellyfish, are all sisters under their skins. They form the *Cnidarians*, as the group is known to science. All use stinging cells to secure their prey and there are a staggering 9000 species of them in the Indo-Pacific region. The box jellyfish, sometimes called a '*Sea wasp'* – scientific name *Chironex fleckerii* – has been responsible for numerous human fatalities in Queensland and Northern Territory waters.

Though no fatalities have been recorded in Western Australia the species is found as far south as Exmouth. The other jellyfish which can cause serious problems for people is the *Irukanji stinger* (*Carukia barnesi*) dreaded by pearl divers. The *Irukanji* is a tiny jellyfish, barely two centimeters in diameter, and its four trailing tentacles – a similar shape to the box jellyfish – are only five to 50 centimetres long.

But this dwarf among jellyfish carries a massive amount of venom for its size. *Carukia* has caused fatalities in Queensland, and its sting is so painful that bathers in Broome have had to be hospitalized. It takes only a fragment of tentacle to cause acute pain.

Pearl divers, protected elsewhere on their bodies by rubber wet suits, are usually stung around the mouth and lips when exchanging mouth-pieces from air hoses to oxygen after a long dive. *'On one occasion I had to bite on a leather strap to stop myself from screaming'* pearl diver Larry House recalls.

The coral reef is important because it provides shelter for so many other forms of life. The coral polyps contribute too with events such as the coral spawning which bring many other species – including the whale sharks – together at particular times of the year.

There are also a myriad other creatures including crabs, crayfish, shrimps, sea squirts, marine worms and hundreds of radically different sea shell mollusks, all of which make their own kind of living in the reef. Creatures living day by day in their own little worlds. We tend, of course, to have our attention distracted by the more highly visible creatures which catch the eye.

In that respect Ningaloo has the full range of seriously large creatures in the great whales. The most commonly sighted are the humpbacks described in detail in the chapter on whaling. But there are also Sperm whales, Blue whales – earth's largest creature -- Bryde's whales and rorquals. There are also the orcas, the killer whales identifiable by their knife-shaped dorsal fins, as well as pilot whales and false killers.

Other large denizens in the reef environment are whale sharks, manta rays, and dugongs. Among the shark family there are tiger sharks, bull sharks, makos, hammerheads, black-tips, white-tips, leopard and nurse sharks, and even the occasional Great white shark on its sinister lonely patrol. Among the bill-fish there are black, blue, and striped marlin, sailfish, and broadbill swordfish.

The familiar bottlenose dolphins can often be seen sporting around the bows of the charter boats. In deeper water there are common dolphins, spotted dolphins, risso's dolphins, spinner dolphins, and in the Gulf itself, the strange-looking Indo-Pacific humpbacked or *'Irrawaddy'* dolphin. The biggest of the boney fishes are the giant cod. Both the Queensland groper and the potato cod beloved of photographers, may reach impressive sizes.

Then there are the reptiles, the green, loggerhead, and hawksbill turtles, and several varieties of sea snakes. In short, Ningaloo has many more species of fishes, sharks, marine mammals, and reptiles than you could attempt to name in a single breath.

How many species?

The Marine Life of Ningaloo Marine Park & Coral Bay by Ann Storrie and Sue Morrison lists 500 species of fish, 600 species of molluscs, and 250 known species of corals. The word '*known'* implying that we may have missed a few. And that's before we start on shrimps, crabs, and lobsters, marine worms, sea stars and urchins. 'Not to mention sea squirts, and cephalopods, barnacles, sea lice, and plankton. We also need to include the plants and seagrasses. All a part of the wonderfully complex undersea world.

The Ningaloo Reef system is the longest shore-fringing coral reef in the world. It stretches 300 kilometres from the Muiron Islands and Sunday Island to Bundegi, around the tip of the Cape and south past Point Cloates and Coral Bay to Amherst Point. It is also the heartbeat of the Exmouth region.

The reef has had its literal ups and downs. In *Ningaloo: Australia's Untamed Reef*, a work in process, Hans Kemps describes how the Cape Range was once a coral reef itself. The Range is a fold in the earth's surface which was once under the sea. Kemps suggests that 14 million years ago tectonic activity pushed the reef upwards until it became first a series of islands, then the hills of the Cape Range which are now 330 metres above sea level.

Sharks' teeth and sea shells embedded in the limestone high above the sea remain to tell the story of those early years.

Sea levels varied greatly in the past due to the Ice Age and other factors. At the height of the Ice Age 18,000 years ago, when Australia was joined to New Guinea and Tasmania, sea levels were as much as 130 metres lower than today.

The area of the present Ningaloo reef would have been dry land. The modern Ningaloo Reef may be quite *'young'* in those terms – perhaps only 7000 to 8000 years old.

If the reef is the living focus of marine life in the region, its pulse is the Leeuwin Current. This slow moving body of water feeds all of Western Australia's coral reefs from Ashmore, Seringapatam, and Scott Reefs in the north, to the Rowley Shoals, the Dampier Archiplago, Monte Bello and Barrow Islands, the Ningaloo Reef, Shark Bay, and the Abrolhos Islands, further south. It stimulates coral growth much further south in Western Australia than on the west coasts of the world's other continents. In Africa and the Americas all the corals are on the east coasts.

The Leeuwin Current is a comparatively narrow band of warm tropical water which originates far away in the equatorial Pacific Ocean. Like an invisible river, it flows down through the Indonesian Archipelago, down the Western Australian coast and around Cape Leeuwin towards Tasmania.

It colonises Australian reefs with organisms brought down from tropical areas. These include, Kemp says, seeds, eggs, larvae, and juveniles of corals, sponges, fishes, invertebrates, sea grasses and algae which have populated the reefs. Ningaloo, which benefited from this transportation of organisms when the shore-line re-submerged after the Ice Age, is now a self-propagating ecosystem, sending its own eggs and juveniles on in turn to more southerly regions.

Most visitors, more interested in visual stimulation rather than the scientific record, look over the top of the staghorns and cabbage corals. They hope to observe some of the large and more spectacular marine animals swimming about over the coral heads. They are seldom disappointed.

Rhincondon typus, the whale shark, has become the popular symbol of Ningaloo Reef diving, as we have already discussed. Certainly it raises the most inquiries at the Exmouth Visitors'Centre, and in season the visitor has more chance of diving with a whale shark off the Ningaloo Reef than anywhere else in the world.

In the circumstances some of the other species, which are just as interesting in their own particular way, may be somewhat overshadowed. Take manta rays as an example. *Manta birostris* shares two things in common with whale sharks – mantas are also filter feeders, eating planktonic crustaceans and small bony fishes scooped into the wide mouth by two strange cephalic lobes.

They are also seriously large, sometimes achieving a maximum width of nine metres across their diamond-shaped bodies, and 1400 kilograms in weight.

Notes provided by the Western Australian Department of Environment and Conservation tell us that nine metres is about the length of two family cars, nose to nose, bumper to bumper.

The larger mantas on the Ningaloo Reef and in Exmouth Gulf tend to be around seven metres body width, ranging down to a mere three metres. The name '*Manta*', is the Spanish for *'blanket'* coming from Mexican fishermen. The English in the Caribbean at one time called them *'Devilfish'* because of a perceived sinister appearance. But in fact the manta does no harm to anyone. It does not even have a sting in its tail like stingrays.

Interestingly mantas have the largest brain of all the fishes. Does that make them smarter? We don't really know. Because they have no commercial value and don't threaten anyone, they haven't attracted a lot of scientific study. We can't even guess about how long they live, whether they have a social pecking order, or much about their migratory habits.

As with the whale sharks, where they happen to be at any one time probably depends on such feeding factors as the coral spawning and the movement of planktonic crustacea.

They make for fabulous underwater photographs, and diving with mantas can be a very rewarding experience. Patience is needed as with all large sea creatures. If the diver chases, or swims fast towards the object of interest, the manta is likely to become *'spooked'* and depart. However if the diver remains stationary there is a good chance that the Manta – a naturally curious creature – will come to inspect him or her, thereby providing the best camera image. That is a rule which also applies to most of the larger fishes, sharks, and rays.

Mantas are often in large groups, sometimes 50 or more individuals wheeling about – a spectacular sight! They play host to sucker fishes and cleaner wrasses, and like whale sharks often have traveling companions of other species, usually juvenile cobia, trevally, or even spotted eagle rays.

Are these *'pets'* in the same way that humans have cats and dogs? The companions, of course, have the protection of the Manta in a symbiotic association.

Different mantas may have different personalities, sometimes banking and looping around a diver, apparently just for fun. They can also be romantic. Department of the Environment and Conservation marine park notes tell us:

'*Mating occurs when one or more males chase a female... He nips the tip of her pectoral fin which impairs her swimming, moves to her underbelly and inserts one of his claspers (like sharks) into her cloaca, thereby mating belly to belly. The male may hold on to the female's pectoral fin for several minutes after removing his clasper, eventually letting her go..'*

'Ain't love grand?'

One of DEC's particular requests to visitors is that, despite the natural human inclination to reach out and touch interesting animals, we keep our hands to ourselves. Mantas, like most fishes, have a protective covering on their skins. If we touch them it may remove the covering and may '*Cause infections and permanent lesions*'. That advice is good for all fishes and sea creatures.

One of the most difficult animals to photograph is the dugong, believed to be the origin of the Mermaid myth. Dugongs suckle their young at the breast like most mammals, and it is said that a dugong and baby on the surface seen from a sailing ship may have started the legend. The sailors must have been a long time at sea!

Because of the story dugongs and their related species around the world – including the manatees of West Africa and the United States – are known as the '*Sirenia'* after the '*Sirens'*, the singing maidens who lured sailors to their deaths in the Greek legends. Dugongs are as different from mantas as the swimming *'Blankets'* are from whale sharks. All of them are part of the incredible diversity of creatures of the coral reef. The three major differences are that dugongs, like seals and sea lions, are mammals, they have hair, they are warm-blooded, and they breathe air. They are one of the larger animals of the Ningaloo Reef, growing to as much as three-and-a-half metres in length and sometimes a respectable 400 kilograms in weight. They may live as long as 70 years.

Like the whale shark and the manta they do no harm to anyone, feeding on sea grasses in the undersea meadows in Shark Bay and between Point Cloates and Coral Bay. Individuals are often seen in Exmouth Gulf. Dugongs have a transverse tail like a dolphin, a thick bulky body and a pig-like head and they *'blow'* when they exhale like a dolphin or a whale. Their shape is more practical than beautiful, though they do move with a certain grace, particularly if you are lucky enough to see a mother and calf together.

As with humpback whales and dolphins, the baby rides on the mother's back with synchronized movements, talking to each other with soft bird-like chirps. If you are a diver, hoping to swim with a Dugong, patience is required.

Dugong are very shy creatures and it is generally hard to get close to them. They are also often found in discoloured water where conditions for photography are less than ideal. However they do tend to move on regular tracks.

If you see a place where they regularly pass by, station yourself along the route. The chances are that if you remain absolutely still a passing dugong will come to inspect you. A good way to find them – and to take the chill out of waiting – is with a surf ski or surfboard. You are better placed to see the distinctive blows as the dugong approach and you can slip silently over the side with your underwater camera at the ready.

The dugong's natural enemy is the tiger shark, but by far its greatest predator through the centuries has been man. A sadly familiar story.

Though their range originally extended through all the tropical reaches of the Indian Ocean to India and Sri Lanka, the Indonesian Archipelago, Malaysia, and the Philippines, dugongs have long since been hunted to extinction in most of those waters. The largest surviving populations are in Australia. They are found in Queensland, and in Western Australia at Shark Bay – 10,000 individuals – and on the Ningaloo Reef as well as the Kimberley coast.

Aborigines hunted them for thousands of years as subsistence hunters without affecting the populations. Dugong bones are still found in the Aboriginal middens in the sand dunes of the Cape Range National Park. The dugong is protected today by State and Commonwealth government legislation.

'What about the sharks?

That's the question many people ask when they first come to Exmouth and unpack their bathing suits and swim goggles. The reply to that may be '*What kind of sharks do you want to see?'*

Exmouth has the full range which you might expect to exist in a sub-tropical coral reef region. The area is prolific in fish of many species, and the natural equation is that where there are a lot of fish there will also be sharks. Some of them, unquestionably, are potentially dangerous to humans. But since the town was first established, in the first 40 years of its history up until 2010 there has been no human fatality resulting from a shark attack.

There have been a number of shark incidents, but they have mostly been connected with spear fishing. Blood in the water and a struggling fish can ring the dinner bell for any sharks in the vicinity. However it is most likely that the shark is only interested in the wounded fish. For those who actually want to see sharks there are a number of options.

Surprisingly -- for most people think of them as a shark of colder southern waters -- Grey nurse (*Carcharias taurus)* are found off the Muiron Islands at the head of Exmouth Gulf. From a diver's point of view they are almost the perfect shark. Grey nurse are territorial and usually to be found regularly in the same area, often in caves. They move slowly, and will usually allow a patient photographer to approach within comfortable range.

Grey nurse appear menacing, with long snaggle teeth in a mouth that is always partly open to show the hardware. They grow to a respectable size, and in appearance they are everything that we would expect of a shark. In pre-diving days they had an undeserved and evil reputation as '*man-eaters*', simply because they look that way. But appearances can be deceptive.

There is no record of an attack on a human being by a Grey nurse shark. In fact the reverse has been true. When divers first found the schools of Grey nurse in breeding situations off Queensland and New South Wales in the 1970s, they decimated the unfortunate sharks in an orgy of killing with explosive-headed spears, colloquially known as '*Smokies*'. The killing reached the point where it was believed that the sharks were threatened with extinction and protective legislation had to be brought in to save the species.

In the ignorance about sharks which was general in the past, Grey nurse usually got the blame for attacks by Whaler and Bull sharks – and there have been plenty of those particular incidents through the years!

Bull sharks are common in all the warm seas of the world. They are found from Australia to India, the Persian Gulf to the Red Sea, South Africa to South America, the Gulf of Mexico to the United States. Wherever they are, Whalers have the darkest record of any shark in terms of the numbers of attacks on humans. Whalers in general are also the commonest sharks in Ningaloo and Exmouth Gulf waters, though only a handful of more than 200 sub-species of their *Carcharhinidae* family are a potential problem for humans.

Bull sharks, *Carcharhinus leucas*, sometimes called Bronze or Black Whalers, are the more dangerous members of the family, and Silver tips, and Oceanic white-tips, can also be a cause for diver concern. Though, as deepwater species they are less likely to be encountered on the reef. Bull sharks are most dangerous of all in water of low visibility, especially the coffee-coloured waters of tidal mangrove creeks or harbour shores.

Shallow water – knee deep – doesn't deter them. Many of the Sydney attacks have been in the shallows and creeks in water less than a metre deep. The safe rule is not to swim or wade in those kinds of dirty-water places, especially down at the bottom end of the Gulf. Sharks which divers can observe without needing to feel nervous include the White-tipped reef shark. *Triaendon obesus* grows to a reasonable size, and has no black-book record of attacks on humans (though they may attempt to seize speared fish).

The name may create a false impression if we equate *obesus* with obesity. White tips aren't fat, unlike grey reef sharks which can be quite chunky. They are actually a long slim shark, slow-moving and relatively unafraid of divers. In that respect they offer a good target for photographers. White-tips can often be seen at the premium snorkelling site of Turquoise Bay on the Ningaloo Reef. Black tip whalers, usually of smaller size, and also harmless, are frequently seen in shallow water just off shore.

One of the common Ningaloo species, often seen from the air, but rarely sighted underwater, is the tiger shark. *Galeorcerdo cuverii* is second in size only to the Great white among the dangerous sharks. Tigers may grow to five metres in length and the species has often been involved in fatal attacks on humans in other areas.

At Ningaloo tigers principally predate on turtles, but they will eat almost anything else if the opportunity occurs. Their diet may include dugongs, dolphins, cormorants and sea birds of all kinds, and even sea snakes. Because they are largely a nocturnal or night feeder, as evidenced by the tiger stripes and the large dark eye, encounters with humans are rare. Tigers actually seem to avoid humans by choice. The best way to avoid THEM is to restrict night bathing to the hotel swimming pool.

Another shark which may be seen by divers is the hammerhead with its strange, almost grotesque frontal lobes shaped, as its name indicates, somewhat like a hammer. Actually the shark's head is more like the suction end of a domestic vacuum cleaner and shaped, perhaps, for similar reasons. Hammerheads eat a lot of crabs, crayfish, and bottom fish, and scientists believe that the curiously-shaped front end has evolved for scouting along the sea bed just like a vacuum cleaner. The electro-sensitive pits, the *Ampullae of Lorenzini* common to all sharks, are spaced in the hammerhead's wide nose to detect the electrical impulses of prey buried below the sand. Despite their sinister appearance and a set of very sharp teeth, hammerheads – like the Grey nurse – have not yet been recorded as attacking a human.

Then there are the beautifully mottled carpet sharks or wobbegongs, bottom dwellers with piggy-eyes and whiskery faces, and grumpy dispositions. They're best not disturbed, poked, or prodded. They will bite as a natural reaction to being annoyed. Leopard sharks, which have a yellow skin with black spots, have a less cantankerous disposition.

There are also Tawny nurse sharks – no relation to the grey nurse—and the tiny epaulette shark, which is often only 75 centimetres long when full grown. Not to mention the dozens of other species of sharks, and rays, large and small, each one adapted to its own particular niche in the coral food chain.

It is unlikely that a visitor would ever get to meet the *Darth Varder* of the shark world. *Carcharodon carcharias.* The Great white shark, with its huge bulk and its sinister triangular flesh-ripping teeth, does visit Exmouth waters, shadowing the humpback whales. Satellite tracking tags have shown regular movement of the species, made infamous by the film JAWS, from South Australia up the Western Australian coast to Exmouth Gulf. One made a rare public appearance in 2004 when a dead whale was washed ashore in the Gulf south of the town.

Whaler and tiger sharks had already taking the opportunity to feast on the stranded carcass, when they were joined by the Big Bad Boy in person. A five metre specimen of *Carcharodon.* When some photographers in an inflatable boat pulled up alongside to take some movie shots, the Great white became irritated at the intrusion, and the apparent lack of respect.

It turned on a flipper, bared its teeth, and petulantly ripped the side out of the inflatable.

The occupants had to be rescued in a hurry by other boats as the *'rubber duck'* lost its buoyancy in a burst of bubbles. Proving – if it needs to be proved -- that it is unwise to take liberties with an apex predator!

Perhaps the most visible visitors to the Ninagaloo Reef, its shores, and the adjacent islands, are the shellbacks, the green and loggerhead turtles. Turtles, like the whale shark and manta ray, have never hurt anyone and are a delight to observe in the water.

Turtles have been hunted mercilessly by humans for centuries and in recent times there have been serious concerns for the survival of creatures which have been physically unchanged for 150 million years since the Age of the Dinosaurs. Snorkellers may see as many as three turtles in a swim in the Ningaloo Marine Park most times of the year.

While they are clumsy and cumbersome on shore they are surprisingly quick and agile in the water. Seemingly *'flying'* on their extended flippers, they are capable of considerable bursts of speed. In summer hundreds of both sexes congregate in the shallows, mating by day with the sun glinting on their shells in an orgy of love-making. It may seem strange to think of cold-blooded reptiles as sensual or romantic. But why should we warm-blooded humans believe that we have the monopoly in that regard?

At night from October to February, the pregnant females climb the beaches to lay their eggs as they have for millions of years. There is no mistaking where the ladies have been. They leave flipper marks in the beach sands like the track of a caterpillar tractor, and great volcano-shaped pits where they have dug their nests.

The mother turtle often digs several nests to confuse predators before she finally lays her clutch of 150 ping-pong ball-sized eggs with papery shells. The eggs take around two months to hatch, the sex determined by the temperature of the nest. The baby turtles are the right size to sit on a person's palm and though they usually hatch at night they have to run a gauntlet of seabirds, fishes, crabs, and sharks, when they reach the water's edge. As few as five percent of hatchlings may actually reach the safer zone of deep water, and perhaps only one female of an entire clutch of eggs will survive to maturity. An extreme example of Charles Darwin's *'Survival of the Fittest'*.

The two main large species of the Exmouth region are the green turtle, *Chelonia mydas*, and the loggerhead, *Caretta caretta.* Geen turtles have incredible homing instincts. The females make a 4828 kilometre return trip from South American shores to the lone speck of Ascension Island in mid-Atlantic Ocean to lay their eggs. How do they find their target?

We really don't know, but scientists theorise that the turtles may use the earth's magnetic field to navigate. Loggerheads are considered endangered worldwide though there is a population of 300 to 500 females which nest and breed in the Exmouth area. Most of these nest on the Muiron Islands at the head of the Gulf. But there are also nesting sites all the way down the west coast of the Cape Range National Park, with Jurabi a major centre for turtle study.

A smaller turtle which is relatively common at Ningaloo is the hawksbill, *Eretmochelys imbricata,* which was been hunted for centuries for the *'Tortoiseshell'* of its carapace. In the 17th and 18th Centuries hawksbill tortoiseshell made European ladies' combs, brooches, and inlays for jewellery boxes. Though all turtles are protected in Australian waters today, hawksbills are still actively hunted in Indonesia for their shells for sales in the Asian market.

The Department of The Environment and Conservation runs tagging programs each year to determine turtle movements. Supervised tours have been available from the Exmouth Visitor Centre since the establishment of the Marine Park. They take place in the summer months and there are strict ground rules for prospective turtle watchers. Females climbing the beaches to lay are easily frightened and turned away by human activity and especially by bright lights or camera flashes. Dragging her weight of 200 kilograms up the beach past the tide mark is an exhausting effort for the mother-to-be. She needs all the help she can get.

Turtle watchers should keep still, silent, and out of sight while the preliminaries take place. Once the turtle begins laying she can be approached with appropriate care and photographs may be taken.

Many of the reef creatures are nocturnal, hiding during the day and coming out to feed and socialize at night. These include crayfish and crabs and shrimps, and marine worms. Most people would be surprised to know that worms are by far the most numerous animals in any coral reef system. There are literally thousands in any coral head. Among the common ones are the delightful '*Christmas tree'* worms. The worm itself is in a tube in the coral. But its feeding tentacles in the shape of a tiny bright coloured tree, wave in the current to trap plankton.

The octopus is a master of disguise and ambush, able to change the colour and even the texture of its skin to match its surroundings. It is a member of the *Cephalopod* ('head footed ') family which has more than 650 members around the world. They include the ocean's largest invertebrate. *Architeuthis princeps* the giant squid, reaches an incredible fully-extended length of 20 metres. This makes it the creature you would least like to meet in your hotel swimming pool!

Can *Architeuthis* be found at Ningaloo?

Very probably large squid do exist in the deep water beyond the Continental Shelf, sometimes coming to the surface at night. The Shelf does come closer to shore near Point Cloates, some five kilometers off shore, than anywhere else in Australia. Tourists are hardly likely to encounter the ultimate monster of the deep. But if they are snorkellers they are very likely to meet up with some of the smaller relations. The octopus, the cuttlefish, or the squid, are all common and visible inside the reef lagoons.

Cephalopods are very intelligent, as scientists have found out in laboratory tests. Cuttlefish in particular can become familiar with divers. If you want to have fun with one take a mirror down with you. The cuttlefish may go bright red and angry, puffing itself up to larger size, if it thinks the image in the mirror is a rival. Or it may fall in love with itself, grasp the mirror with its two long tentacles, and refuse to give it back. Octopuses often have bright sea shells or pieces of coral as decorations outside their holes in the reef and get quite cross if you move them.

The colour changes of octopii (or should we say '*octopuses'* ?) are amazing to watch. I recall a cuttlefish which we befriended as being very impressed by my lady diving companion. Olena Caswell had long blond hair which flowed down her back. The cuttlefish considered this, screwed up its eyes in a visible effort, and then produced a bright yellow streak right down its own back! It was going to be a fashionable *'blonde'* too! .

The *cephalopods* occupy a bewildering number of habitats. Octopuses are basically bottom dwellers though they can propel themselves short distances by their jets. Cuttlefish live in the reef, but they hover and swim quite well, balanced by the internal '*Cuttle bone'* we often see washed up on beaches. Squid are pelagic swimmers pure and simple. The pearly nautilus, with its tentacles, lives in its beautiful striped shell at great ocean depths, while the paper nautilus uses its white crinkly and similarly-shaped shell to sail along the surface of the sea.

Where do you start (and finish!) in describing the fishes of the Ningaloo Reef? Which of the 500 or so species do you include, and who do you leave out? Like party invitations someone is sure to be missed and miffed. The same applies to the molluscs. With 600 species just setting down the names would run this chapter out of space. Then we have the 250 species of corals to consider and the New York telephone book might seem small and uncomplicated in comparison!

When we humans talk of fish we usually think of the ones we consider good to eat. Coral trout, barramundi, Spanish mackerel, pink snapper, blue-bone groper, spangled emperor, King George whiting, and mangrove jack, all win hand claps of approval when brought to the table. There are many others including rankin cod, king snapper, and threadfin salmon, which may be somebody's favourite (we'll step quietly around that argument).

Culinary appreciation often depends on whether the fish is served up fried in batter, grilled, mornayed, steamed, braised, poached, or – marlin and mahi mahi (dolphin fish) go well here – soused in a South Seas or Japanese-inspired sushi and eaten raw. The quality of the chef (cook) and the skill with a skillet is always at least as important as the variety of the fish.

The other fish whose names are well known to us are familiar because of their ability to stretch a line. Black, blue, and striped marlin, sailfish, and broadbill swordfish are probably at the top of every game-fisherman's wish list, and figure prominently in Exmouth's annual *'Gamex'* fishing carnival.

The billfish are followed by wahoo, dolphin fish (mahi mahi), mackerel, queenfish, trevally, and bonefish *'the pocket rocket'*. All of the eating and fighting fish are to be found in Ningaloo, Exmouth Gulf, or Muiron Island waters. However there are hundreds of other varieties which scientists find fascinating but which are lesser-known names to the general public.

Among the novelties are parrot fish which sleep among the corals at night after drawing a blanket of slime over themselves to deter predators. Puffer fish can blow themselves up like footballs to prevent being swallowed. Surgeon fish, as the name implies, have bony protuberances in their tails which are sharp as scalpels and capable of creating a slashing wound (the author has a permanent scar to prove it). Clown fish coat themselves with a protective slime which makes them immune to anemone stings. In a good example of symbiosis a group of clown fish live among an anemone's stinging fronds laying their eggs in safety and driving away the anemone's enemies. The largest clown fish is always a female, with a smaller male, and with neuter non-breeding fish down the pecking order.

If the female dies the male changes sex and becomes female and the largest non-breeder becomes a male.

This weird mix-up occurs -- Storrie and Morrison tell us – so there is always a pair of adults ready to breed. And so it goes on. Offence and defence are art forms among those who live in the shelter of the reef. Only those who do it best survive.

Even tourists who do not dive cannot help noticing the seashells washed up on the beaches. In most cases these are just the houses in which the animals once lived and the occupant has gone – unless someone else, such as a hermit crab or tiny blue-ringed octopus has taken up residence. (Watch your fingers!) Many of the more colourful shells, in particular the cowries, balers, and spider shells, make attractive decorations and the natural instinct in the past was to take them home. Shell collecting was then an acceptable hobby, and people could often be seen turning over rocks at low tide to see what shells might be found beneath them.

Unfortunately a number of problems arose. The shells with the best colour and lustre naturally were *'live'* shells with a living occupant. To keep the shell meant killing the animal. Disturbing the rocks meant removing the protection for other animals which lived in their shelter, especially if the rock were left carelessly overturned and not replaced. For those reasons shell collecting has since been deemed to be now unacceptable, and taking any shells or coral, alive or dead, is expressly prohibited in the Ningaloo Marine Park.

However, on the basis of *'Look but don't touch!'* which applies to most sea life, we can still observe molluscs going about their daily business. There are 600 species of them at Ningaloo, and each one has some special place in the ecological balance.

They range from the biggest of all, *Tridacna maxima*, the giant clam, which at full size may be like a baby's bath and be too heavy for one person to lift. In contrast there are tiny shells smaller than a child's little finger nail. Among the pretty ones are tiger and egg cowries, spider shells, and pearl oysters. North west rock oysters are unmatched for eating. Baler shells, which may be as long as 60 centimetres, were modified by Aborigines and used for carrying water and babies while the tribes moved from place to place. Shells were also used as scoops in digging for water, and remnants of clams and balers can still be seen in old Aborigine camp sites.

Some shells can be dangerous to humans. Among the more innovative adaptations, the Cone shell fires a harpoon from inside its shell which carries a powerful poison.

The Cone shell kills fish much larger than itself and the poison is strong enough to kill human beings. No need to say *'Don't touch'* there! There are other dangers on the reef, and while people tend to worry more about sharks it is worth remembering that there are also little things which can kill, or at least cause injuries of varying severity.

The Blue ringed octopus, tiny enough to sit in a tea-cup, has a potentially deadly poison and there have been a number of deaths in Australia. The Stone fish, named because it is so well-camouflaged that it looks exactly like a stone, has a series of 13 spines which inject a poison so painful that it will put a full grown adult person in hospital. There have been some Stonefish deaths in the Pacific region. When wading be careful where you step, especially avoid treading in little sand holes in the reef! Most divers know the multi-striped Butterfly cod, sometimes called the Scorpion or Lion fish. It has a series of poison spines which it can dart beyond the range of its white-frilled fins.

The Marine Park has a wide range of stingrays from the huge *Dasyatis thetidis* or Harbour ray which can reach more than two metres across, to the frying pan-sized *Urolophus mucosus*. All have poisonous barbs on their tails. Many of the smaller rays can be found in shallow sand flats and it is essential to watch where you step. A stingray spine wound is painful enough for most people to require medical treatment.

NEVER, ever, swim over the top of a large stingray! Big rays have a barb on their tail the equivalent size of a kitchen carving knife. Like all other rays, and most of the poisonous or stinging creatures, the barbs are only used defensively.

But if you swim close above a stingray it may panic – remember a diver with fins is as big as most sharks -- and react with a swishing slash which is almost quicker than the eye can follow. There have been a number of stingray-caused human fatalities in Australia. The most-publicised death was that of Steve Irwin, who had achieved world-wide fame as *The Crocodile Hunter* on international television circuits. He was killed when the barb of a large stingray pierced his chest on the Great Barrier Reef in an unfortunate accident in 2006.

Sea snakes, especially the olive sea snake, *Aipysurus laevis*, are found in the Ningaloo Marine Park, though they are more prevalent around the Muiron Islands. All sea snakes are air-breathers and all have a dangerous venom. This is primarily used to kill fish, but it can also be used in a defensive role and a lot of human fatalities have occurred, particularly among net fishermen in South East Asia. Olive sea snakes are very curious and will often come up to inspect a diver. In the mating season, October-November, they may become confused and make love to boat anchor ropes. They may also become irascible and try to chase divers out of their territory. It is better to leave quietly – the territory usually only extends a short distance.

Modern pearl divers often encounter sea snakes and have developed strategies for dealing with them. Fortunately the snakes have small mouths and teeth and even if they wanted to would find it difficult to bite a wet-suited diver. However the hands are vulnerable, particularly the web between the forefinger and thumb. The natural reaction to an angry snake might be to try to push it away. But putting a hand out would actually be the most dangerous thing to do.

The pearl divers' advice is to clench your fists and put them under your armpits. Put out a fin between yourself and the snake while swimming away backwards. The snake will peck at the fin, but will soon get tired of banging its nose on the rubber and take its bad temper away.

Australia's other most infamous reptile is *Crocodilus porosus* the salt-water crocodile which has a well-deserved reputation as a man-eater. A number of crocodile attacks on humans occur in Northern Australia every year. Generally speaking *porosus* is a tropical animal needing high water temperatures to survive comfortably. Onslow is regarded as the southern limit for the species and unconfirmed sightings are said to have been occasionally made in the mangrove swamps on the eastern side of Exmouth Gulf. However, until 2009, no crocodile had been seen on the western or town side of the Gulf, or along the Ningaloo Reef.

But in May, 2009, a large four-metre Saltwater crocodile made its way down the inshore waters of the Ningaloo reef to Coral Bay and Gnaraloo. It consistently swam within 20 metres of the shore in prime tourist holiday areas. The Department of Conservation and the Environment decided that it was too dangerous to remain in the region in the circumstances, and – after six days of tracking – it was shot. Nobody was happy about that, especially the crocodile. A case of the wrong species, in the wrong place, at the wrong time!

All coral areas have stinging plants and creatures. Delicate white fronds among the corals may be hydroids, which can give a diver a painful but non-serious sting. The same applies to fire coral, *Millepora platyphylla*, a series of smooth yellow brown plates with lighter yellow edges. As a general rule stay clear of all jellyfish, large or small. Among the other '*Don't touch me!*' creatures are devil urchins with their long black spines which pierce gloves or wet suits with ease. The author once had a 2cm piece of spine in his foot for two years as a souvenir of a visit to Tioman Island in Malaysia.

There are many kinds of urchins in Ningaloo waters, including heart urchins, pencil urchins, sea mice, and sand dollars. There are also sea slugs, sea squirts, and many other fascinating animals on the reef. So many diverse creatures that they would require an encyclopedia to list them all. Further reading is strongly recommended.

'GOTCHA!' An osprey falls from the sky like a meteor and splashes down to secure a fish for its dinner.
(Picture: Karin Calvert Borshoff)

PELICAN in a philosophical mood.
(Picture: Karin Calvert Borshoff)

OYSTERCATCHERS have striking red legs and beaks.
(Picture: Hugh Edwards)

NATURE'S DARTH VARDER. Carcharodon carcharias, the Great White Shark, is an occasional visitor to Exmouth waters. (Picture: Hugh Edwards)

LOVE AT FIRST SIGHT. Divers and a Potato cod in a situation of mutual admiration. (Picture: Hugh Edwards)

CYCLONES are a fact of life for Exmouth and the North West Cape. Mega-Storms have included the cyclone which destroyed the pearling fleet in Exmouth Gulf in 1875, the 'blow' which devastated the RAAF base at Learmonth in 1945, and Cyclone Vance with 267 kmh winds in 1999. (Picture: Hugh Edwards)

RED SAND HILL near Bullara Station is a typical feature of the inland countryside. (Picture: Hugh Edwards)

'BIRDS DO IT, bees do it, even educated fleas do it! Let's fall in love!' (Green Turtles pictured by Karin Calvert Borshoff)

I DON'T THINK I should be watching this! (Hawksbill turtle, picture Hugh Edwards)

'STARVE THE LIZARDS! – who was the silly coot who said that?' (Picture: Hugh Ewards)

POINT CLOATES LIGHTOUSE became unstable on sand foundations and was replaced in 1935. Today the ruin stands as a lonely landmark. (Picture: Hugh Edwards)

SNOOZIN' IN THE SUN a Warroora Station lizard takes life easy on a veranda rail. (Picture: Hugh Edwards)

CATALINA FLYING BOATS were the world's most versatile aircraft, in service from the 1930s until the present day. In World War II, they were used for reconnaissance, for dropping bombs, depth charges, torpedoes, and setting down commandoes on covert operations. They were amphibious, equally able to put down on land or sea. During the war Catalinas based on the Swan River, at Perth, were Australia's link with Britain, making the 'Double Sunrise' flight of more than 30 hours from Exmouth to Sri Lanka. (Picture: Military-Aircraft. UK)

ALL THAT REMAINS of the cattle-carrying steamer SS Mildura, driven ashore on the North West Cape by a cyclone on March 12, 1907. The unfortunate cattle swam ashore on the waterless Muiron Islands where they died of thirst. The loss of the vessel resulted in the lighthouse being built at Vlamingh Head. The wreck was used for target practice by Allied aircraft in World War II.

PINCTADA MAXIMA the giant North West pearl shell was a sensation when beds were first discovered in the 1860s. Today Australian pearlers, including those at Exmouth, produce some of the world's biggest and most lustrous pearls. They are marketed world wide as 'South Sea Pearls'.

PEARLS are at their best when offset by a beautiful woman.

THE GIANT SQUID, Architeuthis princeps, is the creature with whom you would least like to share a swimming pool. Huge squid may well exist off the Continental Shelf of the Ningaloo Reef, rising to the surface at night. (Picture: Hugh Edwards)

FEEDING WILD CREATURES can cause problems. If people with-hold food to maintain their attention creatures may become aggressive. Here a large stingray buffets a diver who has failed to deliver the expected morsel. It is better not to raise their expectations in the first place. (Picture: Hugh Edwards)

Have we dwelled too much on the dangers in this chapter? There are many dangerous elements in our own ordinary lives which we overcome quite naturally and just take for granted. Crossing a city street has its own elements of risk, let alone driving a car around a busy city roundabout or on a country trip. The ocean is the same.

The great majority of Ningaloo divers and snorkellers swim without incident through a combination of commonsense and sensible advice from the dive operators. The rewards of experiencing coral reef waters far outweigh the inconveniences of the necessary constraints of caution.

So -- Good luck, and good diving!

Cyclones – Whirling One-Eyed Monsters

Chapter Fourteen

Exmouth Gulf lies in a cyclone belt where some extreme storms have been experienced through the years. Modern records begin with the great cyclone of Christmas, 1875. In Exmouth Gulf it sank the pearling boats *Wild Wave, Lily of the Lake, Ariel, Fairy Queen,* and *Blossom*.

The *Wild Wave, Lily of the Lake,* and the *Fairy Queen*, were large schooners, each carrying more than 30 crew and Malay divers. The death toll was 76 lives – Exmouth's first major recorded loss of life after the wreck of the *Stefano* in the same year.

Cyclone losses of vessels and men would become depressingly familiar on the Western Australian pearling grounds as the years rolled by.

The tropical storms which batter Northern Australia in summer and which we call *'Cyclones'* are known by different names in other parts of the world. They are *'Hurricanes'* in America and the Caribbean, and *'Typhoons'* in the Philippines, Japan, China, and the South China Sea. A case of different names for the same deadly phenomenon.

The name '*Typhoon'* may have come from the ancient Greek myth of a monster called *'Tuphon'* who generated hot and devastating winds in the Mediterranean. It is believed that the name was carried to the Far East in the 1500s by the Portuguese. *'Hurricane'* comes from the Spanish in the Caribbean, and is said to be taken from the name of a Carib Indian storm god named '*Huracen'*. The Australian Aborigines of the Kimberley associated their storms with *'Wandjinas'* and the distinctive *Wandjina* figures with their lightning haloes are found in most of the cave painting sites in the West Kimberley.

In Australia 'Cyclone' is the modern, though perhaps less romantic, meteorological term to describe a whirling tropical storm cloud mass revolving around a low pressure center. The lower the central pressure, recorded on the barometer, the more intense the storm and the stronger the winds. Wherever the storms travel, north or south of the equator, and whatever name they may travel under, they are bad news for mariners at sea.

Vessels may be overwhelmed in huge seas and shrieking winds. Captains and crews drowned, cargoes lost. The storms bring equal grief for the coastal villages, towns, and cities where they come ashore, leaving a trail of death and destruction in their wake.

The storms are all formed in the same way. They are spawned out over the ocean, in a combination of thunderstorms combined with the sun's heat and rising water vapour. A spinning cloud mass is formed around a low pressure center, which generates its own forces as it builds upon itself. Meteorologists tell us that a single Force Five Cyclone-Typhoon-Hurricane generates more energy than all the electrical utilities in the world combined.

Some of the storms listed as tropical depressions (from the fall of pressure on barometers) are hardly more severe than regular storms resulting from ordinary winter cold fronts. But others, like Hurricane *Katrina* which devastated the city of New Orleans in the Southern United States in 2005, killing 1836 people and flooding 80 per cent of the town, may be whirling monsters described as '*super-hurricanes*'.

The origins of these tropical storms are consistent. They are oceanic. But once cyclones get underway the only definite thing which can be said about them is that -- even with all the science available in modern meteorology today including satellite observations -- they are frustratingly unpredictable. A small depression may suddenly intensify and escalate into a killer storm, as Cyclone *Tracey* did with Darwin on Christmas Eve in 1974.

Tracey took the town by surprise and by the time it had swept through the area 71 people were dead and 70 per cent of Darwin's 12,000 dwellings had been destroyed. The official wind speed was listed at 135 miles an hour (217 kph). That was recorded before the instruments stopped registering. But unofficially it is believed that the highest wind gusts may have been in the region of 185 mph or 300 kph. Similarly the death toll may have been higher, perhaps above 100 victims, because who knows how many extra people or vessels might have come to town, unrecorded, on that festive season night?

The town was virtually destroyed. Even the houses which survived were uninhabitable. There was no electricity, no water, and no sewage facilities. Darwin was declared a National Disaster and 35,362 people, of a total of 47,000, had to be evacuated. It took two years to rebuild the town to the most basic level of occupation.

Memories of *Tracey* were rekindled when *Cyclone Vance* swept through the town of Exmouth on Sunday, March 22nd, 1999. On the morning when the storm struck the town, wind speeds reached 267 kilometres per hour, the highest wind speeds ever officially recorded on the Australian continent. Despite that, no lives were lost and while there was major damage, only 12 per cent of Exmouth's houses were actually destroyed. It was a huge disruption for a town whose income was reliant on tourism. But thankfully no-one was dead.

And more houses survived than might have been expected with a storm of such intensity. Overall, despite inevitable pain and suffering, it was an immeasurably better result than occurred with the Darwin tragedy.

Tracey was an example of all the things which frustrate weather forecasters. Darwin had not seen a serious cyclone in 100 years and so people were complacent about the risk. Many houses were not built to cyclone standards. *Tracey* began as a relatively unimportant tropical depression 700 kilometres north of Darwin in the Arafura Sea. Within 24 hours winds had picked up to 63 kilometres per hour – less than Bass Strait gales in the south – but sufficient to qualify as a Category One cyclone. As cyclones often do, *Tracey* followed a random zig-zag path, meandering southwards over several days. '*No immediate threat*' was the call over Darwin's ABC radio.

However, early on Christmas Eve, *Tracey* suddenly took wings. She passed the western tip of Bathurst Island, spun around and headed directly for Darwin, gaining strength along the way as though impelled by some malevolent spirit. It was the worst possible time to strike the northern city. Everyone there was involved in Christmas drinks and Christmas parties. There had been a false alarm ten days earlier when a cyclone designated *'Selma'* was reported to be on track to strike Darwin. *Selma* fizzled, and with the previous record of no cyclone reaching Darwin since the 1890s, people were understandably over-confident. There was an attitude of *'It can't happen here!'*.

Because it was Christmas Eve few people were listening to the weather reports on radio or television. The town with its Christmas trimmings, reindeer ribbons, daddies in Santa Claus rigs (*'Ho, ho, ho!'*), and a *'Jingle Bells!'* celebratory mood, was quite unprepared for the onset of Nature gone berserk.

Few people in Darwin that night, or in Exmouth in March, 1999, had ever experienced a cyclone before. In the aftermath it has often been asked why Exmouth should have done so much *'Better'* than might have been expected, given the ferocity and the fury of Vance? The answer is that the degree of preparation was markedly different in the two towns. That was what made the difference for Exmouth in terms of restricting the damage. The area had a long history of cyclones and that experience was factored in when the town was built.

Houses in Exmouth were deliberately engineered to withstand winds of cyclonic force. There was a well-established emergency procedure. The cyclone took several days to arrive, and people were well and truly ready for it when it did come. Though, despite being forewarned, the wind force still far exceeded their expectations.

In Darwin, besides the 71 officially dead, hundreds received medical treatment in the aftermath for injuries of severity varying from life-threatening traumas and broken bones to flesh wounds. In Exmouth only one man, who cut his foot on broken glass, needed treatment. That is not to trivialize the effect of *Cyclone Vance* on Exmouth. It was a horrific experience, the aftermath, as usual, worse than the storm itself. Like Darwin all civic facilities were put out of action. Those civilised things we all take for granted – electricity, gas, fresh water from the tap, flushing toilets – were shut down for weeks. Most women and children and many men who no longer had jobs or a good reason for staying, were evacuated.

The town's major income was based on tourism, and some of the charter boats had been booked out for the season. The marina was one of the worst hit areas of the town, with boats sunk or smashed against rock walls and pylons. Pieces of painted timber, boat cushions and life-jackets, gaffs, and red plastic fish baskets, all floated together in coffee-coloured water in a mass of debris.

Now all bookings had to be cancelled. Even if boats were repaired or replaced there was insufficient accommodation for those who lived there, let alone for people from outside. There was simply nowhere, for the present, for visitors, tourists, or backpackers to stay. In Exmouth 116 houses were uninhabitable, and 320 severely damaged. None escaped water damage. Most were saturated to the point where some insurance companies tried to cry off responsibility on the excuse of an escape clause of *'flooding'*. Fortunately that gambit did not of itself, hold water.

What was it like to live through a cyclone?

South Perth historian Michal Bosworth did a series of interviews after *Vance*. She captured the sharp edge of the distress, the bewilderment, of people who had had their homes literally smashed around them. She also recorded the resolution and determined commitment of those involved in the clean-up. The good citizens who rolled their sleeves up and took on the daunting task of restoring the town to something approaching its former self.

People like 'Jacko', the proprietor of the *Rock Cod* café who cooked 65 meals a day for volunteer workers. Or the Salvation Army workers who came from Perth, provided 85 meals on their first day, and set up kitchens to feed people who were unable to buy food. With no power, lighting, or refrigeration the local shops were closed down. Or the volunteers on a State Emergency Service committee under former Shire President Doug Bathgate. The SES handled communications and the organization of incoming help from a generous outside world. Or the Shire Council with President Mike Purslow and CEO Kerry Graham who worked tirelessly in the relief process.

Michal Bosworth's interviews, giving a poignant day-to-day picture of a town's recovery from a catastrophe, would be valuable background for anyone involved in future emergency services. Useful for anyone who lives in a cyclone area and who may have to face the same situation at some unspecified time in the future.

Unspecified?

As Shakespeare said ' *Ah! There's the rub!'* Because with cyclones you simply never know quite what to expect.

Of course there is a pool of scientific knowledge to which we can refer. Cyclones require a sea surface temperature of more than 26.5 degrees Celsius to get started. So that means that they initiate somewhere near the Equator. But where they go to after that is anybody's guess.

Where Australia is concerned the high temperature requirement limits them to a 'Cyclone Season', a period over the summer from November onwards, extending through to April. Surprisingly some of the worst Northern Australian ones (like *Tracey*) have been at the beginning of summer, or late in the season in April. Obviously what happens with *El Nino* over on South American coasts also has an influence.

While they have a tropical origin, cyclones generally head across the top of Australia, and duck down through the Coral Sea to dismay Queenslanders. Or they may zig zag down the west coast whirling their untidy cloud masses about them with the distinctive sinister single dark *'eye'* of calm in the middle. A one-eyed monster! Most of the damage is caused when they leave the ocean and cross the coast. While the tracks appear random, some places get hit more often than otherwise.

Broome, for instance seems to have been blessed. In all its century-plus years of modern history it had never experienced a cyclone of the intensity of a *Tracey* or a *Vance*. Though the cyclone of 1910 did sink a number of pearling luggers in Roebuck Bay, and cyclones in 1926 and the 1990s caused structural damage around the town without any lives being lost. Cyclone Rosita in April, 2000, had a similar result with the main force of the cyclone passing south of the town totally destroying the buildings and chalets of the tourist operation at Eco Beach

Through the years areas immediately south, and north of Broome have been struck with direct hits by some savage cyclones. The Eighty Mile Beach has experienced some particularly violent storms. In 1887 the pearling fleet was caught by a late cyclone in April which sank 18 luggers and mother ships, and drowned 140 men. Another cyclone in 1908 sank the fleet with the loss of 50 lives, to be followed by another *'blow'* in December of the same year which caught the fleet off Cape Bossut. Thirty three vessels were sunk with further heavy loss of life.

The worst catastrophe for the Broome pearling fleet was the Lacepede Islands cyclone of March, 1935, when 20 luggers were sunk and 142 divers and crews were drowned just to the north of Broome. It was sometimes called the '*Koolinda'* cyclone because that State ship rescued many of the crews in dismasted or sinking luggers in the aftermath.

Many of the divers and crews who were saved were Japanese, and it has sometimes been said that -- out of gratitude -- Japanese aircraft avoided bombing *Koolinda* in the Second World War even though they had the chance on a number of occasions. In contrast her sister ship *Koolama* was bombed and now lies in a permanent watery grave at the bottom of Cambridge Gulf off the Wyndham wharf.

Port Hedland and Onslow have been hit so often by cyclones in 120 years that they have almost given up counting. The most infamous Port Hedland cyclone, *'The Koombana blow'*, occurred in March, 1912. The captain of the State ship *Koombana*, carrying 150 passengers bound for Broome, decided to head out of port for the open sea when his barometer indicated that a cyclone was imminent.

He was confident that the *Koombana*, a vessel of 3668 tons, could ride out a storm of any severity. *Koombana* was last seen crossing the Port Hedland bar, the swells running ahead of the cyclone lifting her stern so high that her propellers were thrashing out of the water on the crests.

She was never seen again, and to this day her wreck has never been found. It was the highest cyclone loss of life in Australian records. Cyclones seldom seem to travel very far south of the North West Cape, though there have been exceptions. Cyclone *Alby,* in April, 1978, began life north of Australia in the Timor Sea. The storm danced all the way down the west coast, ducked around Cape Leeuwin, and gathered its skirts to whirl off out into the Southern Ocean.

On its journey down the coast, tracking just off shore, *Alby* created 93 mph (150 kph) winds at Fremantle and Bunbury, sinking boats on their moorings, washing large and small craft ashore, and damaging buildings in passing. The unexpected rainfall caused flooding throughout the South West. *Alby* ended by smashing the woollen mills and a lot of other vulnerable buildings in Albany in a last vindictive fling. It was a nasty and totally unexpected event. Albany is WA's southernmost port, in a cold water zone. It is said of the town *'Anyone living south of King George's Sound is a penguin!'*. In short it is a place which could reasonably consider itself immune from tropical cyclones of any category!

But seven people died through *Alby's* romp down the west coast, and the damage bill reached nearly 40 million dollars. The lesson again, was '*Never say never!*' where cyclones are concerned. As an additional concern, Alby arrived at the weekend, and moved so quickly that it caught weather forecasters by surprise. With the result that there was no warning issued for the South West. In that sense *Alby* brought one good piece of news in that it engendered a major upgrading of the cyclone warning system throughout Australia.

The Australian Government Bureau of Meteorology today has one of the world's most efficient cyclone tracking and warning systems. There is an international series of categories which define the danger of individual cyclones, and each one is accorded the courtesy of a name for identification purposes. Useful when you may have the not-unknown situation of two or more systems forming at the same time in the same area.

Category One: Gales of less than 125 kph. 'Negligible house damage. Damage to some crops, trees, and caravans. Water craft may drag moorings'.

Category Two: Destructive winds of 125-169 kph. 'Minor house damage. Significant damage to signs, trees, and caravans. Heavy damage to some crops. Risk of power failure. Small craft may break moorings.

Category Three: 170-224 kph. 'Some roof and structural damage. Some caravans destroyed. Power failure likely'.

Category Four: 225-279 kph. ' Significant roofing loss and structural damage. Many caravans destroyed and blown away. Dangerous airborne debris. Widespread power failure'.

Category Five: Winds of more than 280 kph. 'Extremely dangerous with widespread destruction'.

Cyclone *Vance,* approaching Exmouth Gulf on Saturday, March 21st., 1999, was described as a 'Category Five Tropical Cyclone', likely to be the strongest *'blow'* since 1945, a period of 54 years. Perhaps even the strongest since the 1875 cyclone which destroyed the pearling fleet in Exmouth Gulf.

The town had ample warning as *Vance* tracked down the west coast, threatening first Port Hedland, then Onslow, and finally turning ominously towards Exmouth. For some of the younger blades in Exmouth there was time enough to go surfing and catch the best waves in 12 months. Older people took the opportunity to photograph the most brilliant sunset seen in years. Then there was an eerie period of almost calm overnight as the cyclone approached.

It appeared at first on Sunday morning as a red wall of dust raised by the winds on the outer fringes of the approaching cyclone. Some people remembered *'A red wall of sand coming towards us that you couldn't see through!'*. By breakfast time the cyclone Exmouth people had all been waiting for was upon the town. The sound was horrendous. A ripping, tearing, roaring noise, of incredible volume, that could never be forgotten by those who experienced it.

Indeed the cyclone sound is the thing people always remember, wherever in the world they may have heard it. The noise begins with a low bestial growl like an animal, and quickly grows to a shrieking, irrational din that overpowers the senses, assaults the ears and makes conversation impossible. Some liken it to the noise of a train in a tunnel, others to a Boeing 747, engines at full power just above the roof top.

Houses begin to shake, preliminary to windows bursting in. Trees, and sheds, and pieces of corrugated iron begin flying past outside. Vehicles are flung on their sides. Then roofs begin to peel off, and walls to topple and fall, while occupants huddle in terror in bathrooms or under mattresses and tables.

There is a sudden calm while the 'eye' of the storm passes over. Householders have just time – ten minutes perhaps -- to take a quick disbelieving look at the extent of the damage outside, and then to rush back inside as the noise begins again, this time with the wind coming from the opposite direction.

For the people of Exmouth, when *Vance* struck, each family isolated from the others in their battered homes, each one a fortress against the elements, the agony seemed endless. In fact the storm passed through quite quickly as cyclones go – the maximum wind strength probably lasted for only about an hour. It was generally agreed that if it had continued much longer many more houses might have collapsed and the damage might have been trebled.

The Bosworth recorded interviews tell their own story:

Bernice McLeod was 81 years old and made of the stuff of pioneers. She had seen a cyclone out in 1964 while living in a tent, one of the first families of modern Exmouth. She refused to leave her house despite the pleadings of her son and daughter and other members of her family who lived elsewhere in town. *'I wasn't scared'* she told Michal Bosworth. *'I knew that the Lord would look after me. I thought 'If he takes me that's fine!'*

Bernice was always looking for positives. She felt comforted by the fact that the cyclone came in daylight and there was no need for candles or lanterns in the loneliness of darkness. She was able to have her breakfast. *'I don't have much breakfast, a piece of toast or something. I was very pleased that I had had a shower and a cup of tea'.* She was ready for whatever the day might bring, though with *Vance* it would be rather more than she had anticipated.

'I could see it all happening, but the noise was something I'll never forget. It was tremendous. All the steel power poles bent over along the road. I was watching through the window when I saw what looked like half a house coming this way. I thought, 'Oh, that's good. It will protect the window! Then I noticed that the window was struck by a piece of guttering, and I knew that if the window goes that's when the trouble starts, then –WHOOF! – and I suppose that's when the roof went. Suddenly I was looking up at the rafters. That was a little bit ...well, not frightening, but I thought 'Oh when the rafters fall in I won't be able to hold them up, not with my knees!'

'I was lying down by then because I had this board that I had been holding at the window to stop the window from breaking. But it broke anyway, and down I went with this bit of board on top of me. It was a bit of light fibre-board and it was over me for a long time. But it got heavier and heavier. When the rain came in of course it got wet but after that the wind just threw the board down, of course with me underneath it. I was really protected with that bit of board. I was pushed onto the carpet and between the couch which was there and a marble-topped stool which fell over and gave me a cracked rib. But that was nothing. It actually pinched me in at the back by the couch, which was probably a blessing. Anyway I was there for a long time. I got wet and cold, really cold, at one stage I felt really tired. I thought 'No, I'm not going to go to sleep! I've got to see it all happen!'

By about 1p.m. the winds had begun to ease and people began to move cautiously outside their homes. Bernice's neighbour knocked anxiously on the door of her ruined house.

'I said I can't come to the door, but I'm all right'. It was my neighbour from two doors down and he came and actually took me through, back to his house, I don't know which way we went. I don't think we opened the front door.

'When I looked back the wall was waving like this and there was no glass in any of the windows. I didn't know that before because I was looking the other way. He asked me how I was and I said 'Oh, I'm all right!'

At 81 years of age, lying on the floor of her roofless, windowless house, trapped under debris, soaked to the skin, chilled to the bone, a broken rib, listening to the roar of the hurricane …but *'Don't worry I'm all right!'*.

Another Bosworth interview was with Frances who was with her daughter and son-in-law and grand-daughter at the M.G.Kailis prawn plant south of the town. Their experience was typical of many people in other parts of the town.

'Sunday, 22nd of March, 1999.

'Five a.m., the wind wakes me up. Goodness, the trees are bending in half! Get up to make a coffee. Simon is already up. He is worried too. We both go out and check around the house one more time. It is very, very windy.

'I go to fill the bath full of water as recommended.

'Tanya rings. 'You're on red alert!'

'Thank you. We know'. Turn the radio on. Sit and have our coffee.

'All hell breaks loose.

'What's that noise? – 'Someone just lost their fence'.

'Which way is it coming?

'Up the road –BANG! It hits the electricity pole across from our house.

'Oh God! Robyn's roof is peeling off!

'Simon, the lattice on the patio is flying loose. There goes the neighbours' shed!

'There goes the barbecue, the mower and whipper-snipper together with the lattice. Things are flying everywhere!

'Something just hit the solar panel. Quick get some towels. The water's pouring in through the bathroom vent!

'Come back into the lounge. Quick – get a mattress and sheets. We're being flooded in the kitchen. Oh, how long is this going to last?

'Simon –quick! – the ceiling is caving in! Get some buckets, get things out of the way! The radio's just gone out and it's pouring rain on it!

'Quick, move the television, the videos, and the stereo! Too late. They're all wet and so are the CDs.

'Simon get a double mattress and put it in the hallway, it's the only safe place. Isabelle come away from the window.

'God, what was that! The neighbours' front porch just landed in the back yard and took the aviary with it. It's stopped just short of your car!

'What's happening? It's all quiet. The'phone rings.

'Tanya – it's all quiet'.

'You're in the Eye of the cyclone. You've got 10 minutes. Check outside!'

'Good God! Don't recognize the place! Get back in Simon, it's starting again.

'Here its goes again. Winds at 240 to 260 kilometres an hour! Now the rain is coming through the dining room window. Move everything thing again. My hands are sore. I've got blisters from wringing out towels.

'Suddenly it's over. Simon and Liane take the car and go to see if people need help. Liane comes home crying. 'Mum, it's terrible – the whole town is wrecked!'

'We're dazed, but we're alive. No-one wants to eat. We all go to bed. None of us can sleep!'.

There were many stories recounted in the aftermath. One of the miracles was that the VLF tower complex at Cape Murat survived with damage to only the small towers carrying the counter weights for the antennae – a tribute to American design and Australian engineering. But at one stage men sheltering in a concrete bunker in the VLF complex heard a mysterious noise at the height of the storm. It was loud enough to be heard above the roar of the wind and they described it as like giant footsteps coming towards them ..THUMP! THUMP! THUMP!

They discovered afterwards that it was a glass-bottomed boat designed to take 32 tourists. The boat had been placed under shelter behind a sand dune on its trailer in the hope that it would be safe there. But the cyclonic winds caught it and blew it over and over and over, right across the peninsula. It passed right through the towers without hitting any of them, to finish totally wrecked on the other side.

In the town itself, while the sheer velocity of the wind saw roofs spectacularly torn off, sheds blown away, boats smashed or sunk, a lot of the losses listed for insurance were from water damage. Even in houses which stood up comparatively well in structural terms, rain water was forced through in high-pressure jets through eaves and vents and through nail holes and tiny cracks. Even the smallest apertures resulted in a virtual flood. The water ruined fridges, radios, television sets, stereos, and power tools, and it reached some extraordinary places. Many ceilings were flooded and some collapsed or caved in. In some houses microwaves on top of fridges finished full of water and so did the refrigerators themselves. The water gushing out when doors were opened.

Bedding and clothing were soaked, even garments in wardrobes and chests of drawers did not escape. Since the rain continued for days and there was no sunshine to dry things out, mould rapidly set in and many mattresses and a good deal of bedding and clothing were ruined. The US Navy 'block-houses' with concrete walls and roofs, which some Australians had laughed at as *'Bomb-shelters'* fared best of all the dwellings. None of them were destroyed or even structurally damaged. Kit houses, which had originally been trucked in and set on stumps, fared worst.

The most damage was suffered by pastoralists and caravan parks. Giralia Station took the full force of the storm and saw $ 800,000 worth of damage, a proportion of which – fences and water points – were uninsured. The homestead built early in the century by the Kings was flattened, and 6000 of 25,000 sheep died. Exmouth Station, run by the Lefroys, Yanrey, and Bullara, also suffered considerable damage to buildings, fences, and windmills.

Robbie Atkinson's Lighthouse Caravan Park lost 35 caravans and seven park homes. The asbestos roof of the old lighthouse keeper's quarters where Robbie lived with Kaye and where they had devoted many hours to painting and renovating, disintegrated into thousands of pieces and was blown all over the park.

It was the second time the roof had been lost in a cyclone – in 1945 members of an RAAF radar unit had watched the sheets of corrugated iron from the original 1910 roof being peeled off and whirled away like dead leaves.

'There were bits of asbestos, broken glass, and pieces of caravans all through the park and the surrounding sandhills' Robbie recalled. *'One caravan base was hanging on the clothes line with a bed frame still strapped to it. The place was just covered in junk and broken tree branches. It was heart-breaking after all the work we'd put into it. You couldn't walk anywhere without treading on broken glass. All the trees were stripped of their leaves and a big palm tree came down and smashed the side of the house. The lighthouse quarters themselves were strongly built, and the walls survived. But the rafters were wooden, they'd dried out and become weak from the heat of too many summers and so they went flying off together with the roof'.*

Peter Turner lost 35 of 45 cabins in his caravan park, and his charter boat which had been booked out for the season was also put out of action. The town itself was also a mess of broken tree branches, fallen power poles and electrical wires, broken glass, pieces of buildings and twisted metal from roofs, sheds, and car ports.

The local committee of the State Emergency Service were in action almost as soon as the wind had passed on down the Gulf. They were all volunteers, and had been meeting one night a month for several months beforehand, anticipating that one day they might be needed. They included members of the Shire Council and staff including Chief Executive Officer Kerry Graham, and Shire President Mike Purslow. Jan Hallam the librarian was communications officer. Doug

Bathgate, a former shire president, and member of the Gascoyne Development Commission, was chairman and leader of the group. He was later given a *'Spirit of WA'* award at the Premier's Citizen of the Year awards in Perth. In his response he said that he accepted the award on behalf of the whole SES team.

Gino Garbellini was President of the Exmouth Chamber of Commerce. He was on the Local Emergency Management Committee, known as *'Lemac'* at the time of Vance. *'In a disaster situation like we had'* he recalled for Michal Bosworth ' *You have two phases, and both are fairly critical. They are the ' Response phase' immediately after the cyclone when you deal with immediate problems, and the much longer 'Recovery phase' when you do the repairs and try to get the town back on track'.*

The first step was to find out what was most critical, and devote the initial resources to those areas. *'Sewage, power, and water, were the important things. Without them a town can't function. Even the hospital, which required all three of those things, was out of action. So when we had all kinds of offers of help coming in from outside we had to decide which was to be given priority. The Shire personnel and the SES committee all worked tremendously hard. The quick way of getting out of shock is getting in and doing something. The donations from people in WA and all over Australia were nothing short of marvelous. So was the help offered by people like the Salvation Army'* Gino recalled.

Among the practical help, greatly appreciated, was the Chinese restaurant, Linda and Sandy Moh, sending regular meals out to the workers doing the clean-up at Robbie Atkinson's devastated Lighthouse Caravan Park.

It was two or three days after *Vance* before the roads were open again – the creeks were roaring torrents raging across the main road. But once the floods subsided trucks were able to bring materials, such as tarpaulins to put over roof-damaged houses. Women and children were evacuated from Learmonth in RAAF Hercules aircraft, and helpers from Western Power and other State services came into town to repair civil amenities. The Army sent men to help with the clean up, and Denver and Rae Blake at Giralia Station were grateful for the consideration of the men who helped in salvaging items, some of them deeply personal, from the ruins of the homestead.

In Exmouth town it took the better part of 12 months to get things back to normal. Some people left and never came back. But those who stayed or returned felt stronger for it. Perhaps the worst period was the first two weeks after the cyclone when the streets of the town still looked as though it had been hit by the *'Atom Bomb'* the locals had joked about for years. But houses were repaired, roofs refurbished or replaced. Many trees which had blown down were stood upright again and braced by wire guys to reach a full recovery. The cyclonic rain saw an amazing re-growth of plants and gardens, and within 12 months the whole town was a picture of blooms, palms, and blossoms. All the standing trees had not only recovered but had an added luxury of extra foliage.

Two years after Vance, tourism was back to normal and a visitor would have found it hard to tell that a cyclone had ever torn through Exmouth. The only signs were the wire guys still supporting the trees that had blown over, and a few of the taller palms which had survived by leaning at a slightly odd angle and which had never really got back to the vertical. Though Exmouth had come through the cyclone far better than might have been expected, valuable lessons were learned from *Vance*. The town will be better prepared if there is another occasion.

Which raises the questions remaining in many people's minds: 'Will it ever happen again? Will there ever be another storm like *Vance*?'

The records show that while a Category Five Cyclone is a rare event on Australian coasts, cyclones of lesser severity can regularly be expected in the North in the summer months. Where they will strike and how hard they will hit cannot be answered in the long term. But Exmouth has experienced *'blows'* on a regular basis in its history of a century-and-a-half, with at least two in 1876 and 1945 with winds of similar severity to Vance.

If we were to ask what the *'Average'* expectation of a cyclone in the Exmouth area might be, the answer would probably be meaningless. Western Australia has experienced 10 tropical cyclones since *Thelma* in 1998. But three of these occurred in the two years 1998 to 2000, while there were seven cyclones between 2004 and 2007. Two of the list, *Vance* in 1999, and *George* in 2007, were Category Five storms. Most of the cyclones – eight of them – occurred in the month of March, the exceptions being *Thelma* in December, 1998, and *Clare,* in January 2006.

George, in March 2007, crossed the coast near Port Hedland with 275 kph winds, and smashed mining camps far inland, causing three deaths. However because most cyclone paths in Australia are in places of low population, fatalities have been much lower than in areas overseas.

It is estimated that cyclones, typhoons, and hurricanes, worldwide have caused nearly two million deaths in the past 200 years. The Bhola cyclone which struck the densely-populated Ganges delta in 1970 has been the deadliest on record. The storm surge caused 300,000 recorded deaths and as many as 1,000,000 people may have died all told. Several cyclones since 1900 have each killed more than 100,000 people in Bangladesh. Typhoon Nina killed 29,000 people in China, but another 145,000 died due to the subsequent famine and epidemics.

Research into core samples of debris layers, after Hurricane Katrina, America's worst storm with 1875 deaths, showed that the United States could expect a Katrina about once every 300 years. The research was undertaken on the commendable basis that '*We should know the past before we predict the future'*.

However predictions are difficult to make because Hurricanes-typhoons-cyclones are like shark attacks. They appear to occur on a cyclic basis and no-one knows the reason why there may be few in a 20 year period and then a rush of them in a shorter time. However it does seem likely that El Nino may play a significant part.

Currently Australia is in a period when we are experiencing more cyclones than in the past. That is a worldwide trend. Category Five storms were rare in the past, but there were seven worldwide, including *George* in Western Australia, in the 12 months to the end of 2007. In May, 2008, Cyclone Nargis devastated Burma's Irrawaddy Delta, the storm surge taking 100,000 lives, and leaving 2.5 million people in danger of death by disease and starvation.

It is a concern that natural disasters are being recorded at a six times greater rate today than in the 1960s. This is partly due to the increase in populations, with people being forced to take up land in vulnerable areas, particularly in poorer countries. But there are also more storms of greater intensity. Research has shown that the energy released by cyclonic storms has increased in the past 30 years resulting in a 15 % increase in maximum wind speed and a 60 % increase in storm lifetime. More storms of increased intensity are striking North America. Five of the most damaging and expensive storms in US history, including *Katrina,* have occurred since 1990.

Hurricanes striking the United States should not be confused with tornadoes (the name derived from the Spanish '*tronada*') which are also a swirling, high-wind systems born of thunderstorms. Tornadoes are land storms most often occurring in central areas of the United States such as Oklahoma. Though they cut a narrower path, they have very destructive winds which can reach 480 kph, wrecking houses and causing significant loss of life.

One set of tornadoes in 1974 killed 300 people in the United States, but the annual fatality figure is usually much less. The area of the world which suffers most from tornadoes – sadly – is Bangladesh which is also the typhoon capital of the world! About 180 people a year die from tornadoes in Bangladesh, with 1300 killed in 1989.

'Tempestologists' – scientists who deal with storms, including tornadoes, have attempted to find ways of reducing or diverting tropical storms, including seeding clouds with silver iodide particles. But to date they have yet to report a major success.

Cyclones are not necessarily all bad news.

The scientists tell us that '*They carry energy and heat away from the tropics to temperate zones which make them an important part of the earth's global atmosphere circulatory mechanisms'*.

Cyclonic rains and floods often break droughts. By bringing vast amounts of water to the inland that part of their cycle, at least, is thoroughly beneficial. The perfect cyclone in farming terms, is one that goes over some other fellow's house and drops its rain in your paddock!

In North Western Australia cyclones are a fact of life. The rain is welcome and the winds are not. But it's how you deal with your storm on the day it comes knocking on the door that really matters.

Ask them at the State Emergency Service in Exmouth!

CYCLONE VANCE swirls across Exmouth, March 1999.

Silver Dollars On The Sea Floor

Chapter Fifteen

It was every diver's dream come true – drifting down, down, to a cannon wreck and a sea bed strewn with treasure! Finding encrusted silver dollars looking like biscuits carpeting the seabed -- Surely that could only be the stuff of fantasy?

'Hard to pinch yourself in a wet suit to make sure you really weren't dreaming!' Frank Paxman said later.

But the coins were hard and heavy in the hand, a cold reality. A test with a diver's knife showed the glint of silver, and when a coin was tapped sharply with the knife butt and the encrustation fell away the relief and the inscription were revealed.

On one side was a king's head *'Carolus 1111. Dei Gratia'* the inscription read: *'Charles the Fourth, by the Grace of God'*. On the reverse were the *Pillars of Hercules* -- the Straits of Gibraltar and the symbol of Spain. The king's coat of arms was there too with a castle and a lion representing the kingdoms of Leon and Castile.

Further inscription informed the observer that Charles was the Emperor (*Rex*) of *Hispania* (Spain) and *Ind.* (the Indies). The dates on the coins gripped in divers' gloves ranged from 1759 to 1809. Though the divers were unaware at the time, the coins were Spanish *'pillar'* dollars minted in Mexico as shown by the mint mark, the letters *Mo.* Each carried the figure 8 representing eight reales, and each was that legendary money unit, beloved of princes and pirates alike -- a *Piece of Eight* from the bottom of the sea!

Treasure finding does not get much better than that! It was Neptune's gift, and the divers were stunned by the unexpected nature of the discovery.

'We were absolutely carried away with excitement and amazement' Frank Paxman, the senior member of the team, told the author some months after the event. *'It was so totally out of the blue, that it took us some time to come back to earth and grasp the significance of what we had found!'*

The four divers who accidentally came across the wreck in the shadow of Point Cloates on that day in 1978 were Frank Paxman, his son Barry Paxman, and friends Glynn Dromey, and Larry Patterson. They were not treasure hunters in the accepted sense, though all West Australian divers knew of the Dutch treasure ships, the 1629 *Batavia*, the 1656 *Vergulde Draeck,* and the 1712 *Zuydorp.* In the general brotherhood of divers they knew at least some of those who had been involved in the discoveries of the Dutch East Indiamen and had perhaps envied them a little.

But they had never expected to be in that situation themselves, because the Paxman party were spearfishermen pure and simple. They were some of the elite *'Spearos'* in Western Australia and had taken the sport to a new level.

Where conventional spearfishing had previously been limited to inshore reefs the Paxmans and their friends hunted pelagic fish sometimes as long and heavy as themselves. The main quarry were monster Spanish mackerel, yellowfin tuna, and wahoo, out in open water that was sometimes as deep as 50 metres. All the group were exceptional divers, easily able to dive to the fabled 30 metre mark. The challenge of confronting mako and tiger sharks in their deep water forays simply made life more interesting. They were psychologically programmed to deal with the oceanic predators.

It was the surprise of a treasure which initially threw them off balance.

'We were camped at Jane's Bay', Barry Paxman recalled 30 years later in 2009. *'June 20th, 1978, was the last day of our holiday and we were a bit down-in-the-mouth because the weather had turned nasty. It was blowing from the North West with a big swell, and conditions would have been hopeless outside the reef. The only possibility seemed to be Black Rock Passage at Point Cloates which we thought might be protected from swell and weather from that direction. So we went there, found the edge of the passage and chucked the anchor in on the shallows just before the drop-off '.*

Frank Paxman was last into the water, waiting to check that the anchor was holding in the wind and short chop. Once over the side he drifted down on a baldchin groper, sighting his speargun, as he dived. But suddenly his attention was diverted. Below on the bottom were long bolts, and anchor, and blackened timber. He recognised that he had found an ancient shipwreck. There was more – when he dived right down to the bottom seven metres below he saw scattered on the sand objects which set his heart beating harder.

'They looked like black biscuits!' he said. *'But there was never any doubt about what they were!'*. He said afterwards that his whoop of joyful recognition would have *'Startled the seagulls on the beach two kilometres away!'*

As Barry Paxman swam over in answer to his father's hoarse cry he saw him rubbing at the encrustation on the *'biscuit'* with his thumb. At that moment the sun came out from behind the clouds and lit a bright flash of silver in Frank Paxman's hand

'You figure what the odds were of dropping the anchor in the middle of an old wreck, quite unaware that it was there until we dived?' Barry Paxman said in 2009, with a shake of the head.

Now it was his turn to make a discovery. '*As I swam on the surface I noticed a couple of large bolts standing up from the bottom. One had what appeared to be a washer on top. For some reason it attracted my curiosity. I swam down and twisted the 'washer' off and was amazed to find that in fact it was three silver coins stuck together. They separated quite easily and the inside ones were bright silver'.*

Now there was a very different mood!

Soon they found a regular trove of coins buried just below the sand near some large anchors. They had no SCUBA gear, but as accomplished free divers in water which seemed shallow to them they had no difficulty in bringing up a large quantity of the coins. Joyously bobbing to the surface and tossing them in the boat with the unforgettable tinkle of *Old World Silver.*

The mood of the divers on the way back to camp was euphoric as they compared coins and different dates. But once they had time for reflection the mood became less exuberant.

'There'd been a lot of trouble between divers and the authorities in the past about supposed looting of treasure ships like the Vergulde Draeck' Frank Paxman recalled. As the oldest member of the party the others tended naturally to turn to him for advice.

'The 1964 WA Museum Act by which all ancient wrecks were supposed to belong to the State had been challenged successfully in the Australian High Court in 1976' he said *'New Commonwealth Legislation had been brought in, but we didn't know much about it or where we would stand having raised some of the silver without anyone's permission.*

'So far as we knew this was a wreck no-one else knew anything about. But we had to be sure about that. Maybe it was a bit like a dog chasing a motor car – what would he do if he ever caught it? Well we'd caught our motor car, and we were buggered if we knew what to do about it either!' he said with a grin.

'There was also the fact that when you've found a treasure, albeit quite by chance, you're a bit reluctant to give it up all at once. So we took our time thinking about which way to go' Barry Paxman recalled in 2009.

'In the end we took the problem to solicitors. On their advice we reported directly to the Commonwealth authorities rather than the Western Australian Museum, which was the usual way of doing things'.

Meantime there was a serious complication. The Paxman group had left some of the *'casts'* of coins on the beach near their camp site. The casts were pieces of corrosion which had broken off but which showed imprints of the coins they had formerly surrounded.

Another group of divers came along who were familiar with the 1656 *Vergulde Draeck* wreck and the casts of coins from that vessel. They correctly deduced that they were from a wreck of the early 1800s and reported the finds to the Museum. Under the terms of the old 1964 Museum Ancient Shipwrecks Act the person entitled to a reward for finding an ancient wreck was the first person to report it. It did not matter that he or she might not have been the first discoverer.

Consternation ensued. However it was eventually sorted out, and it was agreed that only the Paxman group knew where the wreck was actually located and that they had taken appropriate legal steps to report it through their solicitors. A meeting was arranged with Jeremy Green and Graeme Henderson of the Western Australian Maritime Museum at Fremantle.

Henderson recalled the event in his book *Unfinished Voyages*: *'We arranged to meet at Frank and Jackie Paxman's house. Barry Paxman showed my colleague Jeremy Green and me into the living room and we all sat on comfortable lounge chairs either side of the coffee table for discussion.*

'Frank Paxman waited until we were all sipping from our mugs and then lifted the lid of the 'coffee table' which in fact was an old trunk. Our jaws dropped as we gazed on around 1800 Spanish silver dollars they had raised from the wreck during the space of just several days while snorkel diving!'

It was the Museum representatives' turn to be amazed. Once the initial excitement had died down the immediate priority became the organising of a formal expedition to the wreck for archaeological recording and scientific excavation. It was agreed that the original finders would be included in the expedition and they were eventually paid a reward for their important discovery. As a senior curator in the Museum's maritime archaeology department Graeme Henderson led successful expeditions to the site in 1979, and 1980.

'The owners of Ningaloo Station, Edgar and Billie and Jane Lefroy, at the point nearest the wreck were very helpful' Graeme Henderson recalled in 2008. *'They'd had divers, including Harold Roberts of the Underwater Explorers Club staying in their shearing shed by the beach*

on a regular basis. They were happy for our team of Museum and volunteer divers to establish a headquarters there. At times we had as many as 35 people including television teams from Channel Seven and Channel Nine, on site. We had the Museum workboat Beagle and several dinghies and runabouts for working the wreck and lots of enthusiasm from all hands, including the volunteers'.

The Museum team consisted of Henderson, photographer Pat Baker, Jeff Kimpton, Myra Stanbury, Mike McCarthy, Jon Carpenter, Bob Richards and Colin Powell. The volunteers included as many as 100 people from all walks of life over the two years, including doctors, pilots, journalists, photographers, architects, lawyers, farmers, your author, and blue collar workers, all with a common diving interest. *'It didn't matter what you did in the real world'* someone remarked *'We all looked the same striding about in wet suits with salty spiky hair'.*

'The mix was an extraordinary success' Henderson reported. *'We had the technical ability of the Museum people who had worked on 'digs' on other wrecks and were familiar with the necessary procedures. Their skills were combined with the raw energy and willingness to help of the volunteers. It was also pleasant from the social point of view with get-togethers in the shearing shed in the evenings. Ningaloo was a good place to be both at work and play'.*

If the discovery of the wreck and its silver was a diver's dream, the archaeology would provide a similar result for Graeme Henderson. The scenario every archaeologist dreads is a wreck which has no name to provide an identity.

Unfortunately and inevitably there are a number of those in the records of lost ships off the Western Australian coast. However if the identity of a vessel can be established it is possible to provide the other vital information adding the human touch which completes the story. With a name as reference it is possible to trace where the ship was built, who the shipwrights were, and who were her owners. We can find the names of the captain and crew who sailed on her, and --most important of all, given the name -- our research can reveal the circumstances which led to the final catastrophe. How our ship came to be lying on a sea-bed perhaps half a world away from where she originally set sail?

For the first two years the wreck at Black Rock Passage remained nameless and frustratingly anonymous. *'The first two sessions of work'* Henderson recalled '*Showed the wreck to be a large full-built armed vessel. Prominent features included two large wood-stocked anchors, and a smaller, iron-stocked anchor, and eight cannon. We raised the cannon from the wreck, and other items brought up included the ship's bell, and European and Asian ceramics. We immediately found more coins – in fact we finished up with more than 19,000 pillar dollars over two seasons of excavation'.*

While the coin was the main talking-point, it was some of the less glamorous finds which would take Henderson on a long journey to the Northern Hemisphere. Among the relics raised were a complete barrel of salt beef, and a number of American dollars – as distinct from the Spanish silver -- with the famous Eagle prominent, as well as small change in US one cent pieces. The lid of the wooden barrel was stamped MESS BEEF BOSTON MASS and a broken piece of stoneware had the name BOSTON in raised letters. So, could that mean that Boston, Massachusetts, was the port of origin of the mystery vessel? And, since the last coin date was 1809, was the ship wrecked soon after that? 'Maybe within a couple of years?

That was a reasonable hypothesis, but there was only one way to prove it. The Museum gave Henderson a return air ticket to Boston in the United States. He anticipated that his search of the shipping records might take some time. With such a mass of information as would be on hand, seeking details of one ship among possibly hundreds or even thousands of vessels, he was anxious that he might not be able to find what he wanted by the end of the two weeks. But that was all the time he had available.

His elation knew no bounds when, on only the second day of his search, he found the name he was looking for! While skimming the shipping columns of the newspapers of the period in the Boston Public Library he found an entry in the *Columbian Sentinel* of August 3rd, 1811 which completely took his breath away.

The newspaper reported: *'Ship **Rapid**, Captain Dorr, of and from Boston has been lost on the coast of New Holland; Captain and crew saved. Captain Dorr and part of the crew of the **Rapid** navigated to Philadelphia in the schooner **General Greene**, she having lost her captain and crew at Batavia. The **General Greene** had a passage of 111 days and arrived last Monday. It has been ascertained that the **Rapid** had on board when she sailed Two Hundred and Eighty Thousand Dollars in specie. If the ship and cargo have been totally lost it must add greatly to the commercial distress already so severely experienced in this town'*.

There was the name, and there was the story. And what a story!

Thirty years later Graeme Henderson vividly remembered that day in the library. *'There was a blood- rush of jubilation at the moment of success. But looking around I saw all the other people with solemn faces hunched over their books as people in libraries tend to be. The atmosphere was hushed in a place where silence is traditionally golden. I had to stifle the natural inclination to shout out with joy. But believe me, that was the way I felt!'*.

The hardest thing was that, as a stranger in a foreign country where he knew nobody, there was no-one he could tell of his triumph.

Nobody? His first 'phone call was to his wife Kandy, back in Bicton, in Western Australia. Kandy Henderson was herself a library research worker from the Battye Library in Perth, who had co-authored his original edition of *Unfinished Voyages*. She understood Graeme's elation and shared the joy of that special moment by long distance telephone.

While the discovery of the short article in the *Colombian Sentinel* was an initial triumph to be celebrated, there was still a lot more to discover. The library of the Boston Historical Society –*'Surely the best historical society library in the world'* – proved to be a treasure trove of information related to the *Rapid,* her owners and her insurers.

The story of an incredible adventure emerged, as reported earlier in this book There were the circumstances of the wreck, the burning of the *Rapid,* the epic small boat voyage to Java – Captain Henry Dorr in the jolly-boat, a leaking cockleshell of 5 metres, with four other men. How the starving sailors ate rats and crabs at Christmas Island, survived a tropical storm when they had to throw even their clothes overboard to lighten ship, and finally reached Batavia (Jakarta of today). There they took over the American schooner *General Greene* whose captain and crew had died of fever in that port of notorious pestilence.

Dorr and his men returned to the United States where the captain and ship owners immediately began to plan the salvage of their sunken treasure at Point Cloates. 'Hoping against hope that it was still lying in the sunken and burned-out hull of the *Rapid* on the desert coast of what was then *New Holland*. Praying that no-one else had found their cache of silver dollars!

The *Rapid* syndicate still had the complication of the fact that the United States of America and Britain were at war and any American salvage ship and its cargo could be seized on the high seas by a British *'Man-o-War'*. But eventually their chartered vessel *Meridian* sailed for Point Cloates and the silver treasure in the hull of the sunken ship. They must have had many anxious moments, but their divers – probably Indonesian free divers – brought up some 260,000 of the original 280,000 silver dollars.

'It would have been no small task' Henderson reported in 2008. *'The silver was usually carried in boxes, with about 5000 coins in each. That means that each box would contain about 136 kilograms weight of silver plus the weight of the box itself. The salvage which apparently* raised 260,000 silver dollars from the Rapid would have taken some weeks of good weather' he said. *'A stable workboat would have had to anchor over the wreck, while the divers cut or blasted their way through any remaining structure above the boxes of specie. Then the boxes would be individually tied and hauled up by hand'.*

Why did they leave 20,000 dollars behind, to be found in modern times?

'They would have been acutely aware of the adverse political situation between the United States and Britain and the risk of capture by a British vessel'. Henderson said. *'The British were now in charge in Batavia, due to the Napoleonic Wars. That situation wasn't settled until 1815, the year of the Battle of Waterloo. So there would have been a degree of nervousness aboard the Meridian, especially when they had the bulk of the silver on board.*

'Perhaps the salvage party were observed by a passing ship which showed curiosity, and they opted not to push their luck any further – deciding to quit while they were ahead, as the saying has it. After all the salvage had probably gone better than expected.

'Or perhaps they just had a run of bad weather, with the concern of a questionable anchorage. Or maybe they were running short of stores, and decided to call it a day. I hope to make another trip to Boston one day, and perhaps I'll find more answers there. I certainly hope so'.

The search for the Portuguese vessel *Correo da Azia* by WA Museum maritime archaeologists was a contrast with the story of the *Rapid* where everything had fallen so conveniently into place in a comparatively short time.

With the American vessel there was the incredible good fortune of the discovery, and the better-than-could-be-expected result of the research. A happy ending to a shipwreck story in all respects. The *Correo* was different inasmuch as the maritime archaeology department at Fremantle knew the wreck was somewhere in the neighbourhood of Point Cloates – described by the castaway captain and crew as *'The island'* – but 20 years of searches failed to find it.

'We had some good research in transcripts of a report from the captain of the Portuguese vessel Emillia and we knew it was in the general Point Cloates area' Jeremy Green, head of maritime archaeology in Fremantle, said in 2008. *'After the wreck the Portuguese governor at Macau sent a pilot named Luis Antonio Da Silva Beltrao in a vessel called the Emillia to investigate the navigational dangers of the Australian coast at Point Cloates, and if possible, to attempt a salvage'.*

The Museum arranged for the purchase of the Beltrao transcript by the State Library of Western Australia. Beltrao also had the skipper of the *Correo*, Joao Joaquim de Freitas and several other members of the crew with him on board. They confidently pointed out what they believed was the site of the wreck and left a description. But there was no record of any salvage.

The *Correo* survivors '*Recognised the position, the exact site of their misfortune, with a bottom of rocks and a circle of rocks similar to a salt marsh. They were then sure that this was the position they sought'.*

The first modern Museum search was made with divers towed behind a boat in 1987. They simply saw a lot of coral and were unable to match the description to any particular location. A second attempt in 1988 was also unsuccessful. Green continued towed searches of divers backed up by a small magnetometer. *'In the process we found one other wreck from the second half of the Nineteenth Century which we believed at the time was the Stefano. But the Correo itself remained elusive.*

'She was pretty important in the scheme of things, as the only Portuguese colonial wreck definitely known to be in Australian waters, so we were never going to give up on her. It was just that 20 years was a frustratingly long time!'

Dr Mike McCarthy, who was the Museum's Inspector of Wrecks at the time, remembers the towed searches well. *'Shipwrecks are generally found by accident'* he recalled in a paper titled *Finding the Stefano. 'Some would argue that the discovery of the Stefano in 1997was an accidental piece of good fortune. Most of the divers on the WA Maritime Museum dive boat Seaspray on that trip actually had their minds set on locating the Portuguese vessel Correo da Azio'.*

'That was not to downgrade the importance of the Stefano', he added. '*While the Hungarian barque was a 'pedestrian coal-carrying cargo vessel' the dramatic story of the survivors and the insight it gave into the daily life of the Aboriginal people of the North West Cape before white settlement, made her extremely important in the historical scheme of things.*

'We took turns in being towed along and around the Ningaloo Reef in pairs or threes, hour after hour, day after day, ten metres or so aft of the boat. 'Trolling' we called it (referring to big game fishing) because in our colourful wet suits there was always a concern that we might prove an attractive, bright lure to large fish species! (Like sharks!)

'There was safety in numbers, we thought, with the best place to be in the middle on a slightly shorter rope than the two outriders! But as we skimmed over what is undeniably some of the most beautiful underwater scenery in the world and some of the most prolific sea life on the planet, our heads were filled with thoughts of the Correo!'

There were some interesting experiences. At Black Rock Museum photographer Pat Baker 'Curious as to why a turtle was eating a strange jellyfish, poked and prodded it, and was then stung by what we now know to be a relative of a box jellyfish'.

He was hauled aboard the *Seaspray* in a state of collapse, in great pain and with breathing difficulties, his face ashen white. The boat began a race south towards the nursing post at Coral Bay 40 kilometres distant. *'As we gathered our senses, Kimpton and I furiously chewed Minties... quietly arguing who was to give our patient mouth-to-mouth resuscitation and who would perform heart massage. Just a few miles out, thankfully, he started to recover'*

Finally on Wednesday, April 9th, 1997, Geoff Kimpton, the Museum's senior diver dropped off his tow, raised his arm and shouted in triumph to the boat. The others tumbled into the water, but if they hoped to see the remains of a Portuguese carrack they were to be disappointed. At the same time they were elated to find a wreck – any kind of wreck! After all it was the last day of a 10 day search, and in two hours they would have packed up and gone home lamenting another unsuccessful attempt. If the boat had been only 50 metres east or west it was likely that the wreck might not have been sighted at all. It was a near thing.

'What we saw' McCarthy remembers *'At first sight was a davit – Geoff's first glimpse -- with mast rings and iron plate. The wreck site covered about 50 metres, the wreck canted seawards, with large anchors and iron knees. There was a great moment when Bob Richards located the ship's bell'.*

It was decided then that the ship was the *Stefano*, an identification that was later brought into question. But the *Correo da Azio* continued, meantime, to remain elusive.

'The main difficulty' Jeremy Green remembers *'Was that the Ningaloo Reef covered a very large area between Point Maud and Point Cloates. Apart from being a long run of reef, north and south, it also formed a particularly wide expanse of flat corals from the outside into the shallows still far from shore'.*

It was quite different from previous sites the Museum had worked at Ledge Point (the 1656 *Vergulde Draeck*) and the Abrolhos Islands (the 1629 *Batavia,* and 1727 *Zeewyk*) where the outer reefs were narrow bands sometimes no more than 50 to 75 metres across. Sites where wreckage was often hung with seaweed but not actually overgrown or swallowed by corals. In contrast the Ningaloo Reef flat top was several kilometres wide in places, and in some instances reef corals had grown completely over sections of wreckage, shielding them from the view of divers on a tow search. While tow searches were an inexpensive and legitimate means of locating wrecks, and had worked well elsewhere in the past, it was obvious that something else was required at Ningaloo.

Over the 20 years of searching for the *Correo* the technical capabilities of finding lost shipwrecks had advanced enormously. When the *Rapid* was first discovered there was no satellite GPS (Global Positioning System). The precise location of a wreck had to be established with a sextant, allowing for possible errors in a tossing boat or the difficulty of a sun sight on a cloudy day. An even less satisfactory option was the age-old method of taking landmarks, assuming that the shore was close enough to make that possible. But if the shore were distant, changes in conditions and even the altering shadows on cliffs or heights, depending on the time of day could make for errors. As any fisherman will tell you.

Side scan sonar and magnetometers (for identifying the presence of iron) had been available for quite sometime. But they were expensive items and generally used from larger vessels.

During the 20 years in question there were some exciting deepwater discoveries of famous ships, most notably the *Titanic, HMS Hood,* and the German battle cruiser *Bismarck* deep down in the Atlantic Ocean. Later, as we have already noted, would come the sensational Australian discovery of the sunken wrecks of *HMAS Sydney* and her opponent the German raider *Kormoran,* off Shark Bay in 2008. However the cost of the equipment used in those searches, and the cost of the expeditions themselves, ran into millions of dollars and were far beyond the resources of the Western Australian Museum or any similar institution.

'But by the time the year 2000 came around many technical aspects had changed' Jeremy Green recalled. *'The GPS made a huge difference. With a simple instrument that you could wear on your wrist like a watch you could find a position accurately within a short distance. It was quite astonishing really'.*

Another important factor was Western Australia's mineral boom. It meant that a lot of the equipment used for locating iron ore deposits or precious metals was in practical use in the State. Some of it, especially high-powered magnetometers towed by aircraft or helicopters, also had a potential for shipwreck searches. Most wrecks had anchors and the older ones had cannon whose iron would readily register as an anomaly on a magnetometer. The Dutch East Indiamen wrecks, for example, had as many as 38 guns per vessel. Tests on the Deepwater Graveyard off Rottnest, where hulks and old vessels have been traditionally sunk over nearly 100 years, showed that they could be readily located as deep as 200 metres.

'We established 18 sites' Green said *'Including HMAS Derwent scuttled by the Navy at the end of her service. So the system worked well enough. There was just one serious snag. 'The cost of chartering an aircraft for a day or a couple of day's flying was still pretty expensive, and well beyond our budget in ordinary terms. But fortunately the Museum had a good friend in Geoff Glazier with connections to FUGRO Airborne Surveys'.*

Glazier, a keen diver himself in his spare time moments, had been on Museum expeditions to Thailand and Sri Lanka as a volunteer. He offered to arrange an aerial magnetometer survey of the Ningaloo Reef area where the *Correo da Azia* was believed to lie. The president of FUGRO, Gert Jan Kramer generously offered to meet the cost of the exercise himself.

Twenty years of frustrations were swept away in 2003 as FUGRO detected four anomalies in the likely area. One of them was the *Correo* (*'At last!'*), and another was a mid 19th Century wreck still to be identified. It was something of an embarrassment of riches because it might well be the *Stefano* which the Museum claimed to have found in 1997.

'We really came into the 21st Century with a bang' Jeremy Green said. *'After all those years, in two days of flying FUGRO had registered four anomalies. On the ground, using GPS it took us 15 minutes to find the first site, and 24 minutes to locate the second!'*

Geoff Glazier came up to Ningaloo to help the divers celebrate with champagne bottles opened and fizzing on the beach. While there was elation at finding the *Correo* the site – continually blasted by heavy surf – was not as productive as had been hoped. It did not have anywhere near the variety of artefacts, or shape of the ship as iconic dive sites like the 1629 *Batavia* with its bronze guns, bellarmine jugs, massive timbers and coin recovery which had so richly rewarded archaeologists in the past.

First swims on the site recorded only two cannon, an anchor, some hundreds of slabs of iron ballast, a couple of sounding leads, and some lead sheathing. There was no shape of a ship. Where the *Correo* had been listed as carrying 106,000 silver dollars of similar origin to the pillar dollars found on the *Rapid* , there was little that was obvious at first. But persistence paid off, and the diving team eventually found a clump of concretion that contained about 700 pillar dollars. With individual coins from sand holes and coral fissures this gave the Museum divers a total of 9013 silver dollars. Their dates of 1789 to 1815 confirmed the wreck site and the coins were similar to those of the 1811 *Rapid.*

'It was pretty clear that coral had grown over a lot of parts of the wreck' Jeremy Green said. 'We expect to have a number of seasons of fieldwork to know more about this historic wreck site. After all it is the only known Portuguese wreck on Australian shores and there's certain to be a good deal more there to be discovered'.

And the unidentified wreck?

'Yes, there's something of a puzzle there' Jeremy Green conceded. 'We thought that the wreck that we found in the old tow search days in 1997 was the Stefano.

'But now we have another very similar mid 19th Century wreck from the FUGRO survey close by. One of them is probably the Stefano, but the question remains which is the other one?

Archaeology is a science and it's facts which are the real requirement. So we'll keep diving and researching until we have the right answers. That's all a part of the fascination of the job'.

If one of the two wrecks is the *Stefano* then the other may be the source of the legend, as told to Charles Tuckey, that people, including women, had come ashore from an unknown wreck – other than the *Emma* – and had been killed and eaten by the Aborigines.

In addition to the *Correo, Rapid,* and (perhaps) the *Stefano*, Museum divers, through the years, have also swum on many others of the known wrecks on the Ningaloo Reef, including the *Emma, Zuir, Perth, Benan, Chofuku Maru, Mildura, and Fynd.*

Are there more wrecks yet to be discovered, perhaps another treasure ship? Past experience says that the possibility should never be entirely discounted. The archives of the Western Australian Maritime Museum in Fremantle list the names of vessels known to have been lost in the Exmouth Gulf-Ningaloo Reef region between 1800 and 1943.

1811: American China trader *Rapid.*
1816: Portuguese vessel *Correo da Azio*
1856: The guano brigantine *Occator*
1867: The coastal cutter *Brothers*
1867: The coastal schooner *Emma*
1868: The cutter *Ariel*
1874: The coastal cutter *Bertha*
1875: The pearling schooner *Fairy Queen*
1875: The pearling vessel *Lily of the Lake*
1875; The pearling vessel *Blossom*
1875: The Croatian barque *Stefano*
1875: The pearling vessel *Wild Wave*
1879: The brig *Cock of the North*
1887: The coastal steamer *Perth*
1889: The three-masted schooner *Airlie*
1889: The British iron-hulled sailing ship *Benan*
1899: The lugger *Don Joseph*
1901: The lugger *GSS*
1902: The Austrian steam-powered vessel, *SS Zvir*
1907: The Australian steamer *SS Mildura*
1910: The lugger *Wyndham*
1915: The motor sailer *Queen of the Sea*
1923: The Norwegian whale-chaser *Fynd*
1931: The Japanese wheat carrier *Chofuku Maru*
1943: The American submarine chaser *SC. 751*

'There were also a number of more fortunate vessels' Dr Michael McCarthy of the Western Australian Maritime Museum advised *'Ships which stranded but which managed to free themselves from the reefs'*. The strandings which are recorded are as follows:

1815: The American China trader *Caledonia*
1818: The American vessel *Ollices*
1870: The 450-ton barque *Strathmore*
1923: The iron barque *Iona*
1931: The Japanese wheat carrier *SS Shunsei Maru*

'The list of wrecks may not be complete' Dr McCarthy suggested. '*Some of them, such as the 1811 Rapid, were unknown until they were accidentally found by sport divers. There may well be other unknowns waiting to be discovered some day in the future'*.

With this in mind, astute readers may have already noticed that while there are many shipwrecks listed after 1800, there are none – except the 1622 *Tryal* at the Monte Bello Islands – on the records as lost between 1616 and 1811. This was a period of almost 200 years when we know that there was quite a lot of passing traffic going by the North West Cape. Chris Halls listed 25 English or English-crewed vessels passing Point Cloates from 1620 to 1811. There were some hundreds of Dutch VOC East Indiamen which sailed eastwards from the Cape of Good Hope on their way to the Sunda Strait and their East Indies capital of Batavia. Many of them would have passed by in close proximity to the North West Cape.

Why the perfect record in the first two centuries, followed by a host of nautical disasters in the next 100 years to 1911?

There was certainly a considerable increase in colonial coastal traffic in the later years. But it would not be surprising if one or more 17th or 18th Century wrecks, with their massive cannon and distinctive vee-shaped anchors – and perhaps another silver treasure trove – were to be located off the Ningaloo Reef in years to come.

Underwater explorers should not give up hope just yet!

Picture: Hugh Edwards

The Cape Under The Microscope

Chapter Sixteen

Shaped like a crooked little finger, the North West Cape extends over a full degree of Latitude -- 22.30 degrees South, to 23.30 degrees. That represents a distance of a little over 100 kilometres from Point Murat at the northern extremity, down to Gales Bay inside the Gulf, and Point Cloates on the ocean side.

Within its natural boundaries it contains a wide diversity of habitats, plants, and animals, the occupants of different living spaces. These, in turn, provide study opportunities for scientists working in fields as diverse as marine and terrestrial biology, anthropology, climatology, and geology.

Studies of creatures as opposite as marine mammals such as the great whales and the tiny *cavernicolous* subterranean fauna living in permanent darkness below the caves of the Cape Range.

'The *cavernicolous* WHAT?'

We may laugh at the unusual name. But the little blind gudgeon fish and prawn-like crustaceans found in the *Karst*, or underground cave and aquifer systems of the Cape are our seniors on this planet by a wide margin. They are survivors of 180,000,000 years living in this earth. Yes, one hundred and eighty million years -- no misprint!

Compare that species life-span with the development of humans. Scientists believe we began our evolutionary journey less than nine million years ago, with *Homo sapiens* (You and me) only emerging in the past 250,00 years!

There are several distinct geographical areas of the Cape. Though they may appear as a single entity when we look at the map, each area has individual natural characteristics quite different from the others.

For instance, if we were to take a wedge-tailed eagle's view of the Cape -- the raptor's ragged-tipped wings soaring on the thermals -- we might start in the west by looking down on the long rollers of the Indian Ocean approaching the shore in marching regiments.

The waves have travelled all the way from Africa, free and untrammelled. But as they feel the drag of the shallows below them, they make the transition from swells with moderate slopes to the vertical faces of rolling surf. Rearing and crashing in explosions of dazzling white foam along the outer edges of the reefs.

Even as the spume clears away the crest of the next wave behind it is already feathering, ready to fall and break in a repetition of its predecessor. Hour after hour, day after day, the pounding continues unceasing as it has for thousands of years. The thunder of the surf is the background music. The ceaseless natural symphony of action and reaction resounding between the sea and the shore.

The natural rampart of the Ningaloo Reef – as already remarked, the world's longest shore-fringing coral reef -- takes the full fury of the ocean swells. It protects an inside chain of bright green and blue lagoons running all the way down the coast.

Sometimes – as at Lighthouse Bay in the north – the reef is right on the shore. At other places such as Tantabiddi or Point Cloates or Mauds Landing further south, the outer reef may be some kilometres from the land. No one place is exactly the same as the others.

Above the tidal edge of the ocean and the beaches run lines of white sand dunes where Aborigines once made their camps and held corroborees. Behind the dunes is a narrow fringe of coastal plain, where kangaroos graze. A kilometre or two inland are the first rugged steps and steppes of the Cape Range. The Cape Range and Rough Range, with their caves, canyons, gorges, and water courses, rise in the centre of the Cape like serrated lizard's backs. We cross over them, observing with our eagle eye, to another coastal plain on the eastern side. That plain, covered in low eucalyptus scrub is divided by dry stony creek beds full of red boulders. The creeks become raging torrents in times of cyclonic rain with the water pouring off the ranges.

A serious challenge for modern road engineers.

Lapping the eastern shore are the shining waters of Exmouth Gulf itself, a vast body of water nearly 70 kilometres deep and 40 kilometres in width. The Gulf encompassing its own world of marine life. Its creatures include the shy dugong, diamond-backed manta rays, and the spectacularly-leaping humpback whales in their winter season.

Nature is old on the North West Cape. Even the first Aborigines arrived there 30,000 years ago. A time when Europeans themselves were clothed in skins, and lived in caves. When our European ancestors had to deal with hairy mammoths and sabre-toothed tigers. In contrast the period of modern occupation of the North West Cape is less than an eye-blink in time. But our eagle would certainly notice significant changes to the landscape, cruising up there, a black cross-like shadow high in a blue sky.

Modern Europeans, the technical champions of the planet, have imposed signs of their activities everywhere on the landscape of the North West Cape. The features are highly visible from the air. As we fly in to Exmouth, looking out of the windows of our modern jet, we see roads snaking across the countryside, the red scars of firebreaks, and the glinting roofs of built-up areas. The most evident changes are on the eastern coastal plain. There we see the spread of houses and civic buildings of the town, with its swimming pools, parks, and sports fields, the boats and prawn trawlers clustered in the marina, and the new canal housing complex.

To the north is the giant VLF tower complex at Point Murat, and Naval Communication Station Harold E. Holt. South of the town are the military and civil aviation aerodromes at Learmonth, the high frequency radio section opposite the Bay of Rest, and the Learmonth Solar Observatory.

Centuries ago the Dutch explorers saw Western Australia with prejudiced eyes. As we remarked earlier, they complained that it was too hot, and there were far too many flies! It also lacked the silks and spices they sought to make themselves and their nation rich. So they called it '*The Miserable Southland!*' and sailed on past its coasts.

Australians today have learned to live with the land and naturally see the arid areas of Australia quite differently from the Europeans who were the first-comers. We actually prefer wide horizons to enclosed spaces. The bright light of summer suits us just fine, even if it does call for sunglasses and sunburn cream. The surf which alarmed the first mariners has become our playground and a major recreational asset.

Visitors from Europe and Asia today are also a different breed from the complainants of the 17th and 18th Centuries. They have the benefit of education and know what to expect before they reach Australian shores. They arrive with a positive approach, looking forward to experiencing the outback, the Range, the Reef, and a landscape quite different from the over-crowded cities and pollution-dulled skies of the Northern Hemisphere.

They want to see kangaroos, and whale sharks too. *'Yes please!'*.

What the French scientist Francois Peron described as '*A frightful desert!*' is far from being a sterile landscape in reality.

Today's marine biologists, blowing bright SCUBA bubbles below the surface, find unceasing wonder in their studies of the myriad creatures of the Ningaloo Reef. The beauty of corals revealed in a living tapestry. But while the Reef is the Exmouth region's most advertised asset, there are other interesting aspects to the North West Cape.

Evolutionary biologists study the subterranean fauna deep in the caves of the Cape Range where bats squeak in the shadows. There in dark pools are pale varieties of shrimps and small fish and eels, almost white, whose ancestors lived so long out of the world of light that their descendants have become blind. The study of the subterranean fauna has only recently begun. But already it has been described as being of world importance.

Some of the terrestrial *troglobitic* fauna including millipedes, are of particular interest -- according to W.F. Humphreys (editor of the *Biogeography of the Cape Range, Western Australia)* -- because of their high degree of adaptation to their underground environment and because they may be related to similar creatures '*Only known from other continents, usually a hemisphere away'*. Their relations may be found as far away as Texas and the Caribbean!

Geologists study the serrated structure of the ochre-red rocks of the Cape Range and the aptly-named 'Rough Range' where Australia's first oil strike was made at Shot-hole Canyon in 1953. Fossil sea shells and extinct *Megladon* shark teeth found on the flanks of the Cape Range tell us that some of the present high ground was once submerged. They are relics of a time when the Continent was still forming, and when the range was a coral reef below sea level. Strange to think that waves once broke over high slopes now grown over with native shrubs and eucalypts.

Anthropologists working in the beach-side middens and remains of old fires in the caves of the ranges, find evidence of the stone tools, and some of the remains of the food Aborigines ate before the last Ice Age. What did they talk about at meal times?

Aborigines themselves came down from the North, and were in Australia when the pre-historic *megafauna* were still living in the continent. It stretches our imagination today to picture a three tonne diprotodon, a wombat-like creature the size of a hippopotamus. Or giant kangaroos and marsupial lions, roaming the countryside. Or the fearsome five metre monitor lizard *Megalana prisca*, which weighed more than 400 kilogram. It must have been the equivalent of a land-going crocodile with a turn of reptilian speed! 'Not a nice creature to meet on a sunny afternoon!

We know that the *megafauna* did exist because we have their bones to prove it. Carbon dating tells us when the owners of the bones were alive and well. None of the bones of the Big Boys have been found in the Exmouth region to date, though there are many areas remaining for archaeologists to examine and anything is possible. But remains of the *Thylacine* – the Tasmanian tiger, extinct in our own era – have been found in several of the caves of the Cape Range. In comparison the dingo, which only came to Australia 4000 years ago is a new arrival.

Dingoes are still present in the region and may occasionally be seen in the Cape Range, sometimes on the outskirts of the Harold E. Holt Communications Centre. Notices on walking trails request people not to feed the dingoes or encourage contact. The advice follows unfortunate incidents at Fraser Island in Queensland where dingoes became over-familiar with visitors and grew aggressive as a result.

Anthropologist Professor Kate Morse of the University of Western Australia and her associates, have been excavating caves in the Cape Range, and Aboriginal middens and campsites on the western Ningaloo sea shore, since the mid-1980s.The excavations have turned up stone tools, and fish, and animal bones, and sea shells that were part of tribal diet thousands of years ago. Professor Morse's most spectacular find to date has been 23 small cone shells which once made up a necklace. They have been established as being 30,000 years old! Proof that even in pre-history days people liked to dress themselves up!

'It is the earliest evidence to date' Professor Morse says *'For the antiquity of human decorative traditions in Australia. They are as old as any of the personal decorative material found in the caves of Europe or indeed anywhere else in the known world'.*

The identification of the beads was an adventure in itself. *'We didn't recognise the significance in the Mandu Mandu cave at the time of excavation'* Kate Morse explains, *'Because the objects and shell fragments from the particular strata were embedded in a sort of paste of red earth. It was only when we returned and the objects were individually cleaned that we realised that the shells had been modified for use as a strand, an arm-band, or more likely a necklace. Whatever the mode of application, they were a human decoration'.*

Because they were too precious for any of them to be crushed into the fragments necessary for age testing, a piece of baler shell from the same strata level was sent for carbon dating. When the result came back Kate Morse and her colleagues couldn't believe their eyes. Surely there was some mistake? Further samples were sent back to repeat the process. But yes! Additional testing confirmed the date!

Who was the person who wore the necklace? Was the owner male or female? What sort of daily life did the people who spent time in the caves lead?

'We can actually tell a good deal about them' says Kate Morse. *'They were hunter-gatherers like the later Aboriginal people the Europeans found when Western Australia was first settled in the Nineteenth Century. They wouldn't have lived in the caves permanently. It was too easy to exhaust the surrounding food and water sources, if they stayed too long in one place. The Aboriginal life-style required them to always be on the move. They would probably have sheltered in the caves when it rained or to escape bad weather'.*

Excavations of the beach middens provided evidence of a people who made a living from their coastal environment. Their diet was largely marine based – fish, turtles, turtle eggs, an occasional dugong if they were lucky, a despised stingray if they were desperate. The animal protein heavily supplemented by plants and seeds.

Aboriginal life depended entirely on the environment, and the physical aspects of the Cape would have changed a good deal over 30,000 years. There were times when it was wetter or warmer, or colder. The fluctuations resulting in changes in the vegetation and perhaps the animal life upon which hunter gatherers depended. In more tropical times, for example, there were stands of mangroves in many of the bays down the west coast and in the Gulf. Mangroves create their own habitat and shelter for fishes, crabs, and shell fish such as *Terebralia palustris* which was eaten extensively by Aborigines.

The taller, bulbous-rooted species of mangroves found north of King Sound today may have also provided timber for building rafts allowing the hunters to venture off shore in pursuit of turtles and dugong.

Today, in cooler times, there are mangroves in only one bay, Mangrove Bay (you guessed it) on the west coast of the Cape. The surviving species *Avicennia marina* that still grows there is a comparatively small and scrawny variety. Though it has edible fruit it is quite unsuitable for raft building.

Archaeological excavations by Professor Morse found that there was a gap of time in the occupation of the rock shelters in the ranges, including the cave at Mandu Mandu where the prize find of the shell necklace was made. But no animal remains from meals or other evidence of occupation was found with carbon dates between 20,000 years ago and 5500 years ago.

It was the time of the most recent Ice Age which lasted for about 10,000 years. The excavations of the rock shelters appear to indicate that during the harsh and arid conditions of the Ice Age Aborigines withdrew from the area, and returned in the Holocene period (the present time) when the climate and food availability were more to their liking.

While the caves also present opportunities for scientists there are others who go underground for the excitement and interest of a different kind of exploration.

'We do it for the excitement and exhilaration and the thrill of it' Darren Brooks, an instructor with the Exmouth Emergency Service Vertical Rescue Team told Gerry Blum in an article for the *Exmouth Expression*.

Brookes and his colleagues have mapped more than five hundred features in caves in the ranges. He said that the longest known cave, '*Wanderer's Delight*' extended underground for an impressive 6.86 kilometres, and some others were as deep as 90 metres. *'Mind you, a lot of Happy Wanderer's length involves crawling. 'Not especially comfortable over a long distance'* he remarked. Other caves such as the *'Anomaly'* cave have spectacular stalactite and shawl formations. Darren Brooks said that he expected that as Exmouth's visitor population increased the popular interest in the caves would also increase. But he warned that caving was physically demanding and that cavers needed to know what they were doing.

'Most of the caves involve vertical descents at the entrances and we abseil to get down into them. Our SES group have attended a number of emergencies' he added. *'Sadly the call outs have involved two fatalities – the only caving deaths in WA'*. He suggested that people wishing to explore Cape Range caves contact local experts for advice. The Exmouth Visitor Centre lists about 800 caves and rock shelters in the ranges.

The caves and the underground streams and sinks which honeycomb the ranges, the interestingly-named '*Stygal* 'realm of darkness below, may tell the most extraordinary Exmouth story of all. Scientists believe that some of the tiny blind creatures, including the shrimps and amphipods – tiny, flattened crustaceans barely 2mm in length, which live in subterranean waterways -- may date from a time before the Australian continent was formed. A time when Australia was part of the legendary *Gondwana Land* and joined to Africa and Asia before the great land masses drifted apart.

Some of the creatures in the bowels of the Cape Range and Rough Range, have relations in other parts of the world, long separated from Australia. Places as incredibly far distant as

Madagascar, the Mediterranean, Texas, and the Caribbean. The age of the original species of 180 million years is such that we find it hard to grasp the concept. But the Exmouth *troglobites* and *stygofauna* are among some of the oldest life forms on earth.

Up above where the sun shines brightly, a good deal of the North West Cape is encompassed in the 50,581 hectares of the Cape Range National Park which occupies about one third of the peninsula. All the animals within its boundaries are protected, and today's tourists, coming from around the world, are pleased to find a profusion of the kind of animals they expect to see in Australia. In the Park red and grey kangaroos are abundant, and there are the rare black footed rock wallabies of Yardie Creek, with their little faces peering down from the cliff caves of the gorge. They often sit with their tails between their legs and out in front of them. Why? Easier grooming, perhaps. But only the rock wallabies really know.

There are also many native animals outside the park and in proximity to the town. Emus walk around Exmouth town as though they own the streets, often trailed by a string of clucking chicks. Bush bustards or bush turkeys, are commonplace on the outskirts, bands of galahs, and screeching corellas fly overhead. There are some dozens of varieties of other birds from honey-eaters to butcher birds, wagtails, and mudlarks, to be seen in parks and gardens and nesting in the gardens of private homes. Their demeanour plainly suggests that they see it as being their town too.

For the visitor taking a morning stroll on one of the walking trails around the town it would not be unusual to find a short-sighted echidna with its '*hedge-hog'* spines ambling on its little short legs across the path. Or an arrogant two metre Perenti lizard, a goanna dinosaur-reminder, may choose to stand his ground and hiss, tail lashing, and forked tongue flickering.

Snakes of all descriptions from death-adders to brown snakes out in the bush, command respect and the sensible walker gives any of them right of way. No need to explain the reason for that!.

In the ranges there may be the rare sight of a three metre rock python slithering across the rocks. On the sea shore, sea eagle ospreys, *Pandion haliaetus*, soar above the reefs and shallows ready to drop from the sky, sharp talons outstretched, onto an unsuspecting fish. The resultant splash momentarily engulfing both bird and prey. Osprey nests top many of the towers and navigation beacons around Exmouth, including spectacular nests at the Tantabiddi boat launching ramp and Learmonth airport.

Seagulls, *Larus novahollandiae,* squabble noisily over fish scraps and picnickers' abandoned potato chips. Gannets patrol the sea lanes with steady wing beats, along with crested terns, frigate birds, storm petrels, and other seabirds. Dusky shearwaters skim the waves, brushing the crests with their wingtips. All winged Nature is on the move, as it has been each day for countless thousands of year. But now the birds are in newer circumstances. Some – especially seagulls -- adapt well to the influx of humans. But others are affected by the loss of nesting habitat or breeding season disturbance.

In the animal scene there are, sadly, also some absent friends. The advance of civilisation, with introduced dogs, cats, rats, and foxes, has seen many extinctions of native animals in the Australian bush. The smaller mammals, such as the central rock rat, have been particularly vulnerable. Nonetheless there is still a large group of survivors, including the visitor's own favourite creature, the kangaroo. In fact there are so many plains kangaroos (*Macropus rufus*) in the lower regions of the National Park, that motorists have to drive with extreme care in the late afternoon and early evening to avoid running into one. There are several species, including the hills kangaroo, *Macropus robustus*, of the ranges. Strangely there are no local wallabies, though the cute little rock wallabies (*Petrogale lateralis*) peering down from the cave shelters of Yardie Creek are a feature of boat tours there.

The Cape has 49 species of mammals, with 38 ground animals, including echidnas, bandicoots, possums, six species of bats, and six introduced animals – feral foxes, cats, rats, goats, and dogs. At one time there were camels on all the stations as well as sheep, cattle, donkeys, and horses. And the arrogantly-named *Homo sapiens* – aren't we mammals too?

While we are talking numbers, there are 84 species of reptiles –lizards and snakes – in the Cape, and about 200 bird species, as well as five amphibians. All typical of semi-arid regions.

The one natural phenomenon that all visitors see but seldom seem to remark on, are the termite mounds prominent on the spinifex plains outside the town. They are highly visible on the surrounds of the main road from Carnarvon, and in the Cape Range National Park. Visitors tend to look past them, their eyes seeking the more mobile kangaroos or emus or perhaps a perching wedge-tail eagle. But the termite colonies are actually one of Nature's marvels.

They are usually described as '*ant hills*'. In fact termites are not ants at all, despite a strong physical resemblance and their erroneous common name of '*white ants*'. They are a different species actually much more closely related to wood-eating cockroaches.

The rough mud exterior of each mound conceals a colony and an organisation which – once we are aware of the facts – most people find quite amazing. There are some 2230 species of termites world wide and 350 of them live in Australia. The nests the tourist sees in the Exmouth region are those of *Nasutitermes triodiae,* the '*spinifex termite*' , which inhabits some of Australia's most desolate sub tropical areas, including the inland deserts. Inside each of the ragged-looking red mounds, in complex chambers and tunnels, there may be a million inhabitants, divided in complicated social orders.

The nest itself is built of a mix of mud and termite saliva, the height increasing one or two centimetres a year. Big nests may weigh a ton or more – imagine the number of workers, each scarcely as long as a finger nail, who have provided the saliva!

The nest has built-in *'air conditioning'* which keeps the interior at a constant 28 to 30 degrees Celsius. Air is drawn in at the base and funnelled out at the peak so there is good reason for the tapering shape. Some of the larger nests may be anything from 50 to 100 years old.

How long the inhabitants live as individuals remains an open question. But scientists studying them have a good deal of other information, because in some other areas – notably Darwin and the Northern Territory – the species there tend to eat houses and furniture, even electrical cables, and whatever else may be around. Not unreasonably they are regarded as pests, and significant sums of money are spent each year on research and in chemical controls.

However only about 20 % of termite species fall into this '*nuisance*' category. Our friend the Exmouth spinifex termite, as its name implies, basically eats spinifex, converting the cellulose into energy with assistance from bacteria living in its gut. Any creature which can find a living from that harsh and spiky plant with its needle-tipped leaves, is to be congratulated!

Worker termites, which make up the bulk of the population in a nest, are mostly blind and white in colour (hence the name *'white ants'*) because, like the subterranean fauna, they never see the sun. However, as with conventional ants, there is a complicated social order. At the top of the hierarchy are the queen, and the king, whose sole task is reproduction. A queen, who may reach 10 centimetres in size, can lay thousands of eggs a day. Next in line are the reproductive class, which have well developed eyes and darker coloured bodies, and grow wings. These become the swarms of *'flying ants'* we see after rain, which leave the nest to start new colonies elsewhere.

The workers forage, building tunnels from the base out to food sources where they harvest grass and plants, including spinifex. They also maintain the nest, repair any damage, and digest the cellulose, passing the digested food on to the queen, king, and other members of the nest including the soldier ants. The soldiers' job, as the name implies, is to defend the nest against enemies, usually conventional ants. Like the other divisions soldiers have distinctive physical modifications. In their case the difference is in the shape of big heads and powerful jaws to deal with intruders. Termite nests in Africa may grow 10 metres high, though North West Cape spinifex termite mounds seldom exceed three metres. Nonetheless, taking the tiny size of the worker termite, that is the equivalent of humans constructing a building more than a kilometre high into the sky!

While termites generally get a bad Press due to the fact that some species chew up our houses, they are generally considered to be good for the countryside creating nutrients which go back into the earth. They provide food for many other insects and animals, and the *'flying ants'* are actually regarded as a culinary delicacy and eaten by humans in many parts of the world. Crushed ant nests provided solid floors in pioneers' houses, and make good compact for tennis courts today. Even the destructive Northern Territory termites have one strike in their favour. They hollow out the limbs of trees from which Aborigines make the didgeridoos important for traditional ceremonies, and which are popular purchases for tourists.

Aside from the termites the North West Cape also hosts a complex web of other insect life, including spiders, scorpions, centipedes, cockroaches, and other winged and crawling creatures.

In fact there is so much that is remarkable about the region in terms of the Ningaloo Reef, the birds, animals, insects, the ancient *stygofauna*, that the area has been recommended for World Heritage status.

TERMITE MOUNDS are a feature of the North West Cape. People often call them "ant hills" but in fact termites are not ants at all but quite a different species of insect. There are 2230 species of termites worldwide and 350 of them live in Australia. Some of them are nuisances to humans because they eat the timber and even electrical cables in houses. But our North West Cape termites are not guilty in that regard. They eat mostly spinifex. There may be as many as a million termites in any mound which you may see on the North West Cape. The mounds are 'air conditioned' at a constant 28 to 30 degrees.

The Song Of The Whale

Chapter Seventeen

Each July, in Exmouth Gulf waters, the humpback whales are leaping. They throw themselves up and almost clear of the water, flippers wide-spread. Forty tons of whale crashing down backwards makes for an awesome splash!

Why do they do it?

We humans, the curious species, like to know the reasons for everything. But in this case though we may seek an explanation for the spectacular breaches, the humpbacks themselves don't need one. All that massive effort is just for fun, for *joie de vivre,* the joy of life. Humpbacks are jolly folk. Affectionate too, as they roll and play together in the waters of the Gulf, frequently touching each other, in a tactile way, with their four metre-long pectoral fins.

Why do they have such long flippers, when other whales such as the right whale and the sperm whale and the mighty blue whale have short stubby ones? We don't know that either. But the physical peculiarity is noted in the humpback's '*Big flipper*' scientific name, *Megaptera novaeangliae.*

For whale-watchers in Exmouth Gulf the sounds associated with the whale frolics are the watery splashes and the hiss of the sheets of foam striking the surface. But there are other sounds below unheard. If their whale-watching vessel were equipped with the hydro-phones used by scientists the people would be able to hear the sounds made by the whales communicating with each other. The strange creaking noises which the scientists dub whale '*Songs*'. The songs vary in different parts of the world, and have improvisations or changes from one year to the next. The '*Humpback hit parade*'!

At Exmouth Gulf the humpbacks have come a long way for their songs and winter sunshine. All summer they have been down in the Antarctic, on the edge of the pack ice, gorging on the '*Krill*', the masses of crustaceans which abound there. When the winter fronts and storms turn southern waters into a hell of howling winds, they head north for warmer climes.

The whales reach the Western Australian coast in May and June, and spout their way up along the shores to the sheltered waters of Shark Bay, Exmouth Gulf, and further north as far as the Lacepede Islands and Camden Sound on the West Kimberley coast. There they spend the winter months calving and mating until September and October when they make the reverse journey down the coast. Cruising back to their familiar realms in Polar seas. Cows and calves always keeping close together.

Western Australia sees several species of whales. Blue whales at a maximum of 120 feet in length, or more than 40 metres, are the largest living creatures on the planet. Their hearts alone are as big as a Volkswagen car. The names of the whales were given to them by whalers long ago. The right whale was the '*right*' whale to hunt because it was slow and easy prey and didn't sink when harpooned. The humpback had a rolling motion when it surfaced to spout. The sperm whale was the only toothed whale, with round ivory teeth and living principally on squid. The other great whales strained krill, plankton, and small fishes through brushes or baleen in their mouths and were called the *Baleana*. In a previous century the baleen was used to stiffen ladies' petticoats.

Sperm whales had the *'oiliest'* and most aromatic oil of all, with a cache of it in the whales' great square head. Blue whales were often a dark blue in colour. Sperms and blues also swim off the Ningaloo Reef, but they tend to be further out to sea and the humpback is the species most likely to be seen by whale-watchers inside the Gulf. Humpbacks grow to 40 feet or 12metres in length and around 40 tons in weight. Their extraordinarily long pectoral fins may be as much as a third of their body length, and it is the pectoral fins which are most likely to catch the attention of whale-watchers. Humpbacks often roll on their backs or lie on their sides, slapping the water with their knobbly pectorals.

Seeing them today, in their obvious enjoyment of each other's company and the winter sunshine of Exmouth Gulf, it is sad to think that they were once hunted by whalers off the Ningaloo Reef and slaughtered in their thousands through the years. Whaling was the original industry of the North West Cape. A whaling station was actually established at Point Cloates in 1912, and because the operators hailed from Norway the locality was re-named *'Norwegian Bay'* – it was originally *'Port Sholl'*. But it was by no means the first appearance of whalers off the Ningaloo coastline. The keels of whale ships had been furrowing the blue waters of the Indian and Pacific oceans since the first days of Australian settlement.

Yankee whalers were off the coast of Western Australia as early as 1789. That was not long after the First Fleet landed its unhappy cargo of convicts at Botany Bay, and forty years before the first settlement at the Swan river in 1829. At the peak of Yankee whaling in 1846 there were 729 whale ships sailing out of east coast American ports. By 1830 there were so many of them in Australian waters that there were 37 American whale ships tied up at one time in the Derwent River in Hobart. The taverns filled with brawling whalemen adventurers.

Whalers and sealers worked all Australian coasts, often setting up shore stations for boiling down blubber into whale oil. Remnants of their shore stations can still be seen at Kangaroo Island, in South Australia, in the islands of the Recherche Archipelago off Esperance, at Cheynes Beach near Albany, and in the Dampier Archipelago on the North West coast.

The Point Cloates area of North West Cape, where the deep water comes closer to shore than any other place on Australian coasts and where the Continental Shelf is at its narrowest, was renowned for the numbers of whales which passed by outside the Ningaloo Reef.

The favoured quarry of the Yankee whalers, was the sperm whale which they sometimes called *Cachelot*. It was preferred because of the finer quality of the oil. Sperms were easily identified from the crow's nest by their thick bushy spout which inclined to the left.

'Thar she blows! B-l-o-w-s!, Blows-oh!'

Records show that between the years 1761 onwards a total of 744 whaling ships sailing from United States made 1665 voyages and captured 36,908 sperm whales around the world.

The most famous whaling port was Nantucket, and the hunt for *Leviathan* – as described in Herman Melville's classic book *Moby Dick* – employed the traditional means used by whalers for hundreds of years. Nineteenth Century whale ships carried up to eight sleek oar-powered whaleboats hung in davits which were launched overboard when whales were sighted. The whaleboats were rowed silently and behind the whale's vision until they were within striking distance.

A barbed harpoon was flung into the whale's back by the headsman, and then the rowers sat tight, oars inboard, while the whale towed them at a furious speed in a '*Nantucket sleigh ride'*. When it exhausted itself it was killed with a long lance driven into its heart and that was the most dangerous time for the hunters. In his book *The Whales' Journey,* Stephen Martin quotes:

'*At this crucial moment the boats are exposed to great danger, for as the whale sometimes turns rapidly in its final flurry it is impossible to tell in what direction he might rush. The headsman shouts hoarsely to the crew ' STERN ALL !' to keep clear of the dying fish. But perhaps a boat gets stove or capsized and its crew struggling in the 'white water' amongst fragments of oars, and planks, and falling gear, is in danger of instant destruction ...'*

The Yankee whalers, whose product of whale oil was principally used for lamps, went out of business in the 1860s because of the discovery of cheaper kerosene, and finally the advent of gas and electricity for lighting. The Norwegians changed the method of world whaling with Sven Foyn's invention of the harpoon gun with its explosive head in 1864. The first question was where to put the gun for best advantage? A design of fast, steam-powered steel vessels with platforms mounted at the bow provided the answer. Foyn's original vessel was called '*Spes et Fides' – 'Hope & Faith'* .

She was the first of a new breed of whale chaser which would introduce modern methods to an age-old hunt. They were so efficient that inside 100 years they would push some species of whales to the brink of extinction. With the advent of the mechanical age, requiring specialised lubrication for mechanisms ranging in diversity from pocket watches to sewing machines, the world price of whale oil – the '*oiliest oil'* -- soared once more. The Norwegians sent their fleets out around the world in pursuit of *Moby Dick's* descendants. They killed whales of all species, including sperm whales, blue whales, sei whales, and minke whales, wherever they found them. But the humpback herds suffered the most because they were at first the most numerous species and a comparatively easy target.

The Norwegians went down to the pack ice in Antarctica in summer with a base at the islands of South Georgia in the South Atlantic. In the southern winters when the whales went north, Australia and South Africa were the favoured locations. The whalers applied to the various governments of the day for licenses to operate shore stations.

Old-time whalers used sailing ships which processed their catch at sea, lashing the whale carcasses alongside. The flensers stood on platforms hoisted out over the ship's side and stripped *'blankets'* of blubber from the dead whale. Raised to the deck by block and tackles from the yard arms, the blubber was chopped up into chunks and boiled down in try-pots amidships. Used blubber went into the fires as fuel, producing thick black smoke in billowing clouds which turned the ship into what was called a ' *Devil's kitchen!*'

It was a very smelly and messy business, but it had the great advantage that it could be carried out anywhere on the oceans of the world. Provided, always that the weather was clement. It gave the whalers an independence of movement. Yankee whalers could be away from their home ports for three or four years before they filled their holds with barrels of aromatic sperm oil. They most often circled the globe, hunting whales in the Atlantic, Pacific, and Indian Oceans, before coming home *'west-about'* around the Cape of Good Hope.

While the modern whale-chasers were much more effective in hunting down whales, their design didn't permit processing at sea. The catch had to be towed to factory ships or shore stations for flensing, the process of cutting up the carcasses and rendering down the blubber for oil. In

1912 the Western Australian Government granted licences to Norwegian companies to establish shore whaling stations at Frenchman's Bay in Albany, and at Norwegian Bay at Point Cloates. The Point Cloates location on the North West Cape was surveyed by Captain Bull of the Spermacet Company, and re-named *'Norwegian Bay'*.

It was the opinion of Captain Bull, a very experienced whaler, that this was the best location for taking humpback whales on the entire Australian coast. Catch figures would prove him right. The two factory ships *Prince George,* and *Vasco da Gama* anchored in the bay while the whale chasers including the *Fynd*, worked outside the Ningaloo Reef. In 1913 the whale chasers took 654 humpback whales and were forced to slow down their operation because the factory ships were full of blubber and could not keep up with the processing. In 1914 the slaughter continued with an extra factory ship the *Rakiura.* From late June to the end of September 1900 humpbacks were killed off Point Cloates.

The Western Australian Government became concerned at the numbers of whales being taken, and whether pregnant females and mother with calves were being killed indiscriminately. A Parliamentary Select Committee was established to discuss these points.

Whaling Captain Carl Andersen was asked by a committee member: *'It seems to me that you fellows go in for wholesale slaughter?'*

He replied *'I never knew any whaler who made any scientific study of a whale'*.

In 1915 the Spermacet Company began building a slipway and shore station at Point Cloates in accordance with their licence. But already the effects of the huge catches were beginning to show. The take in 1915 was 21,300 barrels of oil, only half of that of the previous year. In 1916, it was down by half again, with only 10,000 barrels filled. Faced with the prospect of operating at a loss, the company closed operations and sold out. However the whalers were reluctant to admit that the cause of declining catches was the wholesale depletion of whale numbers. They simply said that the whales had *'Gone away!'*.

In 1921 Point Cloates was re-opened by the North West Australian Company with Australian finance and personnel. It was unsuccessful due to lack of experience, and the Norwegian Bay Whaling Company, with Captain Bull as manager, stepped in to assist. The catch rate improved initially, but once again declined. It was the same story as before. Operations were officially shut down in 1928, though the Point Cloates station was still manned in 1931 in caretaker mode, with engineer Maurice McBolt in residence, when the *Chofuku Maru* was wrecked nearby.

Foreign factory ships with stern slipways continued to operate in the area through the 1930s taking 7000 humpback whales off North West Cape, and Western Australia coasts before the Second World War put a stop to whaling everywhere. After the war, due to a shortage of the fats needed to make margarine the world price of whale oil soared to six times pre-war values. In Perth the Moore brothers trading as the Nor' West Whaling Company obtained a licence to re-open the Norwegian Bay whaling station.

To say that the station was a mess would have been an understatement. Rust and rot had taken their toll and the 1945 cyclone had inflicted what appeared to be terminal damage. But the Moores were efficient engineers and determined people. They chipped the rust off the winches, cleaned out the boilers, rebuilt the flattened buildings, and got the station operational again in a seeming miracle.

As whale chasers they used fast ex-RAAF *Fairmile* air-sea rescue craft, and they brought in experienced Norwegian gunners. Though they were allowed a quota of 600 whales a season, catches were limited by equipment failures and problems related to the remoteness of the location at Point Cloates. At one time a 40 ton humpback whale carcass fell right through the rotting timbers of the slipway, and impaled itself on the supporting piles, creating a major problem for the flensers and the factory.

The Commonwealth Government, making an unusual incursion into a commercial field, also set up a whaling station at Babbage Island in Carnarvon after the Second World War. They hired Captain A.Melsom as advisor. He was a very experienced Norwegian whaler who had gone to sea at the age of 18 and within six years was a captain and a master gunner. Melsom had been whaling in most of the seas of the world including the Indian Ocean off Point Cloates in pre-war days. He was reputed to have personally killed 3850 whales. With everything brand new and the machinery sparkling, Babbage Island at Carnarvon was a direct contrast with the patched-up Norwegian Bay operation with its rust and its ruins in the sandhills at Ningaloo.

Why was the North West coast such a good location for whalers? After 1900 the Norwegians knew more about whale movements than anyone. There was a distinct pattern of movement. The humpbacks migrated north in June and July up the west and east coasts of Australia. Their movements were regular as clockwork. At particular points along the WA coast, in particular the sheltered waters of Shark Bay by Carnarvon, and Exmouth Gulf around the North West Cape, the whales would spend weeks in the sun, sporting and mating. Whether you were a whale or a whaler those were the places to be.

Graham Chittleborough was a young CSIRO scientist allocated to do research at the northern whaling stations. He still remembers his first day on the job. *'I stepped on to the flensing deck for the first time, a fresh-faced 24 year-old, newly kitted out in a spotless blue boiler suit, leather belt holding a handsome sheath knife. I wore shiny Wellington boots'* he recalls in his book *Shouldn't Our Grandchildren Know? ' With a neat black beret jauntily covering my golden locks. In my hand I held a gleaming galvanised bucket containing a new 66 foot measuring tape, callipers, and scientific instruments'.*

At the sight of this splendid creature from another world: *'A derisive cry went up from the bloodied flensers clad only in ragged, blood-stained shorts, and torn rubber boots. I surveyed the deck with great sheets of blubber strewn about, juices still dripping from exposed backbones, enormous whale skulls, the deck awash with blood. At that first sight all seemed total chaos from some gory nightmare'.* Further down the deck an intact whale lay on its side in a clearer area. That looked a good place to start work.

'I began walking down through the blood towards the whale, climbing over blubber, whale meat, and intestines when there seemed no clearer path. After a few slithering steps I made an important observation. The flensers weren't slipping because they had three short spikes screwed into the heel of each boot, gripping the wooden deck safely. These spikes enabled them to run nimbly up the length of a whale, slicing into the blubber with their hockey stick-shaped flensing knives as they climbed. I stifled the impulse to leave the deck until I too had spiked boots. Instead I adopted a skating motion across the slippery areas.

'The boys, however had more in store for me. A blood-blackened, dripping cable 'accidently' dropped across my shoulders as I slithered beneath it. A flenser standing on the whale high above me cut off a four metre flipper just after I had ducked under it, spraying me with blood. A well-judged miss. Then as I waded through another pool of blood, I didn't notice one grinning flenser signal with a finger. A winch driver to one side suddenly threw his steam winch into gear – a

greasy black cable flicked up, hooked the hind foot I was just lifting, flung me into the air and face-down into the gore. I was initiated!

'Lying there, feeling the blood oozing through my new boiler suit and listening to the peals of laughter, I reflected that my next move was fairly important for future relations. Scrambling to my feet and gathering my gear I tried to grin naturally. I made a small bow then continued to collect my samples as the whale was dismembered. The flensers were rough types, but cheerful and good-hearted, and we eventually became good friends.

' Each of them had a nick-name. When they saw me collecting samples of whale testes and ovaries my future nick-name came quite naturally.

'BALLS!' they roared with delight, and 'Balls' was the name I was known by ever after'.

At Point Cloates Chittleborough had one of the more interesting experiences of his scientific career. He was flying in the whale-spotting aircraft with pilot Jim Pekin, *'I was looking at the wonders of the Ningaloo Reef below us and thinking what a great job I had'. Immediately below was a whale that had been killed, pumped with compressed air, and buoyed by one of the chasers. The water around that whale was a writhing mass of sharks'* Graham Chittleborough remembers. *'They were jumping over each other's backs to get to the whale. There must have been hundreds of them in a feeding frenzy. I remember thinking to myself 'I'm glad I'm up here, not down there!'.*

At that moment the familiar throb of the engine of the aircraft stopped abruptly and the motor cut out. In the moment of silence which followed, with just the whispering sound of the wind rushing past the windows, the passenger was naturally thrown into consternation!*'There was an inflatable rubber dingy in a pack behind my seat. I wondered whether we would have time to blow it up before the sharks arrived! Always, of course, supposing that we could get it and ourselves out of the aircraft in what appeared to be an inevitable crash landing in the sea!'*

Jim Pekin kept the nose of the aircraft down in a shallow dive to keep the propeller turning while he fiddled with something below the seat. Meantime he watched the expression on his passenger's face out of the corner of his eye and tried to keep a straight face. Below the seat was a lever which switched fuel tanks -- as the pilot knew perfectly well. Now he pushed the lever over and in a few moments the engine kicked back into life with a cheerful roar and a wide grin from the pilot. *'Later he said that my face was a laughable study!'* Graham remembered.

Graham Chittleborough had been caught again!

Sharks were a constant problem for whalers. The species varied according to regions. Great whites attacked dead whales at Albany. At Babbage Island and Point Cloates packs of whaler sharks shredded whale carcasses, with an occasional tiger shark or two sharing the feast.

'Sometimes, by the time the whale reached the flensing deck all that was left was a head, an exposed backbone, and a tail. 'Not much joy for the company there!' Chittleborough said. Point Cloates was by far the worst place for sharks among the Australian stations, which included Tangalooma in Moreton Bay in Queensland and Byron Bay in New South Wales.

But sharks weren't the only problem. The whaling station operators weren't at all happy with Graham Chittleborough's scientific measurements and organ samples. What they were showing, along with declining catch figures, was that the whales were getting smaller and smaller and less mature. Views from the spotting aircraft showed that the proportion of larger males, the breeding stock, was falling at an alarming rate. Male whales were the main targets for the whale chasers and stations were only allowed a small quota of females. Invariably Chittleborough the '*whistle-blower'*, found that the ones killed were pregnant.

Whaling was a cruel business. British author Peter Lancaster Brown took a job at Babbage Island at Carnarvon to get material for his 1972 book *Australia's Coast Of Coral And Pearl.*

Out at sea on a whale chaser he witnessed one of the more unsavoury aspects of the modern whale hunt. A cow in a pod of humpback whales had been harpooned by the gunner – the captains on whale chasers were always the gunners – and brought alongside the chaser in a welter of blood. The fourth whale in the pod, a large bull, suddenly turned in his course and came plunging back to the side of his stricken mate and lay alongside her.

'Even to the hardened deck crew the sight was a pitiful spectacle. A horrible thought crossed my mind ...Even before it crystallised the harpoon gun barked again and the second harpoon curved the air obscenely and struck the faithful bull with a great thump low down near the head. Driven frantic with pain his great flukes thrashed the air, and frothing blood splashes smothered the for-ward deck in a red squall until the scupper were running red. But the terrible impact of the grenade in the harpoon head soon showed its effect and the wild thrashings gradually lost power until all life had ebbed away. The bull's eyes, dilated and contorted with pain, fixed dreadfully towards its slaughterers.

'A double killing was a common occurrence on the whaling grounds. Man took advantage of the rule of Nature which declared that the male of the species was expendable. The female, producer of life, had a fundamental purpose to live and reproduce. No whale cow remains with her stricken mate. Her primeval instinct is directed to the preservation of the calf in her belly'. On the other hand a male would always come back to a wounded cow, sacrificing his life in doing so!'.

Knowing that if a cow were shot her male mate would remain with her, making him an easy target, the whalers always killed the cow first.

Peter Lancaster Brown did not enjoy that day on the whale chaser.

Dr Chittleborough's figures, which he recalled in his book *Shouldn't Our Grandchildren Know?* were a warning to all involved in the hunt what the outcome would be if the killing continued at the present pace. But no-one wanted to know about that.

The operatives in charge of the stations regarded him with undisguised hostility as an *'Interfering busybody'* and actively tried to get him dismissed from his job. But some of the message may have got through to the Commonwealth Government.

The Babbage Island whaling station was quite suddenly put up for sale in 1955. The Carnarvon operation was eagerly snapped up by the Moores, the operators of the Nor'West Whaling Company. They were only too pleased to give up the decrepit patched-together operation at Point Cloates, close it down, and move into modern quarters next to a thriving town and port.

The conditions were infinitely superior, but the catch figures were about to dive. In 1957 the two stations maintained their catch rate with 1120 whales processed at Babbage Island. But after that the numbers went steadily downwards. Part of the problem was that the Russians and the British fleets were hunting the same whales down in the Antarctic, when they migrated southwards in summer. By 1963 only 87 whales were caught out of Carnarvon of a quota of 550 allowed by the International Whaling Commission.

The humpback whaling industry on both the west and east coasts of Australia collapsed that year because the whale population had been devastated by the inroads of whalers at both ends of the humpback migration. The reason plainly was over-fishing both by the whalers in Australia and the international fleets in the Antarctic. Belatedly, the International Whaling Commission moved to declare the humpback whale a protected species. The year 1963 was the requiem for Australian humpback whaling. After that the thump of the harpoon guns in Shark Bay and off Point Cloates and the Ningaloo Reef would never be heard again.

Whaling continued at Albany with the Cheynes Beach Whaling Company taking sperm whales until 1978. But by then there had been important changes in world attitudes towards whaling. This was especially the case in the United Sates where the slogan *SAVE THE WHALE!* had become familiar. Somewhat ironically America, which was once the world's greatest whaling nation, was now the country most strongly and vociferously opposed to whaling. The United States was a powerful voice on the International Whaling Commission.

It is interesting reading the literature on the subject, from Herman Melville's great novel *Moby Dick* onwards. Until modern times the attitude of writers describing whaling was usually excitement at; what was most often described as *'The World's Greatest Hunt'*. The descriptions were usually in complimentary terms. But there were some exceptions. Steven Martin in '*The Whale's Journey'* quotes Thomas Melville (no relation to Herman) a surgeon aboard the whaling ships *Britannia* and *Speedy* between 1791 and 1796.

'One cannot help admiring the wonderful contrivance of Nature in constructing the Organs of these monstrous Animals so as to render them incapable of noise. Were they favoured with the powers of voice who could stand the dreadful yelling that must be uttered when labouring under such a weight of pain? '

Frank Hurley, the famous Australian photographer who accompanied Ernest Shackleton and Sir Douglas Mawson's expedition to the Antarctic, and was a great First World War correspondent, was an early and almost lone voice of protest after viewing the whale slaughter down by the pack ice.

'I had marvelled at the devices that enabled man's ingenuity to triumph over Nature's moods and most powerful creatures' he said. *'But their ruthless application to such unrestricted devastation provoked sad disillusionment. The absurdly mad scramble for quick money seems a deplorably short-sighted policy. The impossibility of securing international protection means that whaling must succumb in the near future to unreasonable greed'.*

They were prophetic words. But the sentiments were not popular at the time, and his views did not see print until years afterwards. The eminent Sydney zoologist William Dakin too gave early warnings about the vulnerability of whale herds to whalers' greed which were ignored at the time, but which would come back to haunt the whaling industry later.

As someone who studied animals he felt a sadness which he expressed in his writing after witnessing whales killed by our old friend, the chaser *Fynd* working out of Frenchman's Bay, Albany.

'It is always after the excitement is over that regret and depression come' Dakin said. *'I think it would be impossible for even a sea-sick landlubber (* himself *) to miss the thrill whilst a whale hunt is on. But one later has other feelings. No one who has seen a whale die can ever think of it unconcernedly as just a fish'.*

Your author first experienced whaling at Albany in 1962, and later in 1976 to 78 while filming the Great white shark for a television series. I was interested to see the changes in the public perception towards whaling over that period and in my own feelings towards killing whales.

When I first saw whales killed from the whaler *Kos V11* as a young journalist my own attitudes were quite different to my feelings sixteen years later. In 1962 I was in my 20s and myself a keen spearfisherman – a hunter too. Though I recall that my photographer Maurie Hammond, a man of great sensitivity who loved life and animals, wept when it took five shots to kill one whale. The whalers themselves were unhappy about that.

That was the down-side of whaling. When Sven Foyn invented the harpoon gun in a previous century he had hoped that the whale would be killed instantly by the explosion in the harpoon head, and that his invention would take the cruelty out of whaling. The whaling companies always put the legend out that this was indeed the case. Sometimes the whale was indeed killed by the first shot. But too often while the wounded whale struggled stubbornly for life other shots were needed. The gunner fired *'killer'* harpoons which had explosive heads but no barbs for deeper penetration. In those cases a kill could be a very messy and gory business with evident agony for the animal concerned. No-one who has witnessed the hard death of a whale could ever forget it.

By the late 1970s my own attitude had changed 180 degrees. At the time the rest of the world vilified Great white sharks as hideous man-eating monsters, thanks to the film JAWS. But our somewhat-out-of-step view of them from the shark cage alongside dead whales at the Albany whaling station was quite different. The sharks were magnificent, banking past us on their huge pectoral fins like B 52 bombers. Sometimes they showed us their gleaming triangular teeth by biting on the bars of our cage. But even though they seriously frightened us at times by attacking the cage -- presumably with the idea of getting us out of there and eating us -- we couldn't help admiring them as beautiful and impressive creatures. The fact that they were predators and demonstrably dangerous didn't alter that view. After all, aren't humans also predators and dangerous too?

Ask a whale!

Seeing fish, seals, sea lions, and yes – whales too – underwater, had given me a completely different perspective on life in the sea by the 1970s. When you shoot with a camera instead of a gun the world becomes a very different place. I understood by then that I was privileged to observe one of the world's great spectacles in the whale hunt. But now I winced when I saw the harpoons strike home, sending rivers of blood across the surface of the sea. I felt nausea in watching the thrashing of a mortally wounded whale. It transpired that I was not the only person seeing things differently.

The first time I went to Albany the whalers – remembering that whaling was the town's major industry – were home-town heroes. By the end of the whaling era they were beginning to feel increasingly like pariahs. Conservationists around the world were calling for an end to whaling. There was a particularly strong movement in Australia and towards the end of 1978 a huge *SAVE THE WHALE* demonstration was planned for Albany to picket the whaling station. The Commonwealth Government announced an inquiry into the validity of the industry now that effective substitutes for whale oil were available in the form of vegetable oils.

Was it really necessary or desirable to kill whales any more? An adverse finding, the most likely outcome, could have seen the Cheynes Beach Whaling Company operations closed down.

That never happened because a fall in the world price of whale oil persuaded the company to close the station of its own volition.

It was a termination for economic rather than moral reasons. But there is no doubt that the strong anti-whaling attitude of the public reflected in the proposed government inquiry would have had some influence on the decision.

How had this dramatic change in attitudes come about? There is no doubt that the advent of television had played a major part. Animal stories stand up well on TV, especially ones with a *'Feel Good'* theme. Before the popular series '*Flipper'* starring a lovable bottle-nosed dolphin, dolphins in Australia were invariably and incorrectly called *'porpoises'*. Porpoises – including the common *'harbour porpoise' Phocoena phocoena* -- actually only occur in the northern hemisphere. After Flipper our bottle-noses, *Tursiops truncatus*, took on their rightful name of dolphins and no-one now calls them anything else.

Other television series based on the US Sea World aquarium in Florida, and Jacques Cousteau's French diving team aboard his vessel *Calypso,* helped world-wide audiences see ocean mammals as interesting creatures. Aquariums sprang up around the world, including the popular Sea World on Queensland's Gold Coast. For the first time people were relating to oceanic animals, seeing them experiencing the same love, fears, joy, and protective attitudes towards their young, as ourselves. There was also the discovery, new at the time,that humpback whales communicated with each other with strange underwater sounds which scientists called *'Songs'*. How could you fire a killer harpoon into the hearts of creatures that sang to each other?

Now, more than 40 years after they became protected, the humpback whales sport and play off Ningaloo and in the waters of Exmouth Gulf. People today, more than 40 years after humpbacks were reprieved from the slaughter, are largely unaware of how close the species came to extinction. But figures tell the story.

Immediately after the Second World War the migratory humpback herd off the Western Australian coast numbered 16,000 whales. By 1963, after only a few years of whaling, the number was reduced to less than 3000 individuals. Had whaling continued the results would have been even more disastrous, as they had proved for the Australian fur seal which was almost wiped out by sealers in the Nineteenth Century.

In the new millennium humpback numbers are recovering again. The world has changed and we are far better-educated today in terms of living more harmoniously with the creatures which share our planet. Whale-watching will ultimately bring in more money – if that were the only criteria – than killing whales ever earned in the past. But dollars aside, shooting whales with cameras instead of the deadly harpoon gun is a far more soul-satisfying way of interacting with our sea creatures.

When we watch the whales spouting off the North West Cape, the wind blowing the vapour from their spouts high in the air, and marvel at the grace and beauty of such enormous beasts, we still need to reflect from time to time on the errors of the past. To hope that whales are never hunted here again. Not ever!

Unfortunately the moratorium on Australian coasts didn't mean that the same whales might not be in peril elsewhere. Australians generally were dismayed with the news that the Japanese intended to take 50 humpback whales in Southern Ocean and Antarctic waters in 2008. Eventually public pressure persuaded them not to take humpbacks, though they still targeted minke whales.

The new Rudd government came under strong pressure to appeal to Japan for a cessation of all whaling in Australian waters which included the Antarctic.

Today the Norwegian Bay Whaling station north of Point Cloates has relapsed into a set of rusting ruins in the sand hills, Nature reclaiming a little more of it each year.

Though the curious tourist taking a four-wheel drive through the sand hills can still see enough to envisage how the station must have appeared in its heyday. A little to the south, by Frazer Island, the wreck of the whale chaser *Fynd* lies visible on the outer reef. She had probably taken thousands of whales in her long career before falling victim to the sea herself. Now she too sleeps with her memories A reminder of whaling days gone by.

For most of us the world will be a better place when all whaling, everywhere, becomes a memory too.

We Saw It Happen

Chapter Eighteen

The character of any town depends on the strength and personalities of the people who live there. In Exmouth there are still people who lived in a tents and caravans at the time when construction of the Base and the town was under way. Those were the days before there were any completed buildings or even made roads. When the bright hue of red dust or red mud – on the rare occasions it rained – was the prevailing colour of the countryside. Before the sharp silhouettes of the VLF towers pierced the skyline .

Some of the pastoralists such as the Lefroys at Exmouth Station, the Blakes at Giralia, the Shallcross family at Bullara, and the Forrests at Minderoo, remember the North West Cape when there were less than 40 people – including the family of the lighthouse keepers – in the whole of one of Western Australia's most remote regions.

Looking at the region today with the thriving town of Exmouth, the Naval Communication Station Harold E. Holt , the Marina Village, and the international airport, it is sometimes hard to imagine how it must have been before its transformation. The time when the winding gravel road to the Cape was a sea of corrugations and washaways, and there was no town at all.

Times change. Today's bitumen road is smooth as silk and the widely-spread town has an air of comfortable suburbia about it. Modern Exmouth is lush with garden greenery, and colour from red and white bougainvillea vines prolific around the town to jacaranda trees with their bright blue flowers and poincianas with a blaze of scarlet blossoms. Palm trees of many varieties rustle green fronds in the breezes, frangipanis and flowering plants bloom in the gardens. A well-ordered network of streets with wide pavements replaces the straggling eucalypts, red dust, and stony ground of what was once the realm of high-stepping emus and merino sheep.

One of Exmouth's original citizens, Bernice McLeod – 'Mrs Mac' to everyone in town -- celebrated her 90th birthday in 2008, recalling Exmouth's history as it approached its first half century. *'My husband Dudley and myself and our four kids came up here from Margaret River in 1963'* she rememberd *'And I've been here ever since!'*

The McLeod family, Bernice, Dudley, and children Leonie, Keith, Neil, and Lyle, made major contributions to the town through the years, each making their mark in different ways. Bernice was remarkable – apart from her strength of character – in her work for charities such as the Royal Flying Doctor Service, King Edward Memorial Hospital, and Princess Margaret Children's Hospital.

She was recognised in 1982 with the award of an MBE (Member of the British Empire) and in later years became West Australian Citizen of the Year. The honours coming a long time after the McLeods first pitched a tent in what would later become a caravan park. *'We weren't supposed to be here at all!' she remembers. 'The authorities had designated it as a man's town – no women or kids! But we came there just the same, and a lot of other men brought their families up. They couldn't stop us, you see. There was no school then', she said 'Just School of the Air if you happened to have a radio. I had to give my own kids lessons, and in no time at all there were other children sitting in.*

'So I established the town's first kindergarten. The surroundings were rough, but the spirit was willing and we all got along just fine'.

There was a family tragedy when Dudley died suddenly in 1971. He had always been very community conscious and had set up cave tours and initiated a tourist bureau in Margaret River. He had worked hard to create a tourist bureau in Exmouth and was president of the local tourism association. Sadly he died just before it was due to be officially opened. Bernice opened the bureau for him instead.

When her son Neil began operating his Ningaloo Safari Tours among the highlights for visitors in his OKA four-wheel drives, were morning and afternoon teas out on the track. Neil swung the billy can in approved bushland style, and the tourists enjoyed thick cuts of Bernice's orange and fruit cakes made the night before. *' I was always being asked for the recipes' Bernice recalls. 'I never minded giving them to people. I just hoped they enjoyed them'.*

But her more serious work in Exmouth was for charities. She had a big tin shed in Maitland-road, Exmouth, filled with a vast array of second hand goods donated by townsfolk. There were clothes, televisions sets, toasters, vacuum cleaners, pots and pans, crockery and cutlery. They were the kind of things some householders might have no more use for, but which might have value for other people. Exmouth people brought them in to Bernice's shed. So instead of going to the rubbish tip as in other towns, or being put out on the street verge for collection, the goods were recycled into someone else's world at very modest prices.

The amount of money raised by Bernice McLeod and her willing volunteer helpers for her favourite charities in this way was quite astonishing. Between the RFDS, King Edward, Princess Margaret, and St John's Ambulance, more than $20,000 went out in cheques each year.

Lesser spirits might have found the working conditions somewhat trying. The shed was unlined and had no air conditioning. Cool in winter, stifling hot in summer. On the day the photograph in this book was taken the November 2007 temperature was over 40 degrees and climbing. But Bernice was quite unfazed. *'It is a little warm'* she agreed, looking cool as a cucumber *'But it doesn't really affect us here'.*

In a tin shed?

Not surprising perhaps from the tough old lady who – as previously recounted – had her house disintegrate around her in Cyclone Vance in 1999. With the roof gone and all windows blown out, she was lying pinned to her floor by a marble-topped table, soaked to the skin, with broken ribs. Her reply when an anxious neighbour came searching was classic Bernice.

'I can't come to the door. But I'm all right!'

'I'm all right!'. The pioneers were a breed all of their own!

The Bernice McLeod Day Care Centre in Exmouth is named for her, and many of the town mothers remember with gratitude Mrs McLeod visiting with a present -- *'A little something for you, my dear'* -- when their babies were born at the local hospital.

Robbie Atkinson's first visit to the North West Cape was as a 15 year-old member of the crew of the lighthouse supply ship Cape Otway in 1958. *'We went ashore in the longboat'* he remembers *'And loaded up a trolley with the lighthouse stores and fuel. Then six sailors put on harnesses and towed it three kilometres to the lighthouse!'* He had no inkling then, of course, that one day he would become the proprietor of the Lighthouse Caravan Park. Or that the surrounds which seemed so strange when seen for the first time would become very familiar to him in the future.

His next visit to Exmouth was in 1964 working for O'Connor Cranes, driving a crane on the construction of the Navy pier. He followed that by working with 30-ton cranes in the Base construction, eventually becoming the director of transportation.

In April 1967, his friends shook their heads as he gave up a handsomely-paid US Navy job at the Base and took on the lease of Exmouth caravan park.

'I remember it well' he recalls. *'The date was April 1st, and when I walked into the pub feeling pleased with myself they took the wind out of my sails. "Well, here comes a real April Fool!" they said. The construction work was finished, and the workers were all leaving town. The Navy and Australian personnel all had their own accommodation and it was generally thought that the caravan park would become as dead as a dodo. I went down to Perth and bought five caravans, and that was just the start of it. I had the only accommodation in town besides the Pot Shot hotel!'.*

He never looked back, running the town caravan park for the next 31 years, until 1998. At one time, in 1995, he had three caravan parks, Exmouth, the Lighthouse, and Yardie Creek. *'We spent ten years building up the Lighthouse park and then in 1999 Cyclone Vance smashed it to bits. We had pieces of caravans hanging off the trees and lost the roof off the historic lighthouse keepers quarters'.* For Robbie and his wife Kaye it was back to work again rebuilding the park and lovingly restoring the 1912 lighthouse keepers' quarters to make them a showpiece for visitors.

George King was a legend in the charter boat business and so was his boat *The Gun* which took hundreds of divers and fishermen to sea off the Ningaloo Reef through the years. It was only one of a number of vessels in the King family fleet, which included the well-known *Nordon.* But *The Gun* is still the name everyone remembers best. After all George King himself, was '*The Gun'* so far as charter boat skippers went.

Today his son Raymond and wife Branka King keep the family business going. Ray skippers the 22 metre utility vessel *Calypso,* or *The Gun,* or a third vessel the *VG,* on oil and gas contracts, and scientific research. Branka operates *King Dive* and *King's Ningaloo Reef Tours* on the tourism side of things.

'We've seen water tourism develop from very early days' Raymond recalls *'Dad had the first charter fishing boat in WA. We originally started at Coral Bay, then moved to Exmouth, and were there for the start of the whale sharking. They were sensational times with Tony Medcraft organising charters for National Geographic and the Japanese NHK television network, and Rodney Fox, Ron and Val Taylor and other celebrities of world diving coming to Exmouth'.*

There was heartbreak in 1999 when *The Gun* was sunk and badly damaged by Cyclone Vance. *'We took her down to Geraldton and rebuilt her from what was basically just a shell. Today she's still earning her keep as a utility vessel in the oil and gas industry'.*

What of the future?

'We've seen Ningaloo Reef tourism reach unexpected heights since the mid-1990s' Raymond King says. *'But I believe the future will see new levels achieved. When we look back we may see all this as just a beginning. Aside from tourism there will be important developments in the oil*

and gas industry. The keys to expansion will be the major airlines coming in to Learmonth and international direct flights. That will happen one day'.

Leonie McLeod came to Exmouth with her parents Bernice and Dudley, and her younger brothers (she was *'Big Sis'*) in the early 1960s when construction of the base had just begun and the family lived in a tent. *'Dad was a surveyor's assistant working on Area A, where the towers are now' she remembers. 'And where huge scrapers were digging the anchor block holes. I was still only 17 and I was a radio operator ordering the concrete as it was required to fill the massive holes.*

' There were about 1500 men living at the construction site and only four women living in a fenced off compound patrolled by the camp Police Officer. I was by far the youngest female in the camp, and the guys called me 'Little Chick'.

'Breakfast was at 5 a.m. and the other women wouldn't bother, but I was always there because it was my only chance to see my dad. *'I'll never forget one piece of advice he gave me when there was some gossip about me and one of the young workers. He told me to ignore it. "Little Chick" he said " Just remember one thing in this life. All you have to live with is your own conscience". I've always kept that as a yardstick, and tried to pass it on to my own children and grandchildren'.*

Later Leonie worked as a secretary for Ken Murdoch at the time of the formation of the town, and then did secretarial work for a period at the Base before becoming CEO Kerry Graham's secretary in the Shire office for 16 years. In spare moments she began the Chinese restaurant later run by Linda and Sandi Moh, started the *Exmouth Expression* newspaper in 1987, and became a real estate agent first under the Peet & Co., banner, and later the Ray White masthead.

She spent some years as a member of the Exmouth Shire Council, and in between times she managed to get married and have three sons, Stephen, Martin and Murray. Busy days! A later husband described being married to Leonie as *'Like living with a whirlwind'*. She saw it as simply *'Getting done what needed to be done'*.

'The Expression was very important' she said. *' There was no other source of local news or way for people to find out what was happening in Council. The paper had its 21st birthday in 2008, and we were very proud of what it has achieved and is still doing for the community'.*

Warroora Station was a huge step for Leonie. She knew the property well from holiday visits with her children in previous years. She was passionate about protecting the wilderness beauty of the area from *'inappropriate over-development'*. When Warroora came up for auction she determined to obtain the lease and to do so she had to find one million dollars in a hurry.

Friends and relatives lent her the $97,000 deposit, and she was ultimately able to borrow the remainder *'At an exorbitant rate'* after being lectured by the lender that her action was *'Reckless and hopeless'* because the run-down station couldn't possibly be expected repay the debt. However, with the help of her two sons Murray and Martin, and their families in a holding called Outdoor Investments, the property was debt free by 2007 and close to being economically sustainable with a mixture of sheep and cattle, and low key tourism. *'My dream for Warroora was to put the soul back into the country'* she said in 2008. She maintains close links with the Baiyungu Aboriginal people, the traditional owners of the area, who run Cardabia Station to the north of Warroora.

Jan McClelland, Exmouth's long-serving librarian was a woman of two worlds. Her day job was running Exmouth's library and Telecentre. When danger threatened, as in the case of cyclones, or there were injuries or fatalities in the parks or ranges, she was communications officer for the State Emergency Service.

'I always wanted to be a librarian' she recalled as she approached retirement in 2008. *' But it took me a while to get there. As a girl I wasn't able to continue my education to the necessary level to obtain the qualifications. So I spent my first 10 years as a general secretary, then – when my husband and I came to Exmouth in 1977, I was a medical receptionist at the Dispensary at the Base. The chance to become a librarian came in 1992. At that time the library was housed in one of the original buildings, with books in a number of rooms with old wooden shelving, and the adult fiction section was behind the circulation desk. It wasn't at all user-friendly! In 1999 the library was re-located to a far better situation and in 2001 we changed from a manual system to a computerised one. We had a few teething problems, but now it works very well, and we combined the Exmouth Telecentre with our orthodox library services'.*

Jan had a strong interest in Exmouth's local history, and complied an invaluable collection of photographs and information, including wartime material. Some of her most vivid recollections are from her role with the State Emergency Service. She joined when she first arrived in Exmouth in 1977, as a radio operator. In more recent times she was SES Communications Officer. *'As with many other emergency services 99 per cent of the time is in stand-down mode, and one per cent of the time you're so busy you don't know which side is up!'.*

Cyclone Vance, in March, 1999, was a particularly stressful time for everyone in the town. *'It was the strongest wind to hit the Australian mainland'* Jan remembers, *'And the Exmouth SES was inundated with calls during the peak of the cyclone from residents who were extremely distressed as their houses were starting to disintegrate around them. They were worried about possibly having to evacuate and concerned when they couldn't contact other members of their families. It was extremely stressful for us all, having to answer calls from people we often knew, trying to sound calm and in full control of the situation when we were just as apprehensive as the rest of the townsfolk'.*

At the height of the cyclone the SES building itself was showing signs of severe stress. *'At one point it looked as though the front doors were going to blow in. If that had happened the entire structure might have collapsed, because it was entirely possible that the roof and walls would have been blown away. Two of the crew managed to crawl around the side of the building into the full force of the wind and reinforce the doors. The entire operations room was awash with rainwater pouring down the walls. The ceiling was flexing up and down and the whole building was vibrating with the force of the wind!'.*

The SES building survived the force of the storm. But many other building and houses were not so fortunate. One SES officer going out to assess the damage in the aftermath found that his own house had been completely blown away. All that remained were the stumps that had once supported it.

While cyclones were the most spectacular area of SES responsibility there were other demanding responsibilities. *'We had drownings with SCUBA divers, people who got themselves lost in the ranges, or were injured or became fatalities in the caves. There were bushfires which threatened the town. Body retrieval was always distressing, especially if you knew the people concerned. We were involved in the search for the missing ore bulk-carrier Andrew P. which had departed Dampier and had not responded to radio signals.*

' I was involved in the aerial search 150 nautical miles off Exmouth and sighted floating wreckage. It was later surmised that the carrier must have suffered catastrophic structural damage, perhaps breaking in half and sinking without warning with her cargo and crew. Looking

at the wreckage I just wondered what had happened to them down there? Were there still crew floating about in lifejackets after the ship went down?'

Aside from her library, Telecentre, and SES work, Jan McClelland found time to be president of the Red Cross volunteer unit from 1999 to 2008, she was also a St John Ambulance volunteer, and spent three years as secretary of the Exmouth Yacht Club from 1992 to 1995.

Doug and June Hunt first came to Coral Bay in 1967, and returned permanently many years later after long involvement with boats and the marine industry. Doug and his brother Norm first came to Western Australia from Tasmania in the sailing schooner *Patanella.* They ran the famous *Islander* ferries on the Rottnest Island run for a number of years and built the first *Seaviewer* underwater observation craft for the island. They also built fishing trawlers, constructing eight before the recession of 1989 sent interest rates peaking at 23 percent, and the death of the Japanese Emperor disrupted seafood exports.

'It was time to move on' Doug Hunt recalls *'We had been caravanning to Coral Bay for a number of years. In 1993 we managed Coral Bay Adventure Tours for the owners, and finished up buying the business in 1994. It was a decision we've never regretted. The corals and fish life here are absolutely amazing and the nicest people take our tours. We have whale shark and manta ray tours and whale watching, and it has been great for our kids Doriana, Marnie, Brodie, and Yasmin – in fact Yasmin became almost a human fish, she spent so much time on the boats and in the water!'.*

John Hallworth, who helped build the Cape's tall towers, and his wife Poppy, were one of Exmouth's best known couples. John was generally known around town as 'John the Pom'. He literally worked his way up to become supervisor while building the VLF tower complex at the tip of North West Cape.

At the time, with Tower Zero at 396 metres, they were the tallest constructions in the Southern Hemisphere and John went even higher with the jinn pole, spending a good deal of his time at the top end of things. After the completion of the Base tower complex he did high rigging work on contract around the world. But he and Poppy became very familiar figures to most people in town because they purchased the Exmouth taxi service in 1985 and ran it for 18 years, finally selling out in 2003.

'Poppy did the day jobs' John recalls *'And I did the night calls if I was in town. The Americans were our best customers, and the business went down by 50 per cent when they left. But we still did all right. It was a demanding business. Most days you'd be getting calls until after the pub shut and that meant driving until 2 a.m. on Fridays and Saturdays and midnight on Sundays. We had three taxi plates and used other drivers when things got hectic. We delivered meals, babies, kids, and dogs. If we found drunks passed out by the side of the road we'd pick them up and take them home. Next day they always paid.*

'We didn't have too many problems. Some of the workers from the prawn trawlers on nights when the boats stayed in because of the moon went a bit over the top. One night Poppy went down to the Pot Shot to pick a group up and they sprayed the taxi inside and outside with foam fire extinguishers. They thought it was hilariously funny, though Poppy had another view of it'.

John went down in another car in response to their request to be taken back to their base. Instead he took them back to his house, gave them buckets and sponges and told them to clean the taxi they had sprayed. *'They had the option of cleaning the car or walking 25 kilometres home'*

John remembers. *'We were the only taxi company so they cleaned the cab! It was a case of he who laughs last laughs hardest!'*

Occasionally they would get calls to travel long distances, including to Minilya, Carnarvon, Bullara and Winning Pool. *'That was OK, but a long haul could be a problem at weekends when we were flat to the boards with local calls. But we would always try to accommodate a customer'.* In addition to his high–rigging commissions which took him around the world, John started the Exmouth Game Fishing Cub with Wally Williams and was the first president. They began the competition which was first listed as *'Gala Week'* in 1969. It later became *Gamex,* attracting keen game fishermen from all over Australia, and which has continued to be an outstanding success in modern times.

Jeff Napier, like many Exmouth residents, began his acquaintance with the town as a visitor, coming up for holidays with his father in the 1980s. When he grew up he had a refrigeration business in town for a short while, but found himself increasingly drawn to boats and the Ningaloo Reef. For a time he worked with Tony Cooper on the fishing charter boat *Yampi Queen,* went prawning on the trawler *Odette C* for a season, worked for George King on *The Nordon* on sediment sampling for oil searches, and on the pipeline to Thevenard, and went pearling with Ray King.

'I did just about everything nautical available in the area' he says with a laugh. *'Both above and below the surface. Finally I worked for Andy Morgan on the commercial fishing boat St Matthew to get my ticket, and eventually was able to buy my own commercial fishing boat Stacey J and then the charter boat Ningaloo Blue in 1999 just in time for Cyclone Vance -- bad timing!'.*

The boat was flooded, bookings for the season went out of the window, and it took months to refit *Ningaloo Blue* in Geraldton. However in following years the charter business went well, restoring both customer confidence and the cash situation. Meantime Jeff's future wife Jeanie had started an internet café and then gone to work with Leonie Horak at Exmouth Ray White real estate agency. In 2003 Jeanie and Jeff decided to buy the agency from Leonie. They began with five staff including Gabby Morgan, and moved to the main street location.

'In the first year at Ray White we sold 50 houses', Jeanie recalled *'But by 2007 we were handling 150 houses and blocks and business was booming'.*

Exmouth's other major real estate operation was Exmouth Cape Real Estate owned by Carol and Stephen Nagy. *' Our first office in 1997 was our bedroom!'* Carol remembers. *'The phone would start ringing at 7a.m. and the fax machine would be aglow all night. It was a time of humble beginnings. We met our potential customers at our front door, and showed them around town in our old four-wheel drive.*

'We had two small children, one at kindergarten and one in nappies and I was relief teaching at the local school. There was no great pressure in real estate in those days and things moved at quite a relaxed pace. Cyclone Vance changed all that in a hurry. As soon as we woke to the devastation the phone began ringing with calls from anxious landlords who lived out of town and naturally wanted to know if their houses were still standing. There were also tenants without power and water and sometimes without roofs! Ironically the cyclone proved a blessing for Exmouth in one unexpected way. Vance gave most properties a new appearance, whether it was a new roof, exterior paint, or just a new fence, most homes had never looked better. And the huge amount of rain really got gardens going. It seemed that this was the catalyst for the property boom that began soon after. Property values in Exmouth really took off!'.

Exmouth Cape Real Estate went from one staff member besides Stephen and Carol to three extra married couples. The development of the Exmouth Marina Village Precinct A, by Dick Lester, with 129 canal lots, involved four years' work to settlement in January 2007. *'There's an exciting time ahead'* Carol Nagy said *'We celebrate the growth of the town and look forward to a bright future'.*

Gino and Georgie Garbellini came to Exmouth in the early 1990s at the point where the town was making the transition from being a service community for the American Base to becoming a tourist destination. The Ningaloo Reef had been newly discovered by Australian and international visitors. *'We outsiders were part of the migration that came up from the south, bought up the American houses and changed the town's standards of living',* Gino remembers.

'We put up patios, fences, car ports, sheds, and verandas. The major change was when we put in gardens, grew plants and trees, and turned the town green. In that way town was changed from a drab, rather unkempt appearance, to its present attractive condition due to this influx of new people. But there is no doubt in my mind that Cyclone Vance – despite the pain at the time – was the best thing to have happened to Exmouth. It forced the changes that have made this community strong, modern, and proud'.

The Garbellinis had an auction warehouse in the south end of town, and Gino, who had a sheep industry background, was involved in pastoral developments. In 2004 his face smiled from the front page of the northern telephone book in every home from Carnarvon to Broome and Kununurra.

He had received an Innovation Award from the Australian Government for the invention of a *Millrun Range* of computer remote monitoring units for stations. It saved pastoralists having to drive hundreds of kilometres on mill runs on a regular basis checking on windmills, tanks, troughs, and the condition of sheep and cattle.

With the new invention the boss could sit at home with his computer and bring up pictures of mills and animals on the screen. Using his keyboard he could stop and start engines at a distance, and monitor pumps and rain gauges, making huge savings in time and fuel.

The device described as ' *Armchair Farming* ' invented by Gino Garbellini was first tested on Bullara Station run by the Shallcross family and Exmouth Station with Linda and John Lefroy. Georgie Garbellini was also an award winner. She was an accomplished artist who won an Exmouth Shire '*Best Painting Of the Year*' award. Among her many works the wall murals at Sunrise Beach greet the dawn every day.

Eske and Axel Passek who ran the Sea Breeze Resort came to Exmouth from Germany because of the diving. *'We had a lifetime dream to swim with big sea creatures'* Axel said, '*And the Ningaloo Reef with whales and whale sharks and manta rays made the dream come true. This is the only place on the planet where you can have all three extreme experiences'*. Like many other Germans they had travelled extensively before coming to Australia. They learned to dive at Key West in Florida, and later took diving vacations in Turkey, Egypt, and Australia's Barrier Reef. Ningaloo crossed their screen when Tony Medcraft took his films to the famous German boat show, *Bloote,* at Dusseldorf.

'When I asked him about diving in Australia I thought his description of the Ningaloo Reef was too good to be true. But when I came here in 1997 I swam with dolphins, whale sharks, and mantas, and I found that, if anything, what he had told me was an understatement!'

The Passeks arrived in Australia in February with the temperature over the old century mark and no air conditioning in their caravan. Their twin girls Lea and Lisa were only 18 months old and Eske had her hands full. It was a tough beginning. Axel said *'Well we'll give it one year and see how our money lasts'.*

He worked at a number of jobs when they first arrived in Exmouth – including a spell with CALM as an assistant diver, and as a diving instructor with Tony Medcraft. When the opportunity came up, after the American departure, the Passeks applied for and got the lease of Naval quarters at the Base from the Commonwealth Defence Department with the idea of starting a resort of their own. *'Everyone told us it wouldn't work – too far out of town they said'* Axel recalls. *'But we were closer to the best beaches and the diving'.*

Axel carted big stones from the quarry in 43 degrees heat for the garden. They painted walls, decorated rooms, and turned the quarters from their original austere grey Naval accommodation into a bright and attractive venue. *'While we made the place look good, we had to find the customers to appreciate it'.* Axel went back to Germany each year to boat shows with Ningaloo Reef film footage to promote Exmouth. By 2007 the Western Sea Breeze Resort, with its 27 rooms, had seen 13,000 bookings, at an average of 1300 people a year.

In the meantime another daughter, Nami, had arrived. Aside from being a mother and acting as hostess at the resort Eske followed her passion as a sculptor, and became president of the Bernice McLeod Day Care Centre. Axel became chairman of the Gascoyne Small Business Association. *'Exmouth has been so good to us that we were happy to be able to put something back into the community'* Eske said.

Jennie Cary had been working as a marine ecologist in Perth when the position of Manager of the Exmouth District for the Department of Conservation and Land Management (CALM) was advertised.

'I'd been coming to Exmouth on short holidays for 25 years and had dreamed of being there on a permanent basis' she recalls. *'I'd been thinking that it was time to leave Perth and when the job came up in 2001 and I was lucky enough to be selected I was absolutely delighted. It was my sea change in life!'*

However she could never have imagined that the position would land her in the middle of a major environmental controversy. Or the depth of feeling it would arouse among the people who opposed it. *'I was aware, naturally, that the whole Ningaloo area was going through a lot of scrutiny during the SAVE THE NINGALOO REEF campaign, and that this would probably result in planning and changes in environmental policy. But I could never have guessed how intense the spotlight would be on the area in the next few years,*

'I look back on the first three years 2002 -2004 in Exmouth and I'm still amazed at the level of controversy that was generated mainly by the increase in the sanctuary zones (from 10% to 34%) and the negotiations with the pastoralists that bordered the marine park to exclude the two kilometre strip from the leases for inclusion into the marine park'.

Even though all the planning was a broad action by the State Government and its agencies, local DEC staff were the first in the firing line to hear from people opposed to the changes. *'It was not a pleasant experience'* Jennie recalled. *'There were demonstrations outside the Exmouth office, with some pretty emotional language and placards.*

'At the time the ABC 'Four Corners' did a program on the Australia-wide dilemma of regulating camping to protect the environment versus the free and easy lifestyle of the unregulated campers of former days. The problem being, of course, that once there were only a few intrepid souls pushing north into remote areas. But with better roads and access the trickle of people became a flood. When that happened rubbish disposal and degradation of coastal dunes from vehicle tracks needed something done to preserve the area from further harm.

'I've been camping myself for more than 20 years, and I can understand the sense of the loss of personal freedom. In a perfect world everyone would do the right thing, and regulations would be unnecessary. But the reality is that it is an imperfect world and sadly – most often out of ignorance or unawareness of the vulnerable nature of local areas – damage does occur and it needs to be nipped in the bud before it becomes a major problem'.

'It became obvious that camping and fishing on the coast did need some degree of management and regulation to maintain the environment on a stable basis for everyone. We (DEC) are charged to manage the Parks and we prefer to rely upon education and awareness raising and the honour system. Unfortunately, there is a need for regulation and policing to deal with the few whose actions, whether deliberate or in ignorance, are not in the best interests of protecting the Parks. So for me 2001 to 2005 were difficult years while the new order was established.

'By 2008 a lot of heat had gone out of the controversy. The Park belongs to everyone and DEC is simply the manager and interpreter. In that sense we all want the best outcome for the area. Ningaloo has gone from being somewhere that once only a few people knew about, to being well known Australia-wide and internationally. I'm pleased that Government with broad community support, is putting in place the protection the area deserves'.

Jennie Cary has bought a block near the beach a little way south of Exmouth. *'I hope to still be here in retirement. Who wouldn't want that? This is paradise!'*

Neil McLeod of the famous McLeod family went off to see the rest of the world, including America, as a young man, and returned with fresh ideas to set up his own tourist operation. Ningaloo Safaris began with a 12-passenger Toyota, and grew to two OKAs with 14-passenger capacity and greatly increased comfort. In 2001 Neil McLeod and Ningaloo Safaris won the WA Tourist Council's FACET Golden Guide Award presented at the Burswood Resort.

Ningaloo Safaris packed an enormous amount of the Exmouth region into one day for the people taking the tours. After being picked up at 7.30 am, the OKA would go down the road and climb up to the skyline at Shot Hole Canyon and Charles Knife-road.

Then the journey over the Cape Range would take Neil and his passengers '*Over the top*' to the west side looking out over the Indian Ocean and south to Yardie Creek, with stops for lunch and morning tea along the way. At Yardie Creek the passengers would transfer to a boat for a tour up the creek between the spectacular red cliffs, looking out for the black-footed wallabies unique to the gorge. Heading north on the way home there would be a stop for snorkelling at Turquoise Beach which was a highlight of the day.

'You're never too old' Neil would tell his customers. *'I had a lady of 94 put on a mask and fins for the very first try, and she had the time of her life!'*

As a last treat on the way home the OKA would climb the hill at the Vlamingh Head lighthouse to let the visitors see a splendid Indian Ocean sunset and maybe the white flash of a whale spouting far below. In 18 years of running Ningaloo Safaris Neil entertained thousands of customers from all parts of the world.

When he won the award in 2001 he praised his family. *'I'm just the driver'* he said. *'My mum makes the fruit and orange cake, Coralie my wife makes up the lunches, and the kids Daniel, Hayden, Casey, and Lincoln, have spent years cleaning vehicles. Without them all it wouldn't happen!'.*

However he was a lot more than just a *'driver'*. Neil McLeod maintained a running commentary on the geography and geology of the ranges, with introductions to the mammals and reptiles, and the trees and flowers of the area. He had amazing energy, and was always bright and cheerful. In the tourist season there were very long days, often totalling 18 hours each. In the season the OKASs took tours eight days out of every ten Sometimes there were 12 in a row, and the record was 14 successive days. Neil had some famous customers, including super model Elle McPherson, Eagles premiership-winning football coach Mick Malthouse, and WA Governer Sir Francis Burt. Through the years he received some glowing tributes.

The American travel writers Richard and Rachael Heller from Florida, wrote in the visitor's book *'Your standard of quality is unexcelled! We were so impressed with your vast knowledge as well as your dedication and love of the area. You passed that on to all of us on the tour... we will share this most worthy experience with all of our future readers'.*

After 18 years of Ningaloo Safari Tours Coralie and Neil retired – *'We'd done what we set out to do which was to put the four boys through private school'* – and sold the business to Dave and Theresa Mongan.

'We knew Exmouth well' Dave Mongan, a former surveyor, said in 2007. *'My grandfather was here in the RAAF during the war refuelling aircraft. My father Francis William Mongan was the first customs officer at Exmouth, so I'm third generation'.* The Mongan family had been coming to Exmouth since the mid 1980s and had bought a house in town. When they came to live permanently with children Lily and Luke they saw the FOR SALE sign up for Ningaloo Safaris, and now Dave is the man behind the wheel with the OKAs, the hand on the helm with the boat at Yardie Creek, and the fin-kicking leader of the wide-eyed snorkellers at Turquoise Bay.

'We follow the same route pioneered by Neil' Dave Mongan said in 2007. *'But Neil was a one-off and a hard act to follow. For that reason I haven't tried to be a replica or an imitator. I've found it better to be my own man and do it my own way. But I'm forever grateful to Neil for establishing the successful format in the first place'.*

Don Forrest traces his ancestry back to David Forrest, younger brother of Alexander Forrest, and John Forrest.

John Forrest was the Premier of WA in the 1890s and later became a Minister in the first Australian Federal Parliament. He was created Lord Forrest of Bunbury for his contribution to State and Federal politics.

On the other side of politics Alexander became Lord Mayor of Perth as well as being the West Kimberley representative in parliament. Their political success was a far cry from the time when the two brothers worked for the WA Survey Department. They became famous explorers early in their careers. Minderoo Station on the Ashburton River was one of a number of Forrest properties scattered through the North West and the Kimberley regions. The first sheep went to Minderoo in 1878.

Don Forrest grew up on the station in between spells at boarding school. After the usual four years as a jackeroo he returned to become overseer on Minderoo in 1951, and manager in 1952, before buying the station from family interests in 1973. He and his wife Judy had three children, David, Jane, and Andrew. *'Station life was great',* he recalled in 2008 *'Especially for the kids. They had the pool in the Ashburton River to swim in, and horses to ride whenever they wished. They all became very good riders, and have continued the interest into adult life. Like children in all remote areas they had to go to boarding school to further their education. But holidays were very good times'.*

Pastoralists made their own entertainment, often travelling hundreds of miles to bush race meetings, balls, or dances. *'The Winning Pool races ran for 21 years and there were also meetings at Carnarvon, and Exmouth, in later years. In the early days all the stations maintained a lot of horses, both for work and pleasure. Nowadays motor cycles do the job and horses have largely disappeared from pastoral life, though some are kept as riding hacks. It was inevitable, I suppose, but it's a shame to see that happen'.*

Aeroplanes were a boon for covering the miles and Don Forrest flew Cessnas for many years. *'It was handy for us to be able to fly across the Gulf to Learmonth to link up with Skywest flights from Perth'.* The distance would take hundreds of kilometres and many hours by road circumventing the end of Exmouth Gulf. But it only took a comparatively short time in the trusty Cessna. The same formula applied to social gatherings.

John and Josie Barrymore were among the Perth people who bought ex-US Navy properties in Exmouth in the early 1990s. They influenced many of their friends including, Dr Ian Stewart and his wife Jenny, and Barbara and Keith Stevenson, into buying Exmouth houses.

'We've had a love affair with Exmouth for more than 16 years' said John Barrymore in 2008. *'We've seen great changes since we first came here. At that time the town was moon-scape – brown dried out and colourless. There were hardly any gardens or greenery. Unlike the Australians today the Americans spent little or no time outside. When they got home from work they went straight indoors and turned on their air conditioners full bore. They were only here temporarily on tours of duty so you couldn't expect them to be interested in planting things which might take a while to grow and they might never see the result.*

'But when *Australians bought the houses and the blocks were fenced for the first time, people planted trees, extended verandas, and shades, and began to take pride in their gardens. It became a pleasure to sit outside in the evenings. The result has been that the town has become green and beautiful. You wouldn't recognise Exmouth for the same place it was in 1992'.*

One of the Barrymores' interests – aside from being keen fishermen – has been the Vlamingh Head lighthouse. *'It was restored by Ron Campbell and Wayne Briton after cyclone Vance'* said Josie Barrymore. *'But they left town and the tours they set up were allowed to lapse. By 2008 the lighthouse was looking a bit shabby. That was a shame because it's such a great tourist attraction.*

' We hoped that one day Shire and government interest would be revived. After all it's one of the iconic landmarks of the Cape and coming up for its 100 years celebration'.

One of the factors which bound the Exmouth community together was the local newspaper Exmouth Expression, begun by Leonie McLeod in 1987. When she acquired Warroora Station she found it difficult to manage both ends. Looking for a replacement writer she found Gerry Blum. Gerry Blum had spent most of his life in schools as an English literature teacher. During that time as a *'chalkie'* the thought of a possible future in journalism never occurred to him.

Expect the unexpected. He and his wife Doreen spent 15 years in Karratha where Gerry taught at Karratha Senior High School and Doreen became a Community Development officer. Her job also taking her to Tom Price and Parraburdoo. She also found time to become a member of the Roebourne Shire Council for six years.

'Whenever we had holidays' Gerry recalls *'We'd hitch up our old caravan and trundle off down to Exmouth. We found that we liked the place so much that we decided to retire there. We bought a house in Exmouth and I served out the last year of my time with the Exmouth District High School and Doreen did the same as co-ordinator for the Exmouth campus of Central West TAFE.*

' Retirement didn't sit easily because we're both active people. I began writing an Exmouth page for the Northern Guardian, based in Carnarvon. When Leonie Horak had problems in being in two places at once, running the newspaper and her sheep station simultaneously, she asked me if I would write for the Expression and I agreed.

'But at the same time the young lady who sat in the office, typed out the stories, and put the paper together ready for the printers. left unexpectedly. Suddenly there was no-one with the general or computer skills to replace her'.

So, '*by default'* – to use his own words -- Gerry Blum became the journalist, the photographer, the editor, the advertising manager, and the sub-editor all rolled into one. Each month he sent 16 pages fully prepared off to the printers in Geraldton to meet his deadline.

'Fortunately the paper is well accepted by the locals' he says 'And the tourists love it. We have a very satisfactory number of annual subscriptions, and we send monthly copies to readers in all states, We have just about doubled our sales thanks to a supportive community'.

In 2008 Doreen Blum was in her sixth year as an Exmouth Shire Councillor, and in that year was also Deputy President to Veronica Fleay.

By 2008 Sue and Mark Sherwin had spent 22 years teaching at Exmouth District High School. *'It wasn't a job so much as a lifestyle'* Sue recalls. *'We were encouraged to get involved in the community, in sport and other activities, and so we were continually surrounded by school kids and their families. Many have become lifetime friends. In some cases we have taught the entire range of children in a family – brothers, sisters, the lot. The scary part now is that after so many years we are beginning to teach the children of the children we have already taught!'*

'When we first arrived about one third of the children were from American families. Getting to know another culture was always great. We sang both anthems at assembly and flew both flags. Even to this day Halloween remains a tradition in Exmouth and is quite a big event. Obviously a lot has changed through the years. I'm working on a school history, and it's interesting to see how EDHS has developed its own style and personality. There are other changes too – my husband Mark first came up to Exmouth as a physical education teacher. Now his field of expertise is computer studies! But we feel we've been really fortunate having spent our working lives here, and Exmouth is such a special place. In a country town like ours we're well away from a lot of the behavioural problems teachers experience with kids in the city and the bigger towns.

'We're almost in a parental role as teachers and I think the kids appreciate that. Both of our own children have been educated here, and the standard of education is well up to that of the metropolitan area, and thankfully we're without some of the disciplinary problems there that you read about in the newspapers'.

Veronica (she prefers 'Ronnie') Fleay came to Exmouth with her husband Tom and the two youngest of their five children in 1999 immediately after Cyclone Vance. *'Our eldest son Aaron was already living and working in the city and both of our twin daughters, Jasmine and Nicole, had married and settled down. The shift to Exmouth was a huge change in lifestyles for us' she said in 2009. 'I'd come from a pioneering family and grown up on the family farm near Kojonup, and we'd been all our lives in the Great Southern. Tom came from a long line of shearers with Tom's father and grandfather ensuring that the Fleay name featured in historical books on the shearing industry.*

' It was the thought of a sea change and a warmer climate that motivated us to take on a different role in establishing a small business in Exmouth, and we've never regretted the move. Exmouth provided a wonderful opportunity for our children. They were able to become involved in so many varied pursuits. I have always been amazed at the way they adapted to the change. The new environment was something we all delighted in, spending time in and on the water. And of course other family members have always enjoyed visiting us'.

Veronica became involved in community affairs, becoming president of the Exmouth Horse and Pony Club, a member of the St John's Ambulance, the Exmouth Christian Fellowship, the Exmouth Yacht Club, Exmouth Cultural Arts, and the Chamber of Commerce. In 2003 she was elected to the Exmouth Shire Council and a year later she became deputy Shire President.

In 2004 she was appointed to the board of the Gascoyne Development Commission, taking the chair in 2008. In 2007 she was appointed to the West Australian Planning Commission as Regional Representative. Soon after, on the retirement of John Cooper, she was elected Shire President of Exmouth. She was the first woman to hold the position, and though it was a significant change the moment passed without fanfare and with little comment in the local media. *'Council was soon back to a situation of 'business as usual'!*

'I felt very honoured' Ronnie recalled *'And it wasn't at all what I'd had in mind when we first came to Exmouth. But my time on Council has been very challenging and exciting. It has given me the chance to represent the community and the region on many platforms such as the Ningaloo Coast Regional Strategy, and the Ningaloo Sustainable Development Committee which addresses the future of the area. I'm also involved with plans for the Ningaloo Research Centre, the State Council of the West Australian Local Government Association and local committees. It really is a privilege to be involved on so many levels.'*

It was an exciting time to be in an exciting town!

Coral Bay &
'Save The Ningaloo Reef'

Chapter Nineteen

The town of Exmouth and the Harold E. Holt Communications Station are the most conspicuous human alterations to the ancient landscape of the North West Cape. Those changes are clearly visible from the sky to incoming airline passengers. But for people driving up by road signposts along the highway north of Carnarvon and Minilya indicate a number of other potential off-road destinations for the traveller. They include the popular tourist resort of Coral Bay.

Before '*Uncle Sam'* came to the Cape in 1963 and the Americans arrived in numbers for the second time since the Second World War, the names Gnaraloo, Warroora, Cardabia, Bullara, Giralia, Ningaloo, Yardie Creek and Exmouth Station, were all well-known in the wool industry. They were sheep stations pure and simple, the people on them leading a pastoral way of life little changed since the turn of the century.

The bosses, station hands, and jackeroos, sleeping rough in the bush at mustering time, would have laughed heartily over their quart pots of black tea if the notion of *'tourism'* were mentioned. The very suggestion that one day their economic survival might depend on something as '*Sissy'* as what the Americans called a '*Dude Ranch',* would have been treated with appropriate and probably ribald scorn.

But by the advent of the 21st Century, like it or lump it, tourism had become an established fact of station life. Squatters' wives were serving teas to visitors. Where once a stranger was an unusual sight, by 2008 they were arriving by the bus-load. There were a number of factors, following on from the establishing of the US Naval Harold E Holt Communications Station which brought a major flood of population – both permanent and transient -- into the area.

The establishment of the Base and the town of Exmouth involved the sealing of the highway from Carnarvon and eventually Burkett Road connecting to North West Coastal highway. The smooth-flowing black bitumen ribbons allowed visitors easy access to previously-remote areas without the risk of blowing tyres or breaking springs on gravel roads. Or having the mudguards rattle off their caravans and trailers. The travellers' joys of yesteryear.

Falling wool prices in the '80s also caused station owners to look for other ways of supplementing their incomes, and a part-solution lay in the number of visitors pouring into the Gascoyne Region in the winter months. Around 200,000 people a year were arriving after the year 2000, many of them looking to experience some of the atmosphere of the traditional *'Outback'.*

The jewel in the crown of the Ningaloo Reef was Coral Bay. Together with Maud's Landing it was the only really sheltered anchorage between Cape Murat and Carnarvon. Before Exmouth town was built it was perhaps the most beautiful and easily accessible underwater coral landscape in all of Australia.

To go to the Great Barrier Reef in Queensland involved a boat journey out to sea taking up the better part of the day and significant expense. At '*Bill's Bay*', as locals called the future town-site of Coral Bay, all the visitor had to do was stop the vehicle, and walk across the beach with mask and fins. Submerging, they immediately found fish looking at them and wonderful corals under the surface just off the water's edge.

The name '*Bill's Bay*' had a romantic origin. It came from Ruby May Wilson, wife of Charles French, the owner of Cardabia Station which included the bay in its lease. She was affectionately known in the family as 'Aunty Billie'. When Charlie wooed and won her in the 1920s she was a J.C.Williamson singer. He took her to Cardabia which was then one of *'The ends of the earth'*. It was a remote sheep station where she was often left alone in surroundings far different from her previous busy world of cities and theatres. She could still sing but she had only a few thousand head of sheep for company. A herbivore audience which may not have been as impressed by the rich quality of her voice as the theatre-goers of Sydney town..

In short *'Baaah!'* was all the applause available at Cardabia.

As an antidote to boredom Charlie French built Billie a shack on the beach at what would come to be known as '*Billie's Bay*'. It became a favourite holiday spot for pastoralists' families and a local secret. In time the name became corrupted to *'Bill's Bay'*.

The first person to see the tourist potential of the area after the Second World War was Ken Ryan. He was a former chemist with a sense of adventure, who first designed the polystyrene pot floats in the 1960s which became universal in the crayfishing industry. With the establishment of the US Navy base at Exmouth he figured that there would be a rush of American personnel eager to get away from their base in leisure time.

He could see, as a sensible person with scientific training, the dangers of setting up in *Bill's Bay*. Putting the accommodation on top of the unique coral attraction might risk pollution and environmental degradation. His idea was to build a resort at the old Mauds Landing *'town-site'* on Cardabia Station, and have people commute to areas of interest in the surrounding countryside. Including, of course, *'Bill's Bay'*. Here the government stepped in, insisting, despite his pioneering work, that a Maud's Landing resort be put out to general tender. Unfairly, it seemed, someone else got the tender, and eventually failed to go ahead with it.

Undeterred, Ryan gritted his teeth, and finally won permission to set up overlooking *Bill's Bay* instead. There was a carrot dangled by the State Government for people setting up tourist facilities north of the Tropic of Capricorn. They offered a subsidy of a dollar for every dollar of investment. Ryan called his establishment the *'Coral Bay Hotel'*, and waited for the expected rush of American sailors and construction workers from Exmouth. And he waited and waited.

The problem was that United States Navy at the Cape looked after its sailors all too well. They had basketball and tennis courts, a baseball diamond, bowling alley, a swimming pool, library, and chapel, as well as priests, pastors, and psychological counselling should they need it. In the messes and bars there was duty free alcohol with labels like Schlitz, Pabst, Millers, and Lone Star beer, as well as Wild Turkey, Jim Beam, Teachers, and Old Tennessee whisky and bourbon, and Jose Cuervo and Olmeca tequila. There were *'fast foods'* 30 years before ordinary Australians ever heard of a '*Chico roll*' or a '*Big Mac*'.

In short the US authorities successfully sought to create an atmosphere *'Just like home'* for their boys overseas. The result was that the matelots simply preferred to stay on the Base in *'Little America'*, save their money, and enjoy the subsidised benefits.

So far as Australian workers were concerned, most of the construction was finished by the time the Coral Bay Hotel was finally up and running. The remaining tradesmen just wanted to get the job done and go. Their dearest wish was to '*Get the hell out of here*' and back down south to '*cold beer and warm women*' as quickly as possible. The gravel roads from Carnarvon north in any direction were so notorious that ordinary tourists had no inclination to risk knocking their vehicles about by venturing any further. They stayed away too.

The sealed road came too late to save the fast-haemorrhaging Coral Bay Hotel. Ryan's overseas partner Tip Top Travel, a UK firm specialising in exotic locations around the world, collapsed, and so did the *Bill's Bay* venture. So, in a pattern that would become all too familiar in the North in years to come, the Coral Bay Hotel went belly up. Broke.

It so often happened with pioneers from Shark Bay to Broome. Men who could see the *'Big Picture'* up ahead, and who deserved better, were brought undone by mundane matters such as water supply, sewage, and the difficulty of keeping staff in a remote area. And, of course, cash flow to offset the extra expense of setting up in the first place..

Norm Monk, who had established a caravan park alongside the hotel and could see the real potential of the area, stepped in first as a manager for the receivers, and finally became the owner of the hotel. Through the following years Coral Bay – as the settlement was now known – moved on from one difficulty to another. If it had been placed anywhere else it would probably have just disappeared off the map. But its saving grace was the sheer beauty of the corals and the whale sharks, manta rays, and other creatures of the Ningaloo Reef. As the reputation of the area and its attractions spread through the years, an increasing number of people insisted on coming to Coral Bay, no matter what it lacked in accommodation and facilities.

It is interesting to make a comparison between the town of Exmouth and the settlement at Coral Bay. Exmouth initially had the huge benefit of being financed from three sources. The United States Navy, and the Commonwealth Government both gave generously through their respective Defence Departments. The Western Australian Government was also supportive. Huge sums were spent on building and beautifying the town and providing for housing, schooling, civic, and sporting facilities for the population.

Progress at Exmouth continued even after the American withdrawal, with the construction of the marina, the domestic airport terminal, and continued private investment in tourist accommodation.. There seemed to be no problem about unlocking new Crown Land for suitable projects where Exmouth was concerned.

Coral Bay was a direct contrast. Initially there was no proper sewage system. Accommodation expanded with Norm Monk retaining his People's Caravan Park and service station, aided by his two sons. As other tourist accommodation, caravan site and backpacker needs increased every year, charter boat tours also expanded at a proportionate rate. As a result there was a need for living space for the work force. However the Government refused to release any more crown land.

The result was that people working on tourist boats, serving as staff in shops, the hotel, or caravan parks, families of businesses – even though they had a long term commitment to the area – were jammed into a caravan park nick-named '*Little Kenya*' where conditions were well below Australian standards.

In many place the ramshackle dwellings were in touching distance of each other reminiscent of Third World refugee camps. Toilets and rubbish were a continual disgrace. Ordinary visitors to Coral Bay might have looked around, scratched their heads, and asked '*What on earth is the problem?'*.

To anyone taking a practical point of view it might seem that a moonscape of empty land stretches away in all directions from Coral Bay. To the inexperienced eye, a grasshopper might struggle to make a living there. So why was it so precious that a few hectares could not be set aside to provide the normal living conditions most Australians would expect for the workers and permanent people of Coral Bay?

Ask a sensible question and you may get a different kind of answer. The matter was essentially political. In 2008 there were elements in the WA Labor Party and the Government, as well as the 'Green' party, and in 'conservation' circles, who – while mostly unfamiliar with the region themselves -- were vigorously opposed to any increase in visitor numbers to the area.

Their ideas would become summarised under what was declared as the *'Sustainable Development'* policy for the Ningaloo Reef.

What '*Sustainable Development'* means may vary by definition from person to person, and is open to a wide range of interpretations. The general principle is one which everyone would applaud. Namely, that as responsible humans we should try to avoid damage to the reef or its creatures. We should try to maintain an acceptable continuity of sea life and corals. Few would argue with that.

However one of the interpretations, put simply, appears to be '*Too many people are bad for the environment. Let's restrict the access'*. How many people are OK, and how much restriction should be applied is where the arguments begin. There is no actual end in sight.

It is correctly pointed out that *Homo sapiens,* the human race, has been responsible for immense and often unfortunate changes in the natural world around us, especially in the past 100 years. We are all only too well aware of that from our daily newspapers and television programs. The environment and its care (or lack of it) is a constant topic. No argument, again, that we should try to do better, and where possible, make some amends.

The extreme conservation view is that we should keep away from places like the Ningaloo Reef altogether on the premise that people and the environment simply don't mix well. In short the reef is better off without us as it has been for thousands of years. As a compromise it is suggested that conditions should be limited, so that as few people make the effort as possible. Thus the reef is *'protected'*, at least to some degree, and albeit in a negative fashion. That pleases neither the radical '*No go'* conservationists nor those who chafe against regulations of any kind. A compromise is sometimes defined as '*A solution which pleases no-one'*.

There are plenty of horror stories from the past to demonstrate the incompatibility of people and our natural surroundings. Evidence which may seem to support a '*No go'* argument. But while the public is often lectured on its failings from those in official places, it should be remembered that the greatest damage in the past occurred with the approval of the bureaucrats, the relevant departments, and the governments of the time.

In the 1930s Norwegian whalers took more than 7000 humpback whales off Point Cloates under licence from the Western Australian Government. Whaling continued at Point Cloates after the Second World War, again under licence, until 1954, and at Carnarvon until 1963 with catches of up to 1000 humpbacks annually. Whalers were still operating at Albany taking up to 600 sperm whales a year as late as 1978.

In no instance were any of the whaling operations closed down through government intervention. This despite regular submissions from scientists providing research information which clearly indicated the damage which was being done. Warning what the final disastrous result of the over-fishing would be.

The whale fisheries, like the seal fisheries of old, closed of their own volition simply because the operators had killed too many whales and their industries were no long viable. Stocks of the humpback and sperm whales are still recovering nearly half a century later. Surely a black mark against the government agencies concerned?

Perhaps the worst instance of government approving an environmentally unfriendly process at a time when the agency should certainly have known better, was the licensing by the Western Australian Fisheries Department of two vessels, the *East Winds* and *Tringa* in the 1960s to hunt turtles between Point Maud and Point Cloates. The freezer boats processed as many as 100 turtles a day each, and thousands of turtles were killed. They were run down by outboard motor-powered speedboats until they were exhausted, and then, helpless on the surface, they were harpooned. On the processing boats they were dismembered while still alive. It was a cruel way to kill them and to compound the damage they were also taken in their breeding season.

The mistake was realized in 1972 when the licences were cancelled. But it has taken more than 30 years for green and loggerhead turtle numbers -- both species threatened with extinction elsewhere in the world – to recover, and numbers are still well below post-war figures.

In an imperfect world we need to review the mistakes of the past in order to avoid potential wrongs in the future. Ideally to prevent anything like them occurring again. Thankfully government-sanctioned whaling and turtle hunting won't ever take place again in Australian waters.

But some of the problems which have built up over a period of years started from apparently harmless beginnings. Amateur fishermen, for instance, have contributed to an altered state of fish stocks on the Ningaloo Reef. Though the problem hasn't been the ordinary holiday bloke with a tin dinghy, an Alvey fishing reel, a frying pan, and a packet of SAXA salt.

There were other fishermen who fished with nets and long lines and filled mobile freezers. These operators were '*shamateurs*', money-makers, who sold their catch illegally to city and suburban restaurants *'On the QT!'* (old Army term for ' *On the quiet'*) without having to comply with any of the regulations binding licensed professional fishermen.

Further south the result of similar activity saw the collapse of the Shark Bay snapper fishery and the need for severe controls on people taking snapper in Shark Bay. The area had proved surprisingly fragile. The Fisheries Department was remiss for not dealing earlier with the problems there, despite warnings from concerned people long before it became a disaster situation.

At Exmouth the exploitation of the spangled emperor stocks may have had an unexpected result similar to the denuding of the coral on the Great Barrier Reef by the crown-of-thorns starfish. The *Drupella* marine snail lives on coral polyps. Its shell is far too tough for a fish to crack, but the emperor fish lived (among other natural prey) on the soft eggs which the snail laid. So long as there were plenty of emperor fish the snail population was kept in check. But when too many emperor were removed from the system snail numbers exploded. Or so it appeared.

In 1988 whale shark researcher Geoff Taylor going to film previously pristine coral gardens south of Ned's Camp, found, to his dismay, large area of dead white reef where infestations of *Drupella* had killed the coral. ' *The whole area had been decimated. It was just like a graveyard.*

Only a few sticks of live coral remained and there was hardly a fish to be seen. I felt sick in the stomach as I viewed this scene of devastation!'

Was over-fishing (the estimated annual wet-fish catch of professionals and amateurs was then estimated at 100,000 to 200,000 kilos in the Ningaloo Reef area) to blame?

Or was the snail explosion a natural event occurring in cycles even without fishing interference as some might argue? As with the crown-of-thorns starfish on the Barrier Reef there was no immediate or definitive answer.

Whatever the cause, there was no question but that Exmouth fish stocks from 2000 onwards were nowhere near those of the immediate post war years. Old Exmouth hands, can remember the glory days well, and we all have to remember that fish everywhere were protected from 1939 to 1949 simply by the fact that the nation was either at war, or recovering from it.

There were no bag limits in the 1950s. It was generally believed – quite reasonably, it seemed at the time -- that, with 3000 miles between the West Coast and Africa any fish taken would swiftly be replaced by others coming in from the west to fill the gap. *'There's more fish in the sea than ever came out of it!'* is a saying as old as fishing itself.

Sadly the opposite has proved to be the case. Not just at Exmouth and Shark Bay, but Australia-wide and world-wide. Famous overseas fisheries like the Grand Banks off Newfoundland, which had endured for centuries, have crashed in recent years through over-exploitation. Pointing the finger of blame now won't bring the fish back. But experience is relevant today in anglers approving stricter bag limits and sanctuary zones with the minimum aim of at least maintaining current levels of fish populations.

But back to Coral Bay. As early as the mid-1980s, following the initial bankruptcy of the Coral Bay Hotel, the government looked to redeem some of its failed investment in the area amid concerns about environmental difficulties at Coral Bay. The entrepreneurial Labor government, led by Brian Burke in 1987 invited a company called the Coral Coast Marina Development Group to submit plans for a development in the area.

The site chosen was at Mauds Landing, which had been gazetted as a town-site in 1915. A jetty had been built there for ships to take out wool from the sheep stations of the area. For a time, until 1947, there was a wool store, a general store, and an unofficial pub. But the *'town'* itself had never got going and the Nor' West Whaling Company purchased the jetty timbers and other materials for Norwegian Bay after the war. Nevertheless the *'town site'* still remained legally, and apparently conveniently in place. Coral Coast Marina commissioned their architects, completed their own surveys, drew up plans, and submitted environmental proposals which were initially accepted by the government agencies of the day.

The director of the Department of Conservation and Land Management stated then that *'CALM's view is that an effective marina and associated facilities at Mauds Landing would greatly enhance public access to the Marine Park and contribute to the economic development of the region while taking the pressure off Coral Bay'.*

Richard Court's Liberal government replaced an out-of-favour Labor government in 1993, and were also sympathetic to Coral Coast. The developer's plans were approved, subject to some further environmental checks which were not expected to present obstacles. However the scope of the proposal had alarm bells ringing among conservationists. Their complaint was that it was a massive project and was simply too big for a fragile area.

The concept envisaged 250 residential lots for permanent occupation, as well as 1000 resort rooms around a three-story hotel, plus backpacker accommodation and a caravan park. A golf course and a major marina were included. The company said that it anticipated having 1330 guests per day in the '*High season*'. A projected *'Low season'occupancy* rate of 80 per cent was expected to still see 990 people per day through the resort. The resort would cost $200 million, and employ 75 people, with shops, cafes, and bars, to serve visitors. Building it was expected to take place in stages over eight years.

However, for conservationists concerned about the Ningaloo Reef, the most doubt centered around the plans for the marina.

The developer Alan Smith told the Australian Broadcasting Corporation's *'7.30 Report'* in April 2002, *' We anticipate up to 240 boats in the marina'*. It was suggested that as many as 120 boats a day would put to sea. And where would they go except to the Ningaloo Reef?

Oops!

The result was the campaign to *'SAVE THE NINGALOO REEF!'*

It was led by Western Australian author Tim Winton, in combination with other high profile personalities. Basketballer Luc Longley, fresh back from his time with the United States champion team, the Chicago Bulls, joined the protest, together with film star Toni Collette. It was directed by Paul Gamblin who had been involved in a previous successful protest against the development of the Leighton Beach marshalling yards. The idea captured the public imagination in a way unprecedented in WA.

Thousands of vehicle bumper stickers were distributed and an estimated 15,000 people gathered for a rally on Fremantle's Esplanade on December 1st, 2002 to march to the town hall. The Mayor of Fremantle Peter Tagliaferri welcomed the crowd and declared that it was ' *The biggest rally in living memory in Fremantle!'*

An elated Tim Winton said *' The Premier will no doubt be looking at the public mood on this issue. It was an awesome display of public feeling. For every person at the rally we know that dozens more feel the same way!'*

Winton went on to comply with the good-old Australian expression, '*Put your money where your mouth is!*'. When he won the Premier's Prize for Literature in 2002 he donated the whole of the $ 25,000 award to the *SAVE THE NINGALOO REEF* fund. Meantime the Press watched events with a wry grin and a cynicism born of long observation of WA politics. The Geoff Gallop Labor government had toppled a tired Liberal outfit in 2001, with the '*Green Vote*' a substantial factor. Labor's promise to do away with Old Growth Logging of Native forests was a particularly effective vote-catcher.

Suddenly here at Ningaloo was an unwelcome environmental crisis with an election two years away. The Green Vote, plus all those swinging voters emotionally swayed by the *SAVE THE NINGALOO REEF* campaign, could see the government stand or fall. Depending, perhaps, on whether Coral Coast Marina Development plans went ahead.

Tony Barrass in *The West Australian* newspaper of April 14th., 2003, wrote '*If the controversial Mauds Landing proposal fails to get Cabinet approval some will claim that the decision will have little to do with developers failing to follow proper processes and a whole lot to do with backroom preference deals, celebrity politics, and government back-sliding. Whether you believe that the development of the remote coastline is well overdue or are passionately opposed to it, one thing*

END OF A HARD NIGHT'S WORK. Trawlers work the Gulf at night, and their 'day' ends with the sunrise. (Picture: Karin Calvert Borshoff)

THE NEW NOVOTEL NINGALOO RESORT at Sunrise Beach gives Exmouth the touch of luxury which appeals to overseas travellers. (Picture: Hugh Edwards)

GARRY COSSILL with Larry Burkett and Ian Ogden formed Sunrise Beach Resort Pty Ltd to build the Resort, a new upper level of accommodation for Exmouth. (Picture: Hugh Edwards)

DARREN COSSILL was Novotel Ningaloo's first manager. (Picture: Hugh Edwards)

JON WARREN founder of the Exmouth Marina Village stands on site with the Landcorp 'Sydney Harbour 11' bridge in the background. It is the longest single-span bridge in Western Australia. (Picture: Hugh Edwards)

EXMOUTH MARINA VILLAGE sited on canals with boat landings is an entirely new concept for Exmouth, taking advantage of the blue waters of the Gulf.

Bernice McLeod
(Picture: Karin Calvert Borshoff)

Jan Hallam
(Picture: Hugh Edwards)

Jennie Carey (KCB)

Janet Norris (HE)

Andy Morgan (HE)

Geoff Taylor

Coralie and Neil McLeod

Peter Dellar (KCB)

Jeff and Jeannie Napier with Jorjiana (HE)

Josie and John Barrymore (HE)

Branca and Ray King (HE)

Rae and Denver Blake

Andy and Gabby Morgan with Nelson (KCB)

Kaye and Robbie Atkinson (KCB)

Axel and Eske Passek (HE)

Poppie and John Hallworth (HE)

Sue, Chloe and Mark Sherwin (HE)

Tim and Edwina Shallcross with Olivia and Lucy, Bullara Station (HE)

Jennifer and Denver Blake, Giralia (HE)

Linda and John Lefroy, Exmouth Station (HE)

Leonie McLeod, grandchildren
Eva, Sascha, Emma, and dog Ruby (HE)

Ian and Jenny Stewart (HE)

Milton Landon (KCB)

Dave Hall (HE)

John Sullivan (HE)

Gerry Blum (KCB)

is certain ; Maud's Landing, if misread, could spell the end of a Government that surged to power after tapping into another delicate environmental issue, the South West logging debate.

'Just as Labor hard man Graham Richardson delivered to a struggling Bob Hawke an historic fourth term in 1990 after convincing environmental groups that the Federal Government had turned Green, the State Government is desperate to secure Green preferences'.

The article concluded with a swipe at the shabby way in which the negations with Coral Coast Marina Development Pty Ltd. had been conducted. '*The chronological history of the development paints a disturbing picture of government ineptitude, some strange goings on by some public servants and general bureaucratic dilly-dallying'.*

How could the Government extricate itself from a difficult position? It really wasn't as difficult as might be imagined.

Reports about the possible environmental effects of the development, from sources once favourable to the project, now took an entirely negative direction. Some of those in government agencies now questioning the development, were the very men who had once approved it – and that with a degree of enthusiasm at the time!

Of course a good deal of time had passed, and anyone can change their minds (even government-employed scientists) given the light of new information. Was it a matter of science, pure and subjective? Could Tim Winton's passionate rhetoric have reached the men in the white coats? Or were there some other underlying reasons?

Whatever the case, on Friday, July 4th, 2003, the Premier Geoff Gallop and his immediate staff, together with a Press entourage, travelled to Coral Bay. There, with Coral Bay (as it was now known) behind him as a natural stage, he rolled up his trousers to the knee, strode into the water, and turning, dramatically waved a sheet of paper containing his address to an assembled crowd of locals and curious visitors.

'Today I announce that plans for a resort-style marina development at Maud's Landing have been rejected!' he cried as the television cameras rolled.

The statement was greeted by enthusiastic applause from the locals and cynical smirks from the Press. The Premier expanded further '*It is our responsibility to protect the Ningaloo Coast for future generations. We must now ensure that people from all over the world are able to enjoy the area without damaging it'.* He said that his government hoped to *'fast track'* a plan for the region to be granted World Heritage status.

So the Maud's Landing project, after 16 years of encouragement from both Western Australian governments, was scuttled and dead in the water!

Curiously when the South African-based Two Oceans developers and the Hilton Hotels group put up a proposal for a $43 million five star hotel in Coral Bay, with 260 beds and planned to open in 2007, the Government found no difficulty in approving it. Even more curiously there was no demur from conservationists.

To be fair, the proposal – which in the end failed to go ahead -- was for the site occupied previously by the Coral Bay Hotel and the Aspen Ningaloo Resort, so it did not involve further land releases.

So far as the protesters were concerned, Paul Gamblin said after the Maud's Landing triumph, that his group were not against all development. It was the size and style of Coral Coast Marina Development's proposal that had been the issue.

'Fundamentally Ningaloo does need some form of development' he told George Negus in an ABC television interview *'Because more and more people are going up there. It's been discovered by tourists all over the world. But we need low-key environmentally sensitive development and that's the argument that we made'.*

While the Gallop government claimed credit for the final decision some cynics suggested that the decision was made on the grounds of future votes rather than moral conscience. But experience tells us that that is the way of the world in politics no matter which party may be in power. Governments, of course, can claim in those circumstances to be responding to the peoples' wishes. In that respect was Ningaloo the right result for the wrong reasons?

Readers will have to make their own minds up on that curly question.

The positive result of the *SAVE THE NINGALOO REEF* campaign was that it was a people's vote between elections. It would be important too, in defining the future policy for the Ningaloo Reef, resulting in the vision of *'Sustainable Development'* which laid the guidelines for the future. In the sensation of the Government rejection of the Coral Coast Marina proposal it was barely noticed that on July 3rd, 2002 -- significantly the day before Geoff Gallop's announcement at Coral Bay -- a second *'Management Plan for the Ningaloo Marine Park and Muiron Islands Marine Management Area'* had come into effect.

The plan set out *'The main objectives for management of the Park as conservation, recreation, and science and education needs'* until 2015.

The management plan was drawn up by the department of Conservation and Land Management (later to become the Department of Environment and Conservation) and the Marine Parks and Reserves Authority, assisted by the Coral Coast Parks Advisory Committee. The management plan included fishing restrictions and sanctuary areas in 30 per cent of the Park where fishing would not be allowed at all in future. Significantly, a sanctuary zone was declared from Norwegian Bay to Mauds Landing in which fishing from a boat was prohibited over a distance of more than 40 kilometres of shoreline and 10 kilometres out to sea. The very area where the boats from the Coral Coast Marina might have gone for their recreation?

The natural follow-on from the creation of the Ningaloo Marine Park was a State Government proposal to nominate the Ningaloo Reef for World Heritage Listing. In February, 2006, the Minister for the Environment, Mark McGowan, released the outline of a proposal to Exmouth townsfolk. It was received there with serious reservations because there were aspects of Shark Bay's World Heritage Listing in 1993 which locals in that area claimed were less than satisfactory in terms of restricting expansion and commercial activity.

Pastoralists, in the Exmouth region in particular, were concerned about the amount of land which would be taken up. The State Government's proposal outlined by Mark McGowan included only the Ningaloo Reef and the existing Cape Range National Park. Pastoralists said that they had no objection to that particular plan. But the fact that conservationists wanted pastoral leases included raised concerns not only for pastoralists but Exmouth business people as well.

Rebecca Hubbard of the WA Wilderness Society said in a Press release in August 2007 that it was essential that Exmouth Gulf and adjoining land be included in the Heritage application.

'The boundary must be scientifically robust' she said. *'World Heritage listing is a rigorous process and only those nominations that guarantee long term secure protection have a chance of success. Urban development and accompanying pollution, run-off from agriculture, mining*

activities, interference with water flows, and unsustainable levels of tourism all of which involve land-based infrastructure can lead to irreparable damage to reef systems' she concluded.

However including Exmouth Gulf in the listing as suggested, would take in the eastern side of the North West Cape, including the Harold E. Holt Communications Station, the Navy Pier, Exmouth town, the marina developments, and possibly Learmonth airport. That would raise serious concerns for proposals for future building sites and commercial activity.

Where would pearling and prawning fit in with all this? What about off-shore oil and gas projects? For a town basing its economics and individual hopes on expanded tourism, and increased building projects, the concerns were understandable.

Pastoralists had particular anxieties about World Heritage listing. Richard Shallcross, whose family had run Bullara Station for many years, said *'Pastoralists are basically in favour of Heritage Listing so far as it involves the Ningaloo Reef and the Cape Range National Park because that is commonsense. But there's no reason and no need for pastoral properties to be included. We have enough difficulty in dealing with present State Government departments with regard to our leases and other agricultural requirements, without adding another level of bureaucracy based overseas'.*

Conservationists who lived in the south of WA were mainly unaware of the fragile nature of the pastoral country in the North West Cape region.

The properties, most of which had been worked for the better part of 100 years, were all on arid land which was technically semi-desert. Water was scarce throughout and water points were critical to stock numbers. Lease-holders complained that if part of a property were excised, for whatever reason, it could become unprofitable to operate the remainder.

Yardie Creek was the first case in point. It was originally taken up by Julius Brockman of Minilya in the 1880s with a blanket lease that took in the whole of the North West Cape. Tom Carter, the *'Birdman',* established himself at Point Cloates in 1889 on a lease that included Yardie Creek which he called 'Ningaloo' from *'Najendo'* or *'Nose'*, the Aboriginal name for Point Cloates. With successive owners in future years Ningaloo and Yardie Creek were divided into separate properties, and Murray and Trudy Broad bought Yardie Creek from Eric Payne in 1963.

At first it had seemed to be just what they were looking for. A historic homestead, an easily managed property and the beach and good fishing just a few minutes away. However the smiles soon vanished and the initially pleasant prospect turned into a disaster with the unforeseen establishment of the U.S. Navy base and the town of Exmouth.

The best part of the station, including the major watering point of Kuberoo Well, was excised for the Base and the town. Town dogs chased Broad's sheep up into the ranges. Workers trespassed into the property and drove at speed down the west coast disturbing stock. *'They didn't realise'* Broad recalls *'That the clouds of dust they raised on the gravel roads settled on the stock feed and killed the plants'.*

Effectively he had lost half his station and Yardie Creek had become uneconomic, an Albatross. The unfairness of the situation was recognised belatedly by the State government which bought the property from Murray Broad, paying him the price he had paid Eric Payne. In time Yardie Creek Station became part of the Cape Range National Park, and the homestead became a caravan park.

Forty years later the government moved into the pastoral scene again, buying Giralia Station at the foot of Exmouth Gulf from Denver and Rae Blake. The station which had once seen a shearing of 37,000 sheep was de-stocked.

The Blakes retained the homestead and their son Denver and his wife Jennifer continued Giralia traditions with a tourist operation with 3000 visitors, some of them internationals passionate about fly fishing, passing through each year.

Other pastoralists watched the expansion of the national parks and the implementation of the Ningaloo Marine Park Management Plan with varying degrees of nervousness. Three of them, Warroora, Cardabia, and Ningaloo, had frontages to the Indian Ocean, and had tourist regulars paying for camp sites each winter. Tourism was a significant part of their income.

Conservationists urged that the beach front portions of the stations, and some other significant sections, should be resumed by the government and given '*Park Status*' for two kilometres inland. The pastoralists involved protested that this would remove their tourist income and the excisions would make the stock side of their properties unworkable. Jane and Billie Lefroy, whose family had had Ningaloo Station since the 1930s, were offered an excision deal by the State government, but declined on the grounds that the loss of watering points and their campers' income would make the station unsustainable. *'We just like things the way they've always been'* Jane Lefroy said.

Leonie McLeod at Warroora Station spent a good deal of her waking hours on her computer sending submissions to the relevant government departments. *'I realise we have to co-exist with the changes which are occurring' she said. 'Believe me I'm more passionate about the environment than anyone. That's the very reason why I bought the property in the first place. I just want to put the soul back into the place. However I do believe that we can handle things better here ourselves on the spot than bureaucrats managing things at a distance from down in Perth or up in Exmouth'.*

The government held one vital ace in their hand. All pastoral leases throughout Western Australia were due for review in the year 2015. Some 90 pastoral leases were involved. Would the government agree to concessions requested by the pastoralists where remote areas had suddenly become easier of access to numbers of people through good roads and better motor cars?

Or would the interests of conservationists more intent on locking land away prove dominant?

Without a crystal ball or other means of foretelling the future it was impossible to say what would happen. The vital factor, of course, being whether the Labor or Liberal Party with their philosophies poles apart, were elected to office at the time of reckoning. There was a major shock for Labor in 2009 when the Carpenter Government was bundled out of office after unwisely going for an early election.

In a rapidly changing world life on the stations had also changed irrevocably. Motor bikes had replaced horses, wood stoves and Coolgardie safes were gone forever, and station kids ate ice-cream. Their dads had cold beer and their mums dish-washers. TV antennas and satellite dishes sprouted from homestead roofs. Where once there would have been a large labour force now station communities were reduced to a handful of people.

Lonely graves on some stations remained to tell of times when life was very different. In the early days there were many lonely graves in the bush, the majority of them unmarked and forgotten today. Frank Reddy's 1912 grave, with a touching decoration of shells and a cross erected by his mates, by the Vlamingh Head lighthouse quarters is a rare exception.

Dysentery killed Reddy and many others too. But death came, often unexpectedly, from many directions. A rider fell from a horse or was kicked or dragged in the stirrup. Or a teamster fell asleep, nodding while his wagon rolled along the road and fell off his seat and under the wheel of his wagon. Food poisoning took its toll in days without ice or refrigeration, especially among infants and small children. There were drownings at river crossings, deaths in fires great and small. The 1918 influenza epidemic cut a swathe through the countryside even in the most remote areas.

While every death was important to those who lost a loved one, a tragedy in the bush seldom made the city newspapers unless there was some unusual aspect. 'What's the angle?' news editors would ask.

In days immediately after the Second World War when cheap aeroplanes (war surplus Tiger Moths especially) were available many young men in the pastoral industry learned to fly. Roads in the North were still horrendous. But a light aircraft could turn two days of bump and grind behind the wheel (and some seriously bad language) into a three-hour flight with the bonus of an eagle's view of the country below. In that sense flying had a lot to recommend it.

Inevitably there were accidents, and an aircraft crash was one of the incidents guaranteed to raise headlines in the city press. Two of the North West's fatal accidents to attract attention were the crashes of Bill French, owner of Cardabia Station, in 1952, and another involving Perth engineers and entrepreneurs south of Giralia in 1961. The Cardabia crash was a tragedy in several senses. Bill French was a young married man with a wife, Norma, and two young children, Sandy a daughter, and Victor, a son scarcely more than a baby. Bill had acquired an Auster light aircraft, a model well-known for its reliability.

His passengers on the fatal day were a young couple named Cato who worked on the station as stock hand and cook. They had been trying unsuccessfully for a baby for some time, but now believed that they had finally succeeded. Bill French flew them into Carnarvon for a pregnancy test. They were said to be elated at the result!

On his return French flew low over the homestead then circled back in a sweep to drop some items to some fishermen a little further south.

When the aircraft failed to return Norma French's concern turned to worry and then, as hours passed, to desperation. To add to her difficulties the only communication with the outside world, the telephone line, ran through Winning Pool and the exchange was closed that day. Unable to make a call for help anywhere her father Pat Dempster, sought the oldest of station solutions. He mounted a horse and rode steadily south in the direction in which the Auster had last been seen.

'When he got into the sandhill country south of the Cardabia border' Jim Robinson recalled *'He rode over a sandhill and saw the crows circling up ahead. He knew then, what had happened'.*

Bill French and his two passengers were killed. The cause of the crash was never established, but it may have been due to a fuel system failure. Bill French and Jim Robinson had been best friends at school, and Robinson was overseer at Minilya station, still in close contact at the time. After the accident Norma French went back to Perth, and Robinson became manager of Cardabia. In time he married Norma, and bought a share in the property which in its best years shore over 30,000 sheep. Cardabia was taken over by Norma's son and Jim Robinson's stepson, Vic French, in the 1980s.

Jim kept a house in Coral Bay for many years and was a long-time Carnarvon councillor. When he was away on an overseas trip other councillors voted to name Robinson Street in Coral Bay after him. Robinson said later that he would much preferred it to have been named *'French Street'*

In 1998 Cardabia was purchased by the Indigenous Land Council, which had properties around Australia and the property was vested in the Cardabia Pastoral Company Pty Ltd., representing the Baiyungu Aboriginal Corporation which took in the three language groups of the region from North West Cape to the Gascoyne. They were the Thalanji of the North West Cape, Exmouth, the Baiyungu, and Yinggarda people from Carnarvon, historically connected to the area. In 2008 Cardabia was running 14,000 sheep and 1380 cattle, and conducting a limited tourism program on environmental lines.

The aircraft crash at Giralia in December 1961 occupied newspaper headlines in Perth for several days. The aircraft involved was another Auster, ABH, owned by Jim Pekin, a former aerial spotter for Nor' West Whaling who had several aircraft available for charter in Perth.

The pilot was Darcy Devenish, aged 24. The passengers were Bob Saunier 49, Victor McLarty 42, and Tom Snyder.

The aircraft had refuelled at Geraldton and Carnarvon, and left Carnarvon at 12.46 pm, on Saturday, December 16. It was due to arrive at Onslow about 3 pm and when nothing had been heard of it that afternoon or overnight, with no radio inward calls and no response to outward calls the alarm was raised next morning. There was some Press speculation about the purpose of the flight, due to the entrepreneurial nature of the passengers.

Bob Saunier was a crayfisherman who owned a vessel called *Laakanuki* and had various other investments. Vic McLarty was an engineer and a proprietor of the Fremantle engineering firm James McLarty & Sons. Tom Snyder was a very well known professional diver who had first come to WA aboard the famous American submarine *USS Harder* and married a Perth girl. The actual purpose of their visit to Onslow, revealed later, was to examine wartime tanks at Onslow which were believed to still contain a large quantity of fuel.

For several days there was a widespread search for ABH conducted by as many as 11 official and volunteer aircraft as well as ground searchers. Aircraft spent more than 200 hours combing the country south of Exmouth Gulf. The fear was that the pilot and passengers might still be alive and perishing in waterless country with scorching ground temperatures.

But when the wreckage was finally located five days later all those aboard Auster ABH were still in their seats. *'The pilot still had his radio microphone in his hand'* Denver Blake recalled. He was one of the first to the scene on the ground by four-wheel drive. *'The aircraft had been totally destroyed by fire and the bodies were individually unrecognisable. They must have died instantly. It was a shocking sight'.*

The Auster was on Marilla Station about 10 miles south of the Giralia homestead. It was not far off its predicted course for Onslow. So why had it taken so long to find it?

'The Auster was on its back after apparently diving straight into the ground' Blake said. *'Only the frame, the engine, and the bodies remained. From the air it looked just like the blackened remains of a fallen-down windmill, a sight not uncommon in cyclone country'.*

What caught the eye of David Faber and pilot Peter McNeil, in the Nor' West Whaling Company spotter aircraft Piper Apache BUA, on Thursday, December 21st, was not the burned-out wreck but a portion of the wing some distance away. *'We saw something glinting in the sunlight and flew over it'* McNeil said. *'It looked like a piece of a blue and aluminium painted wing'.*

So it proved to be. Once the wing fragment was sighted the wreck of the aircraft itself was soon seen 300 metres away. Obviously losing the section of wing caused the aircraft to crash. But the reason for the structural failure was never established. So the day ended sadly for the pilot and passengers and for their families.

As so often happens, it was the ones who were left behind who had to live with the tragedy.

FRANK REDDY'S 1912 GRAVE at Vlaming Head. (Picture: Karin Calvert Borshoff)

Harvesting The Sea

Chapter Twenty

Pearling is one of Western Australia's oldest and most successful maritime occupations. The industry is still buoyant in the 21st Century, though it has seen many changes and crises over 150 years of operations. Some of the dramas have been reflected in Exmouth Gulf, beginning with the 76 deaths in 1875 from pearling vessels overwhelmed by the great cyclone in Christmas of that year.

The industry is largely based on the northern pearl oyster *Pinctada maxima* -- whose name means, literally *'The Biggest'*. It is the world's largest and most lustrous pearl shell, with some specimens growing larger than twin dinner plates. The pearls, known today as *South Sea Pearls* are equally spectacular.

Pearls, of course, have been considered beautiful and valuable for thousands of years. The Egyptian Queen Cleopatra was said to have dissolved a pearl in a glass and drunk it to impress the Roman general Marc Anthony. Roman emperors wore breast plates studded with pearls from the Red Sea, and the Emperor Caligula had a pearl necklace made for his favourite horse. Aphrodite, the moon goddess of love, was associated with pearls – the symbol of the moon. The Greek name for pearls – *'Margarita'* – became a popular European name for girls, with variations such as Margaret and Margot.

In Tudor Britain King Henry V111's enormous bulk shimmered with pearls. But he was outdone by his daughter Elizabeth 1, *'Good Queen Bess'*, who had more than 3000 gowns decorated with pearls, 80 pearled wigs, and untold chests of pearl ropes, chokers, rings, earrings, and pendants. Pearls later fell out of fashion partly because of the Puritan revolution which frowned on extravagance and displays of opulence.

But the main problem was over-fishing of the pearl oysters of the established centres in Sri Lanka and the Red Sea. In a situation which would become all too-familiar in the future, the beds became exhausted. When the Australian banks of *Pinctada maxima* were discovered in the 1860s they breathed new life into the tired MOP shell markets, and became a new source of large and lustrous pearls. By the time of the First World War in 1914, Broome was Australia's pearling capital and old-time pearling was at its peak. The Japanese were the best helmet divers, and 400 luggers jostled for space in Roebuck Bay, backed by an Asian 'Chinatown' of 3500 people.

While the owners of the luggers were called *'Pearlers'* and fleet owners were *'Pearling Masters'* the real money was in the shell and the occasional natural pearl was a bonus *'on the side'*. Luggers went to sea with mainly Japanese divers and Asian crews working on contract. The white owners of the fleets were known as *'Veranda Pearlers'* because they seldom went to sea themselves. It was too hard a life, and there was no need because the contracted Asian crews did their job very well indeed, and at a significantly lower cost than employing white Australians.

For a time the owners did employ white *'Shell openers'* on the luggers to make sure that they got all the shell and any pearls which came aboard. The practice was discontinued in the

Depression years of the 1930s when money was tight and even minimal European wages were far higher than those paid to coloured crews. In those circumstances the owners were lucky to see a pearl at all.

Why was MOP, *Mother-of-pearl* shell, so valuable? The fact was that MOP, before zip fasteners and plastics, was the natural material from which the buttons of the world were cut.

These included shirt and coat buttons, buttons for men's trouser flies and women's blouses. In fact buttons wherever a shoe or a garment needed fastening. The thought of billions of buttons cut in circular form from pearl shell, each one laboriously drilled with three or four holes to take cotton thread, stretches our imagination!

MOP also had a thousand other uses, in inlays for crucifixes, knife handles, pistol butts, church altars, brooches, walking canes, and reflective decorations of all kinds. But buttons were the major industrial use. Disaster overtook traditional Australian pearling after the Second World War when plastic buttons and zip fasteners came on the market in the United States and Europe in the late 1950s. Overnight the price of MOP collapsed. Broome luggers were drawn up and left to rot on the beach at Roebuck Bay, or sold for rock-bottom prices.

But, in the face of disaster, salvation was already at hand. During the 1920s and 30s the Japanese, with Kochichi Mikimoto the most prominent name, had developed a means of artificially culturing pearls by inserting a nucleus of mussel shell into a pearl oyster. The oyster covered the irritant with nacre and – *Presto!* – a pearl was born. It took years to develop the technique and even longer to overcome European prejudices about *'artificial pearls'*. There was a stroke of luck when a French jeweller sued Mikimoto for '*Fraud'*. But it turned out he actually did him a favour. The judge presiding on the case ruled that the cultured pearls were *'Real'*, and that became an official declaration of authenticity.

After the Second World War Mikimoto, by now a very old man and in his nineties, told Australian officials in Occupied Japan that he believed that the Australian *Pinctada maxima* pearl oyster could be cultured as readily as the much smaller Japanese *Akoya* oyster. If that were the case, he said, it would produce a much bigger pearl and perhaps open up a new world market.

Aware of the looming threat of plastics, Broome pearling master Sam Male, Australian MOP exporter Keith Dureau, and New York importer Alan Gerdau joined forces with Mikimoto's successor, Tokuichi Kuribayashi of the Nippo Pearl Company in Japan. They agreed to set up the first Australian pearl farm at Kuri Bay, north of Broome, where conditions were considered to be favourable. Kuri Bay was immediately successful and the first cultured pearls were produced in 1959, the year of the MOP price crash. They were, as Mikimoto had predicted, the largest and most lustrous pearls in the world and were given the glamour name *South Sea Pearls*.

By 1963 the Duchess of Windsor in Britain was wearing a necklace of Kuri Bay pearls worth millions of dollars. The royal family have continued the tradition of pearls with both Queen Elizabeth 11 and Princess Diana frequently wearing pearl necklaces, earrings, and tiaras featuring Australian pearls. The move from MOP shell gathering to pearl *'farming'* not only kept Australian pearling alive and functioning. It was a changeover which would see a burgeoning export industry of world importance by the arrival of the 21st Century. By 2001 sales of Australian *maxima* pearls were bringing in $ 175,000,000 a year.

Pearling was Exmouth's first industry after whaling, with fleets of schooners and luggers working the Gulf from the 1870s onwards. The industry has always produced strong characters and Alf Morgan was one of the old school of Broome pearling masters. He continued to operate in the traditional way with *'Hard hat'* Malay divers and wooden sailing luggers after the Second World War. When the MOP crash came he saw the need to take a new approach to an age-old industry.

Like other Australian pearlers, the Browns in King Sound and Bruce Farley in Roebuck Bay, Alf Morgan could see that old methods needed to be consigned to the scrap heap and radically new systems applied. From now on, with MOP unsaleable, the industry would have to turn to pearl farming, and operators would become *'pearlers'* in the true sense.

Gone were the days of the copper helmet, the canvas suit, the lead boots. After 100 years of Japanese dominance, Australian divers, mostly ex-spearfishermen and former abalone divers, superseded the Japanese. They used modern wet suits and 'hookah' air compressors as a more efficient means of gathering pearl shell. However Japanese skills were still largely needed for the delicate seeding operations.

Seeded shell in Australia were at first hung from rafts in the Japanese traditional way. But in rougher Australian conditions it was found more practical to hang the shell in panels suspended from long lines or placed on the bottom. It took time to master the new techniques and to find suitable places to set up the pearl farms. With his two sons, Richard and Peter, Alf Morgan tried Exmouth Gulf first. Discouraged by the remoteness and cyclone damage they moved to Port Smith near Broome.

Alf Morgan retired, Peter took up a farm in the south west, and later set up a pearl farm in Shark Bay. Richard Morgan took charge of Morgan & Co. In the 1980s a virus devastated WA pearl farms including Port Smith. Dick Morgan moved his operation out to the Monte Bello Islands and, despite the pioneering difficulties in a remote location – the scene of British A-bomb tests in the 1950s – he at lasted tasted real success.

In the sheltered waters of the Monte Bello Islands some of Western Australia's largest and most robust *Pinctada maxima* pearl oysters grew naturally. Richard Morgan established a floating base, a village on the water, with aluminium houseboat dormitories for divers and workers, and floating pontoons for the *'hands on'* work of cleaning shell and seeding.

Most communication was by air. From Port Smith days Richard Morgan had seen flying as the best way to beat the perennial Northern problem of distances and in any case he had a love of aircraft. He obtained his pilot's license in 1968, and as his success in pearl farming in the Monte Bello Islands grew so he acquired bigger, faster, and more expensive aircraft. He began with a Cessna 272, advanced to larger Cessnas, and a Piper Malibu, and finally a 10-seater Cessna Caravan amphibian which was used for transporting staff and shell. Finally he owned his own corporate jet, a Citation CJ 1, which he based in Onslow.

New techniques continued to evolve in pearl farming. Initially all shell seeded on the farms were *'Wild shell'* picked up mainly off the bottom from the Eighty Mile beach by divers working on contract to the big companies. However research showed that it was possible to grow pearl oysters in laboratories from spat produced by captive shell. The next logical step was to build hatcheries to supplement the intake of wild shell, and perhaps, one day, eliminate the expensive operation of taking wild shell altogether.

The pioneers had the usual problems with maintaining critical water temperatures and combating viruses and mortalities among the spat. Neil Maff set up a hatchery in Carnarvon. He experienced some early difficulties, but Dick Morgan who always took a far-sighted view of pearling, saw the potential and bought the factory in 1995.

The first *'Grow-outs'* were in the Monte Bellos. But it was decided to move that side of the operation to Exmouth Gulf, scene of the original Morgan pearling venture. Andy Morgan, Richard's son who worked with him in the Monte Bello Islands, was given the job of setting up an Exmouth Base with pearl operations down at the Bay of Rest, and an office in town.

'We found that shell raised in the Gulf produced a really nice silver pearl, whereas those in the Monte Bellos tended to have a touch of yellow' Andy Morgan said in 2008. A procedure was established where hatchery shell went first to the Gulf to mature, and were then flown out to the Monte Bellos for *'finishing'*.

'The hatchery process in Carnarvon took five months, we would then give the juvenile shell two years in Exmouth Gulf, before sending them out to the Monte Bellos for seeding and the rest of their time' Andy Morgan recalled.*'We would get about eight years out of a pearl oyster' he added. 'At two years it was ready for seeding for its first round pearl, and would take two years before harvesting. A good oyster could be re-seeded three times. By the third re-seed the loss rate would be up around 30 per cent. But we were having a seeding success rate of 95 percent, and 60 to 70 per cent of the crop would be saleable'.*

And the perfect pearl, the one gem in a lifetime?

'We've had some good ones' Andy Morgan said. *'I reckon we get a really exceptional pearl about once every five years. The top two to five per cent of a harvest provide the gem quality, the rest are used by jewellers in brooches, settings, earrings and so on'.*

Is there any similarity between the 'good old days' of pearling and the modern highly technical age of pearl farming? Andy Morgan laughs at the question. *'Well, we're still essentially dealing with Pinctada maxima'* he says. *'But yes, the old days of the copper helmets, the snide pearl buyers, and 'Veranda Pearlers' that you read about in Ion Idriess' famous book Forty Fathoms Deep are long gone. My father Richard began working Malay helmet divers at Port Smith in the old-time way. He certainly saw some changes and innovated a lot of them himself. But there's no standing on your veranda looking out to sea with a gin and tonic in your hand these days. Pearling is a real hard working industry from owners and top management down to the people in the wet jobs out in the field'.*

There are some extra skills needed by pearlers in the 21st, Century, apart from all the delicate science involved in seeding oysters and growing pearls. Part of Andy Morgan's task at Exmouth was flying a Cessna Caravan 10-seat amphibian aircraft out to the Monte Bello Islands. The aircraft carried stores and staff. But the VIP passengers were shell taken out at 1600 a time in their panels, for a total crop of 25,000 juvenile shell. Flying time was about an hour to the Montes, with three flights a day. Eric Rolston did most of the flying between Exmouth and the Monte Bellos. Andy Morgan also skippered Morgan & Co work boats when the need arose.

Richard Morgan died in 2004, aged 61, leaving an important legacy in Exmouth Gulf and having made a major contribution to the Western Australian pearling industry. Morgan & Co continued at Exmouth and the Monte Bello Islands with a new Chief Executive Officer, Mark Longhurst.

The other name in commercial fishing in Exmouth Gulf was M.G.Kailis, who began prawning in the Gulf before the town or the Base were built. In 2008 Kailis employed 130 staff at Exmouth on boats and in the factory. K-class prawn trawlers brought in 800,000 to 1,000,000 kilograms of catch each year, in WA's second largest prawning operation. It was a far cry from the early day. In the 1960s when a much young Micky Kailis and his mates set up tents on the site of an abandoned fish factory at the bottom end of the Gulf. From there they set out to test the waters.

Michael Kailis had already established himself as a successful rock lobster (crayfish) processor at Dongara after overcoming early hard times. Prawning was already well established in Queensland and the Gulf of Carpentaria. It was showing promising beginnings in Shark Bay with trawlers working out of Carnarvon. While all the licences were taken up there, a look at the map showed that there was another big body of water further north. Exmouth Gulf was virgin ground. In early 1963 Michael Kailis and two of his fishermen Theo Rose and Andy Horne set off in an old red-painted ex-PMG four wheel drive truck to explore Exmouth possibilities. That first trip did not go well. Michael managed to hit a bank and turn the truck over on the diabolical corrugated track that passed for a road at the Exmouth end.

He suffered multiple fractures of his right arm. There was no timber to make a splint so his companions used the cardboard from a carton of beer. They drank the beer by the side of the road while waiting 24 hours for another vehicle to come by and rescue them.

Back in Perth an orthopaedic surgeon screwed the shattered bones to a steel plate. The injury would give Kailis trouble for the rest of his life, and other people might have been deterred by the incident. But *'determination'* was Michael Kailis's middle name and he persevered with the idea of an Exmouth prawn fishery.

Fishing to test the potential began in the 1994 crayfish off-season with four converted cray boats – Manuel Correira's *Costa Rica,* Theo Rose's *Helen 11*, Ken Leach's *Tide Runner 11,* and Clem Hill's *Sea Wyf*. Hill's boat was only 10 metres in length.

Processing was done using an ageing mobile freezer surplus to the Dongara rock lobster plant. A basic processing works was set up on a concrete slab which was all that remained of a fish plant set up by Dan Hunt, of Hunts Canning, Albany. A cyclone had blown the roof and walls over the hills and far away. Other building materials were salvaged from what was left of WAPET's oil drilling camp, which in turn had used left-overs from the RAAF base of the Second World War.

Initially, following some sensational catches in the Gulf of Carpentari,a the emphasis was on daylight trawling for banana prawns, the species *Panaeus merguiensis* . However it was found that night trawling for Western king prawns *Panaeus latisulcactus* and brown tiger prawns *Panaeus esculentus* gave more consistent returns. The catch of tiger prawns peaked in 1975, but by 1983 it dropped to an all time low of less than half of the catch of the previous year, which necessitated a total closure for a period. The problem was the age-old one of too many boats – 23 licences at Exmouth -- fishing one area for too long a season.

The Western Australian Fisheries Department brought in a series of controls, including closed-off nursery areas for juvenile prawns, to stabilise the catch. As described by Dr Mervi Kangas of the Fisheries research section in a paper on the Exmouth Gulf fishery in 2007, a buy-back system was introduced to reduce the number of licences and boats. By 2008 there were only nine prawn trawlers working Exmouth Gulf and all the licences were held by M.G.Kailis Gulf Fisheries.

As with pearling, new systems were continually being introduced into the prawning industry, including *By-catch Reduction Devices*, sometimes known as 'TED's' (turtle escape devices). In prawning's early days there was always concern about the *'by-catch'*. Besides prawns the nets scooped up all kinds of other sea life. Some, including squid, blue swimmer crabs, slipper lobsters, and cuttlefish, were saleable. But turtles, stingrays, sharks, and bottom fish had no commercial value and were often dead by the time the nets were cleared.

There was particular concern about the turtles because green and loggerhead turtles, endangered in the rest of the world, breed in the Exmouth region. The invention of an ingenious By-catch Reduction Device – a grill which allows prawns to pass through into the net but diverts big-bodied animals such as turtles through an escape exit -- largely solved the problem. Kailis were proud of the fact that all their trawls were fitted with BRDs and 97 per cent of by-catch was returned to the sea alive.

While tiger prawns fetched the highest individual prices, averaging 20 per cent higher than kings, it was king prawns which made up the major part of the catch. In 2008 the fishery was already 44 years old and was run in a careful balance. Dr Kangas reported in her 2007 paper on the Exmouth Gulf prawn fishery, that the main aim of research and fisheries practice was to ensure that catch rates did not exceed breeding capabilities. As a result of advanced management practices and the BRDs, the Kailis Exmouth Gulf prawn fishery was officially certified by the Australian Government's Department of Environment and Heritage as *'A sustainable industry'*. The US Department of State also certified the fishery as *'Posing no threat to turtles'* allowing Exmouth prawns to be exported to the United States.

When Mike Kailis first began rock lobster processing in Dongara he and his friend Keith Tocas had humble beginnings. They cooked their dinner on an open fire in half a 44 gallon drum, and slept on stretchers with one blanket each padded out with newspapers to keep warm. With success came creature comforts. By the time Mike Kailis' medico wife, the former Patricia Hurse, came up to Dongara they were living in a new home.

Exmouth prawning pioneering was the same story all over again. Michael and his fishermen lived rough on a sandhill on the edge of the Gulf in the first season using the mobile freezer he had bought in his first days at Dongara. When Patricia Kailis came up she had to wash the babies' nappies in salt water because there was not enough fresh water to go around.

His fishermen from Dongara brought their boats up, and the catches soon justified Michael's hunch that Exmouth prawning would one day be big business. His first fishermen were Jim Bailey, Clem Hill, Manuel Correira, and Ken Leach. Others came up to look at the potential and to lend a hand.

Bob Hugill, a colourful big-bearded crayfisherman from Yanchep took one look at the wind-blown sandy wastes around the living area and declared 'What you need are tamarisk trees! They're the only things that'll grow here!' Hugill brought up scores of seedlings in four gallon kerosene tins. Others shook their heads and opined that nothing would grow in those sandy areas. *'Not even a bloody cactus, mate!'*

Bob planted the tamarisks anyway – as anyone who knew him knew he would -- and the seedlings flourished. In no time at all they were big green trees and they are still there as landmarks on the old factory site, and now the Z-force Memorial site near Learmonth. Like the tamarisks the factory also flourished and expanded and fishermen and workers moved into more civilised quarters. However an unexpected problem arose. The factory discharged prawn heads and offal down a pipe into the Gulf. At the exit end were hundreds of squawking seagulls wheeling about in excited flocks. When the United States Navy arrived and extended the Learmonth airstrip the runway was directly in line with the factory. And the seagulls!

The risk of the big jets sucking seagulls into their engines and perhaps crashing was considered too serious to be allowed to continue. The Commonwealth Government decided that the factory would have to be relocated. A site 10 kilometres closer to Exmouth was selected and M.G.Kailis were given compensation to build a new factory, business premises, and accommodation for his processors, crews, and their families. Despite the temporary inconvenience, with a brand spanking new factory and machinery it was the best thing that could have happened to M.G. Kailis Gulf Fisheries.

In the 1980s two Broome pearlers came to Mike Kailis to ask for financial support in establishing a pearl lease. Michael was always ready to back fishermen he believed had potential into boats and licences, and the idea of pearls intrigued him. When their enterprise failed he took over the licence himself and set about creating a pearling lease in Roebuck Bay with his usual energy. Broome Pearls became another success story. Later a division of Broome Pearls, growing out hatchery spat, was moved to Exmouth in 1995.

By the time he was 40 Michael Kailis had become a wealthy and influential man. In 1979 he was made a Commander of the Order of the British Empire for his services to the Australian fishing industry. He received the Order of Australia in 1993.Despite his various awards resulting from his achievements Michael Kailis was always a modest man. He disliked the description *'millionaire'* and often said *'I may be rich in other ways but I really don't care about counting the money'.*

If it were ever suggested that he was a man of achievement he was quick to point out that he had got to where he was with the help of loyal friends and employees. *'It was always a team effort'* he said.

His biographers Dorothy and Ian Hansen in their book *The Captain's Grandson* recorded many of the names important to Michael Kailis. They included Keith Tocas, '*The brother I never had'*, as well as Peter Parish, Johnnie ('Red') Abbott, Jim Bailey, Terry Hewitt, Clem Hill, Gary Passmore, Angus Callander, Dongara production manager, John Kelly of Broome Pearls, Jan Grieves, Exmouth production manager, and Brett McCallum, personal assistant in later years. They were all part of the extended Kailis family.

As a company M.G.Kailis always encouraged their people to contribute to their local communities. Gary Passmore was manager at Exmouth for 25 years, and spent many years on the Exmouth Shire Council. He was a Life Member of the Exmouth Football Association and a judge at the Exmouth races as well as being on numerous committees. In 1998 Gary Passmore was made a Freeman of the Town of Exmouth, one of only four people awarded that privilege. The other three were Bob Burkett, Doug Bathgate, and Kerry Graham, so he was in good company.

But perhaps the name closest to Michael Kailis was his doctor wife Patricia. She was important in his life in so many ways – as a wife, the mother of his children, and a major contributor of advice and encouragement in his business activities. She sat on the boards of all his companies. At the same time she pursued her own career in medicine, and received her own recognition through the years including the Order Of The British Empire for research with Professor Byron Kakulas in the Department of Neurology at the Royal Perth Rehabilitation Hospital in Shenton Park. She later became Director of the Western Australian Institute for Child Health, but remained on the Kailis company's boards after Michael Kailis died in 1999 from a rare form of cancer.

The name Kailis lives on in Exmouth. The curious visitor will see the lights of the trawlers in the winter time working far out in the Gulf in the evenings. When they return to their marina berths it will be just on daylight, with the first red streaks of the dawn in the eastern sky.

When the blue-hulled trawlers come around the beacons into harbour, the rosy light of the dawning of a new day glinting off their upper-works, it reminds us of the song *'Shrimp boats are a-coming..!'*

The Lights That Shone

Chapter Twenty One

During the Second World War an air link from Britain to Australia was maintained through a Catalina seaplane service from aircraft based at Crawley, on the Swan River in Perth. The aircraft flew through to Ceylon, with refuelling stops at Exmouth Gulf and Cocos Island. The journey was known as the *'Double Sunrise'* flight. A single leg could take more than 30 hours over the seemingly-endless reaches of the Indian Ocean.

When war ended the faithful Catalinas, which had done such yeoman service, were replaced by converted British Lancaster bombers known as *'Lancastrians'*. They made the Qantas hop to Ceylon from Europe. Then they landed and refuelled at Learmonth, before going on to Sydney as the final stage. Later Qantas switched to ex-Liberator bombers which at that time had the longest flight endurance of any aircraft in the world.

With the primitive navigation aids of the time and no landmarks, the pilots of the former bombers steered by compass and took sextant sun and star sights over the Indian Ocean to ascertain their positions. When frustrated by clouds or tropical storms they could be up to 40 miles off course approaching Exmouth Gulf with their fuel levels at a dangerously low point.

But help was at hand. The RAAF radar unit at Vlamingh Head Lighthouse could pick them up 180 miles out to sea and advise Learmonth, who used radio to beam them safely in on a correct heading. During the war the RAAF had taken over the lighthouse at Vlamingh Head. When there was no longer the threat of long-range Japanese bombers, they re-lit the lighthouse, maintaining it and flashing out its message for two years. They were the only air force in the world to have manning a lighthouse as part of their job description!

When they returned the lighthouse to *'It's rightful owners'*, the Commonwealth Lighthouse Service, the RAAF personnel were cheered by the grateful comments and appreciation of the Catalina and Lancastrian pilots. The weary fliers who were so glad to see that welcome point of light flashing in the darkness and which was visible to aircraft from 60 miles out at sea.

At the end of one the world's longest aviation journeys crew and passengers would gather to stand behind the pilots in the cockpit and cheer the first pinprick blink of light that told them that they were nearly home. Sometimes that first evidence of Australia sent tears unashamedly trickling down cheeks for those coming home after years away.

The Vlamingh Head lighthouse keepers returned to resume their duties polishing the lenses, winding the weights, pumping to pressurise the kerosene tanks, and generally keeping the system functioning. The lighthouse, once again, directing its signal to ships at sea after its unique contribution to aviation history. Meantime life on the Cape went back to normal. Sheep, dogs, and horses, and with shearing the high point of the year.

Strange to think that the first blocks of local sandstone were laid for the lighthouse only ten years after the Wright brothers flew the first aeroplane at Kittyhawk Sands in the United States. The date of that historic event was 1902. The men who built the Vlamingh Head lighthouse, and the keepers who first manned it, were all born in days before the first motor cars appeared on the streets and were grown to manhood before the Wright brothers' flight.

Their youth was a time when horses did all the pulling of omnibuses, carts, and buggies. A day when camels ruled the outback tracks, and when any thoughts of men in flying machines were regarded as impractical fantasies.

It was a time when a Clydesdale horse named *Captain* was an integral part of the Vlamingh Head lighthouse team, pulling stores and kerosene lamp fuel from the landing place. No-one then could have imagined that the lighthouse would one day be as important to people flying thousands of feet in the air, as well as to the centuries-old purpose of warning of danger to ships at sea.

In terms of shipwrecks few areas on the Australian coast could have been more in need of lighthouses than the reef-strewn reach of the Ningaloo Reef from Exmouth Gulf south to Red Bluff. Point Cloates which saw the first recorded wrecks in the 1811 American clipper *Rapid,* and the 1816 Portuguese vessel *Correo da Azia,* was considered to be a particularly dangerous area. As a consequence one of the first lighthouses to be built north of Geraldton was at Point Cloates in 1910. The establishment of lighthouses was a matter of politics in the early 1900s, involving careful maneuvering between the State and Federal Governments. While the need for lighthouses along the WA coast was obvious, the *'Swan River Colony'* – as Western Australia was known in early days – was impoverished before the discovery of gold. The purse strings were held tightly by the Colonial Office in London.

There was no money for the urgently-needed harbour at Fremantle, let alone lighthouses in exotic locations. Fremantle was by-passed by steamers of the time because of the exposed anchorage and lack of wharf facilities. Steamships went to Albany instead, and many captains of sailing ships refused to go to Fremantle because of the notorious reputation of Gage Roads and its vulnerability in a winter '*Nor' West'* gale.

The Rottnest lighthouse was a necessity for vessels approaching Fremantle, and the need there could hardly be denied. As a result a lighthouse was built on Wadjemup Hill as early as 1851. As Albany was the major steamer port before the construction of Fremantle Harbour, lighthouses were established at at Breaksea Island and King Point in 1858. Geraldton lighthouse was erected at Point Moore in 1878.

But most other lighthouses would have to wait until the 1890s and into the next century, when there was a flurry of building. There were two reasons for that. With the discovery of WA's rich gold fields at last there was money for public works. This was exemplified in the creation of Fremantle Harbour, the construction of the Goldfields water pipe-line, and with new railways laid to important parts of the State. Lighthouses were put on the list too -- that was what gold, the '*magic metal'*, could do!

On the political scene the creation of the Commonwealth of Australia added another unexpected dimension. It was anticipated that the new Federal Government would take over control over all coastal lights around Australia. It was said in Western Australia *'If we do not get all necessary lights established before that happens it will be difficult to get the Federal Government to put them there later. But if the lights are erected now the Federal Government must continue to maintain them in the future'.*

For that reason while only three lighthouses were built in the ten years of the 1890s, eight others were constructed between 1900 and 1905. A sensible approach was taken in determining locations. Masters of ships plying the Western Australian coast were invited to suggest where they thought the lighthouses should be placed, and a Board of Inquiry ratified their suggestions. Cape Inscription at Shark Bay, Point Cloates on North West Cape, Bedout Island, north of Port Hedland, and Cape Leveque, north of Broome, were unanimous choices.

However, on the day before the report was submitted, on March 12th., 1907, the cattle-carrying steamer SS Mildura was driven ashore and wrecked on the northern tip of the North West Cape. So Vlamingh Head was added to the list.

That was somewhat to the displeasure of the Public Works Department because the State Government had to borrow an extra 10,000 pounds to cover its cost! The other four lighthouses were completed by in the period 1909 to 1910. The Vlamingh Head lighthouse lagged behind for reasons of arranging the finance, and was constructed together with its store and duplex keepers' quarters in 1912. Its 100 year celebration due in 2012.

Since there were no port facilities in Exmouth Gulf and no roads worthy of the name, considerable logistical difficulties had to be overcome in setting up and maintaining the lighthouse. It was decided to land men and materials on the sea side of the Cape, at a point opposite a gap in the fringing reef three-and-a-half miles south of the lighthouse site -- the *Jansz Access* of today. From there a horse-drawn tramway led along the shore and up the hill to the site, the horse no doubt puffing and blowing on the steep ascent. The WA Heritage Council report on the lighthouse records that work began in November – a date that could only have been set by a bureaucracy blind to all physical considerations.

Work would have to be carried on through mid-summer with shade temperatures well over 40 degrees Celsius on most days. Except that there was no natural shade at the site! If a worker put down a shovel or a crowbar in the sun for any length of time and unwisely picked up the tool without care, it could blister his palm, the skin sometimes sticking to the metal and tearing away. Local stone was quarried nearby by hand. It was hard and heavy work and the men working in the sun must have been desperately thirsty.

They were given a condensing plant, but the water was of such poor quality that one of the workers, Joseph Reddy, aged 50 years, died of dysentery and others were severely affected. His fellow workers covered his grave with bright sea shells in a touching tribute to their mate. The baler and conch shells still remain there close to 100 years after the Irishman came to a sad end so far from his home in Shannon Bridge, County Limerick. The white cross over Reddy's grave still stands today, north east of the keepers' quarters. Following his death the workers understandably preferred to cart their water from Yardie Creek homestead.

The construction technique, as with other WA lighthouses, was known as *'shuttered stone'*. Local stone and concrete were set inside a gradually-ascending framework of rough timber. The exterior and interior were then rendered. The interior ironwork, including the platforms and connecting stairs, was manufactured in Perth. But the dome and the lantern were prefabricated in England, by Chance Bros., suppliers of lighthouse lanterns and fittings to sites around the world.

The designer of the Vlamingh Head lighthouse structure was engineer G.E. Farrar of the Harbour and Lights Department in Fremantle, and an engineer called Roland was on site to supervise the construction. He was also responsible for four other lights in remote areas. The result of Farrar's design at Vlamingh Head was a light tower standing 12 metres high on a base of 5 metres across, and sited on a hill 61 metres above sea level. The revolving lantern was powered by kerosene and rested on a bed of mercury. In 1912 G.E. Farrar gave the following description of the light: *'A dioptic double-flash light, comprising optics of four panels, making one revolution in 15 seconds, with two flashes every 7 ½ seconds, the duration of each flash 3/10ths of a second, range of visibility 18 miles ...'*

Quarters for a married family and a single unmarried man were built in a sheltered position below the light house hill. Today they form part of the Lighthouse Caravan Park, which has seen Robbie and Kaye Atkinson as the long-time owners. For many years kerosene for the light and provisions for the keepers had to be brought in by sea and off-loaded into a storage shed on the beach. From there they would be brought up on the tramway on a rail trolley pulled by a plodding Clydesdale horse whose name, *Captain,* is still remembered. Sometimes deliveries were delayed by bad weather.

Access through the Ningaloo Reef was difficult and sometimes impossible if the swell was running high. The original pilotage advice, researched by the WA Heritage Council, issued special cautions to supply vessels:

'The anchorage is to be approached with the lighthouse bearing 80 degrees True (on the compass) keeping the lead going with soundings from 9 fathoms between the 3 fathom bank and gradually shoaling to 6 ½ fathoms at the anchorage when the lighthouse at 60' bears 70 degrees True and the white-painted shed on the beach 134 degrees True. The anchorage at this landing is not safe at all times and care must be taken if remaining overnight.

'Whilst the approach is at times difficult owing to the heavy ground swell which rolls into the anchorage and breaks heavily over the 3 fathoms bank on the outside, the holding ground is good'.

It must have taken some skill to make the passage over the bank in days of sail before engines were fitted to coastal craft. In the early years supplies were off-loaded at Onslow by State ships, and brought 240 kilometres back to North West Cape by schooner. Mail came the long way -- by camel from Onslow around the bottom end of the Gulf.

The Heritage Council records that one of the early light keepers was Sydney Arthur Butler, who took his wife Mary Jane and their five-month old baby to Vlamingh Head in 1914. Not many mothers today would risk taking a new baby to a place so remote. The nearest basic medical help (at Carnarvon) was several days' travel over the roughest of roads by horse or camel. But lighthouse families knew no other option in days without the benefits of radio or telephones.

The Butlers' tenure got off to a bad start. Syd Butler was a tally clerk for the Harbour and Lights Department at Onslow when he was told to report to the Vlamingh Head lighthouse within 48 hours '*For duty until further notice!'*. But when they were ferried across to North West Cape from Onslow in a ketch with a Norwegian skipper and a Malay crew, the resident Naval Reserve lighthouse keeper refused to budge. They had to return to Onslow for '*Official support'*. Mary didn't say whether that involved the constabulary, but she did say of the keeper *'I felt so sorry for him – he didn't even know there was a war on!'.*

Was it a case of '*When ignorance is bliss 'tis folly to be wise!'*

When the Butlers finally got there, Mary Jane described their quarters as *'Excellent with large rooms and verandahs. Unfortunately it was rarely that we could use the verandahs in the evening – the crabs used to come up from the beach in their thousands cleaning up everything in their path. The men used to just kick through them. But I couldn't bear them. My preparation was to avoid contact altogether. The first evening of arrival I decided to rest on a couple of rugs with my five-month-old baby, thinking how lovely and cool the verandah would be during the hot months.*

All at once I found myself screaming madly. I had two wretched crabs hanging off my foot and dozens of others coming on. No-one ever travelled quicker than I did to the safety of a bedroom! It took some time to pick out the pieces of pincer claws. Evidently the crab's motto was "What I have, I hold!".

We may wonder how baby, no doubt at the crawling stage, managed in those circumstances?

The keepers' job was to keep watch through the night, from dusk until dawn. The light was provided by a kerosene-fuelled lantern, like a modern Tilley lantern, and magnified by powerful lenses rotated by gears. Rotation was achieved by a weight in a central column through a series of gears. As the weight descended and turned the prisms it had to be periodically wound back to the top again. The process had to be repeated every two hours or so. Pressure was maintained in the kerosene tanks by hand-pumping. Filling the tanks and general maintenance work was done during daylight hours.

There was no such luxury as holidays for early lighthouse keepers, and there were serious health risks, unrealised at the time, from continual kerosene fumes and – even more dangerous – vapour from the mercury bed on which the lenses rotated. Curtains had to be drawn during the day because the sun reflecting through the magnified prisms could start fires inside and outside the lighthouse.

Keepers' wives were not officially on the Commonwealth Lighthouse Service books (keepers described it as *'Working for the Lights')*. But on occasions when the keeper or his assistant fell ill many a wife hitched up her skirts and went to work a shift or two. Just getting up the hill from the quarters to the light at Vlamingh Head was hard work. *'Some parts of the track were very narrow with the chance of a dangerous fall'.*

Families became proficient at growing vegetables, and keeping goats, hens, and cows. They were usually skilled fishermen, adding fish, crabs, and crayfish to the menu. At North West Cape shell collecting was a favourite pastime. Mary Butler had a herd of goats which provided milk for the baby and the family. She collected turtle eggs from the beach in season, and they were visited from time to time by Aborigines traveling from Yardie Creek to Kuberoo Well. They obtained fresh meat from Yardie Creek Station, their nearest human contact.

'It was two years before I saw another white woman again. Turtle eggs were very plentiful. I prized them highly, they are just like billiard balls only the so-called shell is soft and tough. They make excellent cakes, custards, and omelettes. The whites, however, can't be used.

When the Aborigines, somehow or other, would procure OP rum they would be quite mad and hold a regular corroboree and I would make for the lighthouse! Many a broken head and many cuts have I mended when it was over!'

'Being Scottish I have always set the table on New Year's Eve Hogmany. One year a chap called along with his camel team and told us later that he nearly passed out when he called about midnight. He wasn't sure whether the sun had got him or what had happened!'He didn't know that it was New Year's Eve and in such a desolate place he didn't expect to see a white woman let alone one dressed for a party or a table set for a celebration. Naturally my husband invited him in and later he voted it the happiest New Year's Eve he had ever spent. He could waltz quite well and we were fortunate enough to have an old gramophone and a happy night was had by all! The rest of our time was spent exploring, fishing, bird and turtle watching, and collecting shells'.

Not every occasion was a happy one at the Vlamingh Head light.

In the roasting month of January, 1924, it was officially reported, the lighthouse keeper Ernest Murray McDonald *'Encountered severe pains in his stomach and went to bed. He was seriously ill, and as they had no means of communicating with the outside world his wife flew the lighthouse flag upside down in the hope of attracting the attention of a passing ship. It took nearly two weeks before a ship ventured in close enough to investigate the matter and Lightkeeper McDonald was taken on board and transferred to Onslow Hospital where he died from a strangulated hernia'.*

The poor, poor woman! Imagine the distress of his wife, searching the sea, day after day, with a telescope hoping for a ship. Desperate for help, while her husband lay moaning in agony in their bedroom. Day after day, the nightmare of pain and anxiety, and then at the end of it the unfortunate man died and she was left a widow!

In later years conditions were much better for lighthouse keepers and their families. After the Second World War they had radio and telephones, and the Royal Flying Doctor Service. In WA lighthouse children took part in school lessons – pupils sometimes hundreds of kilometres apart – through the Flying Doctor pedal radio service and School of the Air.

Vlamingh Head was the first Australian light to be sighted by ships coming from Europe through the Suez Canal and steaming via India and Sri Lanka, or vessels coming from Singapore and South East Asian ports. It was the first part of their homeland that the Australians who had been Japanese prisoners of war sighted when they were released and returned home after the victory over Japan. No doubt that tiny blink of light in the darkness – 'AUSTRALIA ! YOU BLOODY BEAUTY!' – would have been a more-than-welcome sight. A star in the night, well worth a hoarse and hearty celebration.

In 1943 the RAAF 31 Radar Unit with 43 personnel, had been sent to Vlamingh Head and the radar unit was set up on the bluff by the lighthouse. The light, of course had been shut down since war was declared on Japan, to avoid giving the location away to the Enemy bombers which visited Exmouth Gulf on several occasions. The unit was heavily camouflaged and theoretically protected by two 18 pounder field guns. The presence of the guns caused some wry amusement among the RAAF personnel. If the Japanese had chosen to invade they would hardly have been able to offer much resistance.

The RAAF lived in the lighthouse quarters and in tents by the beach. The radar units were prone to cyclone damage and – somewhat strangely – to fire. Unit 161 situated by the airstrip at Cape Murat was destroyed by fire in 1944. The 1945 cyclone severely damaged all radar units in the area. For a time after VJ Day the radar unit at Vlamingh Head assisted incoming Qantas flights, but on February 17th, 1946 it too was burned to the ground.

We may have our suspicions. The war had been over for six long months, and the RAAF personnel at Vlamingh Head doubtless desperately wanted to get back to their families and normal life. If the fire was accidental it was a fortuitous occurrence for them.

However they were still running the lighthouse – now back in operation – and they had to wait for civilian lighthouse keepers to take over. Those final searing-hot summer days must have dragged by on leaden feet. They finally left, no doubt with heartfelt thanks that their war was over at last, on March 18th 1946. With their departure the North West Cape was back to its normal population of around 40 people including station owners, managers, and workers, and the lighthouse keepers and families.

When the Australian Government and the United States signed the agreement for establishing the United States naval base in 1963 the days of Vlamingh Head as a functioning lighthouse were numbered. With the erection of the high VLF towers the light was moved to the 304 metre tower, No 11, in 1967. From that time on Vlamingh Head lighthouse and the keepers became redundant. The US Navy lights – one a spare in case of an emergency – employed a new technology, and so the kerosene lantern and all the machinery remained behind *in situ* in the lighthouse at Vlamingh Head. It could still have sent its beams out across the sea if need be.

The first lighthouse at Point Cloates was built two years before Vlamingh Head, in 1910 in the conventional style, using the shuttered-stone technique, with the materials quarried near by. A married couple and one unmarried man were installed to maintain and run the Point Cloates light. The lantern was the usual kerosene–fuelled model supplied by Chance Bros Ltd of Birmingham, with engineer Farrar noting in his usual dry style *'A three-sided optic with flashes of one third of a second duration, and eclipses four and two-thirds of a second'.*

The Point Cloates lighthouse functioned from 1910 until 1935 when an earth tremor caused serious problems with the structure's stonework. Large cracks developed because the foundations were set on the unstable base of a grassed sand hill. It became apparent that the tower could no long be considered a safe workplace. It was decided by the Department of Harbour and Lights to move the light out to Fraser Island, off shore from Point Cloates.

This was closer to the outside reef, and was generally considered an improvement, especially by whalers, because the first lighthouse was sometimes criticised as being too far inland.

At the seabird roosting habitat of Fraser Island, the shearwaters and crested terns, feathers ruffled no doubt, had to make their own adjustments to the new star in their midst. At that stage the island was an imposing landmark with its dune crest 23 ft above the surrounding water. The automatic light was powered by acetylene gas, and the lantern was on top of an impressive 22 metre, metal framework tower, one of the tallest such structures in Western Australia.

Once again the forces of Nature conspired against the engineers. The island began to wear away bit by bit, perhaps because of the new wind patterns created by the metal tower. A huge storm in 1966 washed away the island completely, leaving only a sandspit, and on May 6th the tower toppled and fell full length into the lagoon with a mighty splash.

The engineers went back to their drawing boards, and the result was a new light, re-located back on the mainland on Perth Hill (named after the steamer *S S Perth* wrecked on the reef opposite in 1887). It was a pygmy in size, only four metres high, compared with its predecessors and not nearly as romantic in appearance. In fact it was a fibreglass cabinet, with the light on a stalk rather reminiscent of the Dalek robots from the television series *Dr Who.* Since it was automatic – as are all Australian lighthouses today – it needed no keepers, and because it was in such a remote area its utilitarian design may not have disappointed many tourists.

After all, for those who made the four-wheel drive effort, there was always the spectacular ruin of the original 1910 lighthouse, with its wind-ravaged *'Keepers'* quarters. There was also the collapsed structure out on the reef where the second tower lay growing oysters near the 1923 wreck of the Norwegian whale-chaser *Fynd.*

Heritage Council records show that the first lighthouse keeper at Point Cloates was P.E.Stuart with F. Hill as assistant. They were both there for 14 years, from 1910 until 1924. There was a stir down in faraway Perth when the Premier of WA, John Scadden wrote to the Acting Prime Minister of Australia, Billy Hughes in 1916 complaining that the *'keeper'* at Vlamingh Head and Point Cloates had employed and *'been living with'* an Aboriginal woman for *'a considerable time'* in contravention of the WA Aborigines Act. Because the man was an employee of the Commonwealth it was hoped that the Australian government would take some action.

It was said that the keeper held a permit to employ a male Aborigine, brother of the woman concerned. However the Chief Protector of Aborigines had asked a court to cancel it. The matter was placed in the hands of the WA Commissioner of Police and Scadden warned *'Proceedings may be taken against the Lighthouse keeper in this connection'*. There is no record of who had informed against the keeper or what eventually resulted. The wording of the complaint itself is curious. It complained the lighthouse keeper was *'Living with..'* rather than *'cohabiting'*. Was that taken to mean the same thing?

In any case it was an unusual charge. In the pastoral industry in the Murchison, Gascoyne, Pilbara, and the Kimberley, where white women were rarely seen, relations between white men and Aboriginal women – though technically illegal -- were commonplace and generally overlooked by the authorities in the region. The ladies were usually described as *'cooks'* or *'house girls'* and they played an important part in pioneering days, largely unrecognised today.

Though the Commonwealth Navigation Act covering lighthouses was proclaimed in 1911, the Commonwealth did not actually take control until 1915.

The domes and the complex interior mechanisms of most Australian lighthouses were provided by the famous British firm of Chance Bros. Ltd. They supplied the prisms and lanterns to lighthouses, light ships, and light stations, all around the world.

The Chance family were former farmers who set up in Smethwick in Birmingham in 1824 as general glass manufacturers, eventually becoming specialists in lighthouse glass design. They made their mark as inventors, pre-eminent in designing and producing the optical components and machinery for lighthouses. Their innovations included placing lighthouse lamps inside a cage surrounded by Fresnel lenses which increased the light output and revolutionised lighthouse operation.

They also introduced the concept of rotating optics so that individual lighthouses could be identified by the number of times the light flashed. James Chance, nephew of the founder of the firm was knighted by Queen Victoria for his services to the British Empire. In Britain's glory years it was described as the *'Empire On Which The Sun Never Set'*. It could also be said that there was no ocean in the world where a Chance light did not blink when darkness fell.

In time Chance Bros became the biggest glassworks in Britain. As one historian remarked *'Sand and alkaline came into their premises and wonderful creations in glass, clear and coloured, came out'*. Besides their manufacture of lighthouse components they provided all the glass for London's Crystal Palace for the Great Exhibition of 1851.

The building, 564 metres in length, and 34 metres high, was composed entirely of glass in a wrought iron framework and was a massive undertaking for the glass works. The Exhibition was opened by Queen Victoria herself, and it had many innovative features, including fountains which jetted spray 76 metres in the air, and enclosed live elm trees. It also had London's first public toilets, described as *'Retiring Rooms'*. To gain access people had to pay a copper penny, and 827,000 members of the public took the opportunity during the Exhibition. Hence the origin of the expression *'Spend a penny!'* for those with an interest in such trivia.

Chance Bros provided all the windows for London's Houses of Parliament, as well as the four glass faces of the famous tower clock at Westminster, *'Big Ben'*, whose booming chimes became a national symbol of British spirit during the Second World War. During the war the firm manufactured cathode ray tubes used in radar installations. They also provided the ornamental windows for The White House in the United States.

Today the firm of Chancer Bros Ltd., now combined with the equally famous firm of Pilkingtons, continues its operations with the accent on glass tubing for many applications, and specialising in glassware for laboratory and pharmaceutical use. Their famous speciality of past generations lives on, for visitors to Exmouth today to view, in the glass prisms and rotating mechanism of the 1912 Vlamingh Head Lighthouse.

Today there are 409 lighthouses and light stations in a ring of evening flashes and blinks of light around Australian shores. The first, established on Sydney Harbour heads in 1793 was originally just a beacon with firewood lit by hand. The last Australian lighthouse-keeper retired in 1996, and now all lights are automated, many of them solar-powered. But a considerable number of the original imposing and strongly-built stone structures of the 19th and 20th Centuries are still standing. A number of them have become tourist drawcards, like the famous lighthouse in Byron Bay in NSW, which is now a popular location for weddings. A function, it is safe to say, that would hardly have been thought of at the time of its construction!

There is a romantic appeal about lighthouses, and a surprising amount of interest in their history in Australia. Vlamingh Head Lighthouse at Exmouth has become one of the key tourist attractions of the area.

Both visitors and locals drive up the hill to watch the spectacular sunsets over the Indian Ocean, some hoping to see the white flash of a whale's spout in the distance. The duplex lighthouse keepers' quarters where Mary Butler once lived have become part of the Lighthouse Caravan Park restored by Kaye and Robbie Atkinson in recent times.

The original lantern and kerosene fuelled light are still in working order. Ron Campbell who completed a major restoration of the lighthouse with Wayne Britton in 2003, used to light the lamp twice a year. Once during the school holidays and once on his birthday – a great birthday candle!

For a time he and Britton operated lighthouse tours for the public. Unfortunately the leasing conditions and high insurance premiums ultimately made the operation financially untenable. But that did not dampen his enthusiasm for the lighthouse's important role in Exmouth history. As a confirmed history buff, Ron Campbell tracked down the last lighthouse rail trolley, once pulled by *Captain* the Clydesdale horse. He found it on a rubbish heap south of the lighthouse. He discovered sections of the original railway lines, still in good condition, buried in the sand at the beach where stores once came ashore. Wheels and axles for the trolleys still lie out in the Indian Ocean surf. Greatest triumph of all --- he found a brass breast plate in the sandhills with the name of the Clydesdale horse *Captain* inscribed upon it!

By the side of the road up to the lighthouse today, where it curves at the crest, a ghost from the past remains. A section of the old trolley path is still in place. Cut out of the side of the hill, built up with stones, it shows the huge amount of effort that went into building and maintaining the lighthouse. They must have used the trolley –and *Captain* – to get the stone blocks up the steep hill from the quarry in the early stages of building the lighthouse.

Captain won prizes at horse shows in Britain and was sent out with the original lighthouse prisms and mechanisms to draw the trolley the five kilometres between the landing place and

Vlamingh Head. What did he think as he was landed, perhaps neighing in protest, on a beach blinding white in the sun in such unfamiliar surroundings?

Was he concerned to find himself in a place where spiky spinifex replaced the grassy meadows to which he was accustomed? Was he lonely for the company of other horses in his new environment? Or did his new human friends suffice?

We sometimes tend to forget how important horses, camels, mules, bullocks, and donkeys were to people in pioneering times. Beasts of burden, yes. But they were often companions too, without whom life in remote places would have been lonely indeed. Rest In Peace, *Captain.*

'I'd like to see the lighthouse trolley, some of the rails, and other relics rescued and restored as part of a museum connected to the lighthouse' Ron Campbell said in an interview in 2007 *'And to see lighthouse tours restored. After all Vlamingh Head light is an icon in Exmouth history, and probably 100,000 tourists a year drive up Lighthouse Hill to see the sunset and watch the whales blowing in season. Why not give them more to see in the unique lighthouse interior and an associated museum?'*

Why not, indeed?

THE LIGHT THAT SHONE: Ron Campbell and the Vlamingh Head lighthouse. (Picture: Karin Calvert Borshoff)

Past, Present, & Future

Chapter Twenty Two

It was a sad day at Exmouth when the United States Navy hauled down the *Stars and Stripes* flag for the last time, on October 1st,1992. The Naval Communications Station Harold E Holt, had been the town's *raison d'etre,* its very reason for existence, for the better part of 20 years. As part of a deliberate policy of integration the houses of Australian and American families had been built next door to each other, without fences. They lived side by side in the town as neighbours in spirit as well as proximity.

They shared their holiday celebrations. Christmas Day, Thanksgiving, New Year, Halloween, ANZAC Day, Easter, July 4th, and the Melbourne Cup, were special events. There were organised mixed *get-togethers* both in the town and at the Base. As a social experiment it had all been a huge success. Lifetime friendships had been formed and there were many tears when *'Old Glory'* was hauled down for the last time.

With the withdrawal of the Americans and the termination of the jobs of many of the Australian civil employees who had worked at the Base, the town lost 30 % of its population in one fell swoop. Where the Base at its peak formerly had 480 United States Navy personnel and about 300 Australian employees, numbers were reduced to 40 members of the Royal Australian Navy and about 150 civilians. There were nearly 200 empty American houses where the lights no longer shone at night.

The Base would remain operational, but staff numbers involved after 1992 were a fraction of the previous strength. As a matter of policy, the US Navy had previously included married men with families rather than relying entirely on individual single employees and that had meant for greater numbers of Americans in the town. Now they were gone.

'Sayonara Uncle Sam!'

The American withdrawal affected everyone in town from the shops to the hotel and the taxi service, as well as the butcher, the baker, the restaurants, the hairdresser and the local dress-maker. School numbers too were greatly reduced. Some of the southern newspapers gloomily predicted that Exmouth would erode to eventual '*Ghost Town'* status like Talgarno, the *'Blue Streak'* rocket range settlement. After all, it was asked, apart from a Defence Department role, what did Exmouth have to offer to the world?

Houses were cheap in Exmouth in 1992. When the American houses were put up for public tender after the withdrawal they realized only a fraction of their original cost. They took a correspondingly long time to sell in three tender phases with prices initially as low as $55,000 for a US Navy house.

True, Exmouth did have two industries besides the Navy. Pearling and commercial prawn fishing had both played their own roles in the economy of the town and were a part of its character. However because there was no harbour and no boat slipping or repair facilities in the Gulf, the fleets went south for the summer cyclone season. The employees tended to be transient rather than permanent. But, in fact, by 1992, the seeds for recovery had already been sewn. Indeed some had been planted many years beforehand.

Exmouth's first hardy tourists had begun heading north in the 1960s and 70s, fishing rods on their roof racks, gritting their teeth against the corrugations of the gravel road. When the main roads from Northampton and Carnarvon became bitumen highways in the 1980s, the volume of traffic increased many times over. About 70 per cent of the early holiday makers – according to Shire research – came for the fishing. Some, like Garrick Agnew, Neil Patrick, and Carl Georgeff, from the Perth Gamefishing Club, were among the upper echelon of Australian game fishermen who pursued blue and black marlin in WA and Queensland waters. They were enthusiasts who thought nothing of travelling thousands of miles for a '*Hook up'*.

At the time of the American withdrawal Larry Burkett had been planning significant accommodation extensions to the Pot Shot hotel *'For a moment we were in two minds'* he recalled in 2008. *'Should we go ahead? Or were we about to send ourselves spectacularly broke? In the end we didn't have a lot of choice. Some of the contracts had already been let, and ultimately we really had no option but to take a deep breath, call on all our self-belief and go ahead. We hoped for the best and luckily that's the way it's turned out!'*.

Ian Ogden had become a business partner in 1984 and together they completed the extensions and a new look for the Pot Shot, adding 45 rooms, a pool bar, and a swimming pool, and generally bringing the establishment up to the standards required to accommodate international visitors.

'We were pretty proud of the result!' Larry remembers.

The US withdrawal forced Exmouth to take the direction that was essential for it to not only survive, but to actually thrive in its own right. There was a certain amount of luck involved as well. For a region to succeed in tourism it can be very helpful to have what Professor David Wood of the Curtin University Sustainable Tourism Centre termed an *'Iconic Factor ..A recognizable brand name and point of difference to competitors'*.

What could Exmouth offer visitors that was unique besides some of the best fishing in Australia? The answer to everyone's prayers had been swimming off the Ningaloo Reef for thousands of years, virtually unnoticed for the first 10 years of the town's existence. But the icon for Exmouth in succeeding years would be the giant fish *Rhincondon typus,* more commonly known to the world as the *'Whale shark'*.

Exmouth would prove to be the only place in the world where people could come knowing that they were guaranteed to see and swim with whale sharks in controlled and safe conditions. Western Australian tourism research for the years 2006 – 2007 showed how important the whale sharks were to the Exmouth economy. A survey of tourists visiting Exmouth revealed that 36 per cent of those interviewed said they would not have come to the North West Cape if whale sharks were not present. Another 40 per cent said they would have spent less time in the region. More than 8000 people participated in whale shark tours during 2007, a figure more than double the number ten years previously.

Research by Dr Tod Jones, of Curtin University showed that people who came to dive on whale sharks at Ningaloo in 2007 each spent an average of about $900 in Exmouth per visit and total expenditure was about $6 million. This confirmed that whale shark tours were the region's premier dollar earner. The tourists attracted by the whale shark experience were found to be the source of more than 60 per cent of the money expended by visitors in the town.

Recent figures showed that half of them were international. The United Kingdom provided the greatest number of overseas visitors taking whale shark tours at 33.8 per cent of the total. Germany provided 16.5 per cent, and other European countries 21 per cent.

The German figures were boosted by the proprietors of the *Sea Breeze Resort,* Axel and Eske Passek, who regularly returned to Germany to promote Exmouth and the Ningaloo Reef at diving conventions such as *Bloote 2007* at Dusseldorf.

Interestingly more than half (55.8 per cent) of people taking whale shark tours were female. Their average age was 34, and most were between 18 and 30 years old. Only 5.4 per cent were over 60 years of age.

And what happened to the game-fishing which initially made Exmouth famous beyond its boundaries? In 2009, after more than 30 years, game-fishing was alive and well in the new century. The Shire's official emblem still boasted a black marlin and a prawn on each side of a map of the Cape. Like many tourism activities in Exmouth, fishing went through a process of evolution to meet modern conservation requirements.

Giant billfish, like Garrick Agnew's WA record black marlin of 319 kilograms, caught in 1984, were no longer brought in. No more dead fish, to be hung up by the tail weighed on competition scales, and then sent off to the town rubbish tip. The new policy was '*Tag and release -- Take the picture and the fish swims away!*'.The result was that in the 2007 GAMEX – WA's premier fishing competition held at the end of March every year – only two billfish (one marlin and one broadbill swordfish) were actually brought ashore for scientific purposes. While 169 marlin, 53 sailfish, and 36 sharks were tagged and released by competitors. Five different species of billfish were caught, released and tagged in one day, believed to be an Australian record..

In 2009 there were more than 220 anglers as well as wives, and children, and 69 boats took part in the six day competition. Many boats were towed by road the 1275 kilometres from Perth, and some came from as far away as Broome. GAMEX provided a major boost to the local economy. Jeni Gates, who ran Exmouth Blue Water tackle with her husband Matt Gates, estimated that the game fishing festivals and fishing through the year probably brought between two and three million dollars into Exmouth..

'When you consider accommodation of families, money spent on meals, drinks, and tackle it becomes a significant factor' she said. *'One of the biggest items of expenditure for boat owners regularly travelling distances out to sea is fuel, both petrol and diesel. It's amazing how much fuel even a medium-sized boat can go through in a day, let alone a week!'.*

While fishing had been considered by some to be a declining industry, she said that was not at all the case. Exmouth supported two tackle shops with a total turnover of probably around a million dollars a year each, as well as the bait and tackle sold in supermarkets and caravan park shops. The local community also had a high proportion of people who were recreational fishermen.

'You'll find a fishing rod leaning against the back veranda in most houses around town' Jeni Gates said.

In 2009 the Exmouth Gamefishing Club began work on a new club house in the shape of a boat which would have panoramic views of the boat harbour and the Exmouth Marina Village.

A good deal of research was conducted into Gascoyne region tourism over the period from the mid-l990s, principally by Professor David Wood, and Tod Jones, and James Catlin, of the

Curtin University of Technology. Some interesting figures emerged. For instance the expenditure by visitors to the Gascoyne area ($138,000,000 in 2003) was almost twice the revenue from commercial fishing – principally prawning -- at Exmouth and Carnarvon.

In the modern era what anyone – visitor or resident -- thinks of Exmouth depends largely upon their individual experiences. A visitor may rhapsodise about whale sharks or the coral beauty of the Ningaloo Reef. A scientist might extol the *caverniculous* underground fauna. But if you were to ask a resident living in town with a family what they liked most about Exmouth the most likely answer would be a simple one.

'It's a great place to bring up kids!' they'd say.

When the Americans were in Exmouth they would marvel at the freedom children had to play in parks and playgrounds, sometimes after dark, without the need for adult supervision. That would have been impossible in the cities of the United States, unwise in Australian major cities today.

Exmouth, partly by reason of its geographic location, has significantly less of the crimes which plague other coastal towns. Break-ins and burglaries, car theft, assault, muggings, and police call-outs for domestic violence were all too commonplace in places like Moora, Geraldton and Carnarvon. In Geraldton shop windows in the main streets were often covered with steel mesh to prevent robberies or vandalism.

In Exmouth shops frequently have their goods on display and unattended on racks outside their premises. In Exmouth you could see 100 bicycles stacked outside the school, and none of them have locks. Many residents leave their houses and vehicles unlocked without concern. Something you couldn't safely do in Perth or most other big WA towns.

'We don't have the juvenile crime problems here that are experienced in other places, sometimes resulting from petrol sniffing and drug use' said Alf Iasky, Exmouth District High School principal in 2009. *'That's because we're an isolated community. But it is pleasant to see children coming to school neatly dressed in their uniforms. Kids here have good country-style values in their politeness, courtesy, and collaboration with teachers generally. In that respect they're similar to children in wheat-belt towns where I've taught in the past'.*

The excellent town sporting facilities, including the swimming pool and playing fields dating back to Colonel Ken Murdoch's day, were also helpful in giving Exmouth kids – and their mums and dads – something constructive to do in their leisure time.

In 2010, most people resident in the town knew each other at least by sight and more often on a first-name basis. There was an atmosphere of pleasant familiarity. True, there was not as much social mingling as in the days of the Americans when houses, as a matter of policy, had no fences to divide neighbours. When major occasions such as Australia Day and July 4th festivities were organised on an official basis with government funding. But Exmouth post-2000 still had its Whale Shark Festivals and the Gamex fishing carnivals and a sense of country town togetherness.

Exmouth sense of humour – a sign in Gracies Tavern read *'All unattended children will be sold as slaves or sent away for medical experiments!'*

Exmouth in 2010 was about to undergo a major expansion. The Exmouth Marina Village and other developments were about to significantly increase the number of houses in the town. Part of the finance for the development was a result of a last bequest, a final '*Thank you!'* from *Uncle Sam.* When the US Navy left Exmouth in 1991 the condition in the original agreement with the

Australian government was that the US was '*Required to return Exmouth to the state of Western Australia in the condition in which it was given'*.

This would have meant bulldozing all the US houses, some 200 of them. Obviously that would have been ridiculous! Instead a sensible solution was put forward.

It was determined that instead the houses should be sold off with 75 per cent of the proceeds going to Western Australia and one quarter going to the Navy. The Western Australian share would go to the setting up of an Exmouth Trust Fund, administered by a five-person committee, with Kerry Graham as chairman, and reporting to the WA Deputy Premier, initially Hendy Cowan.

The prices realised for the houses ranged from $55.000 to $120,000, and the proceeds were $13 million, which grew to $33 million with State and Commonwealth Government grants.

The other advantage of the sale was that previously the US Navy and the Defence Department occupants did not pay rates on their houses. But once they were sold the people who bought the houses became ratepayers in the usual way. This meant the addition of another 200 ratepayers putting funds into the Shire of Exmouth's finances.

The Exmouth Trust Fund helped finance the boat harbour which had been sought for a number of years by commercial and residential boat owners.

Other major projects were the development of Learmonth International Air Terminal, and sealing Burkett Road, to connect with Great Northern Highway.

The boat harbour was officially opened in September, 1997, filling an important need for commercial and pleasure craft in Exmouth Gulf. It provided shelter where none had previously existed and as a further benefit it allowed for a canal property development as a second stage.

The Exmouth Marina Village Outline Development Plan was prepared by the Government Agency, Landcorp. The master plan was drawn up by Bill Burrell of Taylor Burrell Town Planning and Design with support from Bowman Bishaw Gorham Environmental Consultants and Cossill & Webley, Consulting Engineers.

The first stage of the Marina Village Canal system created five *Superlots,* which were put out to public tender by Landcorp. The purchasers of the lots prepared their own planning and engineering designs and organised the construction of their own developments. All the residential canal lots were sold off the plan and the Lester Group's 129 lots in Superlot A were sold within 72 hours of their release. A further 40 *'dry'* lots were sold on completion.

Superlot B canals were completed in 2009, and developed by Jon Warren and the City & Suburban Group. The Exmouth Marina Village was planned as a major development which would include retail shops, a liquor outlet, service station, offices, convenience store, and public open space. City & Suburban's project, was designed by planner Larry Smith with Stephen Lubich, CSG's principal architect and development manager.

A spectacular feature of the plan was Landcorp's 80 metre suspended footbridge – a touch of Sydney Harbour as a sunset silhouette. It was the largest single span footbridge in WA, crossing from the Marina Village across to the Novotel Ningaloo Resort and Exmouth Boat Harbour. Among the listed sites for Marina Village properties were townhouses, house and land packages, offices, shops, and mixed-use apartments, and *'icon'* apartments. The overall Marina Village was the biggest development at Exmouth since the Base was built 44 years earlier. Costs were expected to be around $180 million.

The first stage of Exmouth's exciting new development to be completed was the four star Novotel Ningaloo Resort, facing Sunrise Beach. The Resort was opened in December, 2006, and in 2007 it won the WA Tourism Council award for *The Best New Tourism Development.* It also won the WA Hotels Association Award for Excellence in the category of Best Regional Accommodation Hotel-Resort, and received a Gold Award from the WA Spa and Swimming Pool Association for the resort's pool. A good start.

The Novotel was largely the dream of engineer Garry Cossill and hotelier Larry Burkett. As often seemed to happen with developments in Exmouth's history, it all began with a fishing trip. Garry Cossill first went to Exmouth in 1973, staying overnight in a Nissan hut at the old Nor Cape Lodge. *'To be honest I didn't think much of the place, and at the time I didn't care whether I ever went back again'* he recalls.

But in 1992 he was persuaded to go on another Exmouth fishing trip and found a new-look town that had blossomed through the years. *'We stayed at the Pot Shot Resort Hotel and I became friendly with the proprietor Larry Burkett. He told me about the American houses that were being sold off at special prices, and drove me around to show me some. The result was that I bought one with Lyn Ryan – of Rottnest Island fame-- and I've had a strong interest in Exmouth ever since. We caught a few good fish too, on that trip!'*

As a consequence Garry became *'hooked'* himself. He first became involved in the marina development as a consulting engineer and project manager. In the process he and Larry Burkett became interested in the plan for a resort at the site immediately facing Exmouth Gulf next to the marina.

'It was right on the beach, which was really unusual for resorts in Western Australia' Garry Cossill said. *'I knew that building anything there would be a challenge because it was facing Exmouth Gulf in an area which has experienced severe cyclones. But aren't challenges, after all, what make the heart beat faster?'*

He formed a partnership with Larry Burkett which included Larry's partner Ian Ogden. Their operation of the Pot Shot Resort Hotel, the Osprey Villas, and Grace's Tavern had given them long-term experience of tourism in the area. Together they formed Sunrise Beach Resort Pty Ltd., and engaged the services of the architectural firm Oldfield Knott.

'We decided on a mix of self-contained accommodation and studios with some luxury bungalows right on the beach' Garry Cossill said. *'There would be views of the Gulf from wherever you were in the resort -- including the front desk --and where possible we used local material such as natural stones for the polished concrete floors, local crushed stones and rocks and natural plants in the landscaping of the surrounds. We also used local builders and contractors experienced in construction in the area. The builders Brent Bright and Peter Dellar and their sub-contractors did a terrific job and we were more than pleased with the result'.*

'Looking into the future, we anticipate that by 2012 there will be direct flights into Learmonth from other Australian cities and perhaps from overseas. In that respect the link to the worldwide Novotel hotel chain is very important because it gives us access to international advertising and booking systems. We regard international branding as vitally important in the vision for coming years'.

Was building to cyclonic specifications a problem?

'We've mostly been building in Exmouth through the years' Peter Dellar said *'So there was no novelty about the requirements. Basically it's a matter of commonsense, following a design,*

and using only the best materials. Those are costed into the job. People sometimes ask us how we cope with the heat, but once again – we're Exmouth people, and I've lived here all my life. We get a lot of days over 40 degrees and you have to be careful how you pick up metal tools or materials which have been in the sun and you pace yourself when you're working in the open. Commonsense again. Too hot? Get a bigger hat!'

An important emphasis at the Novotel was placed on employing local people. This was not difficult because Exmouth was, after all, a tourist town and there were a lot of people with experience and skills in the hospitality business. Garry Cossill's son Darren was a good example. After completing a degree in environmental science at university he took a job at the Pot Shot Hotel Resort. He worked at all levels from the bottle shop to the dining room and management, and with that experience he became the first choice to manage the new Novotel Ningaloo Resort.

Musing on the effects of his own development, Jon Warren said that the Marina Village concept offered visitors what the town had previously lacked – a picturesque entry view of the Exmouth Gulf.

'Until the Marina Village site was cleared' he said *'And the canals were built, Exmouth was a seaside town where mostly you couldn't see the water. Some of the new houses in the northern sector had blue glimpses, but houses in the original town had no view at all.*

'That situation came about because the town was originally built on a flat space sheltered by the coastal sand hills which are a feature of the North West Cape. They play an important part in protecting the town from storm surges and cyclonic winds, so there was never any thought of bulldozing them. The advantage of having a view would have been outweighed by the negative factors. In any case in the days of first planning the requirements were essentially a practical plan for a no-frills US Base service town.

'No-one was concerned with the aesthetics of a Navy town and the original view was probably that the North West Cape was a harsh desert region which could never be made pretty no matter how hard anyone tried. The designers of 1963 would probably be pleasantly surprised to see the town today with all its attractive greenery.

'The creation of the marina and the canals mean that anyone coming into town will have a quite different view than was possible in the past' he said. *'All visitors, whether arriving in their own vehicles or coming in by tourist coach or the airport bus, have to travel along Murat Road, right alongside the Marina Village. So they'll see plenty of blue water as they arrive.*

' If they are coming out of the rain and cold of a southern winter then the sparkle of the sun on the water will no doubt cheer them up. 'Hopefully a good start to a good holiday!'.

Until comparatively recent times Exmouth was basically a one-level town. Almost everything, including the Shire and government buildings and all the original houses were single storey. By the end of the 90s the Pot Shot Hotel Resort had some two-storey apartments, and there were a handful of two-storey houses at the top end of town. But most parts of the Exmouth town site were low level. One of the original commonsense reasons for keeping building heights low was because of concerns about cyclones. Low building heights provided minimum targets. But modern advances in engineering and strength of building materials have significantly reduced the problem. Some of the buildings planned for the retail section of the Marina Village, combining shops with upstairs apartments and studios, were four storeys high, with wide ranging views of the Gulf and surrounds.

The shape of the new buildings and the style of the architecture were also very different from traditional Exmouth houses. For many years most of the houses in town were either ex-US Navy, or ex-Commonwealth Government buildings. The initial sameness of the block-houses, was transformed through time by individual additions of verandas, patios, and shades. Burgeoning gardens also added a new and pleasing appearance. However the Novotel Ningaloo Resort and the Marina Village offered a contrasting architectural style for the town, and interesting choices for home buyers investing in Exmouth property.

Planning for the marina developments went back as far as 1998. The developers were encouraged by the public demand for housing sites on the water in the canal developments at Mandurah, waterfront developments at East Perth, and the style of architecture at Subi Centro in Subiaco. *'A feature of our section of the Marina Village design'* Jon Warren said *'As at Mandurah, was allowing for canal berths for boats of varying sizes outside properties, since boating is a very important part of the Exmouth lifestyle'.*

Richard Pappas, Sales Director of Exmouth Marina Village, said that he saw an exciting future for the town. *'The development of Western Australia's resources industry and Chinese and possibly Indian contracts will see an enormous expansion of population in the North West'* he said. *'It is likely that many of the new people will be looking for holiday or residential accommodation in a sunny winter climate, and that Exmouth will see a good deal of that demand. In addition there are likely to be significant developments in the off-shore oil and gas industry'.*

The year 2007 saw a significant increase in the value of building licences, due largely to the construction of the Novotel Ningaloo Resort and Exmouth Marina Village Precinct A and B canals.

'Our Development Services staffing numbers have had to grow to cope with the increasing workload' said Shire Chief Executive Officer Phillip Anastasakis, who succeeded Kerry Graham in 2004. *'We've had to put on four additional staff in this area alone to cope with the demand. While modern computer systems have streamlined many of the procedures our people have still been under pressure to keep up with it all'.*

During the period 2001 to mid 2005, the average annual number of building licences was 118, with an average annual value of $5 million dollars each. The second half of 2005 saw a dramatic change in the number and value of buildings being built and approved in Exmouth. The new industrial area had been completed and other tourism, commercial and mixed use lots began being developed in the town site. This saw the number of building licence applications increasing by 20% with the value of works increasing from an average -- up until the middle of 2005 -- of $5 million to $20 million by the end of 2005. In 2006 the average was $23.7, increasing to $71.4 million in 2007.

Phil Anastasakis said that, aside from the private sector, many of the town planning, environmental and building assessment processes had increased in recent years, with the State Government's creation of the Ningaloo Sustainable Development Office, the Cape Range National Park Management Plan and World and National Heritage Listing, all providing land use and development requirements.

'Today the future of Exmouth is bright and assured' Phil Anastasakis said in 2010. *'It has so much to offer. With the emphasis on sustainable management, continued new development will only complement what is already here. Exmouth and the Ningaloo region are a treasure trove of natural wonders, mixed in with an interesting history'.*

One of the economic effects, quite unforseen in the 1990s, was the boost to Exmouth that Western Australia's mining boom would provide. *'I know of at least 50 houses in town that have been bought as holiday homes by people working in Tom Price, Newman, Paraburdoo, and the other mining centres'* said Mark Lucas, of Exmouth's Ray White Real Estate. *'That's a substantial investment. You're looking in the region of twenty to thirty million dollars or the equivalent of five years returns from whale sharks'.*

Retailers too have noticed a difference. *'Once I wouldn't have a dress with a price tag of more than $100 on the racks'* said Janet Norris of the Idaho Boutique dress shop in Exmouth's shopping centre. *'Now there's no trouble in selling $150 garments. The standard of dress has also lifted. As a holiday town most visitors are in shorts and T-shirts during the day, but now a lot more people are dressing up in the evenings to go to restaurants or visiting'.*

Janet and her husband David came to Exmouth from Albany in 1993, the crucial year in which the Americans left town, and have seen many changes since, including the arrival of their children Abby and Reed. *'Once Idaho Boutique was basically a bikini shop and our season was Mothers Day to Fathers Day. The number of residents hasn't increased, but now we have people all the year round from North West towns as well as international tourists escaping the European winter. Swim wear is still an important part of our sales. But now we're selling a lot more up-market clothes, resort and evening wear, and a lot of our customers are from the North West.'*

' The big money in the mining boom is very noticeable' Janet said. *'Once the people from the north used to camp or stay in caravan parks and spend as little as possible. Now they're booked in at the Novotel and drinking chardonnay and champagne instead of beer out of cans'*

A long-cherished dream for the area was the concept of a Ningaloo Research Centre, on the lines of research institutions in Queensland, such as those of the James Cook University of North Queensland, the Australian Institute of Marine Sciences, and the University of Queensland. The Great Barrier Reef has eight major research facilities, but in 2008 there were no similar institutions in Western Australia.

The Ningaloo Reef, the second longest coral reef in the world, and the longest shore-fringing reef, would seem to be a prime area for a world class research centre.

'The idea went back to the time of the American withdrawal' said former Shire President Doug Bathgate. *'The thought then was that the buildings at the Base which would become vacant could be used as the nucleus of a university campus with the emphasis on marine studies on Queensland lines. We pushed the idea hard in 1993 and '94, and we had the support of Curtin University. But at the time we could make no headway with the Defence Department'.*

The idea was revived in more recent years by the Gascoyne Development Commission, with Ian Laurance as chairman, and with the strong support of the Exmouth Shire Council. Veronica Fleay, Exmouth Shire President and chair of the GDC in 2009, said *'It is stating the obvious to say that the establishment of the Ningaloo Research Centre will provide much needed scientific study in the Ningaloo Region'.*

The estimated cost of the research centre was $17.2 million, with funding coming from the State and Commonwealth governments. By 2009 funding had already been provided for a design and a site at the Exmouth Marina. The plan included laboratories, teaching facilities for classes of up to 30 students, accommodation for students, and teachers, a conference centre and a public education and interpretive centre. Besides the Ningaloo Reef Marine Park the centre would also allow research facilities for the Cape Range National Park and regions to the north and south of Exmouth.

'Universities and research bodies agree that the Ningaloo region will continue to require close attention' Veronica Fleay said. *'This is especially important in view of the amount of activity in the region from the oil and gas industry. The Ningaloo Research Centre will be an iconic building which will make a bold statement in the town. It will enable the community and visitors to interact with the scientists who previously tended to come and go unnoticed. The opportunities for further education for local students and the attraction for PhD students from further afield will be significant, as will the role played by scientific conferences. The program may have been a long time coming, but when the dream is realised it will be of major importance for Exmouth and the region'.*

One set of buildings which saw many modifications and extensions on the same site through the years was the Exmouth District High School. The school history, researched by teacher Sue Sherwin, went back to June 13th, 1966, when an agreement was signed between the Western Australian Government and the government of the United States. A school was to provide '*Suitable and adequate education for dependents of whatever nationality, resident in Exmouth'.*

The first schoolmaster was Doug Bathgate, who would eventually become a Shire President. Before a school was built he conducted classes in children's homes. The first school was occupied in May, 1966 with two classrooms, and it was attended by Australian and American children on a ratio of two to one. Classrooms were added and by the end of 1968 there were 12 classrooms. In 1970 the school became a District High School with secondary education to Year 10. By 1981 there were 443 students, and by 1988 the first Year 12s graduated.

It was a mixed-culture school, unlike any other in Australia. With the American children coming from very different education systems – and returning to the US after their parents' 18-month tour of duty – there were natural concerns about the way they were taught, and how they would fit in again when they resumed classes in the United States. The school was run by the WA Department of Education, but was monitored in the early years by the Department of Defence. The operating costs were met by the Western Australian Government, but some monies were provided from US sources, and an American teacher was provided to keep elements of United States education on hand for American children.

'My husband Mark and I began teaching in Exmouth in 1987' Sue Sherwin said. *'We found the American families very eager to be involved with their children in all the activities such as swimming carnivals, fetes, football and other sporting events. It was great getting to know and compare our own traditions with another culture.*

' We raised both flags and sang both national anthems at assembly each morning. It was sad when the Stars and Stripes were taken down for the last time. In a special ceremony it was folded and handed to the principal as a lasting reminder of the only twin-nation school in Australia. It is still treasured at the school today'.

By 2009 the school had seen 15 principals. In that year there were 303 children in kindergarten, pre-primary, and secondary school classes, with 33 teaching staff and 23 non-teaching staff. A feature of the school, often commented on by people passing by, were the wall murals painted by school children under the direction of former artist in residence Ernie Turpin.

Adult crime in Exmouth in the first forty years was at a low level, though the town was horrified by a senseless and vicious murder at Lighthouse Beach in October of 2006. Two backpackers bludgeoned and strangled a man who had given them a lift up from Geraldton, and stole his vehicle, money, and credit cards. They dragged his body down the beach intending that the tide would carry it out to sea. But it was a time of neap tides and the water did not reach him. Instead an early morning beach walker was shocked to find the dead man. The backpackers tried to use his credit card in town and were soon apprehended by the police.

Toby Leigh Fraser, aged 30, an itinerant from Victoria, was sentenced to life imprisonment in the Perth Supreme Court in December, 2007, for the murder of John Blood 44, of Boulder. WA. Judge Peter Blaxell said *'It was an extraordinarily callous and cold-hearted murder with no obvious motive'*.

Fraser's accomplice, Kelly Brown 22, of Melbourne, was sentenced to four years and eight months gaol for her part as an accessory. Though townsfolk were shocked by the crime, there was some relief that no-one from Exmouth was involved. But it raised the question of how long into the future Exmouth's *'Age of innocence'* might continue?

To suggest that the town was without crime at all would be inaccurate. However some of the figures provided by the Western Australian Police Organisational Performance Evaluation Unit do make interesting reading in terms of the respective populations of the other North West towns.

Population: Exmouth – 2000; Carnarvon – 5287; Onslow – 617; Roebourne – 948; Karratha – 11,516; Port Hedland – 11,584.

Offence totals 2002 to 2007: Assault: Exmouth – 95; Carnarvon – 1215; Roebourne – 649; Onslow – 216; Port Hedland – 2514; Karratha – 1286.

Burglary: Exmouth – 98; Carnarvon – 1834; Roebourne – 533; Onslow – 254; Karratha – 1286; Port Hedland – 3336.

Motor Vehicle Theft: Exmouth – 21; Carnarvon – 221; Roebourne – 270; Onslow – 16; Port Hedland – 690; Karratha – 237.

Theft: Exmouth – 423; Carnarvon – 1870; Roebourne – 270; Onslow – 242; Port Hedland – 4436; Karratha – 3291.

The figures confirm that Exmouth does have reduced level of crime compared with towns which are distant neighbours. A sociologist might explain why the figures of assaults, burglaries and thefts, make Carnarvon the crime capital of the north. Or why you are three times more likely to have your car stolen in Port Hedland as Karratha, and twice as likely to be assaulted, though the towns have similar sized populations.

Or why as many vehicles are stolen in Roebourne with 948 people as in Karratha with 11,516 people. At least in Roebourne the thief and the victim are more likely to be known to each other!

In fact, on the figures quoted, the size of a population doesn't necessarily appear to be the key factor.

Though there is no doubt that when towns grow past the size when most people know each other individually, crime rates do increase. It's an inescapable part of the price of *'Progress'* Or so wise men tell us. In practical terms, it seems, *'More isn't always better'*.

When the word *'Defence'* is used in the Exmouth context, most people would associate the term with the US Naval Communications Station Harold E. Holt. However there is another defence capability less conspicuous, but certainly important in its own right.

People coming into Exmouth through Learmonth airport will notice the white domes and associated buildings of the Learmonth Solar Observatory. The complex is perched on the sand dunes by the Gulf a few kilometres north of the airport. It is highly visible to visitors as they take the road into town. The modest collection of buildings and 'dishes' comprises three parabolic antennae, and it would be unlikely that the casual observer would know that an important part of its operation is defined as '*Planetary Defence'*. A '*Star Trek'* description which may raise visitors' eyebrows.

'Defence against what? Are we expecting an invasion from Outer Space?'

The answer to that is, '*Yes, we are!'*.

It is a fact that the earth is under continual bombardment from Space, not by an alien aggressor, but by a sporadic rain of naturally-occurring objects, fragments of Space debris. These range from meteors, large and small, to stellar '*dust'* from other systems in the universe. Rarely there is the occasional major impact of a meteorite which may affect earth's climate and in extreme cases cause animal extinctions. One of the study programs at the Solar Observatory is officially defined as '*That activity concerned with protecting the earth and its inhabitants from destruction due to impact by a large piece of Space debris such as an asteroid or a comet'*.

In those terms the role of solar stations such as Learmonth is far wider than the scope of the VLF station. The Base deals with international political situations on Planet Earth. The other takes in a far wider study of the universe -- including the sun -- for the purpose of defending the earth itself. '*Planetary Defence'* takes in three phases: **Recognition** of the threat or hazard of cosmic impact..**Surveillance** for detection of specific threats..**Deflection** or interception of the threat.

The idea of an asteroid striking the earth with the force of millions of nuclear bombs in a single explosion may seem a science-fiction theme. Something divorced from current reality. The faintest of chances to upset the comfort-zone of our modern age. But it has happened in the past, and there is no reason to be confident that it will not happen again. When it does occur it could have horrendous results for all creatures, including humans, at the time of impact. The devastating result possibly changing the climate and wiping out whole species of animals.

The most famous – or infamous – of these occurrences was the comet which struck the earth 65 million years ago and resulted in the extinction of the dinosaurs. But there have been several lesser impacts in the years since which have also seen major extinctions caused by fire, flood, destruction of habitat, and an altered climate. One asteroid which struck North America 13,000 years ago ushered in a 1300-year ice age and resulted in the extinction of 35 animal species, including hairy mammoths, American camels, the American lion, and the giant beaver. How would the human race fare in a similar cosmic catastrophe to the one which killed off the dinosaurs? Could we – could any animals – survive such a cataclysmic event?

In the past there has been no defence against a cosmic disaster. But it may be that in the future technical advances may enable Mankind to destroy or deflect the threat before the asteroid irrevocably enters our planetary space. To put that kind of defence in place an intensive study of our cosmic neighbourhood is the first requirement.

The emphasis is on the precise mathematical calculations of the orbits of known Space bodies and asteroids, and the identification of new potential threats. That, in a nutshell, is the task of *Project Wormwood* at the Learmonth Solar Station.

The name may send some shivers down the back of readers' necks. It comes from the Book of Revelations in the bible. Turn to the next page if it disturbs you.

'The third angel sounded his trumpet, and a great star blazing like a torch
'Fell from the sky on a third of the rivers
'And on the springs of water
'And the name of the star was Wormwood !'

However the avoidance of future doom – commendable though that may be – was far from being the sole purpose of the Learmonth Solar Observatory.

The observatory was originally established in April 1979, and the site was chosen because it has in excess of 3,500 hours of sunshine per year. It is part of a world-wide network which monitors solar activity 24 hours a day with optical and radio wave-lengths. The facility is jointly managed by the IPS Radio and Spaces Services and the Australian Bureau of Meteorology.

A description states : '*There is a wide range of activities and systems which are affected by solar activity. Examples include short-wave broadcasting, satellite operations, high-frequency communications, manned space flights, geophysical explorations, electricity distribution, and bird migration. High frequency communications probably represent the largest group affected by solar disturbance. In Australia this includes Telstra, Optus, OTC, the Royal Flying Doctor Service, the Army, Navy, and Air Force, Police, Water Authority, Fire Brigades, State Emergency Service, and all commercial airlines'.*

It also includes your fishing or diving weather forecast when you get to Exmouth!

But, aside from these practical day-by-day uses, the information gleaned by the Exmouth Solar Observatory – allied with other similar stations around the world – may one day lead to the development of a defensive technology which could literally save the creatures of the world – including us or our descendants – from an asteroid annihilation.

To balance our views of the present and future we sometimes need to look back to the past. Readers with a leaning towards history may smile at the irony that Perth, the capital of Western Australia, and Exmouth were each established for the same reason. They each owe their origin to the fear of a war that never happened.

The Swan River Colony owed its establishment in 1829 to the British suspicion of French activity in the Indian Ocean following the Napoleonic wars. It was a situation similar to the confrontation which followed the end of the Second World War in 1945 and which peaked with the Cuban Missile Crisis in 1962. After Napoleon's defeat at the Battle of Waterloo in 1815, the British lived with a very real fear of a revival of hostilities with France *'The Old Enemy* across *the Ditch!'*. (The English Channel). Where the vital sea routes to India were concerned, the British were very conscious that, while the Union Jack flew proudly at Sydney and Hobart towns, the pristine coast of Western Australia remained unclaimed by any European power.

The supposedly vacant space (the Aborigines were already there) potentially offered the French a chance to establish a settlement. In the event of any future conflict, that would give them a naval a base, a springboard from which their frigates could threaten the British sea lanes to India, China, and eastern Australia.

French exploration expeditions by Nicolas Baudin, with the *Naturaliste* and *Geographe* from 1801 to '04, and Louis de Freycinet with the frigate *Uranie* in 1818, plastered French names all along Australia's southern and western coastlines, including Cape Murat and the Muiron Islands at Exmouth Gulf.

But the label which most raised British hackles was undoubtedly the title *Terra Napoleon* covering most of the territory of what would later become South Australia.

'Mon Dieu!'.

It created a state of alarm for the strategists in Whitehall, and as a result a regimental party of soldiers were landed at King George's Sound in 1827, to stake a claim on that magnificent harbour. In 1829 the first settlers embarked for the Swan River to cover Cockburn Sound, the only natural anchorage south of Shark Bay. Their official purpose was announced as being purely peaceful, of course. But neither the French nor the British were ever inclined to advertise their true intentions. They preferred the Machiavellian approach to politics in which they said one thing and then did something which was totally different. Sometimes confusing even themselves. A situation which can still occur with modern politicians.

But in fact France was so wounded economically by the campaigns of Napoleon which had bled the nation dry of men and money, and by the destruction of her grand fleet at Trafalgar by Nelson's Royal Navy, that in hindsight we can see that no real threat existed.

But perceptions rather than facts do play their part in politics. The Cold War after the Second World War would eventually peter out and become a damp squib when the Soviets were also brought down by economic circumstances. A wounded rouble, rather than bombs and bullets put the Cold War threat to bed. But the fear of Russia and the threat of communism was real enough at the time the Exmouth base was established by the United States in the 1960s.

As with the Swan River Colony many years before, the official story was that the base was purely for peaceful purposes, in this instance communicating with ships at sea. There was little mention of nuclear submarines because the Australian Labor Party at the time were actively discussing the possibility of legislating to make Australia a *'Nuclear-free zone'.*

While there were no *'nukes'* (nuclear devices) at Exmouth the VLF and HF establishments were clearly there for the purpose of communicating with vessels, both surface and submarine, which did have nuclear capabilities. They were there to relay orders which came direct from Washington and the Pentagon in the United States. The official *Guide to NWC* published in 1966 and describing the functions of the Transmitter & Helix Building was quite specific on the matter. The text concluded *'A vital communication link for the armed forces of the free world was born'.*

Whatever the politics of the case, and the obfuscations put to the nation at the time, Exmouth today owes its existence to those trigger-happy days of the 1960s. It is interesting to consider whether the North West Cape would have remained a collection of sleepy sheep stations at the end of a very long gravel road if there had been no nuclear threat elsewhere in the world?

So what does the future hold for Exmouth?

Broome, *The Port Of Pearls,* has shown the way for international and domestic tourism in Western Australia. Exmouth too has its own iconic attractions of *Rhincondon typus,* the whale shark, the Ningaloo Reef with its corals and marine fauna, as well as the Cape Range National Park. All of them important tourist drawcards. As off-shore exploration continues for oil and gas who knows what the potential there may be later in the century?

Pearling and prawning were well-managed and established fisheries, functioning well before the town or the Base came into existence. They will likely continue that way into the future. It is a safe bet that future governments, whether conservative or left-wing, will continue to be cautious about *'Sustainable Development'* on the North West Cape, especially in the Coral Bay area. But public demand for facilities outside the national parks is likely see more activity in the future.

Is there a potential *Wild Card* out there? Something which will alter previous thinking in the way that swimming with whale sharks took tourism by the scruff of the neck in the early 1990s? An unknown factor not anticipated in current concepts, waiting tantalisingly beyond the horizon?

Who can tell? This book tells what has been, and – for lack of a certified crystal ball -- not what will be.

Readers and the author will just have to cross our fingers. And wait and see.

As this book was ready to go to Press there was a significant echo from yesteryear. The wreck of the gallant little cutter *Mermaid* was located by a National Maritime Museum expedition 20 kilometres south east of Cairns. The important discovery of the vessel, from which the young Phillip Parker King explored and named Exmouth Gulf, was made early in January 2009.

His Majesty's Cutter Mermaid was wrecked on Flora Reef on July 13th, 1829 -- another case of *'The Unlucky Thirteenth'*. In previous years she had circumnavigated Australia with Lieutenant King in command, doing a yeoman job of surveying and chart-making of unknown waters in extremely difficult conditions. Later the tubby little ship -- only 21 metres in length, but with a wide beam and a 40ft bowsprit --went into Colonial government service. While King sailed on again in the larger *HMS Bathurst*, the cutter was re-furbished and re-rigged with an additional mast as a schooner. She helped set up colonies at Norfolk Island, Moreton Bay, and Port Macquarie before sailing with stores for Port Raffles in what is now the Northern Territory.

She departed Sydney in May, 1829, her commander, Samuel Nolbrow, instructed to take the safer but longer passage inside the Great Barrier Reef to the Torres Strait. Instead he steered outside the reef, and despite the protests of his officers insisted on sailing on through the night in coral waters. As a result of that poor decision *Mermaid* struck the Flora Reef just before daylight. Attempts to save the stranded vessel failed, and the crew took to the boats. Luckily for them they were rescued after 11 days by a passing ship, the *Admiral Gifford.*

In recent times divers from the National Maritime Museum expedition found pulley blocks, anchors, copper sheathing, and items of cargo from the wreck.

Mermaid's story remains in the names she left behind, including Exmouth Gulf, Vlamingh Head, the Bay of Rest, and the islands in Exmouth Gulf. As well as a myriad other names recorded in King's log and on the Admiralty charts, from the North West Cape through the north west of Western Australia and the Northern Territory. A boab tree at Careening Bay in WA's Kimberley still bears the legend *'HMC Mermaid'* on its trunk. A crew hand cut the inscription in its bark in 1820 not far short of 200 years ago. Which raises the question – *'How old is the tree?'* The vessel's name is also on Mermaid Reef in Western Australia, and Mermaid Beach on Queensland's Gold Coast.

It leaves us to reflect that history, as demonstrated between these pages, can still be a part of the present.

Exmouth's history will undeniably also be a part of its future.

Recommended Reading

KING OF THE AUSTRALIAN COAST by Marsden Hordern (Miegunyah Press)

THE WRECK OF THE BARQUE STEFANO by Gustave Rathe (Hesperian Press)

THE STEFANO CASTAWAYS by Monte Sala (Warrigal Press)

OUR KING FAMILY by Bill King (manuscript)

HMAS SYDNEY – LOSS & CONTROVERSY by Tom Frame (Hodder & Stoughton)

WHO SANK THE SYDNEY? by Michael Mongomery (Penguin)

SEEKING THE SYDNEY: A QUEST FOR THE TRUTH by Glenys Mc Donald (University of WA Press)

BITTER VICTORY, THE DEATH OF HMAS SYDNEY by Wes Olsen (UWA Press)

SOMEWHERE BELOW by John Samuels (Halstead Press)

THE SEARCH FOR THE SYDNEY by David Mearns (Harper Collins Publishers)

THE HMAS SYDNEY / HSK KORMORAN ENGAGEMENT by Michael McCarthy (WA Maritime Museum)

SEARCH DEFINITION IN THE SEARCH FOR KORMORAN & SYDNEY by Kim Kirstner and John Dunn

SEEKING HMAS SYDNEY by Bret Christian

THE LAST CORSAIR by Dan Van Der Vat (Hodder & Stoughton)

EMDEN by Fransz Joseph (Herbert Jenkins Ltd)

LONELY COMMAND by A.A.Hoeling (Cassell & Co)

KRAIT, THE FISHING BOAT THAT WENT TO WAR by Lynette Ramsay Silver (Sally Milner Publishing)

PRISONER OF THE KORMORAN by WA Jones & James Taylor (Australasian Publishing Co)

THE HEROES OF RIMAU by Lynette Ramsay Silver (Cultured Lotus, Singapore)

KILL THE TIGER by Peter Thompson and Robert Macklin (Hodder & Stoughton)

POT SHOT PROFILE Eric McNabb

THE EXMOUTH RADAR STORY by Morrie Fenton

A HISTORY OF THE NORTH WEST CAPE by J.C.Gordon

WHALE SHARKS, THE GIANTS OF THE NINGALOO REEF by Geoff Taylor (Angus & Robertson)

SHARK BAY THROUGH FOUR CENTURIES – 1616 to 2000 by Hugh Edwards (Scott Print)

A BEER WITH BOB BURKETT by Roberta Edwards (Access Press)

NOR'WESTERS OF THE PILBARA BREED by Jennie Hardie (Port Hedland Shire)

THE HISTORY OF THE NORTH WEST OF AUSTRALIA by J.S.Battye (Hesperian Press)

GONE WHALING by Graham Chittleborough (Picton Press)

SHOULDN'T OUR GRANDCHILDREN KNOW? Graham Chittleborough (Fremantle Arts Centre Press)

GASCOYNE DAYS by Jack Valli (St George Books)

CALLS TO THE DEEP by Brian Humphreys (Defence Publishing Service)

TREASURES, TRAGEDIES, AND TRIUMPHS OF THE BATAVIA COAST by Max Cramer (Scott Four Colour Print)

UNFINISHED VOYAGES by Graeme Henderson -- three volumes (UWA Press)

NINGALOO: AUSTRALIA'S UNTAMED REEF by Hans Kemps

THE BIOGEOGRAPHY OF CAPE RANGE edited by W.E.Humphreys (WA Museum)

AUSTRALIA'S COAST OF CORAL AND PEARL by Peter Lancaster Brown (Rigby)

THE MARINE LIFE OF NINGALOO MARINE PARK & CORAL BAY by Anne Storrie & Sue Morrison (Department of Conservation & Land Management)

SHELL BEADS FROM MANDU MANDU ROCK SHELTER by Kate Morse (WA Museum)

SHELL BEADS & SOCIAL BEHAVIOUR IN PLEISTOCENE AUSTRALIA by Kate Morse & Jane Balme

Index

Symbols

49 vessels 109

A

Aborigines 10, 16 – 17, 19-21, 25, 28, 32 – 36, 38 – 49, 52, 111 – 115, 118, 149, 155, 158, 179, 182 – 183, 185, 188, 239, 242, 257
Adriatic 36 – 37
Adult Crime in Exmouth 254
Agnew, Garrick 246 – 247
Air Raid 75, 77, 109
American Submarines 76, 97
Anastasakis, Phillip 131, 252
Anderson, Reg 60, 72
Aquitania 61, 63
Architeuthis Princeps 153
Arscot, Peter 135
Atkinson, Kaye 238
Atkinson, Robbie 166 – 167, 201, 243
Aunty Billie 215
Australian Commando Association 107
Australian Eighth Division 89
Australian Government 6, 62, 89, 107, 109, 242, 249
Australian Institute of Marine Sciences 140, 253
Australian Maritime Museum 34 – 35, 70, 107, 172, 179

B

Badcock, Captain 32, 35
Baiyungu Aboriginal Corporation 226
Baker, Pat 173, 176
Bangemall Pub 57
Bantam 13, 15
Barbary Coast 27
Barrymore, John and Josie 211
Batavia 11, 12, 20 – 21, 40 – 41, 100, 170, 174 – 175, 177 – 178, 180
Bathgate, Doug 124, 126, 128 – 131, 160, 166, 234, 253, 254
Baudin 22, 24, 257
Bay of Rest 26, 28, 56, 75 – 76, 84, 116, 182, 231, 259
Bedwell 28
Bell, Lieutenant Colonel Hayley 88, 92
Beltrao Transcript 175
Bill's Bay 215 – 216
Birds 23, 25, 52 – 54, 113, 143, 151, 186, 188
Black Rock Passage 171, 173
Blake, Denver and Rae 56, 111, 116, 118, 226
Blamey, Sir Thomas 91
Blum, Doreen 130, 212
Blum, Gerry 185, 211 – 212
Boab tree at Careening Bay 259
Boeing Pty Ltd. 120
Boston 11 – 12, 79, 173 – 175
Bosworth, Michal 160 – 161, 163, 167
Bourne Rig 72
Brand, Sir David 122
Britain 11 – 13, 26, 57, 59, 61, 67, 76 – 78, 87, 89 – 91, 96 – 97, 107, 136 – 137, 175, 228 – 229, 235, 242 – 243
British Empire 88, 91, 200, 234, 242
British Royal Naval Intelligence 71
Britton, Wayne 243
Broad, Murray and Trudy 121, 223
Brockman, Julius 47, 50 – 52, 223
Brooke-Popham, Air Marshall 87
Brooks, Darren 185
Broome 47, 54, 77, 79, 81, 109, 113, 129, 146, 161 – 162, 207, 216, 228 – 230, 234, 237, 247, 258
Brown, Dan 32
Brown, Peter Lancaster 195, 261
Buccich 36
Bulbarli 41, 50
Bull, Captain 192
Bullara Station 1, 118, 166, 200, 206 – 207, 214, 223
Bull Sharks 150
Bundegi 19, 39, 134, 147
Burke and Wills 25, 57
Burkett, Bob 126 – 129, 131, 234
Burkett, Larry 246, 250
Burnett, Captain J 64 – 65, 71 – 72
Burrell, Bill 249
Bush, Robert E. 50
By-catch Reduction Devices 232

C

Caledonia 19, 179
Calliance 31, 34
Campbell Brothers 55 – 56
Campbell, Ron 211, 243 – 244
Cape Farquhar 41
Cape Range 8, 13, 15, 21, 57, 95, 112, 115 – 116, 120, 130, 147, 149, 152, 181 – 187, 209, 222 – 223, 252 – 253, 258
Cape Range National Park 8, 130, 149, 152, 186 – 187, 222 – 223, 252 – 253, 258
Cape York Peninsula 14
Captain, Vlamingh Head Lighthouse Horse 236 – 238, 243 - 244
Cardabia 1, 17, 35, 203, 214 – 215, 224 – 226
Cardabia Station 203, 215, 225
Caretta Caretta 152
Carpenter, Jon 173
Carter, Tom 2, 43, 51 – 52, 54, 112 – 113, 223
Cary, Jennie 208 – 209
Carley Float 62 – 63
Carlo Costa 37
Carnarvon 1 – 2, 39, 47, 50 – 51, 57, 60 – 61, 72 – 73, 75, 111 – 112, 115, 118, 123, 126, 130, 187, 193, 195, 206 – 207, 211 – 212, 214, 216 – 217, 225 – 226, 230 – 232, 238, 246, 248, 255
Carnarvon Volunteer Defence Corps 60
Carpet Sharks 151
Castro, Fidel 4
Caswell, Olena 153
Catalina Seaplane Service 235
Cave 41 – 42, 49, 50, 61, 73, 144, 158, 181, 184 – 185, 187, 201
Cavernicolous 181
Centaur 61, 109
Cephalopods 153
Challi 43, 46, 114
Champion Bay 39
Chance Bros. Ltd. 242
Chapman, Major Walter 99, 102, 105, 107
Charles Knife Road 116
Chelonia Mydas 152
Chester, Major Gort 100
Cheynes Beach Whaling Company 196 – 197
Chinese 15 – 16, 79, 96, 98, 100, 102 – 103, 113, 142, 167, 203, 252
Chittleborough, Graham 193 – 194, 261
Chofuku Maru 112, 114, 179, 192
Christian, Bret 72, 260
Christmas Man 65
Churchill, Prime Minister Winston 87 – 89, 91, 96, 99, 101, 106, 110
City & Suburban Group 249
Civil Commissioner 123, 125
Clark, Dr Eugenie 137
Clifton Downs 50
Clydesdale Horse 236, 238, 243
Cold War 1, 4, 6, 8, 75, 109, 258
Colonial Government 31, 49
Columbia 78, 83 – 84
Columbus, Christopher 14 – 15
Commando Cross of Honour 107
Commonwealth Lighthouse Service 235, 239
Commonwealth Navigation Act 242
Concealed Torpedo Tubes 64
Continental Shelf 153, 190
Cook, Captain James 13, 16, 18, 253
Cooper, John 130 – 131, 213
Coral Bay 8, 132, 140, 146 – 147, 149, 156, 176, 202, 205, 214 – 217, 219, 221 – 222, 226, 259
Coral Bay Hotel 215 – 216, 219, 221
Coral Coast Marina Development Group 219
Corals 12, 143, 145, – 147, 154, 156, 177, 183, 205, 215 – 217, 258
Coral Spawning 134
Coreo da Asio 12
Correo da Azia 18 – 20, 175, 178, 236
Corrugated Iron 52 – 53, 163, 166
Cossack 31 – 34, 39, 43, 49 – 50
Cossill, Darren 251
Cossill, Garry 250 – 251
Court, Sir Charles 122
Cramer, Max 41, 261
Cropp, Ben 132, 137
Cuba 1, 4 – 5
Cuban Missile Crisis 3 – 5, 7 – 8, 119, 124, 257
Cunningham 28
Curtin, Prime Minister John 89, 96, 109
Cyclone 2, 8, 42, 47 – 48, 50, 56, 68, 79, 84, 113, 115 – 116, 118, 130, 158 – 159, 160 – 163, 165, 166 – 169, 192, 204, 206, 211, 226, 228, 230, 232, 240, 245

Cyclone at Exmouth 163
Cyclone Categories 162
Cyclone Damage 160
Cyclone of February 1945 84
Cyclone Numbers 168
Cyclone Tracey 159
Cyclone Vance 56, 116, 129 – 130, 159 – 160, 163, 201 – 202, 204, 206 – 207, 213

D

Dampier, William 22, 143
Darwin, Charles 29, 143, 152
de Freitas, Jao Jaoquim 18
de Freycinet, Louis 22, 257
Dellar, Stan 126, 131
Dench, Dr Alan 43
Department of Environment and Conservation 139 – 140, 148, 222
Detmers, Theodor 61, 63, 71, 73
Detmers, Ursula 74
de Vlamingh, Willem 18, 22
Dirk Hartog 13 – 14, 16, 22, 39, 62, 66, 127
Dirk Hartog Island 13, 39, 62, 66, 127
Discovery 14 – 16, 21, 26, 41, 54, 66, 69, 71 – 72, 134, 137, 170 – 177, 191, 198, 236, 259
Dolphins 8, 23, 121, 146, 149, 151, 198, 207
Domenic Antoncich 40
Domino Theory 7
Dorr, Henry 11 – 12, 174
Double Tenth Massacre 96
Doyle, Des 81 – 82, 85
Dugongs 23, 146, 149, 151
Dutch East India Company 13, 22
Duyfken 14 – 16

E

Eagles 23
ECOCEAN 140 – 141
Ednie-Brown, John 'Buster' 116
Edwards, Roberta 127, 261
Eendracht 13, 16
Emden 59
Emillia 175
Emma 31 – 35, 49, 179
End of the World 57
English Words Adapted 45
Eretmochelys Imbricata 152
Exe 27
Exmouth 1 – 3, 5 – 10, 13, 15, 17 – 19, 21 – 24, 26 – 29, 36, 39, 42, 54 – 58, 72, 75 – 82, 84 – 86, 90, 93, 95, 97, 107, 108, 111 – 137, 142, 146 – 154, 156, 158 – 160, 163, 166 – 169, 179, 182 – 183, 185, – 187, 189 – 190, 193, 198, 200 – 216, 218 – 219, 222 – 224, 226, 228, 229 – 237, 240, 243 – 255, 257 – 259
Exmouth District High School 212, 248, 254
Exmouth Expression 185, 203, 211
Exmouth Future 258
Exmouth Game Fishing Club 206, 247
Exmouth Gulf 1 – 2, 6, 10, 17, 19, 21, 24, 26, 28 – 29, 39, 42, 75 – 76, 78 – 86, 90, 93, 95, 97, 111 – 113, 115, 117, 119, 148 – 151, 154, 156, 158, 163, 179, 182, 189, 190, 193, 198, 211, 222 – 224, 226, 228, 230 – 233, 235 – 237, 240, 249 – 251, 257, 259
Exmouth Marina Village 8, 207, 247 – 249, 252
Exmouth Town 124
Exmouth Trust Fund Committee 129
Exmouth, Viscount 26

F

Fall of Singapore 87 – 99
Farrar, G.E. 237
Fauna 181, 183, 186, 187, 248, 258
Favourite 36, 40
Fencing 53
Finding Sydney Foundation 66 – 69, 71
First Motor Car 57
Fish Species 154
Fleay, Veronica 130, 212, 253 – 254
Flinders, Matthew 18, 22, 24, 28 – 29
Flu Pandemic of 1918 113
Flying Doctor Pedal Radio 118, 240
Folboat 90, 93, 97, 100
Forrest, Don 210 – 211
Forrest, John 58, 210
Fox, Rodney 135, 202
Foyn, Sven 191, 197
France 11, 27, 61, 89, 91, 136, 257, 258
Francis Gregory 3 1, 49
Fremantle 31 – 32, 34, 39, 46, 48, 50, 55, 62, 72, 76, 79 – 80, 86, 93, 100, 102, 105 – 106, 162, 172, 175, 179, 220, 226, 236, 237, 261

French, Bill 225
French, Charles 215
FUGRO Airborne Surveys 178
Fynd 179, 192, 196, 199, 241

G

Galeorcerdo Cuverii 151
Gales Bay 181
Gallop, Geoff 220 – 222
GAMEX 247
Garbellini, Gino 167, 207
Garden Island 67, 99, 100 – 101
Gascoyne Development Commission 130, 167, 213, 253
Gascoyne River 1, 39, 41, 50
Gates, Jeni 247
Gates, Matt 247
Geelvinck 22
General Greene 12, 174
Geographe 22, 24, 257
Georgeff, Carl 246
Geraldton 31, 34, 39, 55, 60, 62, 67, 70, 72, 78, 117, 202, 206, 212, 226, 236, 248, 254
Gerritz, Hessel 15
Giant Cod 146
Giant Squid 153
Giralia Station 1, 55 – 56, 58, 111, 115 – 118, 166 – 167, 200, 214, 224 – 226
Glazier, Geoff 178
Gold Rushes 54 – 55
Gordon, R.C. 76, 112, 121
Gould, John 52
Graham, Kerry 126 – 129, 131, 161, 166, 203, 234, 249, 252
Graham, Ted 66 – 67, 69
Great Inland Sea 25
Great White Shark 146, 151, 197
Green, Jeremy 172, 175, 177 – 178
Green Turtle 146, 152, 218, 233
Greene, General 12
Grey Nurse Shark 150
Grose, Henry 37
Group Captain Rig Bourne 62, 72

H

Hall, Major Tom 106
Hallam, Jan 166
Halls, Chris 22, 180
Hallworth, John 120, 122, 205
Hammerhead 151
Harbour and Lights Department 237 – 238
Harper, Nathaniel 58
Harpoon Gun 191, 195, 197, 198
Hawke, Bob 127, 221
Hawkins, Alf 84
Hawksbill 146, 152
He, Zeng 15
Helix Building 121
Henderson, Graeme 172 – 174, 261
Hill, Clem 135, 232 – 234
HMAS Sydney 11 Cruiser 59 – 60, 61 – 75
HMAS Sydney111 67
HMC Mermaid 29, 259
HMS Adventure 29
HMS Bathurst 25, 259
HMS Beagle 25, 29, 143
HMS Endeavour 13
HMS Investigator 18
HMS Tantalus 105
Holland 12, 15, 21, 23 – 24, 143, 174
Holt, Harold E 7 – 8, 58, 122, 124, 130, 132, 172, 182, 184, 200, 214, 223, 245, 255
HSK Kormoran 60, 69
Hugill, Bob 233
Humpback Whales 149, 151, 182, 189, 192, 195, 198, 217
Hunt, Doug and June 205
Hurd, Thomas 24
Hurricane Katrina 159, 168

I

Ingleton, Major Reginald 100, 102
Inquirer Newspaper 49
International Whaling Commission 195 – 196
Irukanji Stinger 146
Irwin, Steve 156
Islands of Angry Ghosts 21

J

Jack Sue 100, 107
Jack Valli 75, 112, 115, 123, 261
Jacob Remessens River 25
Jansz, Willem 14 – 16

Japanese Bombed Exmouth 81
Jellyfish 51, 145 – 146, 156, 176
Jessie 33, 43, 46, 48
Jinirigudi 42
Jones, Dr Tod 246
Jurich 30, 36, 38, 40 – 43, 45 – 46, 48 – 49

K

Kadaitcha Man 47
Kailis, Michael 128, 232, 234
Kailis, Patricia 233 – 234
Kandy Henderson 174
Kangas, Dr Mervi 232
Kasu 103
Katarshi, Serge 34
Kelly, John 234
Kemps, Hans 147, 261
Kennedy, John F. 5
Kimpton, Geoff 132, 176
King, Branka and Raymond 202, 206
King Family, Joe, Bill Snr, Bill Jnr 55 – 58, 114, 260
King, George 132, 135, 137, 202, 206
Kirsner, Professor Kim 66
Kochichi Mikimoto 229
Kofuku Maru 86, 92
Koolinda 77, 79, 81, 161
Krait 86 – 87, 89 – 95, 99, 107 – 108
Kuberoo Well 114, 223, 239

L

Lady Elizabeth 50
Lake MacLeod 50
Laurance, Ian 253
Lawson, Bruce 144
Learmonth 2, 7 – 8, 77 – 80, 83 – 85, 107, 115, 121, 167, 182, 186, 203, 211, 223, 233, 235, 249 – 250, 255 – 257
Learmonth Jetty 78
Learmonth Solar Observatory 182, 255, 257
Leeuwin Current 136, 147
Lefroy, Billie 172, 215, 224
Lefroy, Edgar 172
Lefroy, Jane 172, 224
Leichhardt, Ludwig 25, 52
Lester, Dick 207
Les Valmadre 137
Librarian 166, 203 – 204
Lighthouse Bay 182
Lighthouse Caravan Park 166 – 167, 202, 238, 243
Light Keepers 238
Lockier Burgess 34
Lockwood, Admiral C.S. 76
Loggerhead Turtles 146, 152, 218, 233
Longitude 131 57
Longley, Luc 220
Lyon, Captain Ivan 87, 91

M

MacBolt, Maurice 114
Mackenzie, Lieutenant Commander Hugh 'Rufus' 105
Madman's Corner 54, 113
Mammals 23, 146, 148 – 149, 181, 186 – 187, 198, 210
Mandu Mandu 184 – 185
Mangroves 184
Manta Rays 146 – 147, 182, 207, 216
Mardsen Horden 24
Marsham, Lieutenant Commander Hubert 99
Mauds Landing 34 – 35, 51, 182, 214 – 222
Mauritius 14, 16, 18
May, Ada 51
McCarthy, Dr Michael 70, 179
McClelland, Jan 203, 205
McDonald, Glenys 66, 69 – 70
McIntyre, Keith Gordon 16
McLarty, Victor 226
McLeod, Bernice 163, 200 – 201, 208
McLeod, Leonie 203, 211, 224
McLeod, Neil 209 – 210
McNabb, Eric 77, 80, 82 – 84, 260
Mearns, David 67, 69, 260
Medcraft, Tony 135, 202, 207 – 208
Megafauna 183
Melsom, Captain 193
Menzies, Gavin 16
Meridian 12, 175
Mermaid 24 – 26, 28 – 29, 58, 148, 259
Mermaid Myth 148
Mildura, Steamship 179, 237
Miller, Bob 51

Miloslavich, Vlaho 37
Minilya 43, 47, 50 – 52, 123, 206, 214, 223, 225
Minilya Station 50 – 51
Missiles 3, 5 – 6, 8, 119
Moh, Linda and Sandi 203
Molluscs 134, 146, 154 – 155
Mongan, Dave and Theresa 210
Monk, Norm 216
Monte Bello, Count 24
Monte Bello Islands 40, 147, 180, 230, 231
Monte Sala 36, 112, 260
Moore, Peter 133
Morgan, Alf 229 – 230
Morgan, Andy 206, 231
Morgan, Gabby 206
Morgan, Richard 230 – 231
Morrison, Sue 146, 261
Morse, Professor Kate 184
Mountbatten, Lord Louis 91, 96, 101, 103, 106
Muiron Islands 24, 26, 36, 40, 93, 147, 150, 156, 222, 257
Murdoch, Colonel Ken 123, 125, 248
Mustika 102 – 104
MV Geosounder 67

N

Nagy, Carol and Stephen 206
Nairn, Charles 32 – 33
Nairn, John 33
Najendo 21, 52, 223
Napier, Jeanie 206
Napier, Jeff 206, 253
Napoleonic wars 12, 24, 26, 91, 175, 257
Navy 5 – 6, 8, 11, 24, 26 – 27, 62, 65 – 67, 69 – 72, 74, 76, 78, 80 – 82, 86, 88, 90, 97, 99 – 101, 105, 107, 119 – 125, 127, 129, 166, 178, 202, 211, 215 – 216, 223, 233, 241, 245, 248 – 249, 251, 252, 257 – 258
Navy 'block-houses' 166
New Guinea 14 – 16, 23, 61, 79, 90, 110, 123, 147
New Holland 21, 23 – 24, 143, 174
New Persevcrant 32
Ngarluma 33, 43
Nickol Bay 32
Nikita Khrushchev 5
Ningaloo 1 – 2, 8 – 9, 12, 16 – 21, 31, 34 – 37, 43, 52, 54, 112, 130, 132 – 137, 139 – 142, 145 – 157, 172 – 173, 176 – 184, 188, 190, 192 – 194, 196, 198, 201 – 202, 206 – 210, 213 – 214, 216 – 224, 236, 238, 246 – 254, 258
Ningaloo Aborigines 35, 36
Ningaloo Marine Park 112, 130, 145 – 146, 152, 155 – 156, 222, 224
Ningaloo Reef 1, 8, 12, 16 – 21, 31, 34, 37, 112, 130, 132 – 140, 142, 145, 147 – 149, 151, 154, 156, 176 – 180, 182 – 183, 188, 190 – 192, 194, 196, 202, 206 – 208, 214, 216 – 220, 222 – 223, 236, 238, 24 – 248, 253, 258
Ningaloo Reef System 147
Ningaloo Research Centre 213, 253 – 254
Ningaloo Shipwreck List 179
Ningaloo Station 1 – 2, 52, 54, 172 – 173
Nor Cape Lodge 127, 250
Norman, Brad 141
Norris, Janet 253
North West Cape 1 – 3, 5 – 8, 13 – 14, 16, 20 – 24, 33, 36, 42 – 45, 47 – 58, 75 – 76, 83, 112 – 115, 119, 121, 123 – 124, 127, 143, 162, 176, 180 – 183, 186, 188, 190, 192 – 193, 198, 200 – 201, 205, 214, 223, 226, 237 – 240, 246, 251, 258 – 259
North West Cape Exmouth Aboriginal Corporation 112
North West Crime 248
Norwegian Bay 10, 113, 132, 190, 192, 193, 199, 219, 222
Norwegian Whalers 217
Novotel Ningaloo Resort 9, 130, 249 – 252

O

Occator 35 – 36, 40, 179
Octopus 43 – 44, 144, 153 – 155
Ogden, Ian 246, 250
Oil 2 – 3, 6, 38, 76, 89 – 90, 97, 101, 115 – 116, 183, 190 – 192, 197 – 198, 202, 206, 223, 232, 252, 254, 258
Ondina 79
Operation Hornbill 96 – 97
Operation Jaywick 86, 91 – 92, 95, 96, 102, 104, 106
Operation Jubilee 97
Operation Kingfisher 100
Operation Pot Shot 2, 77
Operation Rimau 98 – 99, 103, 106 – 107

Ospreys 186
Over-fishing 130, 196, 218 – 219, 228

P

Padbury, Walter 31, 33
Page, Lieutenant Robert 92, 108
Pappas, Richard 252
Parker King, Phillip 22, 24 – 25, 28 – 29, 58, 259
Passek, Eske and Axel 207
Passmore, Gary 234
Patrick, Neil 246
Paxman, Barry 170 – 172
Paxman, Frank 170 – 172
Payne, Eric 82, 223
Pearce, Dr Alan of the CSIRO 136
Pearl Harbour 61, 65, 75, 88, 90, 109
Pearling 228 – 229, 231, 245, 258
Pekin, Jim 194, 226
Pellew, Edward 26 – 28
Pelsart, Franciso 20
Peranich 41 – 42
Percival, Lieutenant General A.E. 88
Peron, Francois 22, 183
Perryman, Lieutenant John, RANR 68
Perth, Steamship 241
Phillips, Fleet Commander Tom 90
Pilbara 31 – 33, 47 – 52, 55, 112, 242
Pinctada Maxima pearl oysters 230
Point Cloates 10, 18 – 22, 32 – 33, 35 – 37, 40, 43, 45, 49 – 54, 114, 132 – 133, 147, 149, 153, 170 – 171, 174 – 175, 177, 180 – 182, 190, 192 – 196, 199, 217 – 218, 223, 236 – 237, 241
Point Cloates Lighthouse 241
Point Cloates Whaling Station 192
Point Maud 19, 41, 45, 49, 177, 218
Point Murat 6, 8, 19, 24 – 25, 40, 119, 181 – 182
Porpoise 76, 99, 101 – 102, 105 – 106
Portuguese 12 – 16, 20, 48, 67, 145, 158, 175 – 176, 178 – 179, 236
Post Newspaper 66, 70, 72
Pot Shot Hotel 124, 126 – 127, 251
Powell, Colin 173
Prawns 232 – 233
Pridmore, Don 66
Prince of Wales 90
Ptolemy 13
Pulimandur 46
Purslow, Mike 130, 161, 166

R

RAAF 60, 62, 72 – 73, 77, 78, 81, 84 – 85, 115 – 116, 166 – 167, 192, 210, 232, 235, 240
RAAF 31 Radar Unit 240
RAAF Radar Unit at Vlamingh Head Lighthouse 235
Rabbit Proof Fence 116
Radar Station 2, 76, 81 – 83
Raider 41 59 – 60, 64, 73 – 74
Raguet, Commander Conde L. 80
Rapid 11 – 12, 18 – 19, 21, 31, 40, 112, 132, 139, 174 – 175, 177 – 180, 236
Rathe, Gustave 36, 260
Reddy 224 – 225, 237
Red Herrings 41
Reptiles 23, 146, 152, 187, 210
Repulse 90
Reynolds, Bill 92, 99
Rhincondon Typus 132, 135, 139 – 140, 142, 147, 246, 258
Richards, Bob 173, 177
Richardson, Dave 130
Rijeka 37
Robinson, Jim 225
Roe 28
Roebourne 31 – 34, 39, 43, 47, 49, 212, 255
Rose 23, 232
Rosette 48 – 50
Rough Range 2, 115, 182 – 183, 185
ROV 69 – 70
Royal Australian Navy 8, 67, 74, 122, 125, 245
Royal Navy 11, 24, 26 – 27, 67, 71 – 72, 99, 101, 105, 258
Royal Navy 'China Station' 71
Russell, Graeme 137
Ryan, Ken 215

S

Salt-water Crocodile 156
Sandakan 100 – 101, 106
Sandakan Death March 100, 106
Sardam 21

Saunier, Bob 226
Save the Ningaloo Reef 208, 220, 222
School of the Air 118, 200, 240
Scurla, Father Stephen 36
Sea Levels 147
Sea Shells 155
Sea Snake 156
Sea Wasp 145
Second World War 1 – 2, 4, 7, 12, 57, 72, 75, 79 – 80, 89, 91, 101, 104, 109, 111, 114, 119, 121, 123, 143, 161, 192 – 193, 198, 214 – 215, 217, 225, 229 – 230, 232, 235, 240, 243, 257 – 258
Secret Ops 86
Services Reconnaissance Department 96
Shallcross, Richard 223
Shark Bay 13, 18, 22 – 24, 36, 39 – 40, 51, 60, 62, 75, 78, 113, 127, 129, 135, 147, 149, 177, 189, 193, 196, 216, 218 – 219, 222, 230, 232, 237, 258
Sharks 8, 23, 35, 51, 132 – 137, 139 – 142, 146 – 152, 155, 171, 176, 183, 194, 197, 207, 216, 232, 246 – 248, 253, 259
Shenton, Sir Thomas 88
Sherwin, Sue 254
Sherwin, Sue and Mark 212
Shipstone, Petty Officer H.B. 74
Shipwrecks, List of 179
Shire of Exmouth 8, 122 – 123, 125, 129, 249
Sholl, Robert 32 – 33, 49
Shot-hole Canyon 3, 115
Shunsei Maru 114, 179
Sieffert, Doug 137
Silver Dollars 11 – 12, 18, 170, 172, 174 – 175, 178
Silver, Lynette 89, 97, 101, 107, 108
Simpson, Dr Chris 134
Singapore 51, 61 – 62, 67, 71, 76, 83, 86 – 94, 96, 98, – 104, 106 – 108, 240, 260
Sirenia 149
Smith, Alan 220
Snyder, Tom 226
South Land 13, 21
South West Pacific Fleet 82 – 83
Spanish 'pillar' Dollars 170
Stanbury, Myra 173
Starling, John 137
State Emergency Service 160, 166, 169, 203 – 204, 257
Stefano 20, 30, 34 – 41, 45 – 46, 48 – 49, 112 – 114, 158, 176 – 179
Stefano Yawl 45
Steiermark 60
Stingrays 144, 148, 155, 232
Stone Fish 155
Stone, Kevin 137
Storrie, Ann 146
Straat Malakka 63, 71
Stratton, Colin 73
Stygofauna 186, 188
Subar Island 103
Sub-Atlantic Comanche 70
Submarine Base 76, 119
Submarines 2 – 3, 5 – 6, 76, 79 – 80, 84 – 85, 92, 97, 99, 109, 119, 258
Submarine Tender Pelias 81
Suicide Pill 93
Sunda Strait 11, 13, 180
Sunk 19, 27, 60, 62, 65, 67, 96, 99, 104, 109, 160 – 161, 166, 178, 202
Sunrise Beach 9, 207, 250
Sunrise Beach Resort Pty Ltd. 250
Sustainable Development 213, 217, 222, 252, 259
Swan River Colony 50, 236, 257 – 258

T

Talanji 42 – 43
Tantabiddi 139 – 140, 182, 186
Taylor, Geoff 132 – 136, 139, 218, 261
Taylor, Ron and Valerie 132, 137
Tays, William 32
Termites 187 – 188
Terra Australis Incognita 13
Terra Napoleon 258
The Big Flap 82
The Birdman 52
The Brothers 33
The Golden West 55
The Raider Kormoran 73
The Swan River Settlement 54
Third World War 7
Thylacine 183
Tiger Shark 19, 28, 149, 151, 194
Tocas, Keith 233, 234
Toma Dediol 38

Torpedo Tubes 64, 71
Tower Zero 8, 119, 120 – 121, 205
Tracking Skills 47
Transmitters, Radio 6, 121 – 122
Troglobitic Fauna 183
Truscott, 'Bluey' 78
Tuckey, Charles 30, 33, 46, 48 – 49, 114, 179
Turnbull, Peter, DFC 79
Turner, Peter 166
Turtles 44, 114, 140, 146, 151 – 152, 184 – 185, 218, 232 – 233
Turtle Killing by License 218

U

United States Navy 6, 8, 76, 80, 86, 90, 119, 122 – 123, 215 – 216, 233, 245
Uranie 23, 257
US Departure 245
US Naval Communication Station Harold E. Holt 124
US Navy 5, 8, 67, 78, 81 – 82, 86, 97, 107, 120 – 121, 123, 127, 129, 166, 202, 211, 215, 241, 245, 248 – 249, 252
US Navy's Withdrawal 129
USN Submarine Tender Chanticleer 86
USS Barbel 80
USS Chanticleer 93
USSR 3
US Submarine Tautog 81

V

Vallero 48
Vespucci Amerigo 14
Vincent, Captain 48 – 49
Vlamingh Head 1 – 2, 24, 57, 81 – 83, 209, 211, 224, 235 – 241, 243 – 244, 259
VLF (Very Low Frequency) 6 – 8, 119 – 122, 165, 182, 200, 205, 241, 256, 258
VOC 13 – 16, 180
Volunteer Defence Corps 60
von Bibra 39
von Humboldt, Alexander 16
von Malapert, Lieutenant 61, 68

W

Walcott, Pemberton 49
Walters , Air Commodore A.T. (Tom) 125
Wandjina 158
WAPET 2 – 3, 115 – 116, 232
Warren, Jon 249, 251, 252
Warroora 1, 17, 41, 49 – 51, 203, 211, 214, 224
Warroora Station 41, 50, 203, 211, 224
Waterman, Stan 137
Water Pipeline to Kalgoorlie 55, 58
Wavell, General 88
Welman Submersible Boat 97
Western Australian Maritime Museum 34 – 35, 70, 172, 179
Whalers 189
Whales 23, 135, 137, 146, 149, 151, 181 – 182, 189 – 199, 207, 217 – 218, 244
Whale Shark 8, 132 – 142, 146 – 149, 152, 183, 205, 207, 216, 218, 246 – 248, 253, 258 – 259
Whaling Station at Babbage Island 193
Willems River 16, 25
Wilson, Barry 130
Wilson, Emily 140
Wilson, Ruby May 215
Windmills 23, 53
Wing Commander Charles Learmonth, DFC 79
Winton, Tim 220 – 221
Wire Fences 47, 53
Witch Doctor 43
Wood, Professor David 246 – 247
World Heritage 23, 188, 221 – 223
World Heritage Area 23
Wrecked 18, 22, 26, 29, 32 – 36, 40, 47, 50, 52, 84, 114, 145, 165, 173, 192, 237, 241, 259

X

X-turret 64, 70 – 71

Y

Yalobia Hill 51
Yandoo Well 52
Yankee Whalers 190 – 191
Yanrey Station 79, 166
Yardie Creek 1, 8, 16 – 17, 52, 54 – 56, 82, 114, 121, 130, 186 – 187, 202, 209 – 210, 214, 223, 237, 239
Yardie Creek Station 8, 52, 55, 82, 121, 130, 223, 239

Z

Z-Force 96

Notes

THE